AN ESSAY TOWARDS THE CONVERSION OF LEARNED AND PHILOSOPHICAL HINDUS

AN ESSAY TOWARDS THE CONVERSION

OF

LEARNED AND PHILOSOPHICAL

HINDUS

REV. JOHN BRANDE MORRIS, M. A.

GYAN

Published by

GYAN

Gyan Publishing House
5, Ansari Road
Daryaganj, New Delhi-110002
Phone: 011-47034999, 9811692060
E-mail: books@gyanbooks.com

Distribution Network
gyanbooks.com
India, USA, Canada, UK, Australia, France

ISBN: 978-81-212-9378-5 (PB)
First Published, 1843

2nd Impression 2023

Printed at: Gyan Press, Delhi.

AN ESSAY TOWARDS THE CONVERSION OF LEARNED AND PHILOSOPHICAL HINDUS

AUTHOR: JOHN BRANDE MORRIS

AN ESSAY TOWARDS THE CONVERSION

OF

LEARNED AND PHILOSOPHICAL

HINDUS:

TO WHICH

THE PRIZE

OFFERED THROUGH THE LORD BISHOP OF CALCUTTA

HAS BEEN ADJUDGED

By the University of Oxford:

WITH

NOTES AND ILLUSTRATIONS FROM THE FATHERS,

AND OTHER SOURCES.

BY THE

REV. JOHN BRANDE MORRIS, M.A.

FELLOW OF EXETER COLLEGE, OXFORD.

Ἡ πίστις διὰ τῶν αἰσθητῶν ὁδεύσασα ἀπολείπει τὴν ὑπόληψιν, πρὸς δὲ τὰ ἀψευδῆ σπεύδει, καὶ εἰς τὴν ἀλήθειαν καταμένει.—S. Clement, *Strom.* ii. § 13.

LONDON:

PRINTED FOR J. G. F. & J. RIVINGTON,

ST. PAUL'S CHURCH YARD,

AND WATERLOO PLACE, PALL MALL.

1843.

TO THE

RECTOR AND FELLOWS

OF

EXETER COLLEGE, OXFORD,

THIS VOLUME

IS RESPECTFULLY DEDICATED,

AS A SMALL TOKEN OF GRATITUDE

FOR THE MANY BLESSINGS,

WHICH HAVE, IN THAT SOCIETY, BEEN ENJOYED

BY THE AUTHOR.

PREFACE.

As a dialogue almost of necessity precludes a systematic treatment of the opinions with which it is dealing, some synthetical account of the doctrines of the Brahmans may appear to be a desideratum in the present volume. It was, indeed, a part of my original design to have attempted something of the kind, until upon further thoughts I was induced to abandon this attempt. The complicated nature of the Indian systems prevents their being handled cursorily; and the translation of the Vishnu Purána, with the valuable notes attached to it, has rendered them no longer inaccessible to those who wish to see further into them. The references and quotations, and glossary, which are found in this volume, will, it is hoped, make it sufficiently intelligible to the general reader, if only he be willing to bestow a proper amount of thought upon subjects unavoidably intricate.

As there are not wanting indications of the existence of pantheistic tendencies in England as well as elsewhere, the conflict here attempted to be exhibited between a pantheistic system and the Christian one may, perhaps, be not altogether useless in this country. The reader will, however, remember, that the book is designed chiefly for India. To explain the Christian system where it clashes with the Brahmanical, and to put together such matter as might be useful to Indian Clergy in dealing with heathens, have been my chief objects. These objects are, it is hoped, in accordance with the purposes for which the prize was offered, if the whole of those purposes be inadequately met owing to deficiencies upon my part.

The passages quoted are given, for the most part, in the originals, as being more satisfactory to those capable of forming a judgment upon the subjects they treat of, than in a translation. Partial knowledge or inadvertency, or strong prepossessions, may make one misrepresent, in a translation, the sense of the original; for which reason also it is more satisfactory to the author, as well as the reader, to give the originals.

Much else might have been expected to be found here, which is purposely omitted. For instance, there is no statement of what the Christian system is, or how its evidences may be best studied, or how far it may accommodate itself to heathen systems by remoulding their existing rites; all which, though very important, cannot be done with conciseness, as any one who has considered the subjects at all patiently, will be fully aware. One reason for omitting such subjects is, because there would evidently be a want of delicacy in treating of them before heathens. Christianity must win upon men, as Christ did, by veiling its majesty before it reveals it. Men of retiring and devotional habits must first attract that majesty to themselves, and then it will draw to them others, upon whom an ostentatious display of knowledge would not have exercised any really beneficial influence.

The Notes and Illustrations (it should be remarked) have been added since the Essay was sent in; the references only, and not the whole of them, existed in the copy sent to the Examiners.

It would be wrong to conclude this preface without expressing my gratitude to friends, to whose assistance I feel that I owe much; and though one is always bound to be fearful of making others seem responsible for one's own errors, I cannot do else than publicly acknowledge the very great obligations this work is under to Professor Wilson, and to the Rev. C. Marriott, of Oriel College.

Exeter College, June 20, 1843.

DIALOGUE I.

ON THE SOURCE OF REVEALED KNOWLEDGE.

יַשְׁפַּר יְיָ תְּחוּמֵיהּ דְּיֶפֶת וְיִתְגַּיְרוּן בְּנוֹהִי
וְיִשְׁרוּן בְּמִדְרְשָׁא
דְּשֵׁם

"May the Lord garnish the border of Japhet, and may his sons be proselytes and dwell in the school of Shem."—*Jon. Ben Uzziel ad Gen.* ix. 27.

ESSAY ON THE CONVERSION,

&c.

DIALOGUE THE FIRST.

LAURENCE. I have long wished to talk over things which have struck me in my travels, most excellent Brahman, with some one versed in your literature.

RA'DHA'KA'NT. In what part has your excellency been?

LAUR. In the North, among the hills of Cashmere, and the mountains of the Himalaya, whence they say that Gotama and other wise men of old came.

RAD. It is generally thought that it was by the river Saraswati, in the Panjab, that the schools of the learned seers of old were frequented, and the Saraswata tribe of Brahmans, even to this day, are in high honour.

LAUR. And the source of the Saraswati is not so far from the foot of the Himalaya mountains; and if the stream of wisdom could not flow through them, it may have flowed along them, and sheltered itself under them. It may be that, as I said, the country of Cashmere was once the nurse of wisdom, where the gentleness of the climate, and the clearly visible Surya, invited men to contemplation.

RAD. So it may have been. But what leads you to say so?

LAUR. It seems that at an early period the wisdom of your ancestors was renowned in the North, and in the West (1); and that the systems of philosophy in Persia were not native to that country, but came into it from India. Now the North of India would be more favourable to the transmission of knowledge into these parts than any more southern part, so that there may have been an early intercourse between India and parts north of the Himalaya.

RAD. That is possible.

LAUR. Do you suppose that the knowledge of those ancient sages, who were masters even of the Persians, was of their own discovering, or that they had it from some other source?

RAD. They are believed by all the schools, Mimánsa and Nyaya, Sankhya and Vedánta, to have had it by inspiration from Iswara; though he may have employed different Munis as instruments in transmitting that knowledge.

LAUR. I see you are looking at things in a far deeper light than I was contemplating at the time; though I know how widely it was believed in the East, that man cannot arrive at knowledge save by assistance (2) from the higher powers: yet, at the time, I was thinking of the outward means, which we see.

RAD. Of old it was counted that the mind was influenced by Iswara, and that the senses were not needed in order to arrive at divine knowledge.

LAUR. Yet surely it may, consistently with this, be allowed, that Iswara did use the senses in conveying divine knowledge to some, at least.

RAD. You make me afraid that I shall not learn things from you that I wished to have learned, seeing you cannot conceive inspiration to go on without the senses: and the sage Vishnu-s′erma says (3), that where there is a close union with the senses, there ambrosia itself is poison.

LAUR. I wish you not to misunderstand me. All which I have said is, that to some, at least, divine knowledge was conveyed not without the aid of the senses. If, for instance, I were to read the Vedas, or the Manava-dharma-sástra, and find in it traces of divine wisdom, I should attain to the end of that knowledge by my mind, though not without the aid of one sense—that of seeing: my eyes would help me.

RAD. Yet still I think the wise men that were of old got knowledge without the aid of the senses.

LAUR. As we seem not to be able to agree upon this, Rádhákánt, let us consider it. Mind is well called Mahat, since it is the great thing in arriving at knowledge; yet surely the senses are of use also. If we go by what we see around us in the case of mortals now existing, you will assuredly allow that this is clearly the case.

RAD. Certainly. Since on the Karma-mimánsa the commentator (4) well says that none of all the ways of knowledge is sufficient without oral tradition; and this oral tradition may be either human, as is a just sentiment, or divine, as is a text of the Vedas.

LAUR. Then we are agreed as to the mode by which existing human beings arrive at knowledge; namely, by something in which the senses are made use of.

RAD. That is no difficulty for me to admit.

LAUR. And if this be so, we allow of one of our senses, that it is useful towards the acquisition of divine knowledge; and this sense is that of hearing. Now let us consider whether another of our senses is not useful to us for the same end; I mean the sense of seeing.

RAD. Certainly it is. When the unregenerate sees Surya in the lordliness of his might, his sight may lead his mind on by degrees till he comes to understand how Brahma shines in the souls of devout Dwijas.

LAUR. A great Western philosopher, Plato by name, taught a doctrine much like that; for he held, as the Vedas teach (5), that what the sun and light are for this visible world, the highest good and truth is for the spiritual and invisible world; but that the one, which the eyes saw, would not be of any great use, unless the sun, which the mind saw, shined also; and that (6) as the eyes might be closed, so the mind might be blind, not seeing the sun for a season; but that it was the two together, which enabled men to see. And our books teach, that the things which are seen helped men to understand the things which are not seen.

RAD. So indeed they taught as our sages taught! Glory to Ganés'a, who in all the world teaches the wise the same truths!

LAUR. Now if this be so,—if, indeed, the outward sun helps men to learn of the inward sun, it will follow that either men immediately, and by themselves, are led by the sight of the outward to think of the inward, in which case the sense of sight alone is employed: or else, that there was some widely spread tradition, which induced men to hold that the outward sun was meant to be a semblance of the inward sun, and that the sight of this outward sun served only to keep the memory alive to a knowledge of the inward sun; and knowledge, in this case, would be conveyed to the mind by another sense—viz. by that of hearing; still it would be conveyed by the sense. Mortals such as we know of, do not come to divine knowledge without the senses, so far as this instance will go. And I think, Rádhákánt, that I can give further reason for thinking that this knowledge of a sun of wisdom in the world unseen did come by this last means to be spread over the world.

RAD. How is that?

LAUR. Plato, the philosopher of whom I spoke, was a Greek; and not being so bigotted as most of his nation, tells the Greeks plainly (7) that they were mere children in knowledge. Now he is himself generally believed to have picked up sundry fragments of knowledge which came from the East, in the course of his travels; and he lived long after the Vedas were written down by Vyasa. So that it is not unlikely that this doctrine of a sun of wisdom had spread by that time far enough for him to have heard of it. Hence, from whatever source the Vedas derived it, he may have heard it in some nation, which had it from them (as in Persia, for instance); in which case the sense of hearing would have been made use of to convey this important piece of knowledge, concerning the unseen world, into the West; and the sense of sight to have it kept in memory amongst the Greeks, whom he so justly and humbly calls mere children in true philosophy.

RAD. But are there any other instances in which there is a similarity between our philosophy and his.

LAUR. Yes; several. The doctrine of metempsychosis doubtless came to them from your fathers, though not immediately; and although I am now bent on more serious conversation with you, I may state, in a general way, that there seems to be a large number of points in which they derived their doctrine from India. Things are scattered up and down in their poets and philosophers, which leave a strong impression upon the mind, when once one knows a little of the Indian doctrines, that the Yavanas of those parts were a most uninventive nation, who treasured up fragments of barbarian philosophy, and were indebted to foreigners for all they knew of the things of the unseen world. This, at least, is what early Christian writers always considered; and one great reason why I think so is, because when one knows more of your systems, particular things can be accounted for in theirs; and the drift and bearing of them can be cleared up. But supposing this were only a fancy, it would serve to illustrate the subject in hand; which is, to show how the knowledge of unseen things is conveyed by hearing. "Faith is the evidence of things not seen," according to our books; and "faith," they also say, "comes by hearing." From which I argue, that the Lord does make use of the senses in conveying His revelations to man, whatever other means He uses in conjunction with them.

Rad. You mean to say, He uses them in transmitting the revelations to others, after they have been once made.

Laur. Well: state it so if you think fit. So far as the question is concerned, as to whether the senses are used in conveying divine knowledge, it comes to the same thing whichever way you state it. Since what I would show you is, that as matter of fact, so far as experience (whether recorded by history or by our own memory) will lead us, the senses are made use of in conveying religious knowledge. Such knowledge, when first transmitted to any nation, is as new and as important to that nation as though it were fresh revelation. And I am not at all denying, that in order to such a transmission being effectual, an influence of the divine Prasada on the minds of men, cotemporaneous with the influence of the things transmitted to the senses, is absolutely necessary. What I am here asserting is, that in all cases to which actual experience reaches, the latter (viz. the external influence of the senses,) has been used, whatever other invisible means were employed at the same time. And if this be the case in all instances coming under our experience, it begets a presumption that it was the case with instances not under our experience, which presumption we ought to be guided by, until we have some other presumption stronger than it, and better evidenced, to oppose to it.

RAD. Would you, then, have me give up as false, the idea that any truth is revealed immediately from Brahma, and yet assert for yourself that the law of Moses, for instance, came by immediate revelation?

LAUR. That shall be discussed by and by: at present I wish to explain further the meaning of what I have said, lest it should leave in your mind a wrong impression as to the amount of influence I intended to ascribe to the senses in the transmission of religious truth. And by the transmission of it, I mean here the conveyance of it to one being from another, whether this being be man or God. And I was disposed to assert, that we do not know of any revelation directly from Him in that sense and manner, that the use of external means operating on the senses is discarded altogether. At some period or other during the existence of a man to whom revelations have been made, he has been formed and trained for it by such external means, whether precisely at the same time or not.

RAD. At some period of their existence! Then do you allow that there have been different periods during which the same soul has animated different bodies?

LAUR. No. I was using the word period in a different way, to apply to the earlier stage of a man's present life; but you have suggested what will serve me as an illustration of what I was about to tell you. Observe only, that it is but as an illustration that I use it. If I do not err, your Pandits thought that the seeds of all knowledge were planted in us during a state of pre-existence.

RAD. Yes; and it is impossible to prove that they were not.

LAUR. It is equally impossible to prove that they were. I grant that some philosophers (8) in the West may have thought that they could prove that there had been such states of pre-existence. And it does not seem incredible that the present system of the world should possibly be the consequence of somewhat past, of which we are totally ignorant (9). But to assert that our souls existed in that system, or those systems, which preceded and possibly gave rise to the present system, is quite another matter, and one not nearly so probable. And therefore, if instead of first imagining a theory, such as to account for our present knowledge, and then asserting that such a theory is true, because either it does account for it, or we think it does, if instead of this, we confine ourselves to that small portion of our existence, with which we are actually acquainted (10) by experience, we shall find that even assuming the existence of those seeds of knowledge to be ever so clearly demonstrated, still they are not made available to us without the use of the senses.

Rad. That would seem true enough in regard to common knowledge; but I was thinking of extraordinary information, such as Brahmá gave to Vyása, Manu, and Valmiki.

Laur. And what I wished to understand was, whether we had any absolutely certain information that he did dispense wholly with the senses, in so enlightening them, or at least in forming them to be fit vehicles for such information. And as I had been informed that the Vedas were of too ancient a date for us to know anything certain about the mode in which they were given to the sage Vyasa; and as, moreover, I am told that Vyasa, however divinely guided in the work, was yet but the compiler and arranger of existing revelations, and the Vedas themselves appeal to the ancients before them (11), it seemed, that as we had no certain knowledge as to the mode of their formation, we must argue from what we know, as Gotama allows we may, to what we do not know. In the conveyance, then, of religious knowledge in that part of the government of

Iswara with which experience makes us acquainted, we find that the senses are made use of; the presumption therefore is, that they were used in the conveyance of it, in the earlier stages of his government, which we are acquainted with, not by experience, but by tradition only. And this tradition, so far from being opposed to that presumption, confirms it; for the arranging of actually existing revelations implies that the arranger had heard or seen them—i. e. that he received them through the medium of the senses from something earlier?

RAD. This seems a strange view for a believer in revelation to take. Explain to me further, whether you think all revealed knowledge comes by the senses?

LAUR. I fear you are altogether mistaking the drift of my remarks. I do not at all deny the absolute necessity of an inward and invisible grace working along with an outward and visible, or audible means. All that I insist upon is, that so far as we know, the senses are necessary to the attainment of divine knowledge. I do not say that at any given time the outward and inward means must necessarily co-exist, or otherwise no revelation can take place; but what I say is this, that so far as I know, no man ever existed, to whom revelations were made, who was not fitted for the reception of them during some period of his existence, by means of information conveyed through the senses (12). And I do think it a thing of the most immense importance to keep very distinctly before us the very great use which Iswará makes of the senses, in conveying all knowledge to us, however shallow and unsatisfactory it be to assert that they are the only means.

RAD. I cannot altogether take in what you mean. Our sages have mostly taught that the objects of our senses are unreal, and mere semblance.

LAUR. However, they also teach that the Brahmachári must hear the instructions of his Guru; so that whatever theory you hold about the senses, he cannot go one step towards the fourth degree without the use of the senses. But suppose we descend awhile from sacred knowledge, and see whether the instances of ordinary knowledge will not serve to make what I mean much plainer. Are there not, then, sundry arts which render life more comfortable to us?

RAD. Certainly.

LAUR. And when we look at these arts we find that improvements have taken place in them, in the course of time. But the steps in them already made are something outward and visible, and the skill which avails itself of these existing inventions is something internal. And the existing inventions often lie hid, for a long time, until some clever person lays hold of them, and turns them to account. Crude inventions are like the actions of a hero unsung by the poet; but when the bard comes to them, then they become glorious, and useful to mortals. Still, had the actions not been wrought, the strain might never have entered the mind of the bard. And when we look to the first inventors of these arts, we find they were beholden to outward and visible things; yet we do not deny them to be inspired, or guided by heaven in their inventions, because we assert that they were assisted by outward things. Whoever among you imagined that Náreda was not guided by Brahmá in the invention of the Viná, because the gourd and other objects of sense were necessary in order to that invention? Those objects of sense could not alone put it into his mind, though they were necessary in order to his achieving the invention. And possibly it was not the eye only seeing the gourd, but the ear also hearing the wind blowing where it listeth, which suggested it to his mind. So that to assert the use of the senses is not to deny the absolute necessity of something more than the senses—as this instance will show, whether you consider this to be a case of common or of sacred knowledge.

Rad. In what you say of wind blowing where it *listeth,* you imply that the wind has a will, and so may have spoken (so to call it) to Nareda.

Laur. That you may call it if you please; but you still imply the uses of senses intervening. And let me just mention here how, in saying that the wind has a will, I did so purposely, because it seems to fall in with your way of thought to represent it so. Even if I thought such a representation of no importance whatever myself, I hope you will see how proper it is for me to try to enter into your ways of thinking, and to notice things which tally with them in the Christian system, though perhaps not much insisted on by that system. Things seem to have been inserted in that revelation which should accommodate themselves to the different ways of thinking which different minds have, so that it becomes "all things to all men," in those points which are not fundamental. And I mention this here, that we may not digress over-much to things foreign to the subjects, concerning which I hope we may go on conversing. What I wished you then to allow was, that in arts of life, discoveries, or revelations (call them which you please), do not go on without the aid of sense.

RAD. Now I see, that so far you are not asserting sense to be the originator of all knowledge.

LAUR. So far from asserting that, you see that the view I take even of the common arts is, that no improvement goes on, even in them, without the aid of something internal, above and beyond the senses, although things beneath the senses are used in order to arriving at such improvements. So that I agree thus far with your sages in representing even these as the fruits of inspiration.

RAD. You would have me, then, conclude that a belief in the agency of an invisible Being is not subverted by your view of the importance of the senses; but that a closer examination of things which seemingly are the mere product of sense, at first sight, shows that even there sense will not account for the whole of the discovery.

LAUR. You quite comprehend my meaning now. Let us take another supposition, about the discoveries in the arts, which make our present life happier—a supposition such, that it shall bring us back to those discoveries of the Divine Will which make our future life also happier. The arts, then, seem to have existed in different degrees of perfection in different nations. E. g. musical instruments (13) were mostly invented in Asia, and retained Asiatic names, even after they had passed into Europe. And supposing we could find out the country in which they were first invented, then we should bestow the honour of the invention on some person of that country. Whatever improvements are made (14), still the first beginnings are the most difficult, and so claim the highest praise. And on the other hand, in other cases, so far from improvements being made, we might find that the instruments have been spoiled, in that people have discarded parts of them (15) which they did not see the use of, or that they have forgotten some things which called into action some powers of the instrument; or we might find that they had asserted that men were the inventors of instruments who only brought them over from some other country, or that they seemed to have been forgotten (16) and invented over and over again, with such and such modifications. In all these cases we should measure out praise or blame, according as they had been improved or injured by different nations; and yet we should say that the first nation who invented them was to be most honoured, wherever that nation dwelt; and we should think the least of those who had lost all notion of the skill it required to invent them, and spoiled them by their own listlessness. And see, Rádhákánt, how in all this I keep to one sense—the sense of hearing; which is the one chiefly concerned in all musical matters, as well as in the transmission of sacred truth.

RAD. But is not the same true of sight likewise?

LAUR. Some men have thought so in regard to one other most useful invention, which has tended to fix down, and give a visible and permanent form to what existed first in sound only. I mean the invention of letters. For as all the letters of the different parts of India may be traced to the Devanágari, so some one has thought that the letters of the whole world may be shown to have in them affinities and similarities (17), when you arrive at the intervening links which explain how one came from another; and although I only know of one nation (18) who have any record, that can be depended upon, of the invention of its alphabet, even that nation had one or two alphabets to build upon; so that I cannot say anyway more of this outward form into which things conveyed by hearing have thrown themselves, than of the songs and instruments yielding divers sounds, that they were ever invented entirely and throughout without some foundation to begin upon (19). And I hold, that as this was the case in common knowledge of sundry kinds, so was it the case also in revealed knowledge. One nation kept it up more purely than the rest; still all drew from one original tradition, and when this tradition ceased to be oral, and came to be written, then according as each nation had been faithful to the original tradition, its written documents tallied with the written document of the nation, which in sacred things holds the place that our inventor of music does in common things. And the nation which had most faithfully kept up the oral tradition had also fresh written tradition given to it. And (20) the writers of this fresh revelation were not taught it all at once, without any previous knowledge of the existing discoveries of the Divine will, but after it. And though the Western nations were so miserably off that they had (21) no Scriptures at all to look up to, yet this was not the case in the East, e. g. in China or India, where the old oral tradition was early committed to writing; was reverenced by all the virtuous, and guarded by an order of men believed to have been divinely set apart for that purpose.

RAD. Then you would have me believe that the Vedas came from oral tradition, and were not revealed to Vyasa?

LAUR. Is not the common name of S'rúti a proof that they came by hearing, from some other quarter, whatever difficulty may exist as to the precise meaning of the term? For Sankara says (22) that he who knows the Vedas, does not set about any arbitrary interpretation of them, but has recourse to his Guru, who knows the eternal and true Purusha, and hath him in his mind. Yet, as the Mundaka Upanishad teaches, he learned it from some other; and the Chandogya Upanishad says that if there were no speech, then it would be impossible to distinguish right from wrong, truth and falsehood, good and evil, friend and foe. Speech, it says, makes the Rich and other Vedas to be known (23). The most ancient account seems, then, to be, that they were received from tradition, and so that they were not born by the river Saraswati, but came from some other quarter. As far as any tradition about them goes, they came from the north of India, not from the south: they came, therefore, from that part of India which is nearest to that in which, as our sacred books tell us, the human race was first dispersed abroad.

RAD. You have told me that you think the Vedas were the offspring of collected traditions, and that those traditions came from some country further off, and that in this last country the human race first took its rise. But you have not said how far you think they kept up that tradition in a pure form. When you spoke of the musical instruments travelling from one nation to another, you remind me of the Chhandas, which is necessary in order to the right reading of the Vedas; but you at the same time also suggested, that as in regard to musical instruments (24), so in regard to sacred truth, some nations through want of right discernment, perverted it. Now how far have the sacred music of the Vedas, their accents, and their singing, kept the doctrine also pure?

LAUR. That, Rádhákánt, is a very wide question, and one which cannot be easily answered; yet I will attempt such an answer as may be in my power. My belief that Vyasa and others received the sacred learning by the sense of hearing, be it remembered, does not imply that I deny that there was some gift of a supernatural kind likewise necessary, in order to lead him to arrange them as he did, or to give him guidance in retaining this or dropping that, so as to make the book serve the ends for which it was designed. Now if you wish to know of what precise kind this supernatural power was, I will tell you what an ancient tradition reports concerning it. After a time men on earth grew wicked, and a flood was sent to punish them; only a few were saved, and they all spoke one language, but as they availed themselves of this for unholy purposes, they lost this oneness of speech; and though a slight resemblance is traceable in languages of the most remote nations, still they were all divided; and the tradition says it was into seventy-two different nations, according to the number of the angels of God. Thus, besides the outward and visible governors of nations, there were certain angels set over them (25). Hence there was a prince of Persia, and a prince of Tyre, and a prince of the Jewish people, among these angels. And according as the angels were mighty or not, they obtained blessings for their nations. Thus the Jews received the Law by the disposition of angels, and so other nations may, according to this tradition, have retained different amounts of true doctrine. And wherever we find true doctrine to have been kept up, there we may suppose an angel to have interfered, and to have been the messenger of true knowledge.

RAD. But what are these angels?

LAUR. They are ministering spirits who wait upon the most high God to execute his commands.

RAD. And do you really believe that the Vedas were inspired by one of them, in so far as the invisible and unseen part of the revelation is concerned?

LAUR. I only said it might have been, that so far as they kept up the truth, a good angel interfered in order to secure to them that amount of truth which they have preserved. But it will be more important for us to consider the external than the internal means of the revelation. We have already made some advances towards showing that the ancient doctrines of your countrymen came from the country of Cashmere, and so probably from some country still further off, which was nearer to the primitive seat of the ancient tradition. And how long your countrymen kept up a communication with this source of primitive tradition I will not venture to determine; though the fact that there is no mention of incarnations in the Vedas, may be perhaps taken to look as if they had had communication with the old centre of traditions mediately, or immediately after Vyasa's time.

I know, indeed, that the doctrine of incarnations (26) was once widely spread over the world (27), east and west; but I believe it came from primitive tradition to you, not through the Chinese (28), who preserved it very faithfully, but through some other source.

RAD. But how can you prove the existence of such primitive tradition at all; or how, if proved, can you show that you do not, by proving it, subvert at once the high claims to inspiration which you assert for Moses?

LAUR. To you, who do not believe in Moses' writings, I may not be able to make out the existence of such early tradition to be more than an hypothesis which will clear up some difficulties; while to myself, who believe his writings and our other Scriptures to be infallibly true, the proofs for it are more than those of a mere hypothetical kind. With the latter proofs, then, at present, I have nothing to do, but the former only; and with regard to your supposition (that by proving that hypothesis to be true I am destroying the claims asserted to Moses as an inspired writer), I think you are mistaken there. For even supposing the whole amount of Moses' writings to have existed in tradition antecedently to their existence in writing (a supposition which I by no means contend for), still there would be room enough for inspiration to guide him in selection, juxta-position, order, language, and many other points. But I merely assert thus much—that there existed a patriarchal tradition, from which Moses in part drew; that in such tradition he was instructed by one of his senses (viz.

hearing), and that there is proof for the existence of such a tradition. But besides all this, it may be observed, that although we have no right to expect that things necessary to our eternal happiness shall be put before us in the way of authoritative command, yet such authoritative command, when given us, does not necessarily increase in amount, though it materially increases in obligation the rules, precepts (29), doctrines, and facts, already existing in tradition.

RAD. But may I ask for some sketch of the proof of this tradition having existed; such as may point out what things I ought to examine into further, provided I wish to feel more convinced about it.

LAUR. The kind of proof may be suggested to you by the remarks already made upon Plato's system, as appearing to agree wonderfully with the Indian system, in several points. The agreement, I will assume, is such as to force it upon my mind that your philosophy and his were drawn from a common source. For after all points of disagreement are dropped, we find many fundamental points in which the two agree; and from that agreement we are led to conclude that both may be traced to one common source. And this would strike us to be so, whatever difficulty we might have in establishing the connecting links, and would hold good even if the doctrines were false. Their truth or falsehood does not affect the proof of their common origin. And this would force itself upon our belief more as we saw that the points of agreement were points which belonged to a system common to both, and are not isolated truths, such as the experience of all nations would arrive at without intercommunion, and embody in the form of wise sayings, and proverbs, unconnected with each other. Now I think that there are certain points in which the books of Moses agree with the Vedas and Manu, as also with those of other countries, and I should argue from that that they drew from a common source. The differences between them do but make this more credible, inasmuch as they show (what, upon the principles already discussed, we might be led from the analogy of the discoveries in arts and sciences to expect,) that in regard to the discovery of the will of Heaven on religious matters, there would be a certain basis alike in all nations which had access to the first discovery, though improved or impaired by subsequent modifications. Now the old Chinese books, as well as the oldest Indian books, agree with the books of Moses in declaring that there is but one God; I infer then that this belief was handed down (30) by primitive tradition to all nations, and that those nations who lost this tradition forgot God. But that which is forgotten, was once known. And if we look to the Egyptians (31), the very ancient people in whose wisdom Moses was learned, we shall find that there are strong traces of this belief having existed amongst them.

RAD. But if Moses was learned in their wisdom, how can it be proved that they were not the source from whence he drew his knowledge? I have heard somewhat of the Egyptians from the Mohammedans, and thought also that they had been great enemies of all true doctrines, according to your views.

LAUR. Not probably in ancient times; and we hold that whatever Moses may have learnt among them, it was Joseph, who originally taught the ancient wise men (32) of Egypt all true wisdom; so that in this case truth came from out of the Jews to other nations (33): and all the early apologists for the Christian religion are of one opinion upon this point, as to much of the information gained by the Greeks at a subsequent period upon religious subjects (34). And my belief is, that the same line of tradition which was kept up by prophets (35) since the world began, and finally subsided, so to say, into writing among the Jewish people, was the original stock out of which all others drew. I have given you some evidence for it as far as regards one nation, the people of Egypt, and trust to give you some proof also that it was the case with other nations.

RAD. I see plainly that hitherto you have only shown that Moses may have been helped in his knowledge of sacred things by an existing tradition from the earliest time; so that if he and Vyasa were both arrangers of existing traditions, and if their inspiration was displayed in the sorting and arranging those traditions, and adapting them to their respective nations, the question will be how we are to discover which nation has kept up the greatest amount of the old tradition; which, in fact, is the truest representative of the ancient system of religion, once (according to you) the property of all the kindreds of the earth. Relate to me, then, what proofs you have to offer in favour of the tradition of Moses above that of others.

LAUR. I wish first to caution you against thinking that I hold that the whole of Moses' inspiration lay in selecting out of existing tradition (36). That I never taught nor intended; still I think that what we have first to dwell upon, is such parts of his system as appear to have been the re-sanctioning of existing tradition. If by taking this part alone of Moses' system, I can succeed in showing that it bears marks of being the truer revelation, then any argument drawn from the character and dignity of the other, and distinctive portions of it, will come in afterwards as corroborative of the former evidence in its favour. And observe how the fact that there are a great many conflicting revelations in the world, of which such parts only can be true as agree with the truth once known (37), shows that something more than the mere sense of hearing is requisite to secure the transmission of the truth. Let us, then—feeling sure that however God may choose, in transmitting the true revelation, to make use of the senses to humble man's spiritual pride, still He accompanies them with inward operations at the same time;—let us proceed to consider the amount of external resemblance between your law and that of Moses. As the two are not likely to have drawn from each other, considering the early date and distance of countries, and other points which might be mentioned, I am now going to consider them as far as they are both drawn (38) from some earlier tradition, and then to examine what likelihood there is that the law of Moses preserves that tradition purer than the law of Manu does. And even if no likelihood can be drawn from any thing observable in the points of similarity, still there will be found other things in which we can discern evidence in favour of the laws of Moses.

RAD. But how are we to arrive at the standard of primitive tradition, in order to compare it with the laws of Manu and those of Moses?

LAUR. We of course think it exists in the earlier history of the world, as related by Moses. But for the present I will merely *assume* that to be true in which they agree. Thus, for instance, the First Book of Moses teaches that at the time of the Flood there existed a distinction between clean and unclean animals: the law of Moses and the law of Manu both keep up such a distinction; and in some cases the animals are the same which are classed as clean and unclean. But as in the one law, so in the other, there is no palpably evident reason why some animals should be assigned to the class to which they are assigned; which in itself, and taken alone, would lead one to think that they so far both kept up faithfully an old tradition, the reasons for which had been lost. For as both codes show marks of thoughtfulness and design, to set aside such distinctions peremptorily, and at once, as absurd, is evident unfairness and self-conceit. Indeed, the whole subject of this distinction between clean and unclean animals evidently runs up into something mysterious, and cannot be reflected on with any degree of seriousness, without at once leading us to feel our ignorance upon the subject, and inclining us to think that a belief so widely spread took its origin in something unknown to us, traditions of which have been perpetuated throughout the whole world. Thus, considering the fidelity of dogs, one does not see at once why they should be the animal selected to express contempt by every nation upon the earth; yet this view of the animal falls in with the language of our Scriptures concerning it, which use it every where as a term of disparagement, and class it amongst the unclean animals. However, to take another instance in which the law of Moses coincides with yours (39), gentleness to animals is prescribed with great minuteness in Moses' law, as well as in yours; which, considering men's proneness to act arbitrarily towards all creatures in their power, seems to be also a remnant of ancient tradition, and belongs to a time when the destruction of living creatures for food was forbidden. And this, be it observed, was a doctrine which was circulated in the West also (40). But as the Maker of the world is the Lord and Proprietor of it, of course He has a right to order a man to take away the life of another man, if it shall seem good to Him so to do; and much more to put the life of brute creatures into the power of man. The exceptions, then, to the Ahinsa in both codes, whether for sacrifice or for other purposes, appear to be further marks of a tradition widely spread. For to deny men's right to kill living creatures for proper purposes is heretical with you, and with us too. Yet as heresy mostly originates in men setting up their own judgment against what is revealed (41), so it does not seem that men would ever have come to assert their right to take away the life of other creatures; but from a revelation handed on from father to son. The coincidence, however, of the law of Moses with that of Manu, in this respect, would not be anything remarkable, were it not for their coincidence in the two former points. Further, as the two codes acknowledge a distinction between different brute creatures, so do they also between classes of men. There is in both a distinct class to which the priesthood is attached: in both, this priesthood is to have no possessions, but to live by the alms of the pious, and to make religion their portion; to offer sacrifices for the other tribes, and teach the sacred books; and to decide about difficult cases in regard to pollutions, the kind of atonement necessary, the mode of dealing with heretics, and the like. And besides, the whole view of pollutions as conveyed from matter (42), especially from persons with a flux of any kind, from dead bodies, the cautions against seeing ordure, and the discrimination of the fitness or unfitness of things for sacrifice (43); the obligation of men confessing to the priest wherein they were polluted, are all points of resemblance too striking to be passed over. The use of water, too, in purifications, and of bathing a prescribed number of times, the duty of kindness to the ox in particular, the forbidding the priests to marry in any other class, and other points, are evidence, when taken together, that the two lawgivers had before them some older tradition, from out of which both drew what they deemed expedient. It may be, that after all the resemblance is only external, like the haggard looks which belong to the ascetic as well as to the man of enjoyment, between which casual observers cannot discriminate; still, all these peculiarities, even if merely external, are something very remarkable. And to this may be added, that there was an ancient tradition with you, that in the Satyakalpa there was no distinction of classes. Now, according to this, the setting apart of Brahmans for the priesthood would tally with what is told us by Moses of the choosing of the family of Shem to be the priestly race for the whole world; for so great ethnographers have thought him to mean. And this sanctifying of his family was not till after the Flood. So that if the Satyakalpa be at all supposed to represent the period before the Flood, this account would tally pretty well with that of Moses. But I think, Rádhákánt, I have said enough to show you how there are many points of resemblance, externally at least, between the two codes, which look as if both had drawn from one common source. And you will have remarked how the books of Moses mention some things which seem to clear up difficulties in your law, to explain, for instance, how sacrifice and Ahinsa are consistent. For the order of nature is the order of things which God has appointed: now it is not conformable to the order of nature for a reasonable being to cut short the life of another, with the whole capacities and destinies of which revelation alone can make him acquainted. But the permission given by the Author of nature, who is acquainted fully with their capacities and destinies, to destroy living creatures, accounts for the seeming violation of what is natural, and that permission is circumstantially recorded by Moses, which accounts for the fact (44) that it is considered allowable to destroy them. For it is heretics only who are for shutting up things where the Lord has left them open. To all these points of resemblance must be added two very remarkable ones besides, which are these:—the Vedas and the Manava-dharma-Sastra, both recognize one self-existing eternal God as the first cause of all (45), the Maker of the universe, which doctrine agrees externally at least with that of Moses, both in character and in the position it holds at the beginning of the codes; and besides this, it appears that from the time of the Deluge, if not from an earlier period, one family was set aside to be the especial minister of God—the family of Shem (46). And as the Brahmans (47) appear to have been at first a colony of priests in the holy land of Brahmavarta (48), some learned men have thought them to be of this very tribe of Shem, who was held to be the father of all the priestly tribes of the whole earth (49). At all events these which have occurred to me must, I think, be allowed to be proofs of a similarity so striking, as to lead one to assume that both drew from one common original tradition, which existed long before letters were invented.

RAD. You have shown me now how the laws of Moses, and those of Manu, by coinciding, presume the existence of some tradition, whence both drew, passing in our case through the Vedas as a preliminary step; which Vedas are, I am told, about as old as the writings of Moses. But what particular evidence there is for supposing the law of Moses preserved the truer tradition, you have not yet set before me.

LAUR. Before I proceed to show you this, I will first ask you whether you have any strong objection in your mind, which would prejudice you against believing that the law of Moses is divine?

RAD. There is, Laurence, one thing which, in my mind, is an insurmountable difficulty against it, and which I do not believe can be got over.

LAUR. Pray tell me it; for I am so convinced of its divine origin, that I will at least endeavour to get over it.

RAD. It is, that there is said to be no appearance whatever of a belief in a future state, the denial of which Manu makes to be a sign of the quality of darkness (50). And all our old books insist very much on this belief as being, what it manifestly is, essential to morality And I believe it to be a mark of an ancient system that it does insist, and of a later one that it does not insist, upon this doctrine.

LAUR. I think, Rádákhánt, that I have much reason to be glad that you have mentioned this objection so plainly, because it will give me an opportunity of discoursing with you upon two points, one of which will furnish a general solution to your question; the other may be called more properly the answer to it. And I will take them in this order, though I know that at first sight I shall seem to be eluding the difficulty, instead of meeting it. And the reason why I do so is, because it will clear our way in case we see fit to continue our conversation together.

RAD. I see that you are using an artifice to keep me longer talking with you, and am glad that you seem to imply, by your wish to interest and detain me, that you think me teachable.

LAUR. Kindly said, my son. However, to go to the point to which I wish to direct your attention. If the Books of Moses are the revealed will of God, or were assumed to be so, then no objection whatever, drawn from any omission of the kind you specify, would be of weight against them. For in case they are His revelation, then we are quite ignorant what particular things ought, or ought not, to be in a revelation; what degree of clearness in setting them forth was to be expected, what difficulties would be contained in it, what would be cleared up by it, and how far its meaning would be clear from the first, or be gradually developed by subsequent means. And there is a particular reason for this to us, who both believe the world to be made and governed by God; who gave what we respectively believe to be revelations. For in this world which we see about us, there are as many difficulties as in the revealed system, which we believe but do not see; although, when we are familiarised with them, we do not notice them, in most cases (51). Now we expect that in this world experience will clear up difficulties of many kinds, which expectation is partially fulfilled, and only partially. Many and great objections, which seem to lie against the declarations of the wise as to the best rule of conduct in this portion of our existence, though not to be removed or answered, seem quite overbalanced by reasons on the other side. Men are left in far greater uncertainty, indeed, as to their rule of conduct (52), than the brute beasts are, and have to arrive by degrees at that discrimination (53) which seems to exist from the first in these creatures. Hence, if this be the case in natural knowledge, it may be also in regard to our spiritual knowledge. The means by which He who is the source of all knowledge guides us to one and the other have many parallels. That the sending or not sending a reasonable soul into a state of probation depends in many, and possibly the largest number of instances, upon mere lust; the use and enjoyment of his highest faculties is often taken away from him by the bite of a brute beast, itself in a state of wildness and madness, are facts which, *à priori*, would have been highly incredible. And so many things of the kind might be brought together as to make it seem to the profanely inclined, that the world was governed upon the most arbitrary principles of indiscriminating despotism, when the other things, which prove the contrary, are put out of sight. Hence it is plainly to no purpose whatever to object to a revelation, that it takes no care whether or no we are sent safely into a future state, since, for all we see, it is a mere matter of haphazard whether we are sent into existence at all. And when in this state of existence experience does not give us better than dark hints about the way in which we are to act in a great many cases of vast importance to us, and after all, by such a mean thing as a brute creature man may be bereft of the only guide which he has among these difficulties—a guide which often seems of no use to him, especially if he allow himself to trifle about things which may perchance be important. So that the means by which the Loid of the world leads us to ordinary knowledge, where the comparatively unimportant interests of this world are at stake, do not seem at all to warrant us in insisting upon clearer evidence, where the far more momentous concerns of the next world, so much more calculated to rouse us, and to make us attentive to weak evidence, are at stake: and especially is it certain that those who make light of the experience of others, run themselves into difficulties and miseries which no future attention will altogether remove. Nor does it seem at all unlikely, considering that this world is a place of trial and probation, that these difficulties should have been purposely thrown into the way of all true knowledge as to conduct in regard to this world or the next, in order that the careful and attentive might be rewarded. Hence it will appear, that if the omission of the doctrine of a future state in the laws of Moses were a difficulty which could not be cleared up at all, still that in itself would be no argument against its being a revealed system: so long, then, as it is under discussion whether or not they are so, a difficulty of this kind cannot be made decisive in the matter. For there are difficulties quite as great in that part of the system of the universe, which becomes the subject-matter of natural knowledge; and difficulties which experience does not remove. We finite creatures are not at all judges how an infinite Being ought to act; and therefore, going by what we see of His government, we cannot argue from that, that any system which came from Him would necessarily take care that we were duly informed about our being brought into a future state of existence, seeing that, to outward appearance, He commits our being brought into this present existence (or, as I should say, into existence altogether) to mere lust and passion, in so many instances. But I will grant that, however little we could assert that a revelation ought, necessarily, to bestow such and such information concerning such and such difficulties, we may reasonably expect that as experience, which is the guide to natural knowledge, clears up certain (though not all) difficulties in regard to our present life, so would a revelation, which is the guide to supernatural knowledge, clear up certain difficulties in regard to our future life. Hence, when we find a revelation which says nothing of what we are all so highly interested in—viz. whether our life lasts beyond the grave, or no—we naturally look out for some grounds for the omission.

RAD. Then you allow, if I understand, most fully my objection, and assert that the mention of a future life is omitted?

LAUR. I certainly feel of the opposite opinion completely, but will nevertheless waive that for the present, and allow your objection to be true as a fact, but to be of no weight whatever.

RAD. I shall be curious to know how, after what you first said of the omission requiring to be accounted for, you contrive to make so light of it.

LAUR. Living creatures, Rádhákánt, of many kinds can be tamed, and made subservient to man, can they not?

RAD. You surprise me with that question! Surely they can, if it behoves me to answer as a dutiful Brahmachári.

LAUR. And when we set about teaching children,

we treat them as if they had some faculties which other living creatures have not: e. g. we do not treat a child as we should an elephant, but as having such and such advantages over an elephant.

RAD. It is so.

LAUR. And if we had to teach a man, we should not treat him as a child, but take it for granted that he knew certain things, which all men, who are not idiots, do know; should we not?

RAD. Assuredly.

LAUR. And if we had to teach a man who, we knew, was a Grihastha, we should not set about teaching him things which he knew already.

RAD. That is so.

LAUR. In imparting natural knowledge, then, we consider the faculties, and advancement, and knowledge of the person to be taught, so that we do not trouble ourselves to teach things which we have no reason in the world to think he does not know.

RAD. That is all most evident.

LAUR. Well, then, have we any reason in the world to think the Jews did not know of a future state after death, at the time when Moses taught them? Let us see how this is. They had been living in a country (54) noted all the world over for its knowledge of a future state, insomuch that some people have said the doctrine was invented there (55), which of course is mere nonsense in the eyes of any one who believes that ancient tradition to have existed which we spoke of, or as Christians do (56), that it was Joseph, an Israelite of far less note as a teacher than Moses, who taught them in these matters. And as for the Jews being a gross people, and set upon things of sight, that is no more than is quite as true of people who have revelation of a future life to guide them. For the attachment to this world evinced by many of them is perfectly unaccountable upon any principles of reason. Supposing, then, that the traditionary teaching of a future state was so well known at that period of the world, that even the Egyptians were aware of it, there would be no use in enforcing what was believed; whereas, in any age, or part of the world, in which men had fallen into a general disbelief of it, the republication of it would be naturally to be expected. But to lay it down to those who knew it, would be like teaching a Grihastha as you would an elephant.

RAD. But you said that you thought that the law of Moses did contain the teaching. Explain, then, how it comes to teach it, as you have now led me to think that the teaching is supererogatory?

LAUR. It does not teach it in the way of formal statement, but seems to me everywhere to take it for granted, as you would wish me to take many things for granted, and not state systematically things which I should state systematically before a child.

RAD. But will you mention to me some of the places in the law of Moses, which fall in with the doctrine supposed to be known?

LAUR. If man was made in God's likeness, as

Moses says, and if, further, the fact of his being so made is the reason why neither brute nor man must slay him with impunity, the smallest possible excellence that would constitute any likeness between a creature and his God must lie in his having an existence prospectively eternal (57): for any other likeness to Him we can conceive of as being altered, but this would endure, for all we can see, in Hell (58). And Enoch is said by Moses to have ascended into heaven, which shows that not only was the soul immortal, but that the body might become so. Men are said also to sleep with their fathers, which implies that they may wake up after that likeness in which they were first made, and also that their fathers existed still; and in the place of your Sraddha they are bid to confess their sins (59), and the sins of their fathers, which would be idle, if their fathers ceased to exist. And Abraham is said to be like a shock of corn, when he dies; now, unless the words of holy writ are mere similes like ours (which it would be highly profane to presume, seeing that we account them God's words), he was to be gathered into some garner as a shock of corn: and God is called the God of Abraham, and Isaac, and Jacob, which would be an unmeaning title if they were not living in another world. And Moses is said to be gathered or added to his fathers, which were of no meaning if they did not exist to be gathered unto (60); especially as their bones were far away from the place where he died. Nor is this an isolated doctrine, which drops with the law, but in our Sanhita of Psalms it abounds every where; and in the book of Job, which is at least as old, if not older, than that of Moses (in all probability), and in all the prophets, this same doctrine is universally implied. Moreover, in certain books which hold a middle place between the times of the prophets and the apostles (61), in the Paraphrases (62) made from the old Hebrew books into Chaldee, and in all later Jewish books, with the exception of those of an infidel sect among them, this doctrine was universally maintained. So that there is not anything which is at all sufficient to ground a doubt upon it as to its ever having been disbelieved. Hence, if this be your only objection to the law of Moses, I think we may go on to show what evidence can be offered to prove that he teaches a truer system than the Vedas. And, indeed, the fact of his writing at a time when a legal enforcement of this doctrine was not necessary, seems itself to be, when taken in conjunction with other things, a proof of the antiquity of the Books of Moses.

RAD. But you taught me to expect that, as experience clears up difficulties of some kinds in regard to our conduct as citizens of this world, so revelation would in regard to our conduct as citizens of a future world. Now, you have shown me that the patriarchs believed in a future state; yet, as it is not a thing plain and obvious how men came into this world, and why they are sent here, can you show me any thing in the laws of Moses which would seem to meet this difficulty?

LAUR. I think I can; and in so doing we shall come to show the point I have just mentioned, viz. the evidence there is that the law of Moses teaches a system which is truer than that of the Vedas. The belief that the world is renewed and destroyed at different periods, is a doctrine which, however likely or unlikely, is one which we cannot prove to any degree of certainty. Now it is likely, as we have agreed, that a revelation would clear up difficulties, and especially difficulties of a practical kind; the world is God's world, and we are His creatures; and though we, as well as you, should allow that a revelation has much which is inexplicable and mysterious in it; still that it should explain matters of high concern to the welfare of man, as God's creature, is natural to expect beforehand; and when found, is an evidence, and perhaps a very high degree of evidence, in favour of a revelation. Now our system contains nothing at all about previous creations, cycles, and periods, during which the Creator was successively asleep or awake: neither does it tell us anything of Munis or any other inferior beings (63) joined in the Creation; neither does it approach to a confusion of the Creator and the created (64), or speak at all as if there was any matter co-existent with Him from eternity; all which, if I am not misinformed, the Vedas do mention, or intimate. Now, in the account of things given by Moses, there is something especially practical; nothing is recorded to gratify curiosity; no co-creators are even hinted at; no confusion is made between Creator and creature; scarce more is told us, in fact, than is necessary for practice, and practice under this part of our existence, with which we are made acquainted by experience. And though it may be true that, in the government of the world, other ministering spirits are employed, still there seems to be some divine foresight evinced in the omission of any specific account of their creation. For as their ministrations were ineffective save through the abiding presence of God sustaining them in existence, the silence upon the subject of their early and remote existence served to fix men's attention on the Creator more undividedly. And when we contrast this silence with the talkativeness of other early books claiming to be revelations on the subject, and consider how such beings so spoken of have subsequently formed the groundwork of polytheistic worship, the silence in itself appears to be no small evidence of the Books of Moses having come from Him who knew before-hand what was in man, and so to be an instance of the practical character of that revelation. Further, there is nothing which can be reasonably looked upon as a mere imagination of Moses to account for the speculative difficulties of curious minds. His way of speaking of things throughout is simple (65), and awful to those only who are seriously-minded, and consider what is spoken of, and how, upon the supposition of its being true, it would be of importance to man. All which things, in themselves, are presumptions of the strongest kind that it is a true revelation, and those consequently which conflict with it not so. And further, it may be shown, in several particulars, that your greatest men have deviated from the doctrines of the Vedas, and that the institutions of Manu are not observed in many things. The theory of the castes in this latter (66) is different from what the Vedas teach; the Kalika Purana (67) recognizes the bloody service of Kali, which is quite contrary to Manu's prohibition of such offerings; laborious penances have been changed into easy repetitions of verses, or chapters of sacred books; Vishnu is repeatedly declared to be Pradhána in opposition (68) to older teaching; the injunction on certain occasions to eat flesh and drink wine (69) is disregarded; the food in the code directed to be given to (70) Brahmans at a Sraddha is given only to the relatives of the deceased; all which are things of some importance, in which you have deviated greatly from older practice, whereas it appears that the Jews were jealous of their law even to the last, so that either you admit the inferiority of your own code to theirs by deserting it, or else are bound to show cause why inferior laws have a stronger claim upon that people than yours upon you. Consider, too, whether any nation which for more than 1500 years adhered to one code, or in case of deviations recurred to that code in order to correct them, and to no other, does not give proof of some special Divine Providence interfering to keep up what He is assumed to have given; which, perhaps, in itself is considerable proof of the majesty of that code, to say nothing of its being held divine by Christians also, and only abused as contrary to the spirit of Christianity (71) by heretics or ignorant persons, who do not understand the Christian sense of particular parts of it. And the permanence of the law of Moses is a proof of its having come from God, of the same kind as is afforded by the permanence of some other systems to their divine origin: for instance, the permanence of the laws of the external world affords a proof of its having come from God, although there are many things in the external world also, which it would be preposterous to apply in the present Kalpa to the same purposes to which they were once applied, whether as remedies of disorders, or contributing in any other way to render life more available for the service of God and our fellow-creatures. So, too, the permanence of the moral law graven in men's hearts affords proofs of its being His will, although, when exerting its influence in the codes of different nations at different periods of the world, the positive forms into which it throws itself, fluctuate according to circumstances. Further, there are a number of particular things which the Books of Moses clear up, and which yours do not, such as the way in which the nations after the Deluge came to be dispersed; the way in which traditions, more or less clear, of a division of the first Purusha into male and female came to be handed down to several nations; the way in which man, originally made upright, came to fall: things of which other books have only dark and disfigured traditions, though the whole of them more or less immediately bear upon practical points. Again, there are several of your rites and ceremonies which the Books of Moses come in to explain, such as a belief in the sanctity of the number seven; the words (72) used in the marriage ceremony while the water is poured on the bride's head; the notion that children (73) contracted sinful taints in the womb of the mother; the idea that man is formed out of earthy particles (74); the notion of a heavenly city, out of which four mighty rivers flowed in four (75) different directions; the belief that the world was created (76) by more beings than One; the notion that a certain plant communicated immortality, or that men were saved from some general destruction: and a number of similar circumstances, which the study of the Books of Moses would clear up to you. But I may add here, a little more at length, one instance in which the account of Moses seems to furnish a clue to the meaning of a kind of tradition existing, not only among you, but also among several other people of the world. It is this:—several nations agree with you in speaking of enormous periods during which the world has lasted; the notion is a favourite one with those (77) who do not admit the teaching of our Scriptures. Now these enormous periods do not coincide with each other, and therefore do not form a universal consent against Moses's account. But it has been thought by some that these enormous periods have concealed in them a near approximation to the Mosaic period: for, according as each nation pleased, they multiplied the truer number by another, which served to conceal that truer one from the vulgar gaze. And, in general (78), some number connected with the position of a star much observed by the nation was selected for that purpose. Now supposing $a\,x$ to represent one of these enormous periods, and that the factor x represents the multiple selected by any nation; dividing by it, you will, in each nation, find that the whole sum $a\,x$ is reduced to a quantity a, which is a tolerably close approximation to the period assigned by Moses for the world's duration.

Rad. I must acknowledge that there is some weight in all these observations, especially when I consider how curious it is that they should all apply to one book.

Laur. That, Rádhákánt, is a most excellent observation, and falls in with what I have before mentioned: viz., that the things relating to our higher and eternal interests were evidenced in the same way as those relating to our present interests. As in our present life we find it is not one proof, but many little circumstances taken together, which forms the evidence upon which we act, and that the weight of that evidence lies in their being taken conjointly. So is it in regard to our future life; we act upon evidence, which is made up of a number of points; and though we might take exceptions, possibly, against each one of them, when taken singly, we could not refuse to feel the weight of them when taken jointly, and to let it influence us, without our giving up all claim to be prudent men. And it should be observed, that the kings of this world often punish men, and that capitally, upon the strength of such evidence, especially when several points coincide in one man: by the voice, colour, countenance, limbs, eyes, and actions (79), they form their judgments. Hence, as our present welfare is made to depend upon such evidence, so may our future and eternal welfare also; and "justice being destroyed will destroy;" but the not attending to these things may destroy justice in temporal, and so also in eternal things. You have, then, to consider whether you are doing justice to the Books of Moses, if you do not weigh well the force of this evidence in their case. For the only firm friend who follows (80) men even after death is justice. If much depends upon evidence in itself uncertain, we are bound to act upon it as certain. If a shower of rain might do infinite harm to a Vaisya in some trade, he would be mad to take no heed of the peacock's cry, or the ants' gathering together of eggs, though Gotama (81) suggests that a man may imitate the peacock's cry, or some other cause set the ants upon so doing. Much more then, where eternal interests are at stake, are we bound to attend to uncertain evidence. The Gospel is, in some things, clearer than the law of Moses, yet if you believe not Moses, neither will you believe the Gospel. That, then, is the reason why I am so urgent about the duty of believing the law of Moses, and on this ground wish to sum up to you what I have been trying to teach you.

RAD. That may, perhaps, much facilitate my coming to a conclusion; for it is impossible, in matters of religion, to enter all at once, by a single hearing, into a great system.

LAUR. The revelation, then, which I have been treating of, claims to be from that God who is the Lord and Proprietor of the whole earth, and who will judge the world by the rule of His revelation: you are therefore bound in prudence not to set it aside until the evidence has been fairly gone into, and weighed with thoughtfulness and prayer. Further, several points of difference have been noticed, with the especial view of showing how much more practical the revelation given to Moses is than other supposed revelations. And as there were several proofs of its length of duration in the world, some of which were alluded to, so the book itself declares that many of its rites were more ancient (82) than Moses' time, which, of course, is proof of still greater permanence in regard to those particular rites. And the objection, from the supposed omission of a future state, was also considered, and shown not to be of weight. Now all these things, taken together, are evidence in favour of the Books of Moses far stronger than what we are often given to act upon in regard to the poor concerns of this life. Much more, then, may it be expected of us that we should be awake to our truer and eternal interest, and ready to attend to the lesser degrees of evidence concerning an interest so important, as to involve no less than the eternal happiness or misery of those who are the subjects of it. Let me, then, entreat you to consider this well; for now that I have put thus much evidence before you, if you make light of it, you will be in a worse state to all eternity.

END OF THE FIRST DIALOGUE.

NOTES TO DIALOGUE I.

NOTE (1.) p. 3.

THIS is the opinion of Professor Wilson, in his preface to the Vishnu Purána, p. lxvii, and is, I believe, that which is generally received. The following passage may be extracted from that work, as being one not within every one's reach:—

"The earliest seat of the Hindus within the confines of Hindusthán was undoubtedly the eastern confines of the Panjab. The holy land of Manu and the Purán'as lies between the Drishadwati and Saraswati rivers, the Caggar and Sursooty of our barbarous maps[1]. Various adventures of the first princes and most famous sages occur in this vicinity; and the A's'ramas, or religious domiciles, of several of the latter, are placed on the banks of the Saraswati. According to some authorities, it was the abode of Vyasa, the [reputed] compiler of the Vedas and Purán'as: and, agreeably to another, when on one occasion the Vedas had fallen into disuse and been forgotten, the Brahmans were again instructed in them by Saraswata, the son of Saraswatí."

The name Saraswatí is also that of the goddess of eloquence, which possibly is a mythical mode of representing

[1] Professor Wilson has furnished other specimens of these barbarisms, Notes 1 and 7, p. 170, &c. These rivers are, it seems, transposed in the common maps.

the view of the origin of learning here contended for. I may also add, what has been also noticed to me by Professor Wilson, viz., that the clothing mentioned in Manu, ii. 41

कार्ष्णरौरववास्तानि चर्माणि ब्रह्मचारिण:
वसीरन्नानुपूर्वेण शाणक्षौमाविकानिच

is evidently of a very warm kind, and so indicative of a northern nation. The dress described in Arrian, p. 539. (ed. Blancard.) and Philostr. V. Apoll. T. ii. 20, seems to have been of a warm kind, though not so warm as this. See, too, Bähr on Herod. iii. 106. Perhaps, however, the alterations in it arose from Buddhist superstitions against animal clothing. Other authorities for the view here given (viz. that the north of India was the original seat of Brahmanical learning,) may be found in Ritter's Erdkunde, iii. p. 1094.

There was a tradition that Pythagoras was a disciple of the Brahmans, (see S. Clem. Al. Strom. i. § 70. Apul. Florid. ii. [p. 130, Bip.] quoted by Brucker, Philostr. Vit. Apoll. T. i. 2. vi. 11. viii. 7, § 4.) which would show that they were supposed, at least, to be early known. Euseb., P. E. p. 511, mentions an Indian as being in Athens in the time of Socrates. Clearchus of Soli, a disciple of Aristotle, in Diogenes Laert. Procem. vi., says, that the Gymnosophists were descendants of the Magians; which would go to show a connexion between the Persians and Indians; while the alledged prohibition to leave India, and the absence of any traces of Indian learning having come from Persia or Egypt, have induced Windischman (p. 614) to hold that the reverse was probably the case, and that the Persians drew from Indian sources. Were the question of the antiquity of the Zend language and books one which I could enter upon, doubtless much might suggest itself as to the priority or posteriority of the Indian to the Persian system. (See Wilson's Ariana Antiqua, p. 122.) For the present I have been content to follow the opinion of Windischman, and will only add here that a system might have been developed in India, and travelled back to Persia, although its *original* basis was, as is below assumed, a tradition drawn from the neighbourhood of Babel.

NOTE (2.) p. 5.

Thus, Borhân Eddîn. p. 19, ed. Caspar. انما يتعلم الانسان بواسطة الملك: and with this agrees the Persian doctrine of the Fervers or lower genii attached to each man. See Creuzer, Symbol. i. 2, § 5, p. 201, and compare Alex. Polyhistor. ap. Euseb. P. E. ix. 17, extr. With this notion the following striking language of St. Cyril, de Ador. in S. et V., may be contrasted, as pointing to the truth contained under this heathen belief. Speaking of Saul, he says, p. 191: τοῖς παροτρύνουσι καὶ καταλυπεῖν εἰωθόσιν ἀποκαλύπτει Θεὸς, καὶ δι' ὧν ἥκιστα χρὴ ἔσθ' ὅτε τὰ ἐσόμενα, ἐνηχούντων κατὰ τὸ εἰκὸς ἁγίων Ἀγγέλων εἰς ἀνθρώπινον νοῦν ἅπερ ἂν εἰ μάθοιεν οἱ φιλοπευστεῖν ἠρημένοι κατατακήσονται λίαν καὶ ἀπαρχὴν ὥσπερ τινὰ τῆς σφίσιν ἐπηρτημένης ὀργῆς τε καὶ δίκης ὑπομενοῦσι τὴν πρόγνωσιν. This passage must be taken here for what it is intended; namely, to bring before the reader the fact that men's minds were accessible to angels, and that they might be instrumental in nurturing with reproof even heathens. Its bearing, however, will appear more fully in the sequel (Note 25).

NOTE (3.) p. 6.

Vishn'u-s'erma is the author of the Hitopadés'a; the line referred to is the 149th:

यत्रास्ते विषसंसर्गो ऽमृतं तदपि मृत्यवे

where the word, rendered in the text "close union with the senses," is hardly expressible in English. "Sinnverschlungenheit" might be a good German version of it, perhaps.

NOTE (4.) p. 6.

Windis. p. 1759. "This simple perception is only one source of knowledge. The Scholiast of the Sutras (i. e. sententious rules) adds other besides to them; viz. consequence, comparison, conjecture, privation, and oral tradition. Of all these, none is a sufficient ground of duty save oral tradition, since the others are all grounded on perception, (here meaning particularly the receiving of the rule by sense,) which in itself is no ground at all." The Mímánsa is a system of interpretative philosophy, and the Karma-mimánsa is such a system in its bearings upon moral and religious obligations.

NOTE (5.) p. 6.

"According to the declarations of the Vedas, what the sun and the light are for this visible world, that is the highest good and truth for the spiritual and invisible world; and as our bodily eyes have a definite perception of the objects which the sun illuminates, so do our souls obtain positive knowledge, through contemplation, upon the light of truth which flows from the Being of beings. This is that Light through which alone our spirits can be led to the path of happiness." Wind. p. 815, where there is a very long passage setting forth this doctrine in all its bearings. Although the passage of Plato alluded to may be a well-known one, it may be added here to show the similarity:—"Οταν δέ γ' οἶμαι, ὧν ὁ ἥλιος καταλάμπει, σαφῶς ὁρῶσι, καὶ τοῖς αὐτοῖς ὄμμασιν ὄψις ἐνοῦσα φαίνεται. Τί μήν; Οὕτω τοίνυν καὶ τὸ τῆς ψυχῆς ὧδε νόει. "Οταν μὲν οὗ καταλάμπει ἀλήθειά τε καὶ τὸ ὂν εἰς τοῦτο ἀπερείσηται, ἐνόησέ τε καὶ ἔγνω αὐτὸ καὶ νοῦν ἔχειν φαίνεται. "Οταν δὲ εἰς τὸ τῷ σκότῳ κεκραμένον, τὸ γιγνόμενόν τε καὶ ἀπολλύμενον δοξάζει τε καὶ ἀμβλυώττει ἄνω καὶ κάτω τὰς δόξας μεταβάλλον, καὶ ἔοικεν αὖ νοῦν οὐκ ἔχοντι. Ἔοικε γάρ· τοῦτο τοίνυν τὸ τὴν ἀλήθειαν παρέχον τοῖς γιγνωσκομένοις καὶ τῷ γιγνώσκοντι τὴν δύναμιν ἀποδιδὸν, τὴν τοῦ ἀγαθοῦ ἰδέαν φάθι εἶναι, αἰτίαν δ' ἐπιστήμης οὖσαν καὶ ἀληθείας ὡς γιγνωσκομένης μὲν διανοοῦ, οὕτω δὲ καλῶν ἀμφοτέρων ὄντων γνώσεώς τε καὶ ἀληθείας, ἄλλο καὶ κάλλιον ἔτι ἡγούμενος αὐτὸ ὀρθῶς ἡγήσει. De Rep. vi. 18. And Eusebius notices, p. 471, that Plato was said to have been a disciple of the Brahmans (x. 4); and at p. 511 he mentions, on the authority of Aristoxenus Musicus, that an Indian had taught Socrates that "to know human things was impossible unless he knew also things divine,"—a doctrine which Plato also taught, as he there remarks (xi. 3). Apul. de hab. doctr. vol. ii. p. 159, says, "Ad Indos et Magos intendisset animum nisi eum bella tunc vetuissent Asiatica." All traditions of this kind imply that he was supposed to be acquainted with Indian philosophy. A residence of several years in Egypt (Tennemann, Platonische Philos. i. p. 37) would have given him ample opportunity for acquiring a knowledge of kindred doctrines; while the account of Aristoxenus, just noticed, would seem to make it probable that he might have had intercourse with Indians, and that in Athens, even if there were no probability that the Egyptians had intercourse with the Indians as well for commercial as for other purposes. But without doing more now than mention so controverted a point, it may be instructive to conclude this note with the words of Lactant. de V. Sap. iv. 2. "Philosophi quoniam peragratis et exploratis omnibus nusquam nullam sapientiam comprehenderunt, et alicubi esse illam necesse est: apparet illic potissimum esse quærendam, ubi stultitiæ titulus apparet; cujus velamento Deus, ne arcanum summi sui ac divini operis in propatulo esset, thesaurum Sapientiæ ac Veritatis abscondit. Unde equidem soleo mirari quod cum Pythagoras et postea

Plato amore indagandæ veritatis accensi ad Ægyptios et Magos et Persas usque penetrassent, ut eorum ritus et sacra cognoscerent, (suspicabantur enim sapientiam in religione versari,) ad Judæos tantum non accesserint, penes quos tunc solos esset, et quo facilius ire potuissent. Sed aversos esse arbitror divinâ providentiâ: nec scire possent veritatem; quia nondum fas erat alienigenis hominibus religionem Dei veri justitiamque cognoscere." (Referred to by Staudenmaier, Encyclop. i. p. 260.)

Note (6.) p. 6.

Not seeing the sun for a season. The Greek here is *ἄχρι καιροῦ*, and the Syriac (which our version *generally* seems to follow) ܥܕܡܐ ܠܙܒܢܐ "until fit time;" on which Origen (Philoc. xxvii. p. 106, Spencer.) asks, What time? does he mean that time when he should be corrected through his sins, and so through repentance should be worthy, in both senses, to see the sun in soul and in body;—[in body,] that the Divine Power might be proclaimed in the restoration of his eyes; and in soul, because he was, by believing, to avail himself of God's religion?

Note (7.) p. 8.

This passage is a very famous one in the Timæus of Plato, § 5. *Ὦ Σόλων, Σόλων, Ἕλληνες ἀεὶ παῖδές ἐστε, γέρων δὲ Ἕλλην οὐκ ἐστίν. Ἀκούσας οὖν, πῶς, τί τοῦτο λέγεις; φάναι. Νέοι ἐστὲ, εἰπεῖν, τὰς ψυχὰς πάντες· οὐδεμίαν γὰρ ἐν αὐταῖς ἔχετε δι' ἀρχαίαν ἀκοὴν παλαιὰν δόξαν οὐδὲ μάθημα χρόνῳ πολιὸν οὐδέν.* And so D. Laertius, init., says, *τὸ τῆς φιλοσοφίας ἔργον ἔνιοί φασιν ἀπὸ βαρβάρων ἄρξαι*: on which Menagius truly observes, "Ita Justinus Martyr, Tatianus, Clemens Alexandrinus, Theophilus, Eusebius, Athanasius, Theodoretus, alii." See Potter ad Clem. Al. Strom. v. § 90, p. 699. Philostr. Vit. A. T. ii. 29. Porphyr.

ap Euseb. Præp. Ev. p. 742, who says that Egyptians, Phœnicians, Chaldeans, Assyrians, Lydians, and Hebrews found paths to the gods, from which the Greeks erred.

NOTE (8.) p. 11.

Orig. c. Celsum, p. 244, Spencer. Φέρε παραστήσωμεν, ὅτι ἀνδράσι, οὐκ εὐκαταφρονήτοις τῆς λογικῆς ἕνεκεν θεωρίας καὶ τῶν διαλεκτικῶν σκεμμάτων, σφόδρ' ἀπεμφαίνοντα λέλεκται. καὶ εἰ χρὴ μυχθίζειν ὡς ταπεινοὺς καὶ γραώδεις λόγους, ἐκείνους μᾶλλον χρὴ, ἢ τοὺς ἡμετέρους. Φασὶ δὴ οἱ ἀπὸ τῆς Στοᾶς, κατὰ περίοδον ἐκπύρωσιν τοῦ παντὸς γίνεσθαι, καὶ ἑξῆς αὐτῇ διακόσμησιν πάντ' ἀπαράλλακτα ἔχουσαν, ὡς πρὸς τὴν προτέραν διακόσμησιν. ὅσοι δ' αὐτῶν ᾐδέσθησαν τὸ δόγμα, ὀλίγην εἰρήκασι παραλλαγὴν καὶ σφόδρα βραχεῖαν γίνεσθαι κατὰ περίοδον τοῖς ἐπὶ τῆς πρὸ αὐτῆς περιόδου.

Chrysippus, ap. Lact. vii. 23, is evidently arguing from premises when he says, Τούτου δὲ οὕτως ἔχοντος δῆλον καὶ οὐδὲν ἀδύνατον καὶ ἡμᾶς μετὰ τὸ τελευτῆσαι πάλιν περιόδων τινῶν εἰλημμένων χρόνου, εἰς ὃ νῦν ἐσμὲν καταστήσεσθαι σχῆμα. See Potter on S. Clement, v. p. 649. M. Anton. x. 7.

NOTE (9.) p. 11.

Butler's Analogy, part ii. c. 6. It is not unreasonable to suppose that the same wise and good principle, whatever it was, which disposed the Author of nature to make different kinds and orders of creatures, disposed Him also to place creatures of like kinds in different situations; and that the same principle which disposed Him to make creatures of different moral capacities, disposed Him also to place creatures of like moral capacities in different religious situations, and even the same creatures in different periods of their being. And the account or reason of this is also most probably the account why the constitution of things is such, as that creatures of moral natures or capacities, for a considerable part of that duration in which they are living agents, are not at all subjects of morality and religion [2]; but grow up to be so, and grow up to be so more and more, gradually from childhood to mature age. What, in particular, is the account or reason of these things, we must be greatly in the dark, were it only that we know so very little even of our own case. Our present state may possibly be the consequence of somewhat past, which we are wholly ignorant of; as it has a reference to somewhat to come, of which we know scarce any more than is necessary for practice. A system or constitution, in its notion, implies variety; and so complicated an one as this world, very great variety.

Note (10.) p. 12.

The theory of pre-existence does not necessarily imply the theory of transmigration. Origen, for instance, held the former, but not the latter. (See Schubert, Gesch. der Seele, p. 659, compared with Orig. c. Cels. p. 203.) The latter will be treated of at length in the sequel.

Note (11.) p. 12.

"Auf Traditionen der Urwelt berufen sich die Vedaschriften ganz häufig." Thus, in the Yajur-Veda, xl. 10. 13,

इति शुश्रुम धीराणां ये नस्तद्विचचक्षिरे

"Thus we have heard from the sages, who have delivered it to us," which has been obligingly pointed out to me by Dr. Mill, and appears to be a formula.

Note (12.) p. 13.

S. Austin c. Faust. vii. fin. "Sed cur non potius de Christo, discipulis ejus qui etiam corporaliter ei adhæserunt credimus, qui non solum per Spiritum Sanctum ab ipso im-

[2] Compare, as explaining this, Mr. Newman's Sermons, vol. iv. p. 356.

pertitum scire potuerunt, si quid lateret in rebus humanis, sed tam recenti et præsenti memoriâ, etiam *solo humano sensu*, genus Christi secundum carnem et totam originem collegerunt?" And with this may be joined an important passage from the same Father, de Cons. Evang. ii. 51, on the mysteriousness of memory, even in ordinary cases. "Quia enim nullius in potestate est, quamvis optime fideliterque res cognitas, quo quisque ordine recordatur; (quid enim prius posteriusve homini veniat in mentem, non est, ut volumus, sed ut datur;) satis probabile est quod unusquisque Evangelistarum eo se ordine credidit debuisse narrare, quo voluisset Deus ea ipsa quæ narrabat ejus recordationi suggerere, in eis dumtaxat rebus, quarum ordo, sive ille, sive ille sit, nihil minuit auctoritati veritatique Evangelicæ." Such passages as Amos, vii. 14, and Matt. xvi. 17, constitute, of course, no real objection, since all the *common* means of knowledge were open to those there spoken of, in the previous part of their life. The following words of St. Clement will throw light on the latter passage: Ἀμέλει καὶ τῶν ἐπιβοωμένων τὸν Κύριον αὐτὸν οἱ μὲν πολλοί· υἱὲ Δαβὶδ ἐλέησόν με, ἔλεγον, ὀλίγοι δὲ Υἱὸν ἐγίγνωσκον τοῦ Θεοῦ, καθάπερ ὁ Πέτρος, ὃν καὶ ἐμακάρισεν, ὅτι αὐτῷ σὰρξ καὶ αἷμα οὐκ ἀπεκάλυψε τὴν ἀλήθειαν, ἀλλ' ἢ ὁ Πατὴρ αὐτοῦ ὁ ἐν τοῖς οὐρανοῖς, δηλῶν τὸν γνωστικὸν οὐ διὰ τῆς σαρκὸς αὐτοῦ τῆς κυηθείσης, ἀλλὰ δι' αὐτῆς τῆς δυνάμεως τῆς πατρικῆς γνωρίζειν τὸν Υἱὸν τοῦ Παντοκράτορος. οὐ μόνον τοίνυν τοῖς ἐπιτυγχάνουσιν ἁπλῶς οὕτως δύσκολος ἡ τῆς ἀληθείας κτῆσις, ἀλλὰ καὶ ὧν τυγχάνει ἡ ἐπιστήμη οἰκεία μηδὲ τούτοις ἀθρόαν δίδοσθαι τὴν θεωρίαν ἡ κατὰ τὸν Μωϋσέα ἱστορία διδάσκει, μέχρις ἂν ἐθισθέντες ἀντωπεῖν, καθάπερ οἱ Ἑβραῖοι, τῇ δόξῃ τῇ Μωϋσέως, καὶ οἱ ἅγιοι τοῦ Ἰσραὴλ ταῖς τῶν ἀγγέλων ὀπτασίαις, οὕτως καὶ ἡμεῖς ταῖς τῆς ἀληθείας μαρμαρυγαῖς ἀντιβλέπειν δυνηθῶμεν. Strom. vi. § 132.

Under the Jewish dispensation, one of these common

means would be the traditions handed on by the Scribes and Pharisees who sat in Moses' seat. Thus St. Gregory, Mor. xiv. 56, " Scribæ itaque et legis doctores, qui erudire populos ad vitam consueverant, quid aliud quam venturi Redemtoris consiliarii fuerunt? Qui tamen dum incarnatum Dominum conspicerent, consiliis suis multos ab ejus diviserunt, quamvis prius ad credendum Incarnationis ejus mysterium per Prophetarum verba multos docuisse viderentur." To the same purpose are the words of Eusebius, Præp. Evang. xi. 5. *Καὶ τὸν λογικὸν δὲ τρόπον τῆς Ἑβραίων φιλοσοφίας, οὐ καθάπερ Ἕλλησι φίλον, δεινότητι σοφισμάτων καὶ λογισμοῖς πρὸς ἀπάτην τετεχνασμένοις δεῖν ᾤοντο μετιέναι, καταλήψει δὲ αὐτῆς ἀληθείας ἣν ὑπὸ θείου φωτὸς τὰς ψυχὰς καταυγασθέντες οἱ παρ' αὐτοῖς θεόσοφοι, εὗρόν τε καὶ ἐφωτίσθησαν, ἐφ' ἣν ἀκονῶντες τοὺς τὰ οἰκεῖα μαθήματα παιδευομένους, λόγων τε αὐτοῖς ἱερῶν ἀπαγγελίας ἱστοριῶν τε σεμνῶν διηγήματα ᾠδῶν τε καὶ ἐπῳδῶν ἐμμέτρους συνθέσεις καὶ ἔτι προβλήματα καὶ αἰνίγματα, καί τινας σοφὰς καὶ ἀλληγορικὰς θεωρίας μετὰ κάλλους εὐεπείας, καὶ τῆς κατὰ τὴν οἰκείαν γλῶτταν εὐφραδοῦς ἀπαγγελίας, ἐξ ἔτι νηπίας αὐτοῖς παρεδίδοσαν ἡλικίας. ναὶ μὴν καὶ τῶν πρώτων μαθημάτων Δευτερωταί τινες ἦσαν αὐτοῖς· οὕτω δὲ φίλον τοὺς Ἐξηγητὰς τῶν παρ' αὐτοῖς Γραφῶν ὀνομάζειν· οἳ τὰ δι αἰνιγμάτων ἐπεσκιασμένα, εἰ καὶ μὴ τοῖς πᾶσι, τοῖς γοῦν πρὸς τούτων ἀκοὴν ἐπιτηδείοις, δι' ἑρμηνείας καὶ σαφηνείας ἐξέφαινον.* This passage will throw light upon what is offered in Note 20.

Note (13.) p. 17.

Thus the words *ναβλὴ*, *κινυρὰ*, &c., are derived from כנור נבל, &c., where see Gesenius. St. Clem. Strom. i. § 71. J. Pollux, iv. 60. 74, &c., mention other instruments taken from Asiatic nations. And Julian, ap. Cyril. p. 178, Spanh., allows that the Greeks had their music from foreigners originally, though he ascribes to them the invention of what he calls harmony. Such instances as סומפוניה, קיתרוס and פסנטרין, which were borrowed from the Greeks at a *later* period, will not prove any thing as to the origin of music, although it seems fair not to omit them.

NOTE (14.) p. 17.

Aristot. Soph. Elench. vers. fin. Τῶν γὰρ εὑρισκομένων ἁπάντων τὰ μὲν παρ' ἑτέρων ληφθέντα πρότερον πεπονημένα κατὰ μέρος ἐπιδέδωκεν ὑπὸ τῶν παραλαβόντων ὕστερον· τὰ δ' ἐξ ὑπαρχῆς εὑρισκόμενα μικρὰν τὸ πρῶτον ἐπίδοσιν λαμβάνειν εἴωθε, χρησιμωτέραν μέντοι πολλῷ τῆς ὕστερον ἐκ τούτων αὐξήσεως. μέγιστον γὰρ ἴσως ἀρχὴ παντὸς, ὥσπερ λέγεται· διὸ καὶ χαλεπώτατον· ὅσῳ γὰρ κράτιστον τῇ δυνάμει, τοσούτῳ μικρότατον ὂν τῷ μεγέθει χαλεπώτατόν ἐστιν ὀφθῆναι, ταύτης δ' εὑρημένης ῥᾷον τὸ προστιθέναι καὶ συναύξειν τὸ λοιπόν ἐστιν· ὅπερ καὶ περὶ τοὺς ῥητορικοὺς λόγους συμβέβηκε, σχεδὸν δὲ καὶ περὶ τὰς ἄλλας πάσας τέχνας. And in his Metaphysics, i. minor. p. 993. b. 11, Bekk. οὐ μόνον δὲ χάριν ἔχειν δίκαιον τούτοις, ὧν ἄν τις κοινώσαιτο ταῖς δόξαις, ἀλλὰ καὶ τοῖς ἐπιπολαιοτέρως ἀποφηναμένοις· καὶ γὰρ οὗτοι συνεβάλοντό τι· τὴν γὰρ ἕξιν προήσκησαν ἡμῶν, κ.τ.λ. What Aristotle here notices of the importance of small beginnings, is thus applied, nearly as in the text, by St. Cyril. c. Jul. p. 154. Εἰ δὲ δὴ σύνδρομα τοῖς Μωσέως εἰσὶν ἐνιαχοῦ τὰ ἐκείνων, εὐδοκιμοῦσι δὲ λίαν, ὅτι τοῖς νόμοις τῶν Ἑβραίων συμφέρονται, πῶς οὐκ αἰσθάνεται τοῖς ἡμετέροις προγόνοις συγκαταψέγων τοὺς ἑαυτοῦ; ἀλλ' ὅτι τοῖς ἀνὰ πᾶσαν τὴν γῆν γνώριμά τε ἐστὶ καὶ τετήρηται τὰ Μωσέως, καὶ οὐδενὶ τὸ σύμπαν ἀπᾴδει, ταύτῃ τοι φησὶ κακύνεσθαι δεῖν αὐτά. καί τοι πῶς οὐ μᾶλλον ταύτης ἕνεκα τῆς αἰτίας ἐχρῆν καταθαυμάζεσθαι πρέπειν, ὅτι ταῖς ψήφοις ἁπάντων τετίμηνται; Ἢ διδασκέτω πάλιν, τί μᾶλλόν ἐστι τῶν πραγμάτων, οἷς ἂν ἕποιτο δικαίως τὸ ἐπαινεῖσθαι δεῖν. ἆρα τὰ πᾶσιν ἀρέσκοντα καὶ οἷς ἂν τὸ εὖ πεποιῆσθαι λίαν ἔχειν τε ὀρθῶς ἐπιψηφίσαιτό τις, ἢ τὰ ὀλίγοις, ἢ καὶ ὅλως οὐδένι. ἀλλ' οἶμαι τὰ πᾶσιν. Ἔνεστι δὲ τοῦτο τοῖς διὰ Μωσέως θεσπίσμασιν. Εἶτα τίνα δὴ τρόπον, δι' ὧν ἦν δήπου καταθαυμάζεσθαι χρῆν αὐτὰ, διὰ τούτων αὐτῶν ταῖς ἐσχάταις διαβολαῖς ἐνίησιν ἀμαθῶς; Εἰ δὲ ὅτι προηγόρευκε μὲν ὁ Μωσῆς, ἀρέσκει δὲ πᾶσιν, ἀποσοβεῖν ἀξιοῖ τοῦ καὶ ἐπαινεῖσθαι πρέπειν αὐτὰ, φαίην ἂν ὅτι καὶ πολλοῖς ἑτέροις οὐκ ἀγεννῆ λαχοῦσι τὴν δόξαν, ἐπιβουλεύσειεν ἂν, εἰκότως τὰ ἴσά τις αὐτῷ φρονεῖν ᾑρημένος. Πρῶτοί τινες τῶν τεχνῶν εὑρεταὶ καὶ ἐπιστημῶν γεγόνασι τοῖς ἀνὰ τόνδε τὸν βίον. οἱ μὲν γὰρ ὑφαντικὴν, οἱ δὲ τὴν χαλκουργικὴν, ἕτεροι δὲ σκυτοτομικὴν, ἰατρικὴν δὲ πρὸς τούτοις, ἕτερά τε πλεῖστα τῶν ἀναγκαίων εἰς ὄνησιν πολλοῖς προσεπενοήθη. ἆρα οὖν εἰ ταῦτα πᾶσιν ἀρέσκει, καὶ ἀναγκαίως ἐπιτηδεύεται, καὶ εἰς δεῦρο κρατεῖ, τοῦ καταθαυμάζεσθαι δεῖν τοὺς ηὑρηκότας ὑποστερήσομεν; ἀλλ' οὐκ ἂν γένοιτο τοῦτο δικαίως. ἁδροτέρους γὰρ μᾶλλον αὐτοῖς τοὺς ἐπαίνους ἀπεργάζεται, τὸ τιμᾶσθαι παρὰ πάντων τῆς ἐνούσης αὐτοῖς εὐτεχνίας τὰ εὑρήματα.

Note (15.) p. 17.

The analogy between Scripture and a harp is thus noticed by St. Augustine, de Civitate, xvi. 2. "Non sane omnia quæ gesta narrantur, aliquid etiam significare putanda sunt: sed propter illa quæ aliquid significant, etiam ea quæ nihil significant adtexuntur. Solo enim vomere terra proscinditur; sed ut hoc fieri possit, etiam cetera aratri membra sunt necessaria: et soli nervi in citharis atque hujusmodi vasis musicis aptantur ad cantum; sed ut aptari possint, insunt et cætera in compagibus organorum, quæ non percutiuntur a canentibus, sed ea quæ percussa resonant, his connectuntur. Ita in prophetica historia dicuntur et aliqua quæ nihil significant, sed quibus adhæreant quæ significant et quodam modo religentur." So, too, St. Ephrem adv. Scrut. xxi. fin. and xxii. init., where he writes as follows: "Praise to the Lord of all, who devised, yea ordered for Himself two harps, of the Prophets, and also of the Apostles: for one Finger struck two different sounds of the two Testaments; and as the harp changes the sounds, while it is the same harp and the same artist, so do the harps of Truth, my son, change their voices while the Truth is One. Yea, one pipe also is able to gender diversities of sound: for the ear of the mature, it singeth mature sounds; for the ear of children, simple sounds; for the ear of the wise, refined sounds: so also those trumpets of the Truth yield perfect sounds for him that is perfect, and for him that is a child, they frame for him promises of milk and honey." See also St. Gregory, Moralia, i. 11.

Note (16.) p. 17.

Plato, de Leg. iii. 1. ΑΘ. Φέρε δὴ νοήσωμεν μίαν τῶν πολλῶν ταύτην τὴν τῷ κατακλυσμῷ ποτὲ γενομένην. ΚΛ. Τὸ ποῖόν τι περὶ αὐτῆς διανοηθέντες; ΑΘ. Ὡς οἱ τότε περιφύγοντες τὴν φθορὰν σχεδὸν ὄρειοί τινες ἂν εἶεν νομῆς, ἐν κορυφαῖς που σμικρὰ ζώπυρα τοῦ τῶν ἀνθρώπων διασεσωσμένα γένους. ΚΛ. Δῆλον. ΑΘ. Καὶ δὴ τοὺς τοιούτους γε ἀνάγκη που τῶν ἄλλων ἀπείρους εἶναι τεχνῶν καὶ τῶν ἐν τοῖς ἄστεσι πρὸς ἀλλήλους μηχανῶν εἴς τε πλεονεξίας καὶ φιλονεικίας, καὶ ὁπόσ' ἄλλα κακουργήματα πρὸς ἀλλήλους ἐπινοοῦσιν. ΚΛ. Εἰκὸς γοῦν. ΑΘ. Θῶμεν δὴ τὰς ἐν τοῖς πεδίοις πόλεις καὶ πρὸς θαλάττῃ κατοικούσας ἄρδην ἐν τῷ τότε χρόνῳ διαφθείρεσθαι; ΚΛ. Θῶμεν. ΑΘ. Οὐκοῦν ὄργανά τε πάντα ἀπόλλυσθαι, καὶ εἴ τι τέχνης ἦν ἐχόμενον σπουδαίως εὑρημένον ἢ πολιτικῆς ἢ καὶ σοφίας τινὸς ἑτέρας, πάντα ἔῤῥειν ἐν τῷ τότε χρόνῳ φήσομεν; ΚΛ. Πῶς γὰρ ἄν, ὦ ἄριστε, εἴ γε ἔμενε τάδε οὕτω τὸν πάντα χρόνον ὡς νῦν διακεκόσμηται, καινὸν ἀνευρίσκετό ποτε καὶ ὁτιοῦν; ὅτι μὲν γὰρ μυριάκις μύρια ἔτη διελάνθανεν ἄρα τοὺς τότε· χίλια δ' ἀφ' οὗ γέγονεν ἢ δὶς τοσαῦτα ἔτη, τὰ μὲν Δαιδάλῳ καταφανῆ γέγονε, τὰ δὲ Ὀρφεῖ, τὰ δὲ Παλαμήδει, τὰ δὲ περὶ μουσικὴν Μαρσύᾳ καὶ Ὀλύμπῳ, περὶ λύραν δὲ Ἀμφίονι, τὰ δ' ἄλλα ἄλλοις πάμπολλα, ὡς ἔπος εἰπεῖν χθὲς καὶ πρώην γεγονότα. Whence Aristotle, Metaph. xi. 8, Παραδέδοται δὲ παρὰ τῶν ἀρχαίων καὶ παμπαλαίων ἐν μύθου σχήματι καταλελειμμένα τοῖς ὕστερον, ὅτι θεοί τέ εἰσιν οὗτοι καὶ περιέχει τὸ θεῖον τὴν ὅλην φύσιν· τὰ δὲ λοιπὰ μυθικῶς ἤδη προσῆκται πρὸς τὴν πειθὼ τῶν πολλῶν καὶ πρὸς τὴν εἰς τοὺς νόμους καὶ τὸ συμφέρον χρῆσιν· ἀνθρωποειδεῖς τε γὰρ τούτους καὶ τῶν ἄλλων ζῴων ὁμοίους τισὶ λέγουσι καὶ τούτοις ἕτερα ἀκόλουθα καὶ παραπλήσια τοῖς εἰρημένοις. ὧν εἴ τις χωρίσας αὐτὸ λάβοι μόνον τὸ πρῶτον, ὅτι θεοὺς ᾤοντο τὰς πρώτας οὐσίας εἶναι, θείως ἂν εἰρῆσθαι νομίσειεν, καὶ κατὰ τὸ εἰκὸς πολλάκις εὑρημένης εἰς τὸ δυνατὸν ἑκάστης καὶ τέχνης καὶ φιλοσοφίας καὶ πάλιν φθειρομένων καὶ ταύτας τὰς δόξας ἐκείνων, οἷον λείψανα περισεσῶσθαι μέχρι τοῦ νῦν. ἡ μὲν οὖν πάτριος δόξα καὶ ἡ παρὰ τῶν πρώτων ἐπὶ τοσοῦτον ἡμῖν φανερὰ μόνον. St. Clement, Strom. vi. § 27, says that Aristotle took τὰ πλεῖστα καὶ κυριώτατα τῶν δογμάτων from Plato; and this is one out of many instances tending to show the truth of his assertion—an assertion which will strike any careful reader of the two philosophers as of much weight, in spite of their great discrepancies. Imagination has its field, whether Plato went beyond it or not; and imagination always precedes induction, which is but a mere organ of proof. Plato may be taken as symbolizing the former, while Aristotle certainly does the latter (induction), whatever people who do not read him may say.

Note (17.) p. 18.

The case of letters will furnish an illustration of the progress of invention noticed in the last note. It should seem, on the whole, that the original of the Hebrew alphabet was something hieroglyphic: for the names of the letters have a meaning which approximates more or less closely to the most ancient form of those letters with which we are acquainted. Thus the ancient *mém* seems to have originally been a symbol for "water," which the word *mém* means. The ancient *nun* resembled a fish, and *tau* in the Phœnician and Hebrew, as given in a table at the end of Ewald's Arabic Grammar, was a cross: the word seems to mean a brand or mark in this form. And the same is the case with other letters. This was urged of old (see Euseb. Præp. Ev. x. 5. Cyril. c. Jul. p. 231.) as a proof of the derivation of the Greek alphabet from foreign sources. And as all tradition ascribes the introduction of them to Phœnicians, we may see how the letters of (probably) all Europe came from a Phœnician source. For whether the ancient Celtic alphabet constitutes an exception, we do not seem in a position to judge at present[3]. And I may notice, too, the use, for a considerable period[4], of the Greek alphabet by the Copts. And if the old enchorial alphabet *was* not taken, as Gesenius (Gesch. der H. Sprache und Schrift, p. 139.) supposed, from the Phœnician, but the Phœnician from it, as Ideler (Hermapion, p. 80. note 5. Tab. ix.) is confident, there will still be but *one* source of all the aforesaid alphabets. Without having gone into all that Ideler says on the subject, I shall add here the words of Eupolemus (ap. S. Cyril, l. c.) Εὐπόλεμος ἐν τῷ περὶ τῶν ἐν τῇ Ἰουδαίᾳ βασιλέων φησὶν ἐναργῶς, Μωσέα δὴ πρῶτον γενέσθαι σοφὸν, καὶ γραμματικὴν τοῖς Ἰουδαίοις παραδοῦναι τὴν τὸ τηνικάδε

[3] See Ad. Pictet de l'Affinité des Langues Celtiques avec le Sanscrit, p. 6. "L'authenticité de cet alphabet (appelé Coelbren y Beirz) n'a pas été établie ni même discutée, sous le point de vue historique ; mais sa perfection, qui égale peut-être celle du Devanágari est une forte présomption en sa faveur." Apollonius, it may be observed, found in Spain characters unknown to him, which Olearius (ad Philostr. V. 5) imagines was Phœnician : would not Apollonius have known these, being from Cilicia? Can they have been Celtic?

[4] Probably from the introduction of Christianity. See A. Peyron, Gram. Linguæ Copt. p. 2.

τάχα που νενομισμένην, Φοίνικας δὲ παρ' αὐτῶν κατακτήσασθαί τε τὴν ἐπιστήμην ἅτε δὴ ὁμόρους ὄντας Ἰουδαίοις· παραδοῦναι δὲ τοῖς Ἑλλήνων παισὶ, Κάδμου δηλονότι παρ' αὐτοῖς γεγονότος καὶ αὐτὰ δὲ διδάξαντος τὰ πρῶτα στοιχεῖα. It seems allowable, when the matter is so obscure, to think there is something in the tradition (Plato, Phædr. § 134. Phileb. § 23. comp. Kennicott, Diss. ii. p. 148.) which ascribed the invention of them to Theuth or Divinity, (see Ast on Phædr. l. c.) indicative of a divine origin, and possibly faintly speaking of Moses as having been the instrument to convey the invention to men. For if, upon looking at the transition from hieroglyphics to letters, as Ideler gives them, tab. ix., such transition should appear easy to us, the first suggester of it must have been no ordinary person (οὐχ ὁ τυχὼν ἀνήρ). It is impossible for us, who have grown up in the habitual use of an alphabet, to form, perhaps I may say, even the remotest conception of the depth of mind required to suggest that transition.

But to return: my main object in the text is to show, by way of illustration, how a great variety of seemingly unconnected forms may be traced to *one source;* and although I shall be extremely glad if future researches tend to prove that that source was a Semitic one, that is not the thing I am concerned to show in order to make my illustration good. I shall proceed, then, to another class of alphabets. At p. 219 of the sixth volume of the Journ. of the Asiatic Society of Bengal, we find the following observations:—"It is worthy of remark, that in this alphabet, which we may aptly denominate the Andhra character, from its locality, may be traced the gradual transition from the more simple Devanágari to the complicated or florid writing of the southern peninsula. On comparing it with the Hala-Canara, or ancient Carnatic, the letters *n*, *t*, *y*, *r*, *l*, *kh*, *th*, *dh*, *bh*, which may be regarded in some degree as test letters, because they have undergone more variation than others in the modern writing of different provinces, are nearly identical. There is also an incipient loop in the lower line of many of the letters, which becomes afterwards more developed in the west and south. The Telinga or Telugu character is one step further removed; but it springs directly from the Hala-Canara, and retains many of the Andhra letters still unchanged, particularly the *dh* and *th.*" Mr. Prinsep then gives a plate, in which any eye accustomed to the Devanágari will readily see, that it is the basis of these subsequent formations. The importance of noticing these transitions may perhaps be greater than at first we should be supposed to surmise, as Grimm is said (by Pott, Etym. Forschangen, p. xii.) to have shown them to be correlative to certain etymological changes. I may also notice, in passing, that it appears as if some mysterious change in the degree of diversity between handwritings has taken place in the course of ages—a subject upon which the reader will find a very curious discussion in De Maistre, du Pape, i. 15, from which I shall give only the following sentence :—" La correspondence mystérieuse entre les langues et les signes de l'écriture est telle, que si une langue balbutie, l'écriture balbutiera de même ; que, si la langue est vague, embarrassée, et d'une syntaxe difficile, l'écriture manquera de même, et proportionellement, d'élégance et de clarté." This remark I think of the utmost importance, and in my own mind is at the bottom of what I am here saying. To proceed: Professor Wilson, in his Ariana Antiqua, p. 242, &c., has discussed the alphabet deducible from the coins found in those parts. At p. 260 he notices the correspondence of some of these with the Hebrew, and observes, p. 262, " At any rate this much is ascertained, that we have on the coins of Menander and his successors one of the earliest specimens of a well-defined alphabet of the Semitic family ;" referring to Gesenius, Mon. Phœn. p. 74. And as this alphabet is, in a plate, compared with the Devanagari, we see another widely extended branch from Semitic sources, besides the Greek already noticed.

Before winding up this note, it may be well to make two remarks:—

1. Those not accustomed to see different alphabets may be reminded, that diversities, seemingly the greatest possible, at the termini (so to speak) will be no argument against an original common source, if we consider that alphabets probably were originally diffused through the medium of inscriptions on stones or coins. These being hard materials, of course drove artists to expedients varying according to their own skill, or the degree of hardness in the material; which circumstance alone, apart from other considerations of climate, moral condition, &c., would introduce almost an infinity of variations.

2. I would suggest whether, as Philostratus (ii. 27) and Suidas (v. γυμνοσόφισται) lead us to think that there was an intercourse between Babylon and India in the third century, it would not be worth some philologian's while to examine the signs used for vowels in early Indian inscriptions, in order to ascertain whether divers Semitic vowel-points may not have been borrowed from them: an investigation of this kind might also throw some light upon the subject of the connexion between Cabalistic and Indian metaphysics.

To conclude: it will not, perhaps, upon mature reflection, seem unreasonable to any one to suppose that there is something very wonderful and mysterious in the signs by which language is, so to say, gifted with a body and permanent shape. He that feels no serious thoughts at these signs[5], considered as a system over-ruled by Provi-

[5] The numeric signs employed by different nations might furnish a similar illustration in some respects to the one in the text. See Humboldt's paper in the Journal of Science for 1830, p. 300.

dence for men's use, will feel no such thoughts at the investigation of language either. The want of this species of awe has perhaps been the ground of many hasty speculations of which it may be hard to divest the subject. Of this, as of many other subjects which men handle now-a-days, I cannot but confess that I would use the words of our great poet: "Blind fear that seeing reason leads, finds safer footing than blind reason stumbling without fear."—Troil. and Cres.

Note (18.) p. 18.

The Armenian alphabet is here referred to. It is said that Mesrop and Isaac invented this alphabet to suit the wants of the language; the Syriac letters, which they had hitherto used, being insufficient. But it is also said, that they put them together out of existing alphabets (Neuman, Armen. Literatur. p. 32). Ideler has somewhere noticed that one of the letters was borrowed from the Coptic; and Petermann (Gr. Armen.) that the order was taken from Dionysius Thrax. At any rate there would be a manifest absurdity in trying to throw a Sclavonic language into a Semitic attitude, so to call it.

Note (19.) p. 18.

Compare note 16, especially the passage from Aristotle there quoted.

Note (20.) p. 19.

I have stated in the text that the nation which most faithfully kept up the oral tradition had also fresh written tradition given to it. It will be my object, in the present note, to show, as concisely as may be, first, the existence of an oral tradition amongst the Jews; and secondly, that there were colleges of prophets, who were trained up in the study of it, and the commissioned teachers of it. The evidence offered for this will, I fear, necessarily admit of cavil, and must not be considered as the whole of what can be adduced in its support, but merely as a sample which will suggest to thoughtful readers of Holy Writ the mode in which such evidence may be continually amassed.

First, then, I think it will be allowed that there is an appearance of ceremonialism, as it might be called, about the law of Moses. The rules and regulations for sacrifices and offerings are numerous and minute, and enforced with very severe sanctions in some instances. And the general way of modern commentators and of some ancient ones, perhaps, is to assume that the prophets gradually abrogated this ceremonialism; and in particular that any sanctions of a temporal kind were spiritualized only after a lapse of ages. I hope I shall not seem opinionated if I state that my own growing conviction is, that such a mode of interpretation is an untenable one. For does it not seem to involve a direct contradiction of such a passage as Jerem. vii. 21—23? "Thus saith the Lord of Hosts, the God of Israel, Put your burnt offerings unto your sacrifices, and eat flesh. For I spake not unto your fathers, nor commanded them in the day that I brought them out of the land of Egypt, concerning burnt offerings or sacrifices. But this thing commanded I them, saying, Obey my voice, and I will be your God, and ye shall be My people; and walk ye in all the ways that I have commanded you, that it may be well unto you." Here, then, we see that the ceremonial law was not the real object of the legislator, even from the very first: the moral law was given first in the decalogue; the ceremonial was added after, because of transgressions. (See St. Irenæus, iv. 17. § 3. S. Cyril de Ador. p. 58, and St. Ephrem and St. Jerome on the place.) But were there any interpreters of it from the first? Jeremiah proceeds, ver. 25, "Since the day that your fathers came forth out of the land of Egypt unto this day, I have even sent unto you all my servants the prophets, daily rising up early and sending them." Here, then, an uninterrupted succession of prophets is asserted. And we find that it is not at a late, but at an early period, that the ceremonial law is disparaged in comparison of obedience.' See 1 Sam. xv. And with regard to the theory of temporal rewards and punishments, is it not Solomon, the most prosperous of all the kings, who teaches that "all things come alike to all; that there is one event to the righteous and to the wicked; to the good, and to the clean, and to the unclean . . . *under the sun?*" Eccles. ix. 2, 3. Is it not David who owns that he is a stranger and sojourner, as *all* his fathers were? Moses, who is excluded from the temporal land of promise? Asaph, who is perplexed at seeing the ungodly in such *prosperity?* Say what you will to good men and saints having so much higher a view as to be able to suffer patiently, as looking to the recompense of reward, still the prosperity of the wicked seems wholly unaccounted for upon the theory of temporal promises. It is in the law that we are taught that the poor shall never cease out of the land; and it is the law which abounds with exhortations to be kind to the poor, and which bids men give temporal goods to those who, upon this theory, do not deserve them. For if poverty, a temporal evil, were a mark of sin, may we not well ask why should such great care be taken throughout the Pentateuch to make men of wealth feel that the poor were objects of love, tenderness, and compassion?

It seems, then, that these things force one upon supposing, *à priori*, that there must have been an interpretative system of some kind from the first, even if the passage just quoted (Jer. vii. 25) had no appearance of asserting it. And Malachi, who at the very last bids men recur to the law of Moses, also tells us that the priest's lips should keep knowledge; to the intent, doubtless, that the dark sayings of the law might not be hid from the successive generations. (See Ps. lxxviii. Mal. ii. 7. iv. 4, and the place of Euseb. given in note 12.). Let us proceed to show, *à posteriori*,

Secondly, That there were schools of prophets, who were trained up in the study of this tradition, and the commissioned teachers of it. With a view to doing so, I may notice, first, that the New Testament recognises the division of Scripture into Law, Psalms, and Prophets, which is a Jewish division; and according to it the historical books are called the Former Prophets. Conformably with this, we learn from 1 Chron. xxix. 29. 2 Chron. xiii. 22. xx. 34. xxiv. 27, that prophets or seers were employed to compose these books, which looks as if they were commissioned to select such facts as had a typical bearing, and group them with a view to that, and with great indifference to chronological order [6]. For the books are styled מדרשים in 2 Chronicles xxiv. 27, and xiii. 22, the root of which word has always reference to somewhat mysteriously concealed and hard to find out, in which sense the Jews used the word itself from of old. If then the historical books are rightly looked upon by the Jews as prophetical [7], we shall have evidence of a perpetuation of the prophetical schools during the time of the kings. And in Saul's time such assemblages of prophets were looked upon as common, and as consisting of men of holy lives: for their habits must have been openly known to be ordinarily holy; otherwise it were no contrast to say, "Is Saul also among the prophets?" Further, the ordinary mode of training

[6] Aretas in Apoc. p. 297, ed. Oxf., well says, *Μηδὲν θείῃ γραφῇ περὶ τὰ χρονικὰ διαστήματα μικρολογεῖται.*

[7] Orig. in S. Joann. x. § 13, *Οὐ νομιστέον τὰ ἱστορικὰ ἱστορικῶν εἶναι τύποις*, &c.

men to be prophets, to be educated by them. For an exception proves a rule to exist, from which rule it is the exception; and Amos (vii. 14) is evidently surprised at his being commissioned to prophesy, seeing he was "neither a prophet nor a prophet's son." Now the *sons* of the prophets would mean those who gave themselves to that office as their proper profession and occupation; after the way of speaking used by all antiquity. (See Stallbaum on Plato's Phædr. § 74; and for an account of the name, Moehler's Patristik. Einleit. § 3, and Pott. in S. Clem. Strom. i. 1.) But he who has spiritual sons must of necessity have something to teach. Thus when St. Austin (c. Faust. xiv. fin.) says, "Quisque pro modulo suo prædicando Christum debet *generare* Christianos," the faith must have been received by hearing, which he is to hand on, in order to have that heritage and gift which cometh of the Lord. And so, too, must the prophets have had a tradition to deliver, else they could not have had sons (1 Kings xx. 35); and if it be needful now to show that they were the ordinary instructors of the people in difficult cases, which the law anticipated the existence of (Deut. xvii. 8—10), it must be obvious, from 1 Sam. ix. 9, that going to the seer was a common way of enquiring of the Lord; so common as to give rise to the ordinary form of expression there specified, even long before Samuel's day: לפנים. Thus much, then, may suffice to suggest evidences showing the existence of such schools, the perpetuation of them from the earliest times, and that they were the usual educators of the prophets ordinarily so called, whether those prophets were laymen, as Isaiah, Amos, &c., or priests, as Jeremiah and Ezechiel, &c. For there may well have been regular and secular priests then, to use the Christian distinction. What has been here said will be found summarily given by St. Hilary in Ps. Prolog. or. Euseb. Præp. Ev. xi. 5. xii. 1, and more at length by

Molitor, Philos. u. Geschichte, i. p. 155, and John Smith, Discourse vi.

NOTE (21.) p. 19.

See Windischm. i. 1. p. 70, who shows how well attested the antiquity of the King, or Chinese scriptures, is; as Colebrook (Essays, i. p. 98) does in a most striking manner for the Vedas. Hence, doubtless, it was that "in their knowledge of the being and nature of a God, they were already in possession of a light which was but faintly perceived even by the loftiest intellects in the best days of Athens," as Elphinstone, i. p. 94, justly speaks. This possession of ancient scriptures constitutes, indeed, one chief difficulty in dealing with the Eastern, as contrasted with the Western forms of paganism. For those against whom the Fathers wrote had no ancient scriptures, and therefore were properly met by exhibiting to them the antiquity of the Books of Moses, &c. It may be said that this is a mere *argumentum ad hominem*, and not therefore a valid criterion of a revelation. But a little thought will, I trust, show any one who reflects upon what goes on in his own mind, that it is not evidence which makes him believe, but somewhat moral which leads him to wish for the truth of what is presented to him. When that has preceded, then arguments serve to exhibit and embody to himself the fact that he believes; but he must *feel* that they are but an inadequate ground for that conviction which results from his whole nature. To try and convince a man upon mere arguments, would be much as if a man should attempt to argue one into a love of one for whose character and ways—to use a homely term—one has no sympathy. Indeed, this illustration holds in the other point noticed. For whoever tries to give a reason *to himself* (i. e. even without attempting to put it into words) for his love of such and such an intimate friend, will feel at once that he can but state a part of the grounds of it, even to himself. Arguments, then, only serve to hold up the truth before the mind, and are in no sense to be looked upon as generating belief; and if so, the Fathers did right in holding up before western pagans the truth by such arguments as presented for the heart's acceptation one property of it,—viz. antiquity. But this is not essential to truth, nor do I believe it was ever insisted on of old as such; it is a probable argument, and as such proper to use in moral matters. Where not available, other probable arguments must be used; and what has been my difficulty in this part of the Essay is, that I have here to deal with a case not contemplated by ancient writers in defence of Christianity, and therefore to find arguments in a great measure of my own choosing, or at least to apply ancient doctrines or opinions in a way that might require some further justification, were the case other than it is.

I ought to add, that this note is suggested by an apparently kindly intended anonymous letter, which acutely states the difficulty just alluded to, though it does not speak, as it seems to me, with becoming reverence of the sainted champions of the faith in early times, nor with sufficient apprehension of the very small importance of the logicalness of arguments as compared with the moral proof (πίστις ἠθικὴ) of Christianity.

NOTE (22.) p. 19.

See Windisch. p. 1684 to 1686, where he says, "Die Autorität der Schrift und Tradition ist also für den rechtglaubigen Brahmanen überall das Entscheidende; 'denn wer die heiligen Bücher genau kennt,' sagt Sankara, 'der stelle keine Untersuchung der Brahma-erkentniss nach seiner Willkür an, sondern ziehe den Lehrer zu Rath. Dieser verkündigt ihm, wenn er bezähmten Sinnes ist, die Brahma-wissenschaft, kraft deren er jenen ewigen wahren Mann (den Puruscha) erkannt.' Der Lehrer aber hat sie wieder von seinem Lehrer und so der Reihe nach: der erste aber hat sie von Brahma selbst (S. Mundaka); denn dies ist der Quell jenes grossen Ganzen von Büchern, das mit dem Rigveda anfängt, und, viele Wissenschaften enthaltend, gleich dem Licht alle Dinge erleuchtet und mit Allwissenheit begabt ist. Nur der Allwissende selbst kann der Urheber davon seyn," &c.

Note (23.) p. 20.

Windisch., p. 1690, 2, quotes the Chandogya as follows: "Die Rede ist grösser als das Wort; die Rede macht erkennen den Rigveda, &c.; wäre die Rede nicht, dann würde sich weder Recht noch Unrecht, weder Wahrheit noch Unwahrheit, weder Gutes noch Böses, weder Freund noch Feind zu erkennen geben. Rede lässt dies Alles erkennen; verehre die Rede," u.s.w.

Note (24.) p. 20.

We probably at no time fairly enter into the feelings of the ancients respecting the importance of music, as bearing on religion and morality. Minds so different as Plato (Lach. 16. 22. Rep. iii. 12, &c.), Aristotle (Polit. viii. 5), Aristophanes (Nub. 950), Thucydides (v. 70), St. Basil (in Psalm. ap. Hooker, v. 38), St. Clement (Pædag. ii. 44. Strom. vi. 90), and of the Indians (Philostr. Vit. Ap. ii. 34), could never have all agreed upon it, were it not something entirely above the conceptions which the generality of men now form of it. Its religious use, as here alluded to, has been paralleled with that amongst the Jews, who were so particular in their accentuation, that Molitor somewhere tells us that a well-instructed ear knew by the tune any verse of the Bible from any other. V. Windisch. pp. 627 and 717, notices that the intonation of the Vedas छन्दस् was an important part of the instruction of a Brahman.

NOTE (25.) p. 21.

The words used in the text are taken from the Septuagint Version of Deuter. xxxii. 8. *Ὅτε διεμέριζεν ὁ Ὕψιστος ἔθνη, ὡς διέσπειρεν υἱοὺς Ἀδὰμ, ἔστησεν ὅρια ἐθνῶν κατὰ ἀριθμὸν ἀγγέλων Θεοῦ.* To give this version full weight, some little discussion may be necessary; but, perhaps, upon reflection, the reader will not think the subject by any means an unimportant one. I shall observe, first, that the chapter is one in which the LXX. make an addition, which is quoted in Hebrews i. 6, and has no existence in the Hebrew Scriptures, although it may be proved by them. This begets some presumption that there may be other things in the LXX. version of the same chapter which may be proved by other Scriptures, although they also do not exist in the Hebrew. Now the Hebrew text has in this place, "according to the number of the *children of Israel;*" and if Israel's children, as here spoken of, were twelve in number, and we learn from Daniel x. 13, that Michael, the prince or chief angel of Israel, was one of more (for he is there styled *one* of the chief princes or archangels, to use the Greek word which would correspond with it); and if, as there is no objection from any thing in the Old Testament to their number being twelve, so in the New Testament there is direct mention of twelve legions of angels: then, if each were presided over by an archangel, this would furnish a number exactly corresponding with that of the sons of Jacob. This, then, if it be but a weak way of arguing, to some minds at least, is yet sufficient to show that the LXX.'s substitution of the heavenly archetype for the earthly counterpart is far from involving in itself any contradiction of the Scripture account of things. If, again, by the number of the sons of Israel is meant the number of those going down to Egypt, still the earthly and heavenly hierarchy might correspond in number. But without going into any discussion as to the subdivisions of this number of angels, which may be requisite to furnish a more exact correspondence to the subdivisions of the nations anciently assumed, it must be evident that *some* relationship between the number of the angels and that of the nations is implied by the language of the Septuagint. Nor, indeed, is it easy to see how the number of the sons of Israel should be the ground of a division of the nations which was so long antecedent to their birth, unless this same number were itself also grounded upon something antecedent and mysterious. If, then, we once assume that the number of the nations was any way dependent upon a number of the angels, the important thing is assumed. For the important thing is, the connexion between the divisions of the heavenly host and that of the divisions of the nations: once grant this, and it is immaterial whether the number prevailing in both is smaller or larger than twelve now; whether there be more or fewer subdivisions; whether they be or be not ascertainable by us, and the like. For, from the assumption of such a connexion, the mind is naturally prepared to expect that the angels will be guardians of the nations, or at least in some way further connected with them. Did Scripture contravene such an expectation, of course we should feel it a duty then to own that we were misled through the feebleness and imperfection of human knowledge. But it is evident that I am only trying here to put down, in the shape of a consistent *theory*, what Scripture, as matter of fact, appears to countenance and fall in with. Let me, then, proceed to put together some passages bearing upon the subject: and to prevent mistake, I will again state that what I consider the important point to be proved is, that there is ground from Scripture for thinking that there are superintending angels charged with the execution of the designs of Providence, in regard to the several nations. I do not enter upon the specific numbers employed—a question upon which I might be apt to become fanciful, or perhaps lead persons to mistake the mere statements of a law of Providence for assertions of some inherent value in the numbers themselves: nor, again, do I at all touch upon the development of the Christian polity as bearing upon, or altering in any way, this order of things in the ancient dispensation. To proceed:—

1. I have already noticed in the text two passages from Daniel (x. 13. 20), and referred to one from Ezekiel, in which mention is made (xxviii. 16) of a covering cherub which God "will destroy from the midst of the stones of fire." I quote this, not by any means as a clear passage to the point, but as seeming to imply that there had been an anointed cherub set over them by God (14), and that they had made an unauthorized image of him after the pattern of the Jewish tabernacle. St. Ephrem on the place notices that the king of Tyre made himself altogether as a proselyte, ܡܬܓܝܪܘ ܐܬܓܝܪ ܗܘܐ; and yet he was not of the true seed of Judah[s]. Verse 14 seems to imply a reality; verse 16 an idolatrous representation of it, and an abuse of knowledge gotten from the Jews. To this may be added Gen. xxxii., where the name Mahanaim, signifying "two hosts," bestowed upon the place where "angels of God met" Jacob, is taken to imply that Jacob passed from one camp of angels to that of another, as he left one country for another. See Corn. à Lapide on the place.

[s] I quote this as coming from one probably versed in the history of those nations. The Syriac differs here from the Hebrew, so far as to prevent our having St. E.'s opinion, in the way one could wish, upon the passage.

2. In the Psalms (lxvi. 7) we read, "His *eyes* behold the nations," עיניו בגוים תצפינה; and in Prov. xv. 3, "The *eyes* of the LORD are in every place, beholding the evil and the good." And in 2 Chron. xvi. 8, 9, Hanani says, "Were not the Ethiopians and the Lubims a huge host, with very many chariots and horsemen? yet because thou didst rely on the LORD, He delivered them into thine hand: For the eyes of the LORD *run to and fro* throughout the whole earth, to show himself strong in the behalf of them whose heart is perfect toward Him. Herein thou hast done foolishly; therefore from henceforth thou shalt have wars." And in Zech. iv. 10, mention is made of seven "eyes of the LORD, which run to and fro through the whole earth." And in Rev. v. 6, the Lamb is said to have "seven horns *and* seven eyes, which are the seven Spirits of God, sent forth into all the earth." This last text seems to show that though the seven gifts of the Spirit rest upon the Lamb, yet also there are seven angelic Beings, who go forth from Him and run to and fro in the earth: and so would seem to point out how the language of Zechariah may be understood of the seven Gifts of the Spirit, though not in such way as to exclude the intervention of ministering Spirits. For though the WORD Himself is said to run very swiftly (i. e. by His operations), yet משוטטים is more naturally understood of Beings than of operations (as of Satan in Job i.). St. Ephrem gives both senses, understanding the passage of the Dispensing Angels, ܡܕܒܪܢܐ, as well as spiritually, also of the operations of the Holy Spirit; of which St. Jerome and others appear to take them exclusively. The passage of Chronicles might seem to imply that the nations should no longer be restrained from falling upon Asa through the instrumentality of these Eyes, which run to and fro through the earth. (See Epiphanius, as quoted presently.) And with these passages before us, we may be inclined to think that

the words of Ps. lxvi. 7, imply something as to the mode in which God exercised His superintendence over the nation—viz. through the instrumentality of angels, or *Eyes* of the LORD [9]. St. Hilar. in loc. "Ergo incorporalis Deus misericordiæ suæ oculis et tanquam ministerio famulantium Angelorum protegit gentes, et in omnes credentes donum Divinæ miserationis effundit." And that the nations were under a dispensation then, we learn from Ps. xciv. 10, and cxlvii. 20, (on which St. Clement, Strom. vi. 63, says, Τὸ "οὐκ ἐποίησεν οὕτως" πεποιηκέναι μὲν δηλοῖ, ἀλλ' οὐχ οὕτως,) as well as from other Scriptures, e. g. Job xii. 22—25. Hence there is some reason from Scripture for assuming the truth of the teaching implied in the passage of Deuteronomy, from which we started, and which was quoted repeatedly by the Fathers, from St. Clement of Rome (i. 29) downwards. Having then stated the hints of such a system given us in Scripture, I shall next proceed to put together some passages from the Fathers which express a belief in it. And while so doing, I must urge upon the reader the duty of patiently endeavouring to enter into expositions of passages, which, as they seem suited to the mind of Orientals, so doubtless were not written without some superintending Providence, whether it be the hints of Holy Writ, or the language of the Fathers about such hints, which we consider. And they will be found some of them to come from minds as different as those of Origen and Jerome.

St. Clement, Stromat. vi. 157. (Pott. p. 822.) Καὶ αἱ τῶν ἐναρέτων ἀνθρώπων ἐπίνοιαι κατὰ ἐπίνοιαν θείαν γίγ-

[9] It may be worth noticing, that there were Persian officers called βασιλέως ὀφθαλμοί, (Aristoph. Ach. 91, and Aristot. Pol. iii. 16, ap. Scholiast. Philostr. Vit. Apoll. i. 21, et seq. ed. Olear.) which possibly were a heathen imitation based upon some tradition of the same thing; for we find that there were seven chief counsellors in Ezra's time (Ezr. vii. 14. Esth. i. 14); and the passage of Aristotle clearly shows that there were more β. ὀφθαλμοί than one.

νονται διατιθεμένης πῶς τῆς ψυχῆς καὶ διαδιδομένου τοῦ θείου θελήματος εἰς τὰς ἀνθρωπίνας ψυχὰς τῶν ἐν μέρει θείων λειτουργῶν συλλαμβανομένων εἰς τὰς τοιαύτας διακονίας, κατά τε γὰρ τὰ ἔθνη καὶ πόλεις νενέμηνται τῶν ἀγγέλων αἱ προστασίαι, τάχα δὲ καὶ τῶν ἐπὶ μέρους, ὧν ἐνίοις ἀποτετάχαταί τινες, where Potter's note may be consulted. Also Strom. vii. 6. (Pott. p. 832.) *Οὗτός ἐστιν ὁ διδοὺς καὶ τοῖς Ἕλλησι τὴν φιλοσοφίαν διὰ τῶν ὑποδεεστέρων ἀγγέλων. εἰσὶ γὰρ συνδιανεμημένοι προστάξει θείᾳ τε καὶ ἀρχαίᾳ ἄγγελοι κατὰ ἔθνη.* Strom. vii. 12. (Pott. p. 835.) *Παιδεύσεις δὲ αἱ ἀναγκαῖαι ἀγαθότητι τοῦ ἐφορῶντος μεγάλου Κριτοῦ διά τε τῶν προσεχῶν ἀγγέλων διά τε προκρίσεων ποικίλων καὶ διὰ τῆς κρίσεως τῆς παντελοῦς τοὺς ἐπὶ πλέον ἀπηλγηκότας ἐκβιάζονται μετανοεῖν.* Also Origen, in Num. xi. § 5. "Ex initio sæculi hujus, cum dispergeret Deus filios Adam, statuit fines gentium secundum numerum angelorum Dei, et unaquæque gens sub illo angelo facta est; una autem fuit, et electa gens Israël, quæ portio Domini fuit, et funiculus hæreditatis ejus." And, In Luc. Hom. 35. (p. 219, Lommatsch.) "'Quando vadis ad principem.' Quisnam iste princeps est? Quando dividebat Altissimus gentes, quando disseminabat filios Adam, statuit terminos nationum secundum numerum angelorum Dei; et facta est portio Domini populus ejus Jacob, funiculus hæreditatis ejus Israël. Igitur principibus, id est, angelis, ab exordio terra divisa est. Daniel quippe manifestius, quos Moses angelos nominarat, principes esse testatur, dicens, 'Princeps regni Persarum, et princeps regni Græcorum, et Michael princeps gentium.'" St. Jerome also paraphrases Isaiah xiv. fin. "Si, inquit, quæsierint angeli gentis Assyriæ; quare solus Judas evaserit?" On xxxiv. 3. "Ita ut sanie earum et spurcitia ac sanguine montes repleantur; sublimes quoque virtutes et angeli qui singulis gentibus præsidebant." On Isaiah xlvii. init. "Significat autem angelum gentis Babyloniæ præsidem, qui cum cæteris angelis loquitur." Again, St. Basil adv. Eunom. iii. 1. Ἄγγελοι πάντες ὥσπερ προσηγορίας μιᾶς, οὕτω καὶ φύσεως πάντως τῆς αὐτῆς ἀλλήλοις τυγχάνουσιν· ἀλλ' ὅμως οἱ μὲν αὐτῶν, ἐθνῶν προεστήκασιν· οἱ δὲ, ἑνὶ ἑκάστῳ τῶν πιστῶν εἰσι παρεπόμενοι. Ὅσῳ μέντοι προτιμότερον ἔθνος ὅλον ἑνὸς ἀνδρὸς, τοσούτῳ δήπου μεῖζον ὑπάρχειν ἀνάγκη ἀξίωμα τοῦ ἐθνάρχου ἀγγέλου παρὰ τὸ τοῦ ἑνὸς ἑκάστου τὴν προστασίαν πεπιστευμένου. Τὸ δὲ συνεῖναι ἑκάστῳ τῶν πιστῶν ἄγγελον, οἷον παιδάγωγόν τινα καὶ νομέα τὴν ζωὴν διευθύνοντα, οὐδεὶς ἀντερεῖ, μεμνημένος τῶν τοῦ Κυρίου λόγων, εἰπόντος· Μὴ καταφρονήσητε ἑνὸς τῶν ἐλαχίστων τούτων, ὅτι οἱ ἄγγελοι αὐτῶν διὰ παντὸς βλέπουσι τὸ πρόσωπον τοῦ Πατρός μου τοῦ ἐν τοῖς οὐράνοις. Καὶ ὁ Ψαλμῳδός φησι· Παρεμβαλλεῖ ἄγγελος Κυρίου κύκλῳ τῶν φοβουμένων αὐτόν. Καὶ, Ὁ ἄγγελος ὁ ῥυσάμενός με ἐκ νεότητός μου· καὶ ὅσα τοιαῦτα. Ὅτε δὲ πάλιν εἰσί τινες ἄγγελοι καὶ ὅλων ἐθνῶν προεστῶτες, Μωσῆς ἡμᾶς διδάσκει διὰ τῆς ᾠδῆς, λέγων· Ὅτε διεμέριζεν ὁ Ὕψιστος ἔθνη, ὡς διέσπειρεν υἱοὺς Ἀδὰμ, ἔστησεν ὅρια ἐθνῶν κατὰ ἀριθμὸν ἀγγέλων αὐτοῦ. Καὶ ὁ σοφὸς Δανιὴλ ἐν τῇ τοῦ ἀγγέλου ὀπτασίᾳ ἤκουσεν αὐτοῦ λέγοντος, ὅτι Ἄρχων βασιλείας Περσῶν εἰστήκει ἐξεναντίας μου· καὶ ἰδοὺ Μιχαὴλ εἷς τῶν ἀρχόντων τῶν πρώτων ἦλθε βοηθῆσαί μοι, καὶ αὐτὸν κατέλιπον ἐκεῖ μετὰ τοῦ ἄρχοντος βασιλέως Περσῶν. Καὶ μετ' ὀλίγα φησὶν ὁ αὐτός· Καὶ ὁ ἄρχων τῶν Ἑλλήνων ἤρχετο. Ἀλλὰ καὶ ἀρχιστράτηγός τις τῆς δυνάμεως Κυρίου λέγεται, ὁ Ἰησοῦ τῷ τοῦ Ναυῆ ἐπὶ τοῦ Ἰορδάνου φανερωθείς. Καὶ πάλιν τινὲς λέγονται λεγεῶνες τῶν ἀγγέλων, τοῦ Κυρίου εἰπόντος τοῖς μαθηταῖς· Ἢ δοκεῖτε ὅτι οὐ δύναμαι παρακαλέσαι τὸν Πατέρα μου, καὶ παραστήσει μοι ὧδε πλείους ἢ δώδεκα λεγεῶνας ἀγγέλων; Ὁ τοίνυν ἀρχιστράτηγος τῶν ἐν ταῖς λεγεῶσι καταπεταγμένων ἀγγέλων, ἄρχων ἐστὶ δηλονότι. Also St. Gregory Nyssen. de V. Mosis, p. 194. Λόγος τίς ἐστιν ἐκ πατρικῆς παραδόσεως τὸ πιστὸν ἔχων, ὅς φησι· Πεσούσης ἡμῶν εἰς ἁμαρτίαν τῆς φύσεως, μὴ παριδεῖν τὸν Θεὸν τὴν πτῶσιν ἡμῶν ἀπρονόητον· ἀλλ' ἄγγελόν τινα τῶν τὴν ἀσώματον εἰληχότων φύσιν, παρακαθιστᾶν εἰς συμμαχίαν τῇ ἑκάστου ζωῇ. ἐκ δὲ τοῦ ἐναντίου, τὸν φθορέα τῆς φύσεως ἀντιμηχανᾶσθαι τὸ ἶσον διὰ πονηροῦ τινος καὶ κακοποιοῦ δαίμονος, τῇ τοῦ ἀνθρώπου ζωῇ λυμαινόμενον. Again, Severus of Antioch, amongst much akin to what has gone before, has the following passage, which contains an *à fortiori* argument from the above quotation from St. Gregory (in Θεοτόκου Σεῖρα on the place). Εἰ δὲ τοῖς καθ' ἕκαστον Ἄγγελον, ὡς ἔφαμεν, ἐπέστησεν ὁ Θεὸς, πῶς οὐχὶ μᾶλλον καὶ ἔθνεσι, καὶ δήμοις, καὶ πόλεσιν; ὃ τοίνυν φησὶ Μωσῆς, τοῦτό ἐστιν· ὅτι διαμερίσας ὁ Ὕψιστος τὰ ἔθνη, καὶ ὅρια πηξάμενος, ἑκάστῳ τῷ τῶν ὁρίων μέτρῳ καὶ ἀριθμῷ Ἀγγέλους ἐπιδιένειμεν. St. Epiphanius, Hær. xxxi. § 34, p. 456, observes, on quoting Apoc. ix. 14, Ἐὰν γὰρ λέγῃ τοὺς τέσσαρας Ἀγγέλους τοὺς ἐν τῷ Εὐφράτῃ καθεζομένους, ἵνα δείξῃ τὰς τέσσαρας διαφορὰς τῶν ἐκεῖσε ἐθνῶν καθεζομένων ἐπὶ τὸν Εὐφράτην, οἵ τινές εἰσιν, Ἀσσύριοι, Βαβυλώνιοι, Μῆδοι καὶ Πέρσαι. αὗται γὰρ αἱ τέσσαρες βασιλεῖαι κατὰ διαδοχὴν ἐν τῷ Δανιὴλ ἐμφέρονται, ὡς πρῶτοι Ἀσσύριοι ἐβασίλευον, καὶ Βαβυλώνιοι ἐν χρόνοις αὐτοῦ. Μῆδοι δὲ διεδέξαντο. μετ' αὐτοὺς δὲ Πέρσαι, ὧν πρῶτος γέγονε Κῦρος ὁ βασιλεύς. τὰ γὰρ ἔθνη ὑπὸ Ἀγγέλους τεταγμένα εἰσὶν, ὡς ἐπιμαρτυρεῖ μοι Μωϋσῆς ὁ ἅγιος τοῦ Θεοῦ θεράπων, τὸν λόγον κατὰ ἀκολουθίαν ἑρμηνεύων καὶ λέγων· Ἐπερώτησον τὸν πατέρα σου, καὶ ἀναγγελεῖ σοι· τοὺς πρεσβυτέρους σου, καὶ ἐροῦσί σοι· ὅτε διεμέριζεν ὁ Ὕψιστος ἔθνη, ὡς διέσπειρεν υἱοὺς Ἀδὰμ, ἔστησεν ὅρια ἐθνῶν κατὰ ἀριθμὸν Ἀγγέλων Θεοῦ· καὶ ἐγενήθη μερὶς Κυρίου λαὸς αὐτοῦ Ἰακὼβ, σχοίνισμα κληρονομίας αὐτοῦ Ἰσραήλ· εἰ οὖν τὰ ἔθνη ὑπὸ Ἀγγέλους εἰσὶ τεταγμένα, δικαίως εἶπε, Λῦσον τοὺς τέσσαρας Ἀγγέλους τοὺς ἐν τῷ Εὐφράτῃ καθεζομένους καὶ ἐπερχομένους ἐπιτρέπειν τοῖς ἔθνεσιν εἰς πόλεμον, ἕως καιροῦ μακροθυμίας Κυρίου, ἕως προστάξει δι' αὐτῶν ἐκδικίαν γίγνεσθαι τῶν αὐτοῦ ἁγίων. ἐκρατοῦντο γὰρ οἱ ἐπιτεταγμένοι Ἄγγελοι ὑπὸ τοῦ Πνεύματος, μὴ ἔχοντες καίρὸν ἐπιδρομῆς, διὰ τὸ μήπω λύειν αὐτοῖς τὴν δίκην, τοῦ τὰ λοιπὰ ἔθνη λύεσθαι, ἕνεκεν τῆς πρὸς τοὺς ἁγίους ὕβρεως. λύονται δὲ οἱ τοιοῦτοι καὶ ἐπέρχονται τῇ γῇ, ὡς Ἰωάννης προφητεύει καὶ οἱ λοιποὶ Προφῆται. καὶ γὰρ κινούμενοι οἱ Ἄγγελοι, κινοῦσι τὰ ἔθνη εἰς ὁρμὴν ἐκδικίας. ὅτι δὲ πυρίνους καὶ θειώδεις, καὶ ὑακινθίνους θώρακας σημαίνει, οὐδεὶς ἀμφιβάλλει. ἐκεῖνα γὰρ τὰ ἔθνη, ἀπὸ τῆς τοιαύτης χρόας ἔχει τὴν ἀμφίασιν. τὰ μὲν γὰρ θειώδη ἱμάτια, χρόα τίς ἐστι μηλίνη, οὕτω καλουμένη ἐρέα. τὰ δὲ πύρινα, ἵνα εἴπῃ τὰ κοκκηρὰ ἐνδύματα καὶ ὑακίνθινα, ἵνα δείξῃ τὴν Καλλαίνην ἐρέαν. A striking passage to this purpose from St. Ephrem, vol. ii. p. 224, has been quoted in Nature a Parable, p. 310, upon Daniel x. 14; a text which is also used by Aretas in Apoc. p. 412, Oxf. ed. Something *externally* similar was held by the Persians; v. Baehr's note on Herodotus, vii. 53: and in 1 Kings xx. 23, it is implied, by what the Syrians say, that they also believed such different apportionments of superior orders of beings to different places. Nor were the Greeks without a similar belief; for in Plato de Legg. iv. 6, we have the following passage: Γιγνώσκων ὁ Κρόνος ἄρα, καθάπερ ἡμεῖς διεληλύθαμεν, ὡς ἀνθρωπεία φύσις οὐδεμία ἱκανὴ τὰ ἀνθρώπινα διοικοῦσα αὐτοκράτωρ πάντα μὴ οὐχ ὕβρεώς τε καὶ ἀδικίας μεστοῦσθαι, ταῦτ' οὖν διανοούμενος ἐφίστη βασιλέας γε καὶ ἄρχοντας ταῖς πόλεσιν ἡμῶν οὐκ ἀνθρώπους, ἀλλὰ γένους θειοτέρου τε καὶ ἀμείνονος δαίμονας, οἷον νῦν ἡμεῖς δρῶμεν τοῖς ποιμνίοισι καὶ ὅσων ἥμεροί εἰσιν ἀγέλαι· οὐ βοῦς βοῶν οὐδὲ αἶγας αἰγῶν ἄρχοντας ποιοῦμεν αὐτοῖσί τινας, ἀλλ' ἡμεῖς αὐτῶν δεσπόζομεν, ἄμεινον ἐκείνων γένος. ταὐτὸν δὴ καὶ ὁ Θεὸς ἄρα καὶ φιλάνθρωπος ὢν τὸ γένος ἄμεινον ἡμῶν ἐφίστη τὸ τῶν δαιμόνων, ὃ διὰ πολλῆς μὲν αὐτοῖς ῥᾳστώνης, πολλῆς δ' ἡμῖν ἐπιμελούμενον ἡμῶν, εἰρήνην τε καὶ αἰδῶ καὶ εὐνομίαν καὶ ἀφθονίαν δίκης παρεχόμενον, ἀστασίαστα καὶ εὐδαίμονα τὰ τῶν ἀνθρώπων ἀπειργάζετο γένη. The following are the words of St. Augustine de Trin. iii. 9, upon the same subject: "Quod ergo de uno sapiente, quamvis adhuc mortale corpus gestante, quamvis ex parte vidente, posuimus exempli gratia, hoc de aliqua domo, ubi aliquorum talium societas est, hoc de civitate vel etiam de orbe terrarum licet cogitare, si penes sapientes sancteque ac perfecte Deo subditos sit principatus, et regimen rerum humanarum. Sed hoc quia nondum est: (oportet enim nos in hac peregrinatione prius mortaliter exerceri, et per vires mansuetudinis et patientiæ in flagellis erudiri:) illam ipsam supernam atque cœlestem, unde peregrinamur, patriam cogitemus. Illic enim Dei voluntas, qui facit angelos suos spiritus et ministros suos ignem flagrantem, in spiritibus summa pace atque amicitia copulatis, et in unam voluntatem quodam spiritali caritatis igne conflatis, tanquam in excelsa et sancta et secreta sede præsidens, velut in domo sua et in templo suo, inde se, quibusdam ordinatissimis creaturæ motibus, primo spiritalibus, deinde corporalibus per cuncta diffundit, et utitur omnibus ad incommutabile arbitrium sententiæ suæ, sive incorporeis sive corporeis rebus, sive rationalibus sive irrationalibus spiritibus, sive bonis per ejus gratiam sive malis per propriam voluntatem. Sed quemadmodum corpora crassiora et inferiora per subtiliora et potentiora quodam ordine reguntur; ita omnia corpora per spiritum vitæ, et spiritus vitæ irrationalis per spiritum vitæ rationalem, et spiritus vitæ rationalis desertor atque peccator per spiritum vitæ rationalem pium et justum, et ille per ipsum Deum, ac sic universa creatura per Creatorem suum, ex quo et per quem, et in quo etiam condita atque instituta est; ac per hoc voluntas Dei est prima et summa causa omnium corporalium specierum et motionum. Nihil enim fit visibiliter et sensibiliter, quod non de interiore invisibili atque intelligibili aula summi Imperatoris, aut jubeatur, aut permittatur, secundum ineffabilem justitiam præmiorum atque pœnarum, gratiarum et retributionum in ista totius creaturæ amplissima quadam immensaque republica."

But it is time to draw this note to a close. I feel persuaded that any person who reflects upon that part of the system of Providence with which experience makes us acquainted, will see no room to object to this doctrine, at least in its main outlines, upon the ground of its opposing that experience. For in that system, as Plato suggests, we are not furnished with blessings without the intervention of others; "since we find by experience that God does appoint mediators to be the instruments of good and evil to us; the instruments of His justice and His mercy. And the objection here referred to is urged, not against mediation in that high, eminent, and peculiar sense in which Christ is our Mediator, but absolutely against the whole notion itself of a mediator at all." Butler, Anal. ii. 5, § 1. So far as this doctrine has been shown to be a Catholic one, so far it will be found to possess that wonderful attribute of all Catholic truths whereby they meet the promptings of human nature, as shown in Pagan systems, and give them the reality of which they had hitherto had but the shadow. Erroneous systems are but imitations of the true: they may be so, either from their being but partial disclosures, or from their being the produce of demonaical foresight. In either case the Catholic system, and it only, can stand among them and try the spirits, whether they be of God.

NOTE (26.) p. 23.

The heathen notion of incarnations is, of course, but a very marred and dark one: the two following notes will show that they involved generally a belief of the frequent repetition of incarnations, the folly of which will be noticed in a note upon the fourth dialogue.

Note (27.) p. 23.

Müller, in his Dorians, p. 330, &c., represents Apollo as born to be an ambassador, intercessor, and prophet with mankind. Mr. Clinton, in his Fasti, i. p. xiii., has rightly objected to the strain he puts on authors to justify some of his splendid expressions; and one cannot but fear he has overstrained them with bad intentions. Still even the Greeks had some kind of belief in such incarnations. Origen (c. Celsum, p. 232) urges some of them, as showing that Celsus could not consistently admit them, and deny the true. And the Egyptians taught that the deity appeared in different forms, sitting on a lotus, &c. (Porphyr. ap. Euseb. Præp. E. p. 198)—a doctrine probably taken from India, as the lotus is not indigenous to Egypt. (See Ideler's Hermap. p. 52, note.)

It is much to be observed, as bearing upon these obscured traditions of an incarnation, how Cyrus, Cypselus, and Romulus, as well as Krishna (see Vishnu Pur. v. 3, 4), are described as concealed and persecuted in their infancy, as though they were in some weak way allowed to be types of the great Lawgiver to come. As this is an important subject, especially to those who have to deal with unconverted Gentiles, I shall offer a few observations upon it here.

First, The truth of the supposition that they were intended to be types of that Lawgiver is not destroyed by the supposition that they were diabolic imitations of true prophecies: for it is quite intelligible that Satan should have been overruled in such way as to force him to minister wholesome teaching to those who, in every nation, were looking after God, to the best of their power, and ruling their lives with a view to finding Him. Nor is it inconsistent with reason to suppose Satan to be conscious of this; since does he seem to desire now to thrust wicked men into the wretchlessness of unclean living, although he must know from experience that the sight of such persons fills the saints with deeper awe [1] and humility, and arouses the undeveloped seeds of grace in the hearts of others. Satan, we know, did go to and fro in the earth of old, and was counteracted in some degree, as we have seen, even then, by the ministry of angels.

Secondly, As we have the authority of Scripture for taking Cyrus to be a type of Christ, (Is. xlv. 1, &c.) so we find things noticed of the Persians which seem to render them particularly fitted to furnish a type of one to come. The seven eyes of the king already noticed (in Note 25) were one thing of the kind, and furnish, as there noticed, a parallel to Zechariah's prophecy. And it seems as though Scripture might have given us this as a clue to guide us in the use of history, so that by availing ourselves of it, *we* might be ever looking towards Christ. Thus it is certainly remarkable that Arrian records of Cyrus (p. 528), that he was *sealed* into his sepulchre by Alexander, a stranger, to prevent his own people from stealing the body. And the fact that prophecy throws such a light upon this history, leads one to think that there may be other histories on which it would throw similar light. For, as antecedently to proof, there might be a strong presumption against God's prophet anointing a Gentile king externally (1 Kings ix. 15), so might there be also against his anointing him internally (Is. xlv. 1), i. e. bestowing any remarkable office upon him, such as that of Cyrus was, when he led the Israelites, the

[1] See Ps. cxix. 53. זלעפה אחזתני מרשעים עזבי תורתך The first word is a very strong one: Kimchi explains it of fear that shakes the whole body. One cannot help remarking, that this fear may hold some especial place in the time preceding the Judgment, such as to supply the place of other preparations for God's presence in those then alive. Satan seems to be ever out-reaching himself, and benefitting the lot of the righteous, on whom his rod does not fall.

type of mankind, out of Babylon, the type of the kingdom of Satan. Hence all that suffered for righteousness sake were in some measure types of Him; and it seems of the greatest importance, in dealing with heathens, to allow for such resemblances, and to believe there may be somewhat mysterious in them; for so we shall escape sometimes from a groundless scepticism in treating of passages in Pagan writers (e. g. Plato, Rep. ii. § 5), and be more likely to win men when we clear up the rude outlines of the shadow by exhibiting the reality. The following passage from Origen is instructive upon this point: (c. Cels. p. 24.) Ἆρα γὰρ οὐκ ἑώρων οἱ τοῦ Ἰησοῦ μαθηταὶ, τολμῶντες οὐ μόνον Ἰουδαίοις ἐκ τῶν προφητικῶν λόγων παριστάνειν, ὅτι οὗτος εἴη ὁ προφητευθεὶς, ἀλλὰ καὶ τοῖς λοιποῖς ἔθνεσιν, ὅτι ὁ χθὲς καὶ πρώην σταυρωθεὶς, ἑκὼν τοῦτον τὸν θάνατον ὑπὲρ τοῦ τῶν ἀνθρώπων γένους ἀνεδέξατο, ἀνάλογον τοῖς ἀποθανοῦσιν ὑπὲρ πατρίδων, ἐπὶ τῷ σβέσαι λοιμικὰ κρατήσαντα καταστήματα, ἢ ἀφορίας ἢ δυσπλοίας; εἰκὸς εἶναι γὰρ ἐν τῇ φύσει τῶν πραγμάτων, κατά τινας ἀποῤῥήτους καὶ δυσλήπτους τοῖς πολλοῖς λόγους, φύσιν τοιαύτην ὡς ἕνα δίκαιον, ὑπὲρ τοῦ κοινοῦ ἀποθανόντα ἑκουσίως, ἀποτροπιασμοὺς ἐμποιεῖν φαύλων δαιμονίων ἐνεργούντων λοιμοὺς ἢ ἀφορίας ἢ δυσπλοίας, ἤ τι τῶν παραπλησίων. Λεγέτωσαν οὖν οἱ βουλόμενοι ἀπιστεῖν τῷ Ἰησοῦν ὑπὲρ ἀνθρώπων ἀποτεθνηκέναι τρόπῳ σταυροῦ, πότερον οὐδὲ τὰς Ἑλληνικὰς παραδέξονται καὶ βαρβαρικὰς πολλὰς ἱστορίας, περὶ τοῦ τινας ὑπὲρ τοῦ κοινοῦ τεθνηκέναι καθαιρετικῶς τῶν προκαταλαβόντων τὰς πόλεις καὶ τὰ ἔθνη κακῶν; ἢ ἐκεῖνα μὲν γεγένηται, οὐδὲν δὲ πιθανὸν ἔχει ὁ νομιζόμενος ἄνθρωπος πρὸς τὸ ἀποθανεῖν ἐπὶ καθαιρέσει μεγάλου δαίμονος, καὶ δαιμόνων ἄρχοντος, ὑποτάξαντος ὅλας τὰς ἐπὶ γῆν ἐληλυθυίας ἀνθρώπων ψυχάς; ὁρῶντες δὲ ταῦτα οἱ τοῦ Ἰησοῦ μαθηταὶ καὶ ἄλλα τούτων πλείονα, ἃ εἰκὸς αὐτοὺς ἐν ἀποῤῥήτῳ ἀπὸ τοῦ Ἰησοῦ μεμαθηκέναι· ἔτι δὲ καὶ δυνάμεώς τινος πληρωθέντες (ἐπεὶ ἔδωκεν αὐτοῖς μένος καὶ θάρσος οὐ ποιητική τις παρθένος ἀλλ' ἡ ἀληθῶς φρόνησις καὶ σοφία τοῦ Θεοῦ) ἔσπευσαν,

ἵν' ἔκδηλοι μετὰ πᾶσιν
οὐ μόνοις Ἀργείοις γένοιντο, ἀλλὰ καὶ πᾶσιν Ἕλλησιν ὁμοῦ
καὶ βαρβάροις καὶ κλέος ἐσθλὸν ἄροιντο.

With regard to Cyrus, the following two passages from St. Cyril of Alexandria may be advantageously consulted: Πῶς δὲ καὶ οὕτω Χριστὸς καὶ ἅγιος, ὡς ἂν εἶναι, λέγοιτο Χριστὸς Κῦρός τε ὁ τῶν Περσῶν βεβασιλευκὼς καὶ μὴν καὶ αὐτοὶ Περσαί τε καὶ Μῆδοι· ὥρα γὰρ εἰπεῖν μηδὲ ἁγίασθαι Χριστὸν ἀνθρωπίνως, καίτοι καταπτάντος ἐπ' αὐτὸν τοῦ ἁγίου Πνεύματος ἐν εἴδει περιστερᾶς. Κῦρος μὲν γὰρ ὁ Καμβύσου κατεστράτευσε τῆς Βαβυλωνίας κατὰ καιροὺς, πεπλάνητο δὲ καὶ τοῖς ἀκαθαρτοῖς δαίμοσιν ἀνετίθει τὸ σέβας. Ἐπεὶ δὲ Θεοῦ παραθήγοντος καὶ διανιστάντος αὐτὸν εἰς ὀργὰς ὀνόματι κοινῷ, καίτοι Πνεύματι τῷ ἁγίῳ μὴ κεχρισμένος, εἴρηται Χριστός. ἅγιοι δὲ οὕτω Περσαί τε καὶ Μῆδοι, οἱ ξυνασπίζοντες αὐτῷ· λελατρεύκασι γὰρ κἀκεῖνοι τῇ κτίσει παρὰ τὸν κτίσαντα Θεὸν, καὶ προσκεκύνασι τοῖς ἔργοις τῶν ἰδίων χειρῶν. Ἐπεὶ δὲ καὶ ἅπαξ κατά τε τὰς ἐν τῷ Μωσαϊκῷ νόμῳ φωνὰς τὸ ἀφορισθὲν τῷ Θεῷ θῦμα κἂν εἴτε μόσχος εἴη τυχὸν ἢ οἶς, ἅγιον ὠνομάζετο· ταύτῃ καὶ διὰ τῆς τοῦ προφήτου φωνῆς ἅγιοι κέκληνται, καὶ αὐτοὶ, διάτοι τὸ ἀφώρισθαι τοῖς θείοις νεύμασιν πρὸς [τὸ?] ἁλῶναι τὴν Βαβυλωνίων. εἴπερ οὖν ἔστιν οὕτω Χριστὸς ὁ Ἐμμανουὴλ, καθὰ καὶ ὁ Κῦρος, καὶ οὕτως ἅγιος καθὰ καὶ Μῆδοι καὶ Περσαί. c. Nest. ii. p. 43. Here he refers to passages where קדש is used of those Gentiles whom God appoints to execute vengeance, e. g. Jer. li. 27. Joel iv. 9; and shows to what Nestorius's mode of speaking will lead to. The other passages in the Glaphyra upon Gen. p. 53, where, after quoting Is. xliv. 24, he says: Ἀκούεις ὅπως ἐναργῶς τὸ οὐκ ᾔδεις με, φησίν. οὐδὲ ἐν τοῖς εἰδόσι Θεὸν τὸν οὕτω περιφανῆ κατατάττειν ἀξιῶν, ὃν αὐτὸς ἐτίθει καὶ βασιλέων κρείττονα καὶ μυρίων ὅσων ἐθνῶν δεσπότην, τύποι γὰρ ἦσαν τὰ ἐπ' αὐτοῦ τῶν διὰ Χριστοῦ κατορθωμάτων. Προηγόρευσε μὲν γὰρ ὡς αὐτὸς διασκεδάσει τὰς Βαβυλωνίων ψευδομαντείας καὶ τὰ τῶν ἐγγαστριμύθων σημεῖα· τὰς δὲ τῶν ἰδίων προφητῶν οὓς καὶ ἀγγέλους ἐπωνόμασε βουλὰς, ἤτοι προαγορεύσεις, οὐ διεψευσμένας ἀποφανεῖ. Προκαταμεμήνευκε δὲ ὅτι καὶ τὰς τῆς Ἰουδαίας οἰκοδομήσει πόλεις, καὶ τὴν ἄβυσσον ἐρημώσει καὶ πάντας αὐτῆς καταξηρανεῖ τοὺς ποταμοὺς, ἄβυσσον οἶμαί που τὴν Βαβυλῶνα λέγων, διάτοι τὸ πλῆθος τῶν κατοικούντων ἐν αὐτῇ, ποταμοὺς δὲ αὐτῆς τὰ ἔθνη τὰ συῤῥέοντα πανταχόθεν εἰς ἐπικουρίαν. Ἀλλὰ φέρε λέγωμεν τὰ ἐπὶ Κύρῳ σαφῶς μεταπλάττοντες εἰς τὸ Χριστοῦ μυστήριον τὰ δι' ἐκείνου κατωρθωμένα. Γέγονε τοίνυν ὁ Κῦρος μητρὸς μὲν Μανδάνης τῆς Ἀστυάγου θυγατρὸς τοῦ Μήδων ἐξάρχοντος, πατρὸς δὲ Καμβύσου Περσοῦ μὲν τὸ γένος, ἐπιεικοῦς δὲ λίαν τοὺς τρόπους· ὅθεν τινὲς τῶν ἀρχαιοτέρων ἡμίονόν τε καὶ ἑτεροφυᾶ τὸν Κῦρον ὠνόμαζον διά γε οἶμαι τὸ πατρὸς καὶ μητρὸς ὡς ἐν τῷ γένει διάφορον. Πέρσαι γὰρ δὴ παρὰ Μήδους ἔθνος ἕτερον. Ἴδοις δ' ἄν τι τοιοῦτον καὶ ἐπὶ Χριστοῦ· μητρὸς μὲν γὰρ γέγονε κατὰ σάρκα τῆς ἁγίας παρθένου, καθ' ἡμᾶς τε οὔσης καὶ ἀνθρώπου τὴν φύσιν, πατρός τε τῶν καθ' ἡμᾶς οὐδενὸς, ἀλλ' ἵν' οὕτως εἴπωμεν ἑτεροφυοῦς εἰς ἅπαν καὶ ἀνῳκισμένου τὴν φύσιν καὶ πᾶν ὑπερθρώσκοντος τὸ τελοῦν ἐν τοῖς γενητοῖς. It is evident that St. Cyril here insists upon parts of Cyrus's history not alluded to in prophecy, as having a typical meaning to be elicited by that clue which prophecy has given to such meaning: and this is what has been here also insisted on as allowable, and as a useful means for leading Gentiles towards the truth. And it may be a question whether the fact that occasional statements of this kind occur in the Fathers is not to be taken as showing that such a view of things was recognised by them, although they had no occasion to avail themselves of that view, when writing against such Gentiles as had no books looked upon as canonical. The reader may compare Menard's note on the Epistle of St. Barnabas, cap. xii., and Bishop Fell on St. Cyprian's Test. i. 21.

Thirdly, If it be said that the stories of the infancy of Romulus, Cypselus, or Cyrus, might have been taken from some loose account of Moses's childhood, this will not alter the state of the case: for it is not so material what the fact was, as what the general belief was. If any influence, good or bad, induced men to believe generally that account, then it was a preparation for belief of the truth with good minds, and with bad for disbelief of it. Bad minds were thus enabled to classify the truth and such accounts alike under the fabulous,—good, to see the reality they pointed towards. (Compare Plato's account of a bad man's death-bed, Rep. i. 5, Οἱ ΜΥΘΟΙ περὶ τῶν ἐν ᾅδου . . . . καταγελώμενοι τέως τότε δὴ στρέφουσιν αὐτοῦ τὴν ψυχὴν, μὴ ἀληθεῖς ὦσι.) The case of Socrates, "a preacher of righteousness," in his measure, is noticed by St. Justin Martyr, Apol. i. § 5, (or p. 55,) and of course is not open to such an objection as that just mentioned. His words are as follows: Ὅτε δὲ Σωκράτης λόγῳ ἀληθεῖ καὶ ἐξεταστικῶς ταῦτα εἰς φανερὸν ἐπειρᾶτο φέρειν καὶ ἀπάγειν τῶν δαιμόνων τοὺς ἀνθρώπους, καὶ αὐτοὶ οἱ δαίμονες διὰ τῶν χαιρόντων τῇ κακίᾳ ἀνθρώπων ἐνήργησαν ὡς ἄθεον καὶ ἀσεβῆ ἀποκτεῖναι λέγοντες, καινὰ εἰσφέρειν αὐτὸν δαιμόνια. Καὶ ὁμοίως ἐφ' ἡμῶν τὸ αὐτὸ ἐνεργοῦσιν. Οὐ γὰρ μόνον Ἕλλησι διὰ Σωκράτους ἠλέγχθη ταῦτα ἀλλὰ καὶ ἐν βαρβάροις ὑπ' αὐτοῦ τοῦ Λόγου μορφωθέντος καὶ Ἀνθρώπου γενομένου, κ. τ. λ. Compare ii. 8—10.

Fourthly, The credibility of such a system of things as the one here supposed, (viz. that even among the Gentiles there were providentially appointed types of Christ, however feeble,) is materially increased by reflecting that different rites were to be found throughout the world, the meaning of which could only be ascertained by the introduction of Christianity.

They were types of Christian sacraments and ordinances, and had their origin doubtless in primeval times. Thus, in the Hindu marriage-ceremony, the bridegroom says, "I unite thy breath with my breath, thy *bones with my bones*, *thy flesh with my flesh*, and thy skin with my skin." (Colebr. Essays, i. p. 224.) This may serve as a specimen; since, if it could be traced to Genesis, it is *explained*, as well as the passage in Genesis, only by the Christian doctrine of marriage. And one cannot see why, when imitations of such high truths come into the Gentile dispensation, imitations of the highest should not also exist under it.

Fifthly, The idea of such a dispensation having existed is rendered further credible by considering, that trade, which *as far as* it is the offspring of covetousness [2], is of the devil, has ever been the forerunner of the Gospel. Men were fishers for gain before they were "fishers of men." The traffic of Tyre, and her whoredoms (as Scripture calls them), which constituted her the type of Antichrist, (see Ezek. xxviii.) did but form connexions with other nations, which in many ways facilitated the spread of the Gospel. Thus does it seem that while Satan, as Leviathan, taketh his pastime in the great and wide sea, he does it but to be mocked by Him whose kingdom is also like, in another sense, to a merchantman. Covetousness goes (if one may say so) before man's redemption, false merchandise before the true riches, imitation of an Angel of light before the Very Light of Light.

Note (28.) p. 23.

The following is a note in Windischmann, p. 364, on the Chinese traditions of an incarnation: "Die Vorstellung von

[2] It is plain that conquests might have been noticed here as a species of covetousness, if not that for gain. E. g. Alexander, who set himself up as God (like Antichrist), spread that Macedonian Greek abroad in which the Gospel was afterwards written.

einer jungfräulichen Mutter des Heiligen kommt nicht blos in der Tradition, sondern auch in dem King sehr häufig vor. Die Heiligen, die Weisen, die Befreier der Völker werden von Jungfrauen geboren. Die Heiligen und Weisen, sagt das Schu-wen, würden Gottessöhne (Himmelssöhne, Thian-tseu) genannt, weil ihre Mütter sie durch die Macht des Himmels empfangen hatten. Kog-jang-tseu sagt noch klarer: 'Der Heilige hat keinen Vater; er ist durch die Wirksamkeit des Himmels empfangen.' Diese Vorstellung wird so hoch gehalten, dass jede Dynastie gerne ihrem Stifter dieselbe Ehre vindicirt. Es ist für uns genug, dass dieses Bedürfniss einer reinen Empfängniss und Geburt ausgesprochen ist, hier wie in Indien. Auch die Namen der reinen Jungfrau sind bemerkenswerth; sie heisst die erwartete Schönheit, die Aufsteigende, die reine Jungfrau, die allgemeine Glückseligkeit, die grosse Treue, die an sich selbst ihren Schmuck hat. Das Schi-king singt von der Mutter Hoang-ti's, 'Sie brachte ihr Gebet und ihr Opfer dar, dass der Ersehnte kommen möge, und indem sie von diesem Gedanken erfüllet war, erhörte sie Schang-ti, und in dem Augenblick und auf der Stelle fühlte sie ihre Eingeweide erschüttert und war durchdrungen vom Schauer der Ehrfurcht. So empfing sie den Hoang-ti, und gebar, da ihre Zeit gekommen, ihren Erstgebornen, wie ein zartes Lamm, ohne Verletzung, ohne Anstrengung, ohne Schmerzen und ohne Befleckung. Himmlisches Wunder! Aber Schang-ti hat nur zu wollen—die zärtliche Mutter gebar ihn in einer Hütte am Weg; Ochsen und Lämmer erwärmten ihn mit ihrem Hauch; die Bewohner des Gehölzes liefen trotz der strengen Kälte herbei; die Vögel flogen nach dem Kind hin, um es mit ihren Flügeln zu bedecken; er selbst aber liess seine Stimme weithin hören,' &c. Dieser und andre ähnliche Gesänge des Schi-king zur Feyer jungfräulicher Mütter und von ihnen geborner Himmelssöhne sind, nach den sorgfältigen Forschungen eines mit dem Alterthum sehr vertrauten Missionars, wohl nichts anders als Anwendungen einer alten Weissagung, deren Spuren wir bei den gebildeten Völkern des Morgenlandes, ja selbst bis nach Amerika hin, nebst vielen andern Traditionen antreffen. Ein Glossar zum Schi-king fügt noch hinzu, 'Der Thian will seine Macht offenbaren und zeigen, um wie viel der Heilige über andre Menschen ist.' Der Name der Mutter Hoang-ti's—Kiang-jneu—ist übrigens aus zwei Charakteren componirt; der erste begreift in sich Lamm und Jungfrau, der andre Quelle und Jungfrau. Der character Niu, der hier doppelt vorkommt, bezeichnet ein Mädchen von reiner Tugend, die Hände gefaltet, bescheiden sitzend, still und nachsinnend."

Note (29.) p. 24.

Clem. Strom. ii. 100. Τῶν πρὸ νόμου νομίμως βεβιωκότων αἱ πράξεις νόμοι γεγόνασιν εἰς ἡμᾶς. We find, indeed, that the customs of the Patriarchs were gradually adopted as laws: neither does it seem right to assume that the Jewish people were miraculously and suddenly transferred from a natural system to a supernatural one wholly distinct from it, unless we were positively told so. Rather, ancient usages, in *several*, though not in all instances, gave rise to the subsequent laws. Circumcision, for instance, was of the Fathers; abstaining from the sinew which shrank, was of the Fathers; the distinction between clean and unclean animals, was of the Fathers, as were the sacrifices of certain animals, the washing of clothes before sacrifice, the anointing of things in order to consecration, the marriage of brothers' widows, the rite relating to it, and other things. (Vide Grabe ad Test. XII. Patriarch. vi. 3.) In St. John vii. 22, our blessed Saviour appears to reason with the Jews thus, if one may venture to paraphrase His words: "Ye observe a patriarchal law, to the neglect of the Mosaic[3] institution of the Sabbath; why, then, complain of Me for doing an act of mercy upon that day? If the priority of patriarchal laws gives them a title to preference, much more will the law of nature written in the heart, which is prior to both patriarchal and Mosaic laws, be entitled to preference." And if so, it would be plain that laws said to be laws of Moses might have yet been of prior existence, and only re-sanctioned by him. And so it would not be wrong to speak of the institutions here alluded to as "of the Fathers." Yet perhaps it may be right to profess myself unable to conceive of a nation *at once* set down (so to speak) among institutions perfectly new to them, as of an individual born into the world full-grown; the absurdity of which Bishop Butler has shown in the Anal. i. 5, p. 123. Such an account of Moses' legislation seems to me to betray an ignorance of the original text, the words and phrases of which often point most significantly to those older customs in which the laws took their rise. It were much to be wished that men would make themselves acquainted with that text before they speculate upon the law it contains: for else they run into that censure which Aristotle bestowed upon a system not intended for this world, though he represents it as such: *δεῖ μὲν ὑποτίθεσθαι κατ' εὐχὴν, μηδὲν μέντοι ἀδύνατον.*

NOTE (30.) p. 25.

Ps. ix. 17, "All the *nations* that *forget* God." Ps. xxii. 27, "All the ends of the world shall *remember* and turn unto

[3] D. Justin. Mart. c. Tryph. p. 236, ed. 1686. Καὶ γὰρ μὴ σαββατίσαντες οἱ προωνομασμένοι πάντες δίκαιοι τῷ Θεῷ εὐηρέστησαν καὶ μετ' αὐτοὺς Ἀβραὰμ καὶ οἱ τούτου υἱοὶ ἅπαντες μέχρι Μωσέως. A common argument this against Judaism in the Fathers. See Tertull. adv. Judæos, c. iv. The same interpretation of St. John vii. 22, is given, I see, by St. Cyril in his commentary on the place, p. 419.

the Lord." "Si autem reminisceris, profecto redis in memoriam tuam, et in eâ invenis quod non fuerat penitus oblivione deletum," says St. Augustin, de Trin. xiv. 17, who quotes these passages; and St. Clement, (Str. vi. 64) of Ps. ix. 17, says, Ἐπιλανθάνονται δὲ δῆλον ὅτι οὗ πρότερον ἐμέμνηντο, καὶ ὃν πρὶν ἢ ἐκλαθέσθαι ἐγίγνωσκον, τοῦτον παραπέμπονται· ἣν ἄρα εἴδησίς τις ἀμαυρὰ τοῦ Θεοῦ καὶ παρὰ τοῖς ἔθνεσι· referring, probably, to Aristotle, Rhet. ii. 19, εἰ ἐπιλέλησται καὶ ἔμαθέ ποτε τοῦτο. And in Isaiah xxxvii. 26, Sennacherib is reproved for forgetfulness; ("Hast thou not heard long ago?" &c.) and in xl. 21, the nations in general ("Have ye not known? have ye not heard? hath it not been told you from the beginning? have ye not understood from the foundations of the earth?") See, too, Rom. i. 28, οὐκ ἐδοκίμασαν τὸν Θεὸν ἔχειν ἐν ἐπιγνώσει· and 2 Pet. iii. 5, λανθάνει γὰρ αὐτοὺς τοῦτο θέλοντας. To the same purpose St. Irenæus, cont. Hær. ii. 9, "Omnibus hominibus ad hoc demum consentientibus, veteribus quidem et in primis a primoplasti traditione hanc suadelam custodientibus, et unum Deum fabricatorem cœli et terræ hymnizantibus; reliquis autem post eos a Prophetis Dei hujus rei commemorationem accipientibus: ethnicis vero ab ipsa conditione discentibus. Ipsa enim conditio ostendit eum qui condidit eam; et ipsa factura suggerit eum qui fecit; et mundus manifest ateum qui se disposuit." St. Augustin, c. Faust. xx. 19, "Gentes non eo usque ad falsos deos sunt delapsæ, ut opinionem amitterent unius veri Dei ex quo est omnis qualiscumque natura." The general principle is concisely stated by Tertullian, "Quod apud multos unum invenitur, non est erratum sed traditum." Præs. 28. See also St. Cyril, c. Jul. p. 16, Ἔνθα μὲν γὰρ τοῖς τῆς θεοπνεύστου γραφῆς συμφέρονται λόγοις, ἑαυτῶν ὄντας ἀμείνους κατίδοι τις ἂν καὶ ὁμολογοῦντας ἀλλήλοις· ἔνθα δὲ τῶν οἰκείων ἕκαστος εὑρημάτων ποιεῖται τὴν ἀπόδοσιν, διαφόρους τε ὄντας καὶ ἀλλοκόταις δόξαις καταμεθύοντας καταδεῖξαι ῥᾷον. οὐ γὰρ ἦν ὅλως καταθρεῖν δύνασθαι τὰ ὑπὲρ νοῦν καὶ λόγους τοὺς ἐν ἡμῖν, μὴ οὐχὶ τοῦ πάντων κρατοῦντος Θεοῦ, καὶ φῶς ἐνιέντος εἰς νοῦν καὶ σοφίαν ἐντίκτοντος, καὶ γλῶσσαν εὐρύνοντος, καί τι τῶν ἀποῤῥήτων περὶ αὐτοῦ κατά γε τὸ ἐγχωροῦν ἐφιέντος αὐτοῖς καὶ νοεῖν καὶ φράσαι.

NOTE (31.) p. 25.

V. Procl. ad Tim. p. 30, and Plut. de Is. et Osir. p. 354, C. Τὸ δ' ἐν Σάει τῆς Ἀθηνᾶς (ἣν καὶ Ἶσιν νομίζουσι) ἕδος ἐπιγραφὴν εἶχε τοιαύτην, Ἐγώ εἰμι πᾶν τὸ γεγονὸς καὶ ὂν, καὶ ἐσόμενον· καὶ τὸν ἐμὸν πέπλον οὐδείς πω θνητὸς ἀπεκάλυψεν. ἔτι δὲ τῶν πολλῶν νομιζόντων ἴδιον παρ' Αἰγυπτίοις ὄνομα τοῦ Διὸς εἶναι τὸν Ἀμοῦν, (ὃ παράγοντες ἡμεῖς Ἄμμωνα λέγομεν,) Μανεθὼς μὲν ὁ Σεβεννίτης τὸ κεκρυμμένον οἴεται καὶ τὴν κρύψιν ὑπὸ ταύτης δηλοῦσθαι τῆς φωνῆς· Ἑκαταῖος δὲ ὁ Ἀβδηρίτης φησὶ τούτῳ καὶ πρὸς ἀλλήλους τῷ ῥήματι χρῆσθαι τοὺς Αἰγυπτίους, ὅταν τινὰ προσκαλῶνται, προσκλητικὴν γὰρ εἶναι τὴν φωνήν. διὸ τὸν πρῶτον Θεὸν τῷ παντὶ τὸν αὐτὸν νομίζουσιν, ὡς ἀφανῆ καὶ κεκρυμμένον ὄντα, προσκαλούμενοι καὶ παρακαλοῦντες ἐμφανῆ γίγνεσθαι καὶ δῆλον αὐτοῖς, Ἀμοῦν λέγουσιν. And Apollonius, ap. Philostr. Vit. p. 337, says, Τὸν δὲ λόγον ὃς ἐς τὸν δημιουργὸν εἴρηται οὕτω τι ἐπαινοῦσιν [οἱ Αἰγύπτιοι] ὡς καὶ ἑτέροις διδάξασθαι, Ἰνδῶν ὄντα. ὁ λόγος δὲ τῆς μὲν τῶν ὅλων γενέσεως καὶ οὐσίας θεὸν δημιουργὸν οἶδε. This may, indeed, be a pantheistic statement; but surely pantheism implies the pre-existence of a monotheism, of which it is the corruption. Porphyr. de Abst. ii. 26, extr., well illustrates how pantheism again paved the way to polytheism: Αἰγύπτιοι τοσοῦτον ἀπεῖχον τοῦ φονεύειν τι τῶν λοιπῶν ζώων, ὥστε τὰς τούτων εἰκόνας μιμήματα τῶν θεῶν ἐποιοῦντο· οὕτως οἰκεῖα καὶ ξυγγενῆ ταῦτα τοῖς θεοῖς ἐνόμιζον εἶναι καὶ τοῖς ἀνθρώποις. Thus were they led by confounding the creature with the Creator, to passing into idolatry—a fearful judgment from Him to whom all judgment is committed, for corrupting traditions of Him who one day would unite the creature with the Creator without confusion!

NOTE (32.) p. 26.

This is said with reference to Ps. cv. 22, חקניו יחכם.

NOTE (33.) p. 26.

And Aristotle, Metaph. p. 981, b. 23, notices how mathematics were first learnt in Egypt: *ἐκεῖ γὰρ ἀφείθη σχολάζειν τὸ τῶν ἱερέων ἔθνος·* on which words Asclepias Trallensis rightly observes: *οἱ ἱερεῖς τὰ ἀναγκαῖα εἶχον ἄλλοθεν αὐτοῖς παρεχόμενα καὶ ἐσχόλαζον μόνοις τοῖς μαθήμασι·* which quite falls in with the Scripture account of the immunities bestowed upon the priests in Moses' days. Cf. Diod. Sic. Biblioth. i. 21, and 73—4. Porphyr. de Abst. iv. 6. That Pythagoras and others drew from Egypt is generally allowed, and thus a link is furnished by Egypt with other nations.

NOTE (34.) p. 26.

Potter ad S. Clement. Strom. i. § 9, p. 321, gives some passages in proof of this, which St. C. asserts in his Pædagog. ii. § 100. Strom. v. § 90, &c. See also Tertullian, Apol. 47, where Dr. Pusey has given a collection of references. Eusebius, in particular, as there cited, gives a long comparison between Plato's doctrines and those contained in the law.

NOTE (35.) p. 26.

This is twice asserted in St. Luke's Gospel, i. 70, and xi. 50, and is to be found stated in several authors, both Jewish and Christian. The motto of this dialogue is an expression of the Jewish opinion upon the subject, which will be found stated more at length in Molitor. Phil. d. Gesch. i. § 196, &c. Indeed, were there no evidence of a historical kind for such a system of things, we might, or rather must, assume that some creed was handed down of the Creation, of the Unity of GOD, of the fall, and other doctrinal points; which, like every thing dogmatical, necessarily implies an order of men to propagate it. Ἀεὶ γὰρ ὁ Θεὸς τῷ ἑαυτοῦ Λόγῳ κατὰ γενεὰς εἰς ψυχὰς ὁσίας μεταβαίνοντι καὶ φίλους Θεοῦ καὶ προφήτας κατασκευάζοντι ἐπανορθοῖ τοὺς ἀκούοντας τῶν λεγομένων· as Origen well replies (p. 163) to Celsus, who urged that Christ, if God, might have amended man's estate without coming down to men. And St. Athanasius, de Decr. S. N. § 5, writes thus: Ἃ γοῦν Μωσῆς ἐδίδασκεν, ταῦθ' (sic) Ἀβραὰμ ἐφύλαττεν, ἃ δὲ Ἀβραὰμ ἐφύλαττε, ταῦτα Νῶε καὶ Ἐνὼχ ἐγίνωσκον, διακρίνοντες καθαρὰ καὶ ἀκάθαρτα, καὶ εὐάρεστοι γινόμενοι τῷ Θεῷ· καὶ γὰρ καὶ Ἄβελ οὕτως ἐμαρτύρησεν ἐπιστάμενος ταῦτα, ἅπερ ἦν μαθὼν παρὰ τοῦ Ἀδὰμ, τοῦ καὶ αὐτοῦ μαθόντος παρὰ Κυρίου, ὃς καὶ ἐπὶ συντελείᾳ τῶν αἰώνων ἐλθὼν εἰς ἀθέτησιν τῆς ἁμαρτίας ἔλεγεν, Οὐκ ἐντολὴν καινὴν δίδωμι ὑμῖν, ἀλλ' ἐντολὴν παλαιὰν ἣν ἠκούσατε ἀπ' ἀρχῆς. 1 John ii. 7. And to the same purpose are the words of St. Ephrem, ii. p. 494:—

ܢܒܝܐ ܐܫܠܡܘܗ ܠܫܠܝ̈ܚܐ: ܒܪܝܟ ܗܘ ܡܪܐ ܕܝܘܒܠܐ: ܡܢ ܐܕܡ ܐܝܬܝܗ ܠܢܘܚ· ܡܛܐ ܕܝܢ ܠܐܒܪܗܡ· ܘܡܢ ܐܒܪܗܡ ܥܠ ܡܘܫܐ·· ܘܡܢܗ ܠܡܘܫܐ ܕܝܢ ܕܘܝܕ· ܘܡܢ ܕܘܝܕ ܠܘܬ ܫܒܝܬܐ· ܘܡܢ ܒܒܠ ܕܝܢ ܠܦܪܘܩܢ܀

i. e. "The prophets delivered it to the Apostles. Blessed be the Lord of successions! He handed it down from Adam even to Noah: it reached from Noah to Abraham, and from Abraham on to Moses, and from Moses unto David, and from David again to the Captivity, and from Babel to our Redeemer." The same is also said by S.

Methodius, Conv. Virg. vii. 4—7. Archel. Cascharensis, c. Manet. xxviii. And Melchizedek, Abimelech, and Job, are instances serving to show that this tradition was widely spread over the East; two of whom were kings, priests, and prophets, and, as such, might have been urged above (Note 27) as notable Gentile types of Christ.

It may, perhaps, be as well to observe in this place, that any rites existing among the Gentiles which Moses adopted, are not here noticed for anything more than the external resemblance. And admitting such resemblances to have been ever so common, they will still be merely external ones, whereas the Revelation given to Moses breathed an internal life into those rites, which, though invisible from without, wholly altered them in consideration of their prophetic character, for those within. This may be illustrated from the later revelation, the Gospel: under it certain outward signs found already existing in the world, valueless in themselves, yet not wholly devoid of mysteriousness, became the vehicles of the highest Christian doctrines. And what words were in this instance, that other outward signs, viz. ceremonies, were in the former. Profane people, under either dispensation, would see nothing but outward signs in them, and consider them, not in the aspect of sanctified things, but as mere human forms; not as expressions for doctrine held from the first, but as importations of Gentile theories or ceremonies, as the case may be.

Note (36.) p. 27.

St. Cyril, c. Julian. p. 9, notices, that Moses made the wisdom of Egypt, which was human, a *προγύμνασμα* to things divine. And of course what he received (as observed by St. Ephrem and St. Athanasius in the last note) from the patriarchs could be but an imperfect sketch of that great mysterious Temple to be reared in the earth by

Christ, which Moses saw in a figure upon the Mount. The idea of a visible Church to come is given by this vision to Moses, with a minuteness of detail such as nothing preceding that vision appears to have disclosed. Take away from the Pentateuch this description of the Tabernacle, and with it you ruin the whole edifice of subsequent prophecy. Any Hebrew scholar knows that Isaiah, for instance, without the references to the Pentateuch, would cease to subsist.

NOTE (37.) p. 27.

Aristot. Eth. N. i. 8. Τῷ ἀληθεῖ ταχὺ πάντα συνᾴδει τὰ ὑπάρχοντα· τῷ δὲ ψευδεῖ ταχὺ διαφωνεῖ τἀληθές. Origen, c. Céls., well observes, p. 361, Εἰκὸς μείζονα μὲν ἢ κατ' ἀνθρωπίνην φύσιν εἶναι τὴν γνῶσιν τοῦ Θεοῦ· διὸ καὶ τὰ τοσαῦτά ἐστι περὶ Θεοῦ σφάλματα.

NOTE (38.) p. 28.

Mr. Elphinstone, Appendix i. p. 429, is of opinion that the laws of Manu were in force in the ninth century before Christ: the date of the Vedas has been shown by Colebrooke, Essays, vol. i. p. 98, to be nearly the same as that of Moses. Of course, in the present argument, what is generally believed by Hindus forms a tolerable substitute for what is true; and therefore I content myself with this, without entering into diversities of opinions which may exist as to the real degree of antiquity to be assigned to the books in question. And, indeed, persons who argue for the much later date of Manu's laws do so on grounds which would lead to the discussion of subjects very foreign to the present. Remusat, for instance, in his Nouveaux Mélanges Asiat. ii. p. 334, argues, from the mention of the Chinese, that the book must have been later than the dynasty which gave them that name. But as the name (Sin) occurs in Isaiah, it could not have been so late as he places it. Yet the mere mention of these two facts will show the reader that it would be endless to discuss the date of this or that book, even were I competent to the task. And of course the laws of Manu, as well as any other laws (see above, p. 99), could not have been given all at once. The Greek account (Strabo xvii. p. 1035) that they had no written law, though possibly originating only in their getting the name Smriti etymologically interpreted to them, is worth noticing here, as suggesting evidence that there had been a time when the laws existed only as oral tradition.

NOTE (39.) p. 29.

Joseph. c. Apion. ii. 29. Οὕτως ἡμερότητα καὶ φιλανθρωπίαν ἡμᾶς ἐπαίδευσεν, ὡς οὐδὲ τῶν ἀλόγων ζώων ὠλιγώρηκεν· ἀλλὰ μόνον μὲν ἀφῆκε τούτων χρῆσιν τὴν νόμιμον, πᾶσαν δὲ ἑτέραν ἐκώλυσεν. Ἃ δὲ ὥσπερ ἱκετεύοντα προσφεύγει ταῖς οἰκίαις, ἀπεῖπεν ἀνελεῖν. Οὐδὲ νεοττοῖς ἐπέτρεψε τοὺς γονέας αὐτῶν συνεξαίρειν· φείδεσθαι δὲ καὶ ἐν πολέμῳ τῶν ἐργαζομένων ζώων, καὶ μὴ φονεύειν. And so St. Clement, Strom. ii. § 92, p. 477, Pott: Αὐτίκα τῶν γεννωμένων κατά τε τὰς ποίμνας, κατά τε τὰ αἰπόλια, καὶ βουκόλια, τῆς παραχρῆμα ἀπολαύσεως μηδὲ ἐπὶ προφάσει θυσιῶν διηγόρευσεν ἐκγόνων τε ἕνεκα καὶ μητέρων εἰς ἡμερότητα τῶν ἀνθρώπων κάτωθεν ἀπὸ τῶν ἀλόγων ζώων ἀνατρέφων. Χάρισαι γοῦν, φησὶ, τῇ μητρὶ τὸ ἔκγονον κἂν ἕπτα τὰς πρώτας ἡμέρας· εἰ γὰρ μηδὲν ἀναιτίως γίνεται, γάλα τε ἐπομβρεῖται ταῖς τετοκυίαις εἰς διατροφὴν τῶν ἐκγόνων, ἀποσπῶν τῆς τοῦ γάλακτος οἰκονομίας τὸ τεχθὲν ἀτιμάζει τὴν φύσιν. Δυσωπήσθωσαν οὖν Ἕλληνες, καὶ εἴ τις ἕτερός ἐστι τοῦ Νόμου κατατρέχων, εἰ ὁ μὲν καὶ ἐπ' ἀλόγων ζώων χρηστεύεται, οἱ δὲ καὶ τὰ τῶν ἀνθρώπων ἐκτιθέασιν ἔκγονα, καίτοι μακρόθεν καὶ προφητικῶς ἀνακόπτοντος αὐτῶν τὴν ἀγριότητα τοῦ νόμου διὰ τῆς προειρημένης ἐντολῆς. One might also notice other instances in which the law provided for cattle, e. g.

the command that they should share in the rest of the sabbath, that they should be rescued when in danger, or when sunk under a burden.

With regard, next, to the use made in the text of these prohibitions to injure brute creatures, it will be proper again to remind the reader that the similarities noticed are there represented as *external* ones. The internal scope of the law of Moses in such prohibitions may have been, and doubtless was, most essentially different. Thus it seems to have been a favourite heathen notion to represent brutes and men as beings of the same class, and to contend that kindness to them was a duty, on the ground of a fellowship with them. This is acutely defended by Porphyry, (de Abstin. lib. iii.) the fallacy of whose reasoning seems to lie in his assuming that the foresight, memory, and skill of brute creatures is their own, which we cannot prove. And although wanton cruelty to animals can hardly be reprobated in too strong terms, it may be a question whether some persons now-a-days do not speak of the duty of a gentleness to them in a way which originates in some feeling akin to the pantheistic one just noticed. The conduct of our Lord, in bidding St. Peter take a *hook* and cast it into the sea for a fish, would be condemned upon the theory of such persons, though practically they might shrink from condemning it. Yet it may be quite intelligible that the permission to kill living creatures did not at once remove the backwardness in doing so which must have been felt at first, and therefore intelligible, how (as stated in the text) some cases of kindness towards them should be represented as originating with a tradition of the antediluvian system. For if it be not absurd to suppose, as Aristotle does (vide note 16), that remnants of arts and sciences were handed down from that period, then neither is this supposition absurd.

Note (40.) p. 29.

St. Clement, Strom. ii. 91, says: ἐμοὶ δὲ δοκεῖ ὁ Πυθαγόρας τὸ ἥμερον περὶ τὰ ἄλογα ζῶα παρὰ τοῦ Νόμου εἰληφέναι.

Note (41.) p. 30.

The Bauddhas or Buddhists, and the Jains, both condemn the practice of sacrifices and other ceremonies which the followers of the Vedas perform (see Colebrooke's Essays, ii. p. 192): and in a kindred spirit Porphyry, de Abst. ii. 9, contends that sacrifices of animals were an innovation upon the sacrifices of fruits, &c. He notices (ii. 25) that no animal was sacrificed which men could not eat; and thus, while he would argue that the defenders of animal slaughter only made sacrifices a plea for their lust after flesh meat, he incidentally shows how faithful the universal tradition of the world was in keeping up the doctrine of a sacrifice to come, of which also they "have a right to eat" who are Christians. So essential does the ceremony of eating of the sacrifice seem to have been, even to the heathen notion of a sacrifice, that some Americans ate of their human sacrifices. See Carli Rubbi Lett. Americane, Opere xi. p. 170. Yet Satan seems to have tried, under the pretence of abstinence from flesh and greater sanctity, to persuade heathens everywhere to drop this vestige of more ancient doctrine. Thus true is St. Austin's teaching (de Civ. Dei, xv. 1) that the Civitas diaboli, set up from the first against the Civitas Dei, began with Cain,—the first gainsayer of sacrifices in which blood was shed! For though Porphyry would say in words, that he considered abstinence from meat to be the duty of priests only, and not binding upon all, (see Van Rhoer on i. 27,) yet the whole way of speaking of the eating of flesh as unholy (see ii. 31 particularly, and 46) shows what his bias was, viz. to deny the lawfulness of the act, and set aside the permission to kill and eat as far as possible. That nothing but a divine permission to kill and eat will fully account for the eating of animals, is also, I think, made out from what the objectors themselves say; for they urge well against those who opposed them, that the thing to be accounted for is, not how Pythagoras and others, who borrowed from Eastern philosophy, came to give up eating flesh, but how the eating of flesh first came in at all. (Porph. de Abst. ii. 1, &c. Plutarch. Mor. p. 993.) Plutarch also argues that if the doctrine of Metempsychosis, or more strictly of Metensomatosis [4], be not demonstrable, still it ought to have a moral cogency. Τῆς λεγομένης ταῖς ψυχαῖς εἰς σώματα μεταβολῆς, εἰ μὴ πίστεως ἄξιον τὸ ἀποδεικνύμενον, ἀλλ' εὐλαβείας τε μεγάλης καὶ δέους τὸ ἀμφίβολον. (p. 993, c.) Now a revelation, as has been suggested in the text, is a full answer to all difficulties of this kind; for they are based upon the fact of our ignorance of the whole destiny of a brute creature; whereas a revelation as coming from God, who *is* acquainted with their destinies, is a sufficient guarantee for our destruction of them. For antecedently to the knowledge of such a revelation, Plutarch's is evidently the religious way of arguing against the Stoics and Peripatetics; the only question being, whether the Gentiles ought not to have "retained in their knowledge" that revelation, or rather whether they did not retain it, as Heraclides Ponticus ap. Porph. (i. 4) seems to imply. In this case, of course, the deviations from the revelation would come under the censure in the text: men would be acting upon their own judgment against universal tradition. I will conclude this note with quoting St. Paul's words to the

[4] Metempsychosis is the belief of the wandering of souls into other human bodies; Metensomatosis, into the bodies of other animals.

Colossians, ii. 21, which appear to some, at least, in the Greek, to point out very strikingly the distinction between abstinences resulting from the heathen principle of contagion from matter, and those resulting from the Christian principle of voluntary offering and humility of mind, leaving it to others to decide whether the words do convey that impression or no. Εἰ ἀπεθάνετε σὺν Χριστῷ ἀπὸ τῶν στοιχείων τοῦ κόσμου, τί ὡς ζῶντες ἐν κόσμῳ δογματίζεσθε, ‘ μὴ ἅψῃ, μηδὲ γεύσῃ, μηδὲ θίγῃς,’ (ἅ ἐστι πάντα εἰς φθορὰν τῇ ἀποχρήσει) κατὰ τὰ ἐντάλματα καὶ διδασκαλίας τῶν ἀνθρώπων; ἅτινά ἐστι λόγον μὲν ἔχοντα σοφίας ἐν ἐθελοθρησκείᾳ καὶ ταπεινοφροσύνῃ [καὶ] ἀφειδίᾳ σώματος, οὐκ ἐν τιμῇ τινι πρὸς πλησμονὴν τῆς σαρκός.

Note (42.) p. 30.

Joseph. cont. Apion. ii. 24. 26, notices how pollutions of the body were thought, from its connexion with the soul, to affect it also. And whoever will compare the words of Moses, Levit. xv. 4, &c. with Manu, ii. 181, will find a similarity between the pollutions there specified and the rite of purification. In Deut. xxii. 8, we find that men are to beware of *bringing blood* upon their house, by so constructing it that a person may fall from the roof. In Manu, iii. 68, 69, we find that five sacrifices called Mahayajna are appointed for the expiation of such guilt as is brought upon a house by the killing of living creatures accidentally in it. In Manu, iii. 132, we read:

न हि हस्तावसृग्दिग्धौ रुधिरेणैव शुध्यतः

"for hands stained with blood are not to be purified by [mere] blood," and this as a reason why they must go to a learned Brahman, which implies, of course, a pollution coming from the blood, though it is also important as showing the obligation to go to the priests. In Manu,

v. 64, 65, mention is made of the pollution from touching a corpse; and in 85 it is said that one who has touched a corpse is made pure by bathing; which may be compared with Numbers xix. 11—13, where purification by water is also specified for the same pollution. Comp. Eccl. xxxiv. 25. In like manner abstinence from intercourse with a menstruous woman is enjoined, as in Levit. xv. 19, 20; so in Manu, iv. 40. xi. 174. But the comparison cannot be carried to a greater length without giving more time to it than is necessary for the present purpose.

NOTE (43.) p. 30.

This right of discriminating between the fitness or unfitness of things for sacrifice seems everywhere implied in the law of Manu (see iii. 128. 135. 168. 185. 253. iv. 81, &c.); though I cannot specify a definite statement of it. "The Ved says (observes Rammohun-Roy, p. 21) that he who has true faith in the omnipresent Supreme Being may eat all that exists, i. e. is not bound to inquire what is his food or who prepares it. Nevertheless the Vedánt limits that authority thus. The above-mentioned authority of the Ved for eating all sorts of food should only be observed at the time of distress"—a common limitation to many permissions in Manu's laws, and parallelled by what David did when he was an hungred, in some measure. And in Manu, v. 23, we read, "Doubtless in the ancient sacrifices and in the offerings of Brahmans and Xhatriyas there were sacrifices of such birds and beasts as may be eaten." A remarkable passage, both in connexion with the admission of Porph. de Abstin. ii. 25, noticed in p. 108, and also for its assertion of the antiquity of the sacrifice of animals! However, it is here produced as a limitation on a different ground to that of the Vedanta just cited, and illustrates our present subject. For the verse before says that the best kinds of birds and beasts

प्रशस्ता मृगपक्षिण:

may be killed by the Brahmans for sacrifice; which of course constitutes them the judges of what are the best. Akin to this is what we read in Levit. xxvii. 11: "If it be any unclean beast of which they do not offer a sacrifice to the Lord, then he shall present the beast before the priest, and the priest shall value it whether it be good or bad: according to the estimation of the priest, so shall it be."

In Manu, iv. 49, we read thus: "Let him void his excrements, having covered the earth with wood, potsherds, dry leaves, and grass:" and 77, "Never let him look at urine or ordure." Parallel to this is Deut. xxiii. 13, 14: "Thou shalt have a paddle upon thy weapon; and it shall be, when thou shalt ease thyself abroad, thou shalt dig therewith, and shalt turn back, and cover that which cometh from thee: for the Lord thy God walketh in the midst of thy camp, to deliver thee, and to give up thine enemies before thee; therefore thy camp shall be holy, that He see no unclean thing and turn away from thee." Such passages as these, which blend thus fearlessly the mention of things now accounted obscene with the name of the Most High, are indeed a searching warning against all impurity of heart, but may perhaps be noticed also not irreverently, as far as it is to these in particular to which we find parallels in the older heathen systems, as well as to other enactments. Porphyry, l. c. ii. 50, says: *οἱ τῶν τῇδε ἱερεῖς . . . . καὶ τάφων ἀπέχεσθαι κελεύουσιν ἑαυτοῖς τε καὶ τοῖς ἄλλοις καὶ τῶν ἀνδρῶν ἀνοσίων καὶ ἐμμήνων καὶ συνουσιῶν καὶ θεᾶς ἤδη αἰσχρᾶς καὶ πενθικῆς*, κ.λ., which need not necessarily allude to the Pentateuch, as similar observances occur elsewhere. E. g. Carli

R. says, vol. xi. p. 184, of the Peruvians: "I tempi de i naturali spurghi muliebri erano, per legge quasi universali, interdetti alla congiunzione."

In Manu, xi. 227, occurs the following rule: "For sins not public the assembly of priests must award them punishments with holy texts and oblations by fire. By confession, by repentance, by [austere] devotion,

ख्यापनेनानुतापेनतपसा

by reading of Scripture, a sinner may be released from his guilt," &c., with which Levit. v. 5—8, may be placed in juxtaposition: "It shall be that when he shall be guilty in one of these sins, that he shall *confess* that he hath sinned, and shall bring his trespass offering unto the LORD. . . . . and the priest shall make an atonement for him concerning his sin." Compare Josh. vii. 19. "My son, give, I pray thee, glory unto the LORD God of Israel, and make confession unto Him; and *tell me now* what thou hast done; hide it not from me;" a notion likely to be prevalent where much importance is attached to a visible channel of grace. But perhaps I have put together a sufficient number of instances to illustrate what has been said in the text.

NOTE (44.) p. 32.

Justin Mart. c. Tryph. p. 237. Τῷ Νῶε συγκεχώρηται ὑπὸ τοῦ Θεοῦ δικαίῳ ὄντι πᾶν ἔμψυχον ἐσθίειν, πλὴν κρέας ἐν αἵματι, ὅπερ ἐστὶ νεκριμαῖον. Gen. ix. 3. "Every moving thing that liveth shall be meat for you; even as the green herb have I given you all things. But the flesh with the life thereof, which is the blood thereof, shall ye not eat." On which Jarchi observes: שלא הרשיתי וגו׳. "In that I gave not the first man power save over the green herb, to you have I given, as the green herb which I left open to the first man, to you have I given all." And Hizkuni: "*As the green herb.* There are herbs that be fit to eat, and there are that be unfit to eat: thus of cattle, birds, beasts, and fishes, there are that be fit to eat, and there are that be not fit to eat. '*Have I given them all unto you.*' After they were rescued in the ark, and by your hands the rescuing came to them, behold they are in your hands, to do with them as it is good in your eyes." And that this permission was necessary may be argued even from what Porphyry says, ii. § 13. *καὶ γὰρ ἄλλως πάντα μὲν τῶν Θεῶν ἐστιν· ἡμῶν δὲ δοκοῦσιν εἶναι οἱ καρποί· ἡμεῖς γὰρ καὶ σπείρομεν αὐτοὺς καὶ φυτεύομεν καὶ ταῖς ἄλλαις ἐπιμελείαις ἀνατρέφομεν.* If, then, they—or, as we should say, He—whose they are, give the permission to slay, how is this less just than for us to give permission to gather the fruits we have made ours by sowing, as he would have it? In truth we might well answer in the Apostle's words: *Ἄφρον, σὺ ὃ σπείρεις .. οὐ τὸ σῶμα τὸ γενησόμενον σπείρεις, ἀλλὰ γυμνὸν κόκκον .. Ὁ δὲ Θεὸς αὐτῷ δίδωσι σῶμα καθὼς ἠθέλησε, καὶ ἑκάστῳ τῶν σπερμάτων τὸ ἴδιον σῶμα.* So plain is it that we have no right whatever to the things in the world except as a grant from Him who is "Possessor of heaven and earth."

NOTE (45.) p. 32.

See the passage given by Rammōhun Roy, p. 22, and the opening of Manu's laws, which begin with the creation of all things by GOD. The reason why this is so striking is, that so many of the Greeks omitted to notice GOD at all in their speculations upon the Creation. Eusebius, P. E. i. 8. p. 25, c. *Τοιαύτη καὶ τῶν πανσόφων Ἑλλήνων, τῶν δὴ φυσικῶν φιλοσόφων ἐπικληθέντων, ἡ περὶ τῆς συστάσεως τοῦ παντὸς καὶ τῆς πρώτης κοσμογονίας διάληψις, οὐ δημιουργὸν ἢ ποιητήν τινα τῶν ὅλων ὑποστησαμένων, ἀλλ' οὐδ' ὅλως Θεοῦ μνήμην ποιησαμένων.* Thus Homer seems to look on the gods as a sort of secretion from the ocean, *Ὠκέανόν τε θεῶν γένεσιν*, Il. Ξ. 201; and Aristotle, Ethics, iii. 5, gives *ἀνάγκη*, *φύσις*, and *τύχη* as the principles of causation; and in his Physics, ii. 4, 5, expresses his surprise that none of the ancients insisted enough upon chance as one of them, although he is aware that there are people who say that chance is a cause indeed, but one obscure to the mind of man as somewhat divine and superhuman. *Εἰσί τινες οἷς δοκεῖ εἶναι μὲν αἰτία ἡ τύχη, ἄδηλος δὲ ἀνθρωπίνῃ διανοίᾳ, ὡς θεῖόν τι οὖσα καὶ δαιμονιώτερον.* Compare Metaph. xi. 3. p. 1070. a 5, and what he says of Anaxagoras, p. 985, a 18. That I may not be overhard upon the Greeks, I again state the language of St. Cyril, c. Jul. p. 16. *Χρῆναι δὲ φημὶ μετὰ τοῦτο τὴν Ἑβραίων ἡμᾶς πολυπραγμονῆσαι δόξαν, ἣν ἐσχήκασι περὶ Θεοῦ καὶ τῆς τοῦ κόσμου γενέσεως, ἤτοι κατασκευῆς· εἴθ' οὕτω καί τι τοῖς Ἑλλήνων ἔδοξε σοφοῖς ἐμφανὲς καταστῆσαι ἐντευξομένοις. Ἔνθα μὲν γὰρ τοῖς τῆς θεοπνευστοῦ γραφῆς συμφέρονται λόγοις, ἑαυτῶν ὄντας ἀμείνους κατίδοι τις ἂν καὶ ὁμολογοῦντας ἀλλήλοις· ἔνθα δὲ τῶν οἰκείων ἕκαστος εὑρημάτων ποιεῖται τὴν ἀπόδοσιν, διαφόρους τε ὄντας καὶ ἀλλοκόταις δόξαις καταμεθύοντας καταδεῖξαι ῥᾷον.*

Note (46.) p. 32.

St. Ephrem, Præf. ad Gen.:—

ܘܡܢ ܡܓܕܠܐ ܕܒܒܠ ܠܡܘܫܐ ܟܪܘܙܘܬܗܘܢ ܕܗܠܝܢ ܒܒܢܝ ܫܡ ܠܐ ܥܬܩܬ:

i. e. "From the tower of Babel to Moses the preaching of these things among the sons of Shem wore not out." He also says, (i. p. 466.) "Ophir was a mountain in the East by India, (ܒܡܕܢܚܐ ܠܘܬ ܗܢܕܘ :) where dwelt the sons of Joctan, son of Heber." This would bring a Semitic fountain close to India, unless the ܗܢܕܘ of St. Ephrem be, as seems unlikely, different from the Hodu[5] of Esther.

Note (47.) p. 32.

Windisch. p. 978. Braunschweig. Umrisse, p. 92. "Die Braminen, als einer besonderer Priester-kaste, bildeten sie aus den alten Semiten und deren Fürstenfamilien." One could wish this thoughtful author had given his authorities for many of his statements. However, it may not be amiss to add one or two reflections which suggest themselves upon the supposition of the truth of his statement.

1. We find it to have been a common thing for priesthoods of different gods to be confined to families, not only among barbarians, but also among Greeks, (see Wesseling on Diodorus, i. 73.) and even where this was not the case, that *sacra privata* existed, which, as being confined to families, appear to be traces of and witnesses to the principle of confining priesthoods to certain families. Lands were set apart for them, as in Egypt (Gen. xlvii. 20. Diod. Sic. i. 21. 71), in Cappadocia (Strabo xii. p. 809, as there cited), and it should seem in Ethiopia, (Diod. Sic. iii. 3, says: *τὰ συστήματα τῶν ἱερῶν παραπλησίον ἔχει τάξιν παρ' ἀμφοτέροις τοῖς ἔθνεσιν*, i. e. Egyptians and Ethiopians,) and in Chaldæa (ibid. ii. 29).

2. Besides this general principle, we find, as reference to the passages of Diodorus and to Philostr. ii. 29. Porphyr. de Abst. iv. 8, p. 320. Vit. Pythag. p. 12, (Kiessling,) will show, that they handed on a system of doctrine from father to son, analogously to what was the case amongst the Jews, and which may have been a feature in the family of Shem—

[5] The *o* seems to have originated in a nasal pronunciation of Hendu, or Heandu, as it is called in the Zendavesta. Gesen. Lex. Maj. p. 366.

a natural tendency, of which providential use was made in the Jewish dispensation.

3. We find a reason for thinking that the Chaldeans[6] and Ethiopians were Semitic tribes (although some have thought otherwise) in their language; and if this is ever shown to be the case, we can see that these two centres would abundantly account for the transmission of Semitic families through the world. For the Ethiopians claimed to be the instructors of the Egyptians, and seem to have been known in Homer's days as the blameless Ethiopians, in some way specially connected with the gods. (Diod. Sic. iii. 1.) And the Chaldeans, whose name became synonymous with soothsayer, (Wess.[7] ad Diod. Sic. ii. 29.) were known through the world as such. (See Cato de R. R. p. 14, Bip. Arrian, p. 196. 478. St. Basil, Hex. vi. 5. Aul. Gell. i. 9. Olear. ad Philostr. vi. 41.) At all events, if not belonging to the Semitic family, they had means of access to that family, and may have copied from them. I ought to add, that I merely put these few observations together in the hopes that some abler person may investigate the subject. To my own mind the idea seems antecedently probable, and to gain some confirmation from the consideration that St. Ephrem's statement, quoted in the last note, was probably wholly unknown to Braunschweig.

NOTE (48.) p. 33.

See the passage from Professor Wilson in Note 1.

[6] I see not myself why מוליך כהנים שולל, Job xii. 19, should not be taken with the Septuagint and St. Ephrem of Gentile *priests*, which of course would be an early and authoritative recognition of their existence as a common order, and as under God's providential government; and also as an object of spoil, possibly as having lands, as described in Diodorus.

[7] Ἔθνος and *natio* (see Vales. de Harpocr. p. 297) were used of classes of artificers, &c. Does not this imply that they were originally kept to distinct nations, as they even now are in some instances?

Note (49.) p. 33.

The Jews (see Eisenmenger Entd. Judenthum, i. p. 319) and certain heretics (Epiph. xxxv. 6) held Melchizedek to be Shem. He who has thought at all upon many *apparent* absurdities in Jewish tradition will, perhaps, be disposed to allow that it was common for later writers to take up as realities what were only intended for symbolical representations. If this be so, then the Jewish tradition about Melchizedek could only be a symbolizing of their belief that even priests external to the covenant were of Shem's family.

Note (50.) p. 34.

Windischm. p. 1665, so explains the word नास्तिक्यं in Manu, xii. 33, on the authority of the commentator Kullúka Bhatta, if I am not mistaken. The quality of darkness was supposed to be the prevailing and characteristic quality of the last age.

Note (51.) p. 35.

This is frequently observed by St. Austin: thus, upon Ps. xc. En. ii. § 6. "Ipse fecit de quinque panibus multum panis, unde saturaret tot millia, qui facit quotidie in terrâ de paucis granis messes ingentes. Ipsa enim sunt miracula Domini; sed assiduitate viluerunt." It may be observed, as bearing upon the text, that the book of Deuteronomy may be considered as a development having a character of its own, and containing in it much that throws the law into a new light. As such, it would have cleared up the difficulties of serious minds; and as such, if we may venture to notice it, it seems to have been frequently cited by our blessed Saviour. Its conclusion is such as to force upon men's minds that Moses looked for a recompense of reward not to be found on earth. The mention of Hell in xxxii. 22, is very awe-striking, as indeed the whole prospect of future retribution there spoken of must have been to such as were "wise and would consider their latter end."

NOTE (52.) p. 35.

Aristot. E. N. vi. 9. Ἔτι τὰ αὑτοῦ πῶς δεῖ διοικεῖν ἄδηλον καὶ σκεπτέον. See the Analogy, ii. vi. p. 307—8.

NOTE (53.) p. 35.

Aristot. Analyt. Post. ii. 19. φαίνεται τοῦτο πᾶσιν ὑπάρχειν τοῖς ζώοις· ἔχει γὰρ δύναμιν σύμφυτον κριτικὴν, ἣν καλοῦσιν αἴσθησιν. In the Hitopadesa, i. 690,

परिच्छेदो हि पाण्डित्यं यदापन्ना विपद्दशा
अपरिच्छेदकर्तॄणां विपदः स्युः पदे पदे

"Discrimination is a thing to be learnt, when misfortunes have been fallen into. Of them who act without discrimination, mischances will be the lot from time to time."

With regard to what is noticed presently, namely, the mere arbitrary passion which seems to give us our present being, and certainly is *instrumental* in giving it, the following passages of St. Austin are, I think, worth the reader's attention. De Trin. xiii. 23. "Melius judicavit de ipso quod victum fuerat genere assumere hominem Deus, per quem generis humani vinceret inimicum; et tamen ex virgine cujus conceptum Spiritus non caro, fides non libido prævenit. Nec interfuit *carnis concupiscentia per quam seminantur* et concupiunt cæteri qui trahunt originale peccatum, sed eâ penitus remotissimâ credendo non concumbendo sancta est fecundata Virginitas: ut illud, quod nascebatur ex propagine primi hominis tantummodo generis, non etiam criminis, originem duceret. . . . Quamvis enim carnali concupiscentiâ quæ inest genitalibus membris bene utatur castitas conjugalis; habet tamen motus *non volun-*

tarios, quibus ostendit vel nullum se in paradiso ante peccatum esse potuisse, vel non talem fuisse, si fuit, ut aliquando resisteret voluntati. Nunc autem illam talem esse sentimus, ut repugnans legi mentis, etiam si nulla est causa generandi, stimulos ingerat coeundi; ubi si ei ceditur *peccando* satietur," &c. c. Jul. Pelag. ii. 32. "Dicit beatus Ambrosius.... omnes homines sub peccato nasci quorum ipse ortus in vitio est; qui quia *concupiscentiæ voluptate* concreti prius subirent contagia delictorum quam vitalem de hoc aere spiritum ducerent." iii. 49. "Malarum cupiditatum una est concupiscentia carnis *ex quâ* et cum quâ nascuntur et propter quam renascuntur infantes." iv. 34. "*Ideo* sub diabolo sunt qui de corporum commixtione nascuntur, antequam per spiritum renascuntur; *quia per illam nascuntur concupiscentiam*, quâ caro concupiscat adversus spiritum, et adversus se coget concupiscere spiritum." Indeed, much of the Pelagian controversy necessarily ran upon this point, which has elicited from St. Austin many observations useful to those who, whether in single *or* married life, covet earnestly that most excellent gift of chastity, yet dangerous to those who not only think that much that is incident to married life is not venial sin, (see iv. 33, &c.) but even count mortal sins before marriage to be venial. One more passage shall be added, for the fearful thoughts it ought to suggest to sinners. It is from the same treatise, vi. 43. "Non habitat Deus in corpore subdito peccatis, et tamen operatur hominem in utero meretricis. Adtingit enim ubique propter suam munditiam, et nihil inquinatum in Eum incurrit. Et quod multo est mirabilius, aliquando adoptat in filium, quem format in utero immundissimæ fœminæ; et aliquando non vult esse filium suum, quem format in utero suæ filiæ. Ille quippe ad Baptismum nescio quâ provisione pervenit; iste repentinâ morte non pervenit. Atque ita Deus, in cujus potestate sunt omnia, facit esse in Christi consortio, quem formavit in diaboli domicilio; et non vult esse in regno suo, quem formavit in templo suo."

Note (54.) p. 39.

Molitor, Phil. der Gesch. i. § 561. "Allein eben das Beispiel der Zaduzäer beweist gerade für die Existenz einer Tradition im Judenthume. Denn wo ist wohl ein Volk, welches nur auf der ersten Anfangs-Stufe der Cultur stehet, ohne den Glauben an Unsterblichkeit gefunden worden? Haben nicht alle Völker rund um die Juden herum den Glauben an Unsterblichkeit gehalt, der selbst dem rohesten und sinnlichsten Menschen ein Bedürfniss ist. Haben namentlich nicht die Egyptier, von denen man doch vorgiebt, dass Moscheh bei ihnen alles entlehnt, an Unsterblichkeit geglaubt? Und wie sollte denn Moscheh, selbst wenn man ihn blos als politischen Gesetzgeber betrachtet, dieses grosse in der Sehnsucht der menschlichen Natur gegründete Motiv in seiner Religion aufzunehmen versäumt haben? Ist also Israäl das von Gott auserwählte Geschlecht, wie lässt es sich wohl denken, dass Gott seinem eigenen Volke diesen einzigen und hochsten Zweck für den der Mensch auf Erden lebt, für den er durch die Religion soll erzogen werden, verborgen haben würde? Aus diesem Allen gehet also klar hervor, dass, obwohl zwar nirgends mit deutlichen Worten von einem jenseitigen Leben, sondern immer nur von irdischen Vergeltungen die Rede ist, jene sinnlichen Bilde nichts anders, als blos mystische Symbole gewesen sind, deren Aufschluss nothwendig einer Tradition voraussetzt." To this may be added the practical remarks of the venerable Pocock, which are very instructive, even if somewhat diffuse. On Hosea, vol. ii. p. 39 of his Works, he says: "Those that Christ had to call into His kingdom were such, for the most part, as had little or no knowledge of God and of the world to come; and therefore, agreeable to His purpose, was it expedient that he should take chief care, that He should instruct them concerning those spiritual things and concerning the other life which they were ignorant of, and give them such laws which might conduce to their attainment thereof and their well-being therein; and ratify them with such promises and threats as might have respect thereto; yet so as to let them know, too, that His law did concern their well-being in this world as well as in that other world; and that godliness had the promise of this life also as of the life to come, under the Gospel as well as under the Law, though the promises to it of the life that now is were more clearly and frequently expressed under the Law, and those of that which is to come, under the Gospel. And this consideration will afford us a plain and easy solution to the question why, under the Law, the promises and threats, blessings and curses, on obedience or disobedience, were as *to the letter* more temporal and carnal, under the Gospel more spiritual, and concerning things eternal,—and show the cause to be not so much by reason of the dulness, grossness, or carnality, of the minds of the Jews above other people, as some are apt to say; which reason I think ought not to be pressed far, except it could be made appear that such to whom the Gospel with its promises and threats hath been preached, have showed themselves as dull of hearing, as refractory and as stiffnecked as ever they under the Law were: nor doth this difference of promises, threats, blessings, and curses, under the Law and the Gospel, show that they under the Law were ignorant of the other life, and those eternal rewards and punishments in it, or left in doubt of them, but give us rather to suppose that they *were instructed in those things from the Father's*[8] *time*, even before the giving of the Law, and *that it was given to them as supposing that they were so*, and well aware of them.

[8] See Job xxi. 29, 30.

However, in process of time, there rose up among them sects that doubted of, yea plainly denied, that future state of reward to the godly, and punishment to the wicked,—as particularly the Sadducees."

So, too, Origen c. Cels. p. 260. *Ὁποῖον δὲ ἦν παρ' αὐτοῖς τὸ ἐξ ἔτι ἁπαλῶν ὀνύχων διδάσκεσθαι, ὑπεραναβαίνειν μὲν πᾶσαν τὴν αἰσθητὴν φύσιν καὶ μηδαμοῦ αὐτῆς νομίζειν ἵδρυσθαι τὸν Θεὸν, ἄνω δὲ καὶ ὑπὲρ τὰ σώματα ζητεῖν αὐτόν; πηλίκον δὲ τὸ καὶ σχεδὸν ἅμα γενέσει καὶ συμπληρώσει τοῦ λόγου διδάσκεσθαι αὐτοὺς τὴν τῆς ψυχῆς ἀθανασίαν, καὶ τὰ ὑπὸ γῆν δικαιωτήρια, καὶ τὰς τιμὰς τῶν καλῶς βεβιωκότων.* Holding to this most firmly, I wish also not to be misunderstood as if the existence of temporal promises under the Law were denied in these notes: that was not intended to be done, but to assert that more was meant by them than things temporal; that a Law of God's government, applicable to all times and nations, was *distinctly revealed* in the Pentateuch, the seeming contradictions to which Law had a place amongst the Jews as well as elsewhere, and were in themselves enough to force upon them the expectation of a future state of rewards and punishments. And that the existence of such a Law[9] was so vouchsafed to them by revelation, must have removed many doubts, and left the mind free to reflect upon the heart-searching rule by which God, even in this world, judged mankind. The riches and wealth which have made themselves wings, and fled from the Christian Church, do in a like way force upon us that she has not been covetous, above all things, of that holiness to which God by His prophets and by His Son promised that all these things should be added. Both we and the Jews have this law revealed to us; and are consequently driven, by its non-fulfilment, to search our own hearts for those sins which God

[9] Ps. cxlvii. 20. "He hath not so dealt with any nation, neither have the heathen knowledge of His Laws."

seeth there, if we will not. Thus, in each case the *certain knowledge* of the existence of such a law, in regard to temporal goods and ills, helps us to prepare for things eternal. The heathen had not knowledge of the laws by which God does govern this world, and so were in a worse state for preparation for the next.

Note (55.) p. 39.

Herodotus, ii. 123, has been taken by some to assert this, though it seems that he may have meant that they were the first who taught a metensomatosis. His words are, *πρῶτοι τόνδε τὸν λόγον Αἰγύπτιοί εἰσι οἱ εἰπόντες, ὡς ἀνθρώπου ψυχὴ ἀθάνατός ἐστι· τοῦ σώματος δὲ καταφθίνοντος ἐς ἄλλο ζῶον αἰεὶ γινόμενον ἐσδύεται.* I cannot say that the words seem to me to do else than imply that the Egyptians first taught *both* the immortality of the soul as one thing, and its migration as another; though the commentators appear to think otherwise. I am not aware myself, indeed, that the immortality of the soul was ever taught by earlier heathens apart from the doctrine of transmigration (see Note 63), so that we should come to the same point in the end. Aristotle, indeed, *argued against* the doctrine of metensomatosis (de Anima, i. 3); but then he held but very loosely to the other doctrine (de Anim. iii. 5), as Atticus, an acute Platonist, well urges against him (ap. Euseb. P. E. p. 810).

Note (56.) p. 39

The reader may compare the remarks of Molitor, i. § 270, who points out that Jewry knew not of any mysteries in the heathen sense of them; had nothing, that is, exclusively confined to the priests, but consisted of an exoteric and esoteric, which were but slightly separated from each other, and that in such a way that the former was a step to the latter. The priests of Egypt, on the contrary, seem to have kept to themselves whatever Joseph, who had procured them their immunities, taught them. Yet still the doctrine of the soul's existence after death was attested to the people by a public ceremony. See Diod. i. 72.

Note (57.) p. 41.

This is noticed by R. Menasse de Resur. Mort. cap. x. Euseb. P. E. p. 550. Methodius, Conv. Virg. vi. 1. λογικὴ καὶ ἀθάνατός ἐστιν, καθ' εἰκόνα δημιουργηθεῖσα, &c.

Note (58.) p. 41.

For this remark I am indebted, I think, to Tertullian, but am unable to refer to it again: it seems, however, to carry its own proof with it.

Note (59.) p. 41.

This we find in the collection of Jewish prayers published by Landau, p. 393, יזכור אלהים נשמת וגו״. "May the Lord remember the spirit of my father that taught me, who hath gone to his own world: because that I vow alms for him, by this price may his soul be bound in the bundle of life with the spirits of Abraham, Isaac, and Jacob, and with the remnant of the righteous men and righteous women that are in the garden of Eden. And let us say, Amen." And in the same way, in Nachmanides' form of prayer for the dead, given by Pocock, vol. i. p. 209, Not. Misc. cap. vi. יהי רצון מלפני וגו״. "May it please the Lord our God, our Creator, our Holy One, the Holy One of Jacob, who formed all the children of his covenant in judgment, and gave them life in judgment, and killed them in judgment, who shall also raise them to the life of the world to come, and knoweth the number of them all, that He would haste and speedily raise up our lord and doctor, this illustrious one, or this righteous man or wise rabbin, whose body dwelleth in this tomb, whose bones are resting amid these stones, and quicken him with life everlasting, that hath no death after it—the life that swalloweth up all death, that blotteth out all tears," &c. &c. With regard to confessing sins of the fathers, one may notice how Daniel, ch. ix., was continually used in the Selichoth or litanies, of which several MSS. occur in the Oppenheim Collection, now in the Bodleian. Several of the things instanced here are taken from R. Menasse de Resurrectione Mortuorum.

Note (60.) p. 41.

Calov. on Gen. xxv. 8, notices how even bad men are said to *sleep* with their fathers, whereas 'to be gathered to their fathers' is said only of the good. St. Clem. Strom. ii. § 28. p. 444, (Potter) Εἰ δὲ αἱ αὐταὶ μοναὶ ἡμῖν τε καὶ τοῖς πατριάρχαις καταγγέλλονται, εἷς ἀμφοῖν ταῖν διαθήκαιν δείκνυται ὁ Θεός. The application in the text is from R. Manasse.

Note (61.) p. 42.

Austin. c. Faust. xix. 31. "Dicitur quidem ibi, (in veteribus Hebræorum libris,) Diligite sapientiam, ut in æternum regnetis (Sap. vi. 22). Et ipsa vita æterna si non illic in manifesto prædicaretur, non diceret Dominus etiam malis Judæis, Scrutamini Scripturas in quibus vos putatis vitam æternam habere; ipsæ testimonium perhibent de me. Quo enim nisi ad hoc pertinet quod ibi scriptum est, Non moriar sed vivam, et enarrabo opera Domini: et, Illumina oculos meos ne unquam obdormiam in morte; et, Justorum animæ in manu Dei sunt et non tangit illos tormentum (Sap. iii. 1). Et paulo post, Illi autem sunt in pace, et si coram hominibus tormenta passi sunt, spes illorum immortalitate plena est: et in paucis vexati, in multis bene disponentur. Et in alio loco, Justi autem in perpetuum vivent, et apud Dominum est merces eorum, et cogitatio eorum apud Altissimum; ideo accipient regnum decoris, et diadema speciei de manu Domini (Sap. v. 16). Hæc et alia multa, sive apertissima sive subobscura, inveniuntur illic testimonia vitæ æternæ. Et de ipsa corporum resurrectione non tacuerunt Prophetæ. Unde Pharisæi adversus Sadducæos," &c.

Note (62.) p. 42.

Chald. Paraphr. Deut. xxxiii. 6. יחי ראובן בחיי עלמא ומותא תנינא לא ימות. "May Reuben live in life eternal, and not die the second death." Job iii. 17—19. תמא רשיע". "There the wicked that have done penance cease from the turmoil of hell; and there rest the disciples whose might hath been spent in toiling at the Law: at the same time, they that are bound to the schools [of the prophets] are at peace; the babes of the rabbin's house hear not the voice of their master. Jacob, that is called the Small, and Abraham, that is called the Elder, are there, and Isaac, the servant of the Lord, that went forth free from the bond, from his master [1]." The reader will observe how Abraham, Isaac, and Jacob, occur frequently as chief among the dead (see Note 60); as in St. Matt. viii. 11, &c. Ps. lxiii. 4, 5. ארום טב וגו". "For better is the mercy that Thou wilt do unto the righteous in the world to come, than the life that Thou hast given to the wicked in this world: therefore my lips shall praise Thee. I will bless Thee in the life of this world; in the name of thy Word (comp. St. John xvi. 23) I will spread forth my hands in prayer for the world that is to come," i. e. for the kingdom of the Messiah. Jer. li. 39. "I will bring upon them trouble, and they shall be like unto drunken men, seeing they shall

[1] One suspects the reading here should be מן קיוס ידיה instead of קיריס, which would be 'from the tying of his hand.'

not be strong, and shall die the second death, and shall not live in the world to come, saith the Lord." Zech. iii. 7. "Thus saith the LORD of Hosts, If thou wilt walk in upright paths and keep the commandment (Ch. *keeping*) of My Word, then shalt thou also judge them that minister in My sanctuary and keep My courts, and in the resurrection of the dead I will give thee feet that walk among these Seraphin." The Chaldee paraphrast is well worth a careful perusal—a much more careful one than I can own to having given it. Yet the reader will, I think, feel that these passages which I have selected are remarkable for this, that they are paraphrases of passages which do not force the future state upon the mind, and which could not therefore have been so paraphrased, save by persons fully possessed with the doctrine beforehand. Tradition certainly does something towards the interpretation of Scripture: and I may suggest, by way of parallel, that the passages in the New Testament in which we rightly find the doctrine of the Holy Spirit's Divinity, or of infant baptism, do not *force* such doctrines upon misbelievers.

NOTE (63.) p. 43.

This seems to have been adopted from heathenism by several heretics, as by Saturninus (see St. Irenæus i. 24, where Saturninus is said to argue from Gen. i. 26, in proof of his doctrine), and by Basilides (St. Clem. Strom. ii. § 38. p. 449, Pott.), and Bardesanes, of whom St. Ephrem, ii. p. 444, A, writes thus:—

ܩܕܚܬ ܒܒܪܕܝܨܢ ܛܘܥܝܝ ܕܝܘܢܝܐ:

"In Bardesanes flamed forth the error of the Greeks (i. e. heathens) who taught that the universe was created by several essences and formed. Marcion and Bardesanes bear witness and blasphemously say that there is not one

Creator only: The things made by their Maker they attribute to those He made." And so Archel. Caschar. c. Manet. cap. x. says of Manes, that he attributed the creation of Adam to the chief Angels: δεῦτε . . . ποιήσωμεν τὸν ἄνθρωπον κατὰ τὴν ἡμῶν τῶν Ἀρχόντων μορφὴν, καθ' ἣν εἴδομεν ὅ ἐστι πρῶτος ἄνθρωπος. Julian also complains of Moses for having omitted to say anything of the Creation of Angels (Cyril c. Jul. p. 98, c. coll. p. 102). This, indeed, seems to have been a masterpiece of Satan, as will appear in the sequel perhaps more clearly.

NOTE (64.) p. 43.

Greg. Nyss. de V. Mosis, 193, d. Ἔστι γάρ τι τῆς φιλοσόφου γονῆς ἐν μαθήμασι σαρκῶδές τε καὶ ἀκρόβυστον, οὗ περιαιρεθέντος, τῆς Ἰσραηλιτικῆς εὐγενείας ἐστὶ τὸ λειπόμενον. οἷον ἀθάνατον εἶναι τὴν ψυχὴν καὶ ἡ ἔξωθεν φιλοσοφία φησίν. οὗτος εὐσεβής ἐστιν τόκος· ἀλλὰ μεταβαίνειν ἀπὸ σωμάτων εἰς σώματα, καὶ ἐκ λογικῆς φύσεως εἰς ἄλογον αὐτὴν μεταφύεσθαι, τοῦτο ἡ σαρκώδης καὶ ἀλλόφυλός ἐστιν ἀκροβυστία· καὶ ἄλλα τοιαῦτα πολλά· Θεὸν εἶναί φησιν, ἀλλ' ὑλικὸν αὐτὸν οἴεται· Δημιουργὸν Αὐτὸν οἴεται, ἀλλ' ὕλης πρὸς τὴν δημιουργίαν δεόμενον. ἀγαθόν τε καὶ δυνατὸν εἶναι δίδωσιν, ἀλλὰ παραχωρεῖν ἐν τοῖς πολλοῖς τῇ ἀνάγκῃ τῆς εἱμαρμένης. With this account of heathenism the ancient religion of the Hindus falls in, if according to Colebrooke, i. p. 27, it recognises but one GOD, yet does not sufficiently discriminate the creature from the Creator. The whole of the Essay of Colebrooke referred to may be consulted, though it must be confessed that we yet want an accurate account of the theology of the Vedas. Parts of them are now in the course of publication. Dr. Stevenson, Pref. to Sama Veda, p. xi., mentions that at the Pralaya (the destruction or absorption of all things) Soma only is said to remain, and the womb of Ocean (as in

Homer[2], Il. xiv. 201) to contain all the gods. Yet he observes, that "nothing definite can be learnt from this and similar expressions as to the particular scheme of Hindu philosophy taught in the Vedas."

NOTE (65.) p. 44.

Longinus, in the well-known passage, page 70, Toup, notices this of Moses. After saying of Homer, *πολὺ τῶν περὶ τὴν θεομαχίαν τὰ ὅσα ἄχραντόν τι καὶ μέγα τὸ δαιμόνιον, ὡς ἀληθῶς, καὶ ἄκρατον παρίστησιν*, he adds, *ταύτῃ καὶ ὁ τῶν Ἰουδαίων θεσμοθέτης οὐχ ὁ τυχὼν ἀνὴρ, ἐπειδὴ τὴν τοῦ θείου δύναμιν κατὰ τὴν ἀξίαν ἐχώρησε κἀξέφηνεν, εὐθὺς ἐν τῇ εἰσβολῇ γράψας τῶν νόμων εἶπεν ὁ Θεὸς, φησὶ, τί; 'γενέσθω φῶς, καὶ ἐγένετο,' κ. τ. λ.* And it was the same simplicity that won for the Christian Church one whom St. Austin and St. Jerome looked upon as one of the great lights of the West. "Hæc multaque alia cum animo reputans," he says, speaking of the way in which the inconsistencies of pagan systems struck him, "incidi in eos libros quos a Moyse atque a prophetis scriptos esse Hebræorum religio tradebat, in quibus, ipso Creatore Deo testante de Se, hæc ita continebantur, 'Ego sum qui sum.' Et rursum, Hæc dices filiis Israel, 'Misit me ad vos is qui est.' Admiratus sum plane tam absolutam de Deo significationem, quæ naturæ Divinæ incomprehensibilem cognitionem aptissimo ad intelligentiam humanam sermone loqueretur." S. Hilar. de Trin. i. init. A striking contrast this language with the heartless dignity of Longinus' unpractical admiration!

[2] Would not a comparison thoughtfully and diligently executed between Homer and several of the ancienter Hindu books show him to be the great preacher of pantheism in the West? Strabo, at least, lib. i., thought him to have travelled where he might have met with doctrines *derived from* India; and are not his epithets explicable by reference to such a system? I can only offer this suggestion now, which with me is not an off-hand one.

Note (66.) p. 45.

See Windischmann, as above, p. 947.

Note (67.) p. 45.

Ibid. p. 851. "Das Indische Gesetz hat sie denn (die Menschenopfer) für den weitern Verlauf des Zeitalters, in welchem Unglück und Vergänglichkeit herrscht (des Kali-yuga) untersagt, weil Männer und Frauen der Sunde ergeben (und daher kein angenehmes Opfer für Brahma,) sind. Um so mehr haben wir es als einer der vielen Abweichungen vom Gesetze des Manus zu betracht, wenn selbst Brahmanen den blutigen Dienst der Kali angenommen und durch besondre Ritualien ihn geregelt haben."

Note (68.) p. 45.

See the Vishnu Purána, Pref. p. lx. "The course of the elemental creation is in the Vishnu, as in the other Puránas, taken from the Sánkhya philosophy; but the agency that operates upon passive matter is confusedly exhibited, in consequence of a partial adoption of the illusive theory of the Vedánta philosophy, and the prevalence of the Pauránik doctrine of Pantheism. However incompatible with the independent existence of Pradhána or crude matter, and however incongruous with the separate condition of pure spirit or Purusha, it is declared repeatedly that Vishnu, as one with the Supreme Being, is not only spirit, but crude matter; and not only the latter, but all visible substance and time. He is Purusha, 'spirit;' Pradhána, 'crude matter;' Vyacta, 'visible form;' and Kála, 'time.' This cannot but be regarded as a departure from the primitive dogmas of the Hindus, in which the distinctness of the Deity and his works was enunciated, in which, upon his willing the world to be, it was," &c.

Note (69.) p. 45.

See ibid. p. 300, note 2.

Note (70.) p. 45.

Ibid. p. 317, note 8. "The food directed to be given to Brahmans is given in general only to the relatives of the deceased, who are already unclean. In this respect our text and the modern practice seem to differ from the primitive system as described by Manu, iii. 187," where not only is the gift limited to Brahmans, but the particular description of Brahmans is specified. The remark at the end of the sentence is taken from Josephus, c. Apion. ii. 38. Εἰ δὲ φαύλοις οὕτως ἡμᾶς ἐμμένειν ὑπολαμβάνουσι, τί οὐκ ἂν αὐτοὶ δικαίως πάθοιεν, τοὺς κρείττονας οὐ φυλάττοντες; Ἐπεὶ τοίνυν ὁ πολὺς χρόνος πιστεύεται πάντων εἶναι δοκιμαστὴς ἀληθέστατος, τοῦτον ἂν ποιησαίμην ἐγὼ μάρτυρα τῆς ἀρετῆς ἡμῶν τοῦ νομοθετοῦ καὶ τῆς ὑπ᾽ ἐκείνου φήμης περὶ τοῦ Θεοῦ παραδοθείσης. Ἀπείρου γὰρ τοῦ χρόνου γεγονότος, εἴ τις αὐτὸν παραβάλλοι ταῖς τῶν ἄλλων ἡλικίαις νομοθετῶν παρὰ πάντας εὕροι τοῦτον. Compare St. Cyril against Julian, p. 154, D, above p. 63.

Note (71.) p. 46.

This was the case with Marcion, the Manichees, and others, who rejected the Law as contrary to the New Testament, because they would not recognise the principles of typology.

Note (72.) p. 47.

The words alluded to have been given above, in Note 27, p. 96.

Note (73.) p. 47.

Colebrooke, i. p. 225. "Among the Hindus a girl is

married before the age of puberty. . . . Because the bridegroom, too, may be an infant, it is rare that a marriage should be consummated until long after its solemnization. The recital of prayers on this occasion constitutes it a religious ceremony; and it is the first of those that are performed for the purpose of expiating the sinful taint which a child is supposed to contract in the womb of its mother." The author might have recollected Ps. li. 7, "In sin hath my mother conceived me"—a text of considerable consequence against the Pelagians.

Note (74.) p. 47.

Windischmann, p. 1911. "In der Lehre vom Körper haben die Anhänger der Nyaya das Eigenthümliche, dass sie ihn blos aus Erdtheilen, nicht zugleich aus den übrigen Elementen bestehen; diese aber nur als accidental gelten lassen, mit ausdrücklischer Polemik gegen andre Ansichten, nach welchen er aus Erde, Wasser und Feuer, oder aus diesen und dem Wind, oder aus allen fünf Elementen, als eigentlichen Bestandtheilen zusammengesetzt ist."

Note (75.) p. 47.

Vishnu P. p. 169. "On the summit of Mount Meru is the vast city of Brahmá, extending 14,000 leagues, and renowned in heaven; and around it, in the cardinal points and the intermediate quarters, are situated the stately cities of Indra and the other regents of the spheres. The capital of Brahmá is enclosed by the river Ganges, which issuing from the foot of Vishnu, and washing the lunar orb, falls here from the skies; and after encircling the city, divides into four mighty rivers flowing in opposite directions." The notion of the *fourfold* division of the earth, mentioned by Strabo (i. p. 59, ed. Amstel. 1707), as held anciently, and the notion that there were but *four* winds (A. Gell.

ii. 22), are witnesses, in their measure, to the existence of some tradition of the same kind.

Note (76.) p. 47.

The passage alluded to in Note 63 would furnish a source for such a notion, which is thus expressed in the Bhagavat Purána, iii. xii. 5. "To these his sons the Self-existing said, Men do ye create, my sons;" which is expressive of the belief, in spite of the context in which it occurs. The fact that heretics argued as they did from the passage of Genesis seems very instructive: for as there can be no doubt that heretics learnt their creed from heathens, the mode in which the former dealt with the sacred text may show the way in which heathens would have dealt with the creed conveyed in that text to us, but existing in tradition to them. What the servants of Satan did in latter times may perhaps have been so overruled as to disclose to us what they did in earlier times. And as there is every appearance of his carrying on his aggressions upon the truth *on a system*, and as there is a duty lying upon us to be 'not ignorant of his devices,' it is a part of that duty to avail ourselves of the lessons to be drawn from the parallelisms, so to say, traceable in his mode of government in early and later times. That government may have been carried on upon a certain amount of prescience of things to come; or at least (where such prescience was very indistinct) upon the hopes of subverting the Divine system, in case it turned out to be such-and-such. Hence the skirmishes (if one may use the word) between his servants and those of the Truth in earlier times may have their character and bearing explained from the arrayed battle between the heretics and the Church. The history of heresy may reflect a lurid light upon the history of pagan error: the simultaneity of attacks through heresies really of one kind, though outwardly multiform,—and the preparation made for one heresy by another, which was its seeming opposite,—are features of his government strongly brought out in the history of the Church, yet existing as certainly, though less palpably, in his mode of conduct against the Truth in the old dispensations. These remarks, though raised upon a single instance, are yet of so strong a bearing upon much said in this work, that I hope it is unnecessary to apologize for their introduction here. When Shakspeare said that 'the devil can cite Scripture for his purpose,' he uttered a truth which common minds often will not grasp, and therefore use for profaneness. What is contended here is only an extension of his remark to those that are "of their father the devil." And fearful reflections it must suggest to all who are mindful of their own liability to forfeit that image of which the text in question speaks; from which heretics argued for a plurality of Creators,—the orthodox, for the Equality of Persons in the Most Holy Trinity, to whom be all worship and honour, Amen.

The notion of a plant conveying immortality was found not only in India (where it was ascribed to the Soma plant); but also in America, China, Egypt, and elsewhere, similar notions occurred. (See Carli Rubbi, xi. p. 192. Windisch. p. 255. Euseb. P. E. p. 48.) St. Jerom, p. 137, Erasm., on those words of Isaiah, "Bread shall be given unto him; his waters are sure," says, "hæc gentilium fabulæ in ambrosia et nectare intelligunt;" and St. Justin Martyr, p. 296, explains it of the Eucharist, the new Tree of Life.

Note (77.) p. 47.

In St. Cyril against Julian, p. 106, the Apostate says, περιεῖδεν ἐτῶν μυριάδας, εἰ δὲ ὑμεῖς βούλεσθε, χιλιάδας.

Note (78.) p. 48.

The statement made in the text is, it must be remembered, *only one* out of several instances in which the account of Moses comes in as an umpire and explainer of heathen traditions. Hence, if great chronologers of the present day dispute it, their opinion only impairs one amongst several such instances, and so weakens the aggregate of evidence but very slightly. The sort of thing, however, which is referred to in the text, may be understood from the following passage of Jackson's Chronological Antiquities, ii. p. 98.

"The [Egyptian] chronicle contained a term of 36,525 years, which was made out of the famed period of 1461 years, multiplied by a cycle of 25 years, and contained the whole Egyptian chronology, from the beginning of their computation to the end of the reign of the last king of Egypt. The part of it from the gods to the Cynic circle was merely fictitious, to make the Egyptian nation as old as Berosus made the Chaldean, and to commence before the flood, which was absurd in the Egyptians to pretend to; but the rest, from the Cynic circle to the end of the Egyptian empire, is founded upon their ancient records and monuments. It has been before observed that the Egyptians, whose complete year consisted of 365 days and six hours, never intercalated the odd quarter of a day, so that the beginning of the year was removed back a quarter of a day in every year, and was in four years one day less than the Julian year. These quarters, in the space of 1460 years, made 365 days, so that in the space of 1461 years the Egyptian and Julian year coincided and began in the same point of the zodiac; and 1461 Egyptian years were equal to 1460 Julian years. The period of 1460 Egyptian years was called the great year, the canicular and Sothiac year; and also the year of the god Sol, and hence the heliacal year. It was called the canicular year or period because in

Egypt it began with the heliacal rising of the dog-star on the day of the new moon, which was called Thoth, from the Egyptian Hermes or Thoth. . . . . . The grand period of the zodiacal revolution, or 36,525 years, was formed of the two great cycles of the sun and moon multiplied into each other; and this sum was also made to comprehend the whole of Egyptian chronology."

Here we see a process which was regular and systematic in itself, and concealed a real under an enormous fictitious number, which fictitious number might have the appearance, to those not in the secret, of being intended to be one really maintained. There is evidence also to show that the Indian numbers were formed upon some system, though I am not able to say whether the rational number has yet been limited from them. Ideler, in the Preface to his "Mathematische und Technische Chronologie," gave up the discussion of these and the Chinese, whatever he has done since. He notices, however, (ibid. i. p. 214) quoting Euseb. Chron. i. p. 27, that the 432,000 years of the Chaldeans was thought to have contained similarly a shorter number under it. Windischmann (p. 12) observes, that in China the same monstrous periods appeared, which, though originally only symbolical expressions, in time were mistaken for real numbers. This is, however, too wide a subject to discuss at length in a note; and I shall therefore content myself with the general statement of Windischmann upon a subject of which I must confess my inability to give a full and satisfactory account. His opinion is thus stated, p. 12. "Thus much is deducible at once from the closest investigation of the Chinese numerical system, and the chronology of this kingdom, that the Mosaic account, even in the most trifling point, is just as little injured thereby as by the Indian, Babylonian, or Egyptian, which, in their astronomical signification and value, are throughout perfectly accurate calculations." And to this I may add, to prevent persons arguing at once in favour of the Septuagint calculation, from its apparently closer conformity to the numbers deducible from heathen calculations, the following passage from Schubert's Gesch. der Natur, vol. i. p. 176. "Eine der am nächsten liegenden Ausgleichungs-perioden ist das vom Alterthume oft erwähnte zehn-monatliche Jahr (Censor. de Die Nat. viii. xxi. &c. &c.) welches zugleich als eine für die Entwickelungsgeschichte des Menschenleibes, da er die Zeit der Schwangerschaft, die Zeit der Ausgestaltung des im Leibe der Mutter, umfasset, die des zehn-monatlichen Jahr bestund nämlich nicht aus zehn synodischen, sondern aus zehn siderischen oder Knoten-monaten. Hiermit wurde es eben zu einer Ausgleichung des Sonnenlaufes mit dem Mondenlaufe. Denn am 274sten Tage endigt der zehnte siderische, und zugleich auch der 9te Sonnenmonat, öder das 9te Zwölftheil der Sonnenjahres. Es scheint daher dieser dem Menschen so nahe liegende Ausgleichungsperiode im frühesten Alterthüme öfters zum Behuf einer *künstlicher Zeitrechnung* gebraucht worden zu seyn, deren Spuren wir in Septuaginta und in anderen chronologischen Systemen finden (m. v. meinen Lehrbuch der Sternkund. zweite Auf. in dem Abschnitt, die Zeitrechnung der Völker)."

Note (79.) p. 49.

Manu, viii. 25, 26. "By external signs let him (the judge) discern the inner being of men, by voice, colour, gesture, attitude, eyes, and action. From the attitudes, gestures, motion of the body, and the speech, and the changes of the eye and the face, is discovered the inner mind." See Cicero pro Rosc. Amer. cap. 23.

Note (80.) p. 49.

Manu, viii. 17. "Verily justice is the only friend who, even in death, follows one: all others perish along with the body." The other passage just alluded to is from v. 15.

Note (81.) p. 49.

Windisch., p. 1909, gives these instances from Gotama.

Note (82.) p. 50.

See the instances referred to in p. 98. I may add here, that the same view of ancient tradition as that there given, is taken also by H. J. Schmitt, "Uroffenbarung," Pref. pp. iv. v., a work I had not then seen, but the design of which, judging from the Preface, is one which it were to be desired he might carry out. The published portion of it is confined to the Chinese.

END OF NOTES TO DIALOGUE I.

DIALOGUE II.

ON THE SOUL'S MANIFOLD RELATIONS TO MATTER.

ܥܝܢܐ ܘܪܥܝܢܬܐ ܡܠܦܢ ܚܕܐ ܠܚܕܐ:

S. Ephrem. adv. Scrut. xlv.

'The eye and mind each
One another teach.'

DIALOGUE THE SECOND.

Laur. You have seen, Rádhákánt, how it may be that in your ancient books there is kept up a part of an ancient tradition, which contains the true doctrine, more or less disfigured: and one reason why so much of it has kept up in India, doubtless was the austere habits of your ancient seers. For by abstinence from the good things of this life, the soul is purged to see the good things of another life. Calmness of the mind, with fitness for receiving the good things of another life, cometh out of the devotion of the Sannyasi, who leaves father and mother, and houses and lands, and all that is dear to him, for the mere hope of seeing what he believes to be truth. But to Christians who so act, our Master promises an hundredfold in this life, that is, through joyous calmness of mind, and in the world to come life everlasting. I have said that your ancient sages, through Tapas, attained to the sight of much holy truth, being fitted for the transmission of it from the discipline they observed, and able to see and understand it, because they were not a dissolute set like the Greeks, whose very priest class were frequently licentious, and did not seek chastity and holiness by stern discipline, but by sundry devices which it were shameful even to speak of (1). Hence one of them, who was a very shrewd and sagacious person, thought that your philosophy and that of the Jews was all one; and another, who belonged to the same school (2), said that all the wisdom of the wise in deep things was derived either from the Jews (3) or the Indian Brahmans, for he mentions them by name. Plain, then, it is, that even in the West you were looked upon as inheritors of great wisdom; and doubtless, if there were a common source of all wisdom through tradition, then you and the Jews may well have had much in common.

RAD. But will you again go over your doctrine about this common source of knowledge, whence, even before the art of writing was known, men of old drew all wisdom, in order that I may see better if I understand what you mean?

LAUR. I have been thinking, since our last conversation, of a fable to illustrate the subject of it, which I will now proceed to tell you. There was once a time when all the rivers in the world met under the earth, to hold a conversation upon certain phenomena which they had observed, and had now and then talked one by one with their sisters[1] about, but could not quite understand without a general council. They had observed that there grew upon the banks of each river certain crystals of anomalous

[1] Rivers are feminine in Sanscrit.

shapes, which their own waters could not melt at all. There were many which they did dissolve with ease, many which after a long time they succeeded in drinking into their own essence, but some still remained which they could not solve at all. Whereupon one or two of the great rivers of Europe came to a certain very large river, whose mouth and face were always looking towards Asia; and brought her some of these crystals; and she found that she could dissolve several of them with great ease, but that some still remained which defied her powers of solution, would not be absorbed into her essence, but clung sulkily to the banks whenever they could, and resisted all the coy embraces and wheedlings of her sportful wave. This odd circumstance led the European rivers to consider further whether anything else occurred along their banks which would throw any light upon the subject, as they were unwilling to trouble their Asiatic sisters to come to a general meeting, and many of them lived so far off that they would have a long way to come, and were also not very likely to bring the refractory crystals into that dissolved state in which their character could be examined. The European rivers, therefore, considered whether the trees which grew on their banks had any part in the crystals' conspiracy to resist their combined powers. Upon comparing notes, they found that though the trees upon their banks were a good deal alike, yet there was some dissimilarity too, which possibly might affect the soil upon which these crystals grew, and in some cases was found especially to have done so. They then began to think that if they could classify these varieties of trees, and reduce the different species each to his proper genus, they would perhaps be able to analyze the whole difficulty, and find out what prevented their dissolving these refractory crystals. This process was next entered upon, and it was found that, sure enough, it answered in a great many cases. When the influence of one genus of trees upon the soil was examined, it explained how such and such crystals were formed, and in consequence suggested a mode for solving them. But this did not satisfy them; there evidently was still a cloud hanging over the whole subject, and they therefore agreed that a general council of all the rivers in the world was the only thing which would perfectly clear up the difficulties as to the crystals and as to the trees. As, however, this would have been an awkward thing to manage, they appointed deputies; and though I cannot remember the names of them all, I will mention a few of the most prominent. There was the Thames for England, the Rhone for France and the rest, the Danube for a very large tract of country, the Tiber—who had turned his back upon Asia so long that he was afraid to come almost, besides several Russian rivers of high rank and importance. In Asia the Oxus, the Ganges, the Euphrates, the Indus, and several others, which will readily suggest themselves to your memory. After several attempts made by the Euphrates, she found that she could not effect any thing like a perfect solution of the crystals; here and there they yielded to her solicitations, but for the most part they could not be made to do more than show some faint lines which pointed out in which direction they would break; and in a still greater number of instances not even this was effected. Passing over other attempts, I shall not surprise you when I tell you that the Ganga explained how all of them might be solved, and how the trees on the shores had influenced the growth of these crystals, which none of the rivers of the West could at all explain.

RAD. The fable is one which has pleased me; but now relate to me what the fable means, what the rivers are, what the trees, and what the crystals.

LAUR. Thus let it be heard! The waters (4) of the rivers are the nations of the earth, and the crystals are their languages, which, when one nation cannot furnish roots to explain, then recourse must be had to another; and when the smaller waters and those which are less ancient will not explain the difficulties of a language, then recourse must be had to another. The ancient language of the Goths will explain the difficulties of many languages of Europe, by furnishing older words and forms of nouns, which have dropped into disuse in other nations. This, then, Rádhákánt, is the meaning of the solving of the crystals. But the difficulties of the language of one people cannot always be explained by the language of another: we must also consider how the trees which grow on the banks may affect the soil. And these are the customs of different nations, their laws, usages, and religions. These, then, will explain much more; and sometimes those of the most ancient nation will explain things in the languages of the less ancient. The Danube may represent the Gothic language, the Thames the Anglo-Saxon, the Rhone the Celtic, and the Tiber the Roman; which mightily influenced (5) all the languages of Europe. But by the Danube, or so as to have connexion with it, dwelt a people called the Hyperboreans (6), and they were, according to a most learned geographer, a priest-class who brought their learning from India. Along with these may be reckoned the Sacæ, who also came and spread Indian learning through the world, pure or impure, corrupted or not. So wide did the name of these spread, that the Egyptians style a wise scribe Sach (7), and in Latin the word *sacer* is used for *holy*. But though the examination and comparison of these languages did much towards attaining some clearer notions of their structure and formation, and setting the study of language upon a surer footing; still, until they went to Ganga, which the Vayu-Purana well calls the assemblage (8) of all holy waters (for the name well suits with our Myth), nothing comparatively was done towards clearing up the difficulties, both as to the formations of words and to the customs to which allusions were contained in divers languages. Like a mighty solvent, the Sanscrit language, although unknown for so many (9) centuries in the West, and itself in fact ceasing to be spoken commonly when Greek was first in full vigour (10), made the crystals melt before it; like the universal solvent of the alchemist, the institutes of Pán'ini made the sturdiest of them crumble before them. The customs of the ancient Indians served to explain sundry things hitherto unexplained; and the people of the West saw how vain it was to go to the waters of Babylon (11) to have the difficulties of European languages clearly solved. The Myth, O Rádhákánt! and the explanation thereof, is ended, is ended.

RAD. But what has this to do with the subject of which we were talking—the propagation of sacred knowledge in the world?

LAUR. Thus let it be heard. There is an explanation of the explanation. The Ganga is said to be the river which cleanses (12) away all sin; and so also do sacred words (13) cleanse away sin. Ganga is said to have sprung from (14) Siva's foot, or finger, according to different accounts. Let it be the finger then, for the sake of the explanation; and let it be remembered, that language was the vehicle of tradition, and, according to Gotama (15), came from the gods, and was an inspiration. If, then, the true and ancient doctrine was pointed out to man (16) first by the finger of GOD, it may be not amiss to make the Ganga here the representative of that pure and ancient doctrine which, by its fulness, explains the difficulties and perplexities of all nations, and wherein they but lisped imperfectly, and had dark, or exaggerated, or disfigured, accounts of the truth, it was able to speak plainly. For what fruit (17) of its long travails did philosophy show forth? what worth so many and so great labours? Were they not all pregnant with nought but wind, and unable to bring to the birth what they had conceived? They had but abortions till they came to the light of the knowledge of GOD. The ancient tradition in the books of Moses was able to clear up sundry things which were like the truth; and by so clearing them up, to show wherein also they were but false shows and unreal resemblances of the truth which the other nations of the world possessed: for the object of this ancient tradition was to lead men to GOD. And in vain do men think to worship GOD, save when they worship Him as He has revealed Himself. And like as the Sanscrit language made it possible to trace and clear up many things in the languages of Europe which will probably facilitate the communion between the nations, lead towards peaceful intercourse, and so eventually be a great blessing to those nations, although it was so long unknown, having first ceased to be a spoken language about 400 years before Christ, and then being, for almost 1000 years more, scarcely heard of in Europe; so will the true revelation, though long unknown to the other nations, at last work out great and inestimable blessings, inestimable blessings.

RAD. You have explained to me how there came to be similarities between Moses' law and that of other nations, upon the supposition of an ancient tradition kept up with greater or less purity by different nations; but you have not explained how it came that there were these similarities, seemingly of a different kind, of which you now speak.

LAUR. I taught you, if you recollect, how that it was not the whole of that revelation which was conveyed to men by tradition, but only certain seeds and beginnings of it, which, for all we know, are absolutely necessary in order to the attaining of true and Divine knowledge. Instances may exist of nations who, without alphabets or letters, have kept up by memory (18) a larger share of truth than even others with better means: but no proof, as far as I know, exists of these elementary principles ever having been reasoned out, whatever reason may have done to confirm them when known. If, then, they came to men through the sense of hearing, which is the means, according to our books, divinely employed for communicating the substance of things unseen, they may, through want of listening, gradually have been lost. But the sins of men make them by degrees indisposed to listen to religious truth, and so they drop parts which, being omitted, distort the whole. This, then, would be one account of the distortions of the truth which we find among other nations. As, then, according to our books, death first entered in by the ear (19) of our first parents, so by the ear it kept entering in, and by the ear, too truth must enter in, and life.

But there was also another source from which these semblances of the truth arose. For the same evil spirit who at the first deceived Eve, the mother of all living, did also contrive perverse resemblances of the truth to deceive them further. When once the nations were split into different languages for a great sin, the report of which has of old been kept up in China (20), then they could no longer so easily have recourse to Shem's race, the preachers of the true doctrine; and so Satan availed himself of this confusion entailed by sin, to lead men further and further from the truth: for this confusion befel men while they were attempting to build a tower to defy heaven; and it seems likely that they then changed the tongue they all had in common for several new ones: for unless their former language had perished, their work would not have been brought to a stop. It was, then, by the loss of that language that was lost by all other races, and was left with one only, that the building was stopped; and because by the new tongues they were estranged from each other, neither could they hear each other, they had wars among themselves, and occasions of separations, which the tongues occasioned among them (21). Hence they were not only unable, but also unwilling, to receive truths at the hand of each other, and were more easily a prey to error, and less able to return from it when they had fallen into it. Hence evil spirits seeing that other nations had no access to the Hebrew, in which, by the race of Shem, the truth was kept up, put into men's hearts sundry semblances which, from their likeness to it (22), might weaken the credit of the truth, or rather gain it over to their own side: and as they knew which was the truth, and had much to fear from its success, they seem to have been especially careful to put into men's minds sundry doctrines of incarnations (23) throughout the world: and hence, though the Vedas say nothing, I believe, of incarnations, ten are mentioned amongst you. Of these, that of Chrishna has in it certain points calculated to deceive. He is mentioned to have been brought up among the kine, and to have given in his youth early proofs of his supernatural strength: things these which bear a rude likeness to the accounts of Him who was really incarnate. Other things might also be mentioned; but I am afraid of comparing things sacred to me, even in this way, with things which to me, of course, when so compared, cannot be else than profane. If, however, this suggests the kind of thing to you, we should then have considered another of the ways in which tradition, which came by hearing, was interfered with. And in such a case it is plain that we ought to consider not only what information for the truth has been brought to men by means above the senses, but also what has been brought to men against it by the like means.

However, having, I trust, now made this pretty

clear, I may go on to insist upon the importance of the senses. I hope that you will no longer fancy that I deny the absolute need of supernatural assistance in order to arrive at knowledge concerning the invisible world, seeing that I assume (what all nations have believed more or less) that there are evil spirits (24) who work upon our minds, and present to them distorted views of moral and religious truths, as well as a good spirit, who presents them with right views. And as Kanáda (25), as well as Gotama (26), allows that we must fall back upon something more than the senses ultimately for rules of Dharma, we may consider that as a settled point, and proceed further to consider the use made by the Lord of the creation of the senses, in bringing His creatures to divine knowledge. Only I again and again assert the absolute need of the divine Prasáda along with them. First, then, I shall proceed to show how there is this mutual co-operation of the two in common things. Now, we find that our memory is capable of containing in it a vast number of cognitions. No one can enter into it and feel out where they are. They (27) take up no room in it, though they abide in it without wearying out the vigour or elasticity of it; and though man is but a single being, and of a single nature, so far as his soul is concerned, still the memory is at times as good as ignorant of things which yet afterwards prove to be retained in it, though we cannot be properly said to know them at those times. For there are particular occasions on which we are unable to call a thing to mind without some external aid from the senses. The slightest outward and visible thing is sometimes, for all we see, absolutely necessary as a condition upon which alone the inward and invisible faculty of the memory (28) will perform its functions at all. Again, there are many discoveries important in order to man's welfare, which, for all we know, the mind could never have struck out without the aid of some silly thing which occurred to the senses at the time. Analogy, then, would lead us to think that we might be greatly beholden to the senses in order to our arriving at supernatural truth, seeing that the method by which the Lord leads us to natural truth involves the use of these external things, in spite of the co-existence of the greatest internal gifts.

2. The body, also, must be in a certain degree of health in order to the full vigour of the mind; and I say *a certain degree* (29), because I think the full vigour of both at the same time perfectly incompatible: still, this shows further how we depend upon our bodies.

3. These things, taken along with the following considerations, may perhaps prove important. The whole way of thinking and acting in the concerns of our present life is as if our bodies and the things about us were real; therefore, for all practical purposes they may be considered as real. It seems, then, to me vain to imagine a philosophy so impractical as the Vedánta sometimes is, which contradicts the

whole system under which it has pleased Providence to put us. For we find that even for the most sacred science we are made to depend upon our senses, which seems very much as if the senses were intended to be looked upon as having a reality about them, and as if the objects of them were real; so far, at least, as we are concerned with them. We are placed in a system in which mankind will deal with us, and we must, in spite of all theories to the contrary, deal with mankind, as if the objects of sense were real. Hence it does, I own, seem to me an unpractical philosophy, which leads men to treat these things as if they were unreal.

4. And a further confirmation of the idea, that we were intended by Providence to treat matter as if it were real, is, that He has not placed within the reach of our knowledge, so far as I know, any one single instance where it can even be surmised that matter of any kind whatsoever (30) is annihilated: while, on the contrary, the fact that matter is susceptible of such prodigious changes in the mode of its existence, as we see it is in several cases, e. g. in the case of ice, which is convertible into steam; of several gases, which, by being generated under sufficient pressure, may be made fluids, while the essence of the gases in this case, and of the water in that, remains unimpaired:—this fact, I say, is a direct presumption that matter is susceptible of yet further and more wonderful changes without its undergoing

annihilation. And therefore, if a revelation treats of the senses or the body in general as a necessary condition, or as a vehicle of the means of salvation in all ordinary cases, our experience in fact offers absolutely nothing at variance with this teaching, whatever our theories may do. And as experience is our guide, and not theory, in practical matters; as, further, men often entail upon themselves, and even upon others, very great misery indeed, even in this life, by obstinately following their own theories of things in opposition to the teaching of men of experience; it becomes a very serious question for you whether you ought not to be able to prove the Vedánta system far more demonstratively, before you let it have the least influence upon your practice. And the choice between Christianity and Brahmanism is a practical question, and one which you will find, the more you know of Christianity, to be materially affected by the view you take of our relations to matter. And let me add, by way of caution, that I am not at all stating that matter is indestructible, or that it will or will not be in fact destroyed; but what I now urge is, that if particular things in a revelation seem in our present state of insight into that revelation to be built upon the supposition of matter lasting for ever, we cannot (if we go by what we actually experience of God's government of the world, and not by our theories of what it may be) make such particular things any objection whatever to that revelation. Still less can we make it any objection to the revelation, if we find it insists on the necessity of matter or of the senses, during that present dispensation under which we are living in a state of trial.

RAD. There are in all this several things which make me distracted with new and divers thoughts. But one thing I wish much to ask, viz. why it is that, if you insist so much on the senses, you object so much, as Christians do, to worshipping idols. It seems to me, that if the senses are so important in order to keeping up religion in the world, here is just a case in which full use is made of them. May I, then, ask how it is that you seem to hold here such contrary opinions?

LAUR. If, Rádhákánt, you can prove that these idols were set up at the command of revelation, then I shall be bound to answer that question; but if they are only the produce of your own imaginations, then I am in no way bound to answer it. For it is right to show that what we experience under GOD's natural government does not contradict, but fall in with, what we are told of His revealed government. But it is to no purpose to show that under His natural government there are things which fall in with inventions of man's own, in order to serve (31) Him or other beings. When He discloses to us a part of His invisible government, then it is dutiful to trace out similarities in that part of it which comes under our experience; but it is not right for man to decide for himself, and by his own invention, what the invisible system of things is, and then to make out that it squares with the visible, since this would be to make ourselves gods, and assume that we knew what His unseen government was. The Vedas, I believe, make no mention of the worship of idols, so that your oldest revelations would be here agreed with ours (32) in rejecting them.

RAD. You before let me see that you were determinately opposed to Polytheism; but I should much wish to know what other objections you have to it, save the one you have now intimated, that you think it is not revealed to man. I do not at all wish to justify a belief in (33) more than one Supreme Being, although our practice is to worship other beings also; and it still seems to me that what you have said of the importance of the senses, goes towards justifying this practice.

LAUR. I think there are most numerous objections, though perhaps the chief one in my mind is, that it appears that there were no images in any country till religion came to be corrupted: the tendency of men is certainly to degenerate (34), and along with that degeneration the adoption of images (35) has been prevalent, which does seem to me a most cogent presumption against the use of them. All men look back to earlier ages as more pure than their own, and our Master spoke (conformably to what your books say of the Kaliyuga) (36) as though when He came to judge mankind there would hardly be any faith left on earth. At sundry times, when by His judgments upon the earth He has made men's consciences tremble with the expectation of some more final judgment to come, He has punished nations most severely for worshipping them, and by such severe punishment alone has He cured the Jewish people of this practice. But our books especially represent the worship of idols as having a connexion with the unseen world, and putting men into a fellowship with devils (37), which of course may in fact be the essence of idolatry, if, according to your own views of it, it does not lie so much in worshipping the visible image, as in reverencing the unseen beings they represent. If, then, these unseen beings are the creations, or what seem to be the creations, of your own fancy, though they are really inspired by these wicked beings, how dreadful will it be to risk even the danger of supposing them gods, which are men departed at best, or perhaps evil spirits, who are glad enough that you should fall down and worship them, and believe that they can give rain and increase, though really they have no such power. I know, indeed, that when people have long worshipped idols there is in them some wonderfully infatuating power (38) which binds the soul down to them, and which only the more convinces me that they are, as our books represent them, connected with evil spirits. Here, then, is what should seem to be an instance of man selecting for himself a relation to matter, into which God has not put him—for it seems to me impossible to get over the fact, that so many nations plead guilty to having invented idols, when the simple worship of their fathers died away along with their simpler manners. To say that what suits one age may not be fit for another, is only smothering the truth that a corrupt Kali age does not worship as spiritually as a simple Sạtya one. This, then, Rádhákánt, seems to me a thing in which your ancestors were nearer the truth than you now are by many degrees. They may, indeed, have paved the way for your present system, as I before hinted. And indeed I think that this is in itself a proof of there being a great evil spirit, the ruler and manager of a counter system to the truth, who at different ages of the world seems to have contrived to carry out his system by false oracles, gradual encroachments on the truth, lying wonders, and other stratagems. Neither do I know that it would be wrong to think that where he found he could get no hold of some virtuous heathen, he may have left him unmolested with the purpose of letting him serve the better to deceive others, who should mistake such a man for the true Messiah, the great pattern of all holiness. Hence those who have yielded themselves to him as his servants, have in very many instances put on an air of sanctity, and made conscience and religion a plea for wicked deeds. And the reverence which men came to pay to ancestors departed, or to other beings besides the Supreme God, looks like an act of a dutiful and religious kind at first, and may, I freely allow, be plausibly defended as not interfering with the reverence due to Him only; but the history of the world, which is the record of experience, tells sadly to the contrary, and is the best answer to all theories and excuses of the practice. No where amongst the nations did idolatry come in till men had lost the austere simplicity of early piety; and never, as far as I know, has it thriven without doing mischief to the idolater's mind.

RAD. Then you mean me to conclude, from all you have said, that though we are put into sundry relations to matter affecting our religious interests, this is not one which can be proved from reason or antiquity. And if this is your way of arguing, and you set reason aside where antiquity is clear, how comes it that the particular relations to matter, into which Moses' law put you and Manu's law us, are now quite discarded by Christians, who eat flesh like Pisáchas, and have no idea that pollution of any kind comes from matter?

LAUR. That question, Rádhákánt, is, I suppose, tantamount to asking how it is that the Mosaic law is in one sense no longer binding upon Christians: at least I take it that you feel that I ought in fairness to account for this, as I have allowed that your own law agreed with the law of Moses in several of the points in which Christians now discard it. Or at all events I must own that *I* see this, that your question ought to be fairly met and answered, and that I cannot give it an immediate answer, but must, upon attempting to answer it, be directly driven upon the wider question, "Why Moses' law is no longer binding?" When this difficulty is solved, the particular difficulty about pollutions from matter will be solved also. Let us, then, bear in mind what has made us digress from the subject of our relations to matter, in order that when the question of the abrogation of Moses' law has been discussed, we may return to what we were before conversing upon.

RAD. I long to hear how you will answer this, but will not forget what we digressed from.

LAUR. All society is bound together, is it not, by law?

RAD. Assuredly so.

LAUR. And if we look to the common little civilities and courtesies of life, we shall find them in effect to be laws resulting from the law of nature which makes men social creatures; is it not so?

RAD. Certainly it is.

LAUR. But the modes of expressing civility are merely conventional signs; nobody thinks himself obliged, now-a-days, to salute people of station precisely as Ashtavakra did Rama and Sita in the Uttara Rama-Cherita (39), or to invite suitors to the Swayamvaram precisely as Bhima did the Heroes in the Nalopakhyana (40). In fact these are (are they not?) things which may alter without impairing the duty of civility, of which they are the vehicles.

RAD. This, too, is clear.

LAUR. Laws, then, are of two kinds; positive, which are mutable at the will of the authority who institutes; and moral, which are not mutable at the will of the authority who institutes them; because (whether or no, as matter of fact, such laws flow from the will of the authority) by a moral law, we mean one in which that will exerts itself uniformly; and therefore, without entering into the further question, whether moral law is in any way dependent upon arbitrary will (41), we may have a notion of it sufficiently clear for the present purpose if we suppose that that Will which originally constituted it, is one from which there is no appeal whatever, and which does not alter or change. Thus we can conceive of the duty of civility, abstractedly from and wholly independent of any particular forms in which it is expressed, and as a duty of permanent obligation. This, then, is, I trust, clear.

RAD. It is so.

LAUR. The code of Moses, then, is made up of these two kinds of law, positive and moral; and though, indeed, so far as mortals are concerned, all laws seem (42) to fluctuate, moral as well as positive; as, for instance, the laws relating to so solemn a thing as marriage (43), still there is such a thing as a notion of right and wrong, which cannot be effaced from men's minds,—which is the common property of all men in all ages and countries,—through which alone we are able to enter in some degree into the feelings of all human beings whatever. Now this notion of right and wrong is such, that obedience and disobedience to it are connected with hope and fear of something (44) further, which hope and fear make up, in fact, a part of the system of retribution in this present life, and last on up to the hour of death in such a way as to make it appear, in several instances, that they are likely to last beyond the grave. Hence, going by what we see, and acting up to what, upon this knowledge, is the safe course, we may conclude that the things condemned or approved by this internal monitor will be condemned or approved in a future state also, or in other words that the obligation to obey is a permanent one, to last through the whole of our duration, as far as we can learn. Thus if any one were to say that the misery of an idolater on his death-bed is an argument against idolatry, it is equivalent to saying that there is a permanent law of GOD against our being idolaters; and supposing we saw this misery continually happening, we should conclude that men on their death-bed, foreseeing (45) the punishment to follow, did, with the unerring instinct of impiety, fixing upon that which it hated and dreaded, single out the truth. Such laws, then, would be permanent laws of nature, not positive or mutable ones. And any code coming from the Author of nature must of necessity not gainsay them. And see how the law of Moses would confirm what anciently most nations seem to have felt, in that it is so severe as it is against all worship of the likeness of anything in heaven or in earth. However this may be, certain it is that Moses' law does embody all the moral (46) code of other nations, so far as nations in general are agreed. And the way in which it begins with the worship of one God and forbidding of the worship of any others, is perhaps unparalleled by the laws of any other nation. And this being so, its very majesty and moral fitness become a reason for taking the positive laws upon trust, as having something further in them which may be of importance to all ages.

RAD. However, that the Vedas teach all moral law perfectly is my belief, and therefore why is it that we have not the same right to alter and depart from their positive (47) institutions in the course of time as you have to depart from those of Moses? If the law of Moses and the Vedas both teach the same fundamental moral truths, I must have some further reason for thinking the mutable and positive parts of the law of Moses, in all their particulars, much better than those parts in ours, before I can give the one up for the other.

LAUR. The law of Moses, in all its positive parts, prophesied until John, the forerunner of Christ; and by looking to the analogy of discoveries in the arts and sciences, we have certainly abundant reason for thinking that the whole bearing of a revelation of this kind would not be apparent at once (48). Let us, then, proceed to consider what evidence there is that the positive enactments of Moses contain in them some further and more durable meaning than appears on the surface. If we examine the last of all the prophets, he does not draw the attention of the Jews to the later of the prophetical books, as the best preparation for the Messiah's coming, but to the law of Moses. And when the Messiah came, He also told the Jews that if they believed not Moses, neither would they believe Him. Here, then, is something remarkable, and requiring to be accounted for, since it would seem from this and other parts of the New Testament, that each and every portion of the Law was replete with instruction for Christians. Add to which, the law itself intimates,—what Samuel and all the prophets, as many as followed after, seem to have preached,—that it was not sacrifice and burnt offering as such, but obedience which GOD looked favourably towards. Thus one of the prophets said, "I spake not to your fathers in the day that I brought them out of the land of Egypt (49), concerning burnt offerings and sacrifice; but this word did I speak unto them, saying, 'Hear ye my voice, and I will be unto you a GOD, and ye shall be unto Me a people.'" This, then, puts it beyond all doubt that, from the first, preference was given to the moral law—to obedience, not to sacrifice. And if this is so,—if the positive part of the law yielded to the moral,—the same reasons for which the obviously positive part yielded to moral ends also operated in some cases to make the less obviously positive yield. For it is plain that all moral law may also have a positive character. Thus, in relation to the ordinary course of things, the commandment not to kill is a moral law: but in relation to a supernatural course of things it is not so. For as it is in GOD's power at any time to take away life, He may at any time disclose to any particular person that He wills the life of such and such another person to be brought to a close; and in reference to this course of things the obligation to abstain from killing is only a positive law. Life, and houses, and lands, and wives (50) and children, are all conferred upon men by GOD, and He can revoke the grant of them when He chooses. Such a system of government as continually offered instances of such interference would indeed not be the natural and present course of things; yet it is plainly supposable, without involving any violation of the moral sense in order to its being carried on. But if the disclosure of His will may alter in particular cases what in ordinary cases is a moral law, much more may the merely positive ones be altered at His command. Supposing, then, it is His will in some particular case to foreshadow somewhat to come, we can easily see how, in order to foreshadow such a thing, laws which, in either of the above specified senses, are positive, should be suspended. Hence we find that when it was His will that a future event should be foreshadowed, this actually was the case. Whenever, in fact, we see such violations, we may presume they were designed (51) to make thoughtful and attentive Jews see that something further was foreshadowed, and so learn that the ritual, so far as it was positive, was not to last. Thus the commandment not to make any image was violated by Moses in the letter, or positive sense of it, when he set up the brazen serpent in the wilderness. The command to hallow the seventh day was violated by Joshua (52) when he went, seven days running, round Jericho, not to mention a great many other violations of the law, in so far as it was positive, when something future was being foreshadowed. But while this was the case, the Israelites were not left at all in doubt that these ordinances were but for a time; though the carnally-minded among them might have looked for temporal blessings from obedience, as carnally-minded persons always do. But so far was this from being the thing intended, that that very king among them who carried their temporal prosperity to its greatest height, (though their empire was but a narrow one at the best, compared with other empires, which shows that the end of Moses' law was not temporal promises,) that very king, I say, speaks most distinctly upon the point; "There is one event," he says, "to the righteous and to the wicked; to the good and to the clean, and to the unclean; to him that sacrificeth, and to him that sacrificeth not: as is the good, so is the sinner; and he that sweareth is as he that feareth an oath. This is an evil in all that is done under the sun; also the heart of the sons of men is full of evil, and madness is in their heart while they live, and after that they go to the dead." Moreover the prophets, not once only or twice, but in a very repeated and marked way, speak to the same effect. Thus (53) Ezekiel calls them "statutes that are not good;" Jeremiah says that God spake not to them concerning sacrifice and offering; Isaiah that their new moons and sabbaths were an abomination; David that God delighted not in burnt offerings; Samuel that he had not as great delight in them as in obeying His voice: so that you see all the prophets warn them of the transitory nature of these statutes, while they also tell them that to obey the law is their great duty and privilege. If, then, these rules were oracles of God, foreshadowing some great thing to come, it would be easy to reconcile what these passages teach with the fact that the having the law is viewed as a privilege. For it were reasonable to say that you have not only a law which republishes and sanctions the law of nature, which alone if you had, it might with truth be said that "He hath not dealt so with any nation, neither have the heathen knowledge of His laws:" but you have also a ritual which does not end in itself, but which is a continual prophecy, and therefore keeps you continually looking forward to some fresh mercy of God to come, some new dispensation, which will alter the heavens and the earth and all that is in them, as far, at least, as they bear on you. Accordingly all things under the law are to be looked on as shadows of good things to come, when the eternal God should make some fresh disclosure (54) of His nature, and old things should pass away and all be made new. When, then, all was made new, all that was under Moses' law ceased not to be the voice of God, but on the contrary became more precious to those who learned the new dispensation, in that it enjoined to them not burdensome ceremonies, the meaning of which they did but darkly apprehend, and were not able to fulfil, but spoke to them new and joyous commands, while they felt within that strength was supplied them to fulfil these very old commandments in their new and spiritual sense. They were unto them as the words of a preceptor to a child, when he has come to man's estate, and sees the drift and meaning and use of what he could not understand, and from not understanding fancied he should never be able to practise. The law then, Rádhákánt, was, you see, a schoolmaster to the Jews, to bring them to something to come.

Rad. Are you now, then, in a condition to answer my question, as to why the distinction between clean and unclean flesh is done away? It seems, from what you have told me, that this must have been meant also to foreshadow something to come, although I cannot help thinking that, from the fact of Moses' law agreeing with ours herein, there is a strong presumption in favour of there being something real in the pollutions from these animals.

Laur. Let us then try, Rádhákánt, to see how far this may be the case. There seems, then, once to have been a time when the orders of the creation were not at such a distance from each other as they now are. Brute beasts used formerly to speak to men without surprising or frightening them by so doing. And holy saints and ascetics (55) were hospitably received unawares, and angels became the guests of men. And the sons (56) of God went unto the daughters of men and had giants by them, and great confusion at last ensued, and the flood came over the world: and though this interçourse was now and then kept up still, yet by degrees it died away. The older the nations are upon earth, the more traces we find of it amongst them. Hence the Ahins'a among you may be a trace of this primeval state of things; and I would not at once say that there might not be something real, as you suggest, in this distinction of animals into clean and unclean, although we know very little of the case. However, bearing in mind what I told you of the partaking with devils through things offered to idols, and of the way in which they set up false oracles to look like the true, we shall see that if they availed themselves of these animals for false oracles and divinations, so that these animals came to be sacred to them, there was a reason why these same creatures should be accounted unclean by Moses' law, seeing they were connected with (57) unclean spirits. Thus that law served for a reproof to the Egyptians, when it afterwards came to be known to them through the medium of the Greek version. But though these might in themselves, for all we know, be sufficient reasons for the distinction, yet we must look upon it also as foreshadowing something further to come, in which light it yields a proof that the law is divine, seeing it is permanent. For as those who are eminent for virtue (58) upon earth are inclinable to build up, not such buildings as make a great display for a time, but such as last long and benefit many ages; so God, from whom also they gain this slight resemblance of His excellent goodness, is wont to give revelations of an enduring and imperishable nature, and thus in this new and typical relation the law of Moses (59) may endure for ever in heaven. Considering it, then, in this light, and remembering further, as I do, how all nations are wont by a sort of natural fitness in the animals themselves to select those pre-eminent in their country as the types of men of certain moral characters (60), as you in India do the tiger, our forefathers did the wolf, the Persians the lion, for types of men of strength and courage, and other animals for other (61) virtues; considering, too, how in Scripture subsequent to Moses, the lamb is made a type of Christ, the ox of the clergy, the ass of the laity, and other animals of other things, there being types of this kind for all characters but idolaters, to show, it may be, how idolatry, as involving (62) all sin, excludes from the ark; and also considering how, in our prophecies, the different nations are sometimes represented by different living creatures; and considering how our ignorance (63), in many points, prevents our seeing the meaning of some of these;—considering all these things, I think you ought not to be surprised at being told that these animals were meant to foreshow the distinction between clean and unclean men, and that after a time God intended to remove this distinction; and to show those to whom He committed His new and final dispensation that they were not to call any man common or unclean any more. Thus you see, Rádhákánt, that this distinction in Moses may have meant something further; and we Christians think, and have thought in all ages, that they did mean something further, which is profitable to us upon whom the last dispensation is come. I have therefore, I trust, proved to you two very important things; one is, that the law of Moses, in the positive parts of it, has a meaning still, in which meaning it is still binding upon Christians. Whether or no careless or ignorant or misinstructed Christians neglected it, that is nothing to the purpose; for if they hold all Scripture to be the work of God, then they must hold it to be done for ever, that men may fear Him[2], or else be inconsistent. Observe, then, how this is a proof of its divinity, in that it is so wonderfully permanent. And the other thing is, that there is a very good reason why those relations to matter in which the law of Moses placed men should not be binding upon Christians, seeing that they were not relations which can be shown to have flowed from any belief that pollution was inherent in matter, but were relations which were necessarily temporal, because instituted for a certain purpose, viz. that of foreshowing somewhat to come which, when it was come, could no longer be foreshowed.

[2] Eccles. iii. 14.

They had left speaking to hope, and addressed themselves to gratitude.

RAD. There are in your discourse sundry things which puzzle me, and not the least of them is this:—I remember that we are again to return to the subject of our relations to matter; still this difficulty occurs to me. Here you say that the relations to matter in which Moses' law placed men were only for a time, and also say that this was the case in regard to the relations to unclean animals. But you seemed very unwilling to allow that there was any real difference between the animals, as neither between the kinds of matter, which were pure or impure. And yet you say, what is far harder to believe, if I am not misunderstanding you, that there is a difference between one nation and another, which that distinction of animals only foreshadowed. Now how comes it, Laurence, if this is so, that you object to a particular nation having different castes in it? It seems to me as if you had got yourself into an inextricable difficulty here, and that you must either admit the rightness of our system of castes, or else give up all your apologies for the Mosaic law, and own fairly that it is not more permanent than that of Manu, and so lose one of your great arguments for its wonderful and divine character, viz. the fact that it is still acknowledged by all Christians as part of Revelation, and looked to for guidance, in consequence of such acknowledgment, by Christians who are devout and in earnest. If you can get out of this difficulty, I shall then begin to think there must be some truth in a system which can extricate itself from such weighty objections.

LAUR. Oh Rádhákánt, I am not the least dismayed by your objection, though I confess it is most ingeniously urged. I will begin to meet it, not with saying, as I might, that you display not sufficient attention to your Guru's words, but with a quotation from one of the commentators on the Bhagavata and Vayu Purana, who says that, "whatever (64) differences are observed in the different Puranas, is ascribed by the pious to the differences of their ages." All, then, that I had said would not amount to more than this; and the very thing that I wished to insist on was, that under our dispensation distinctions might be sanctioned, which distinctions were, however, to pass away. I, then, am the last person to be puzzled with the difficulty you suggest.

RAD. How can that be?

LAUR. Because I should fully allow that the institution of castes is one which might have been at one period divinely sanctioned, but under another period divinely abrogated. What can be simpler than this?

RAD. But what proof can you give for the one or the other, consistently with your views of things?

LAUR. You set me such hard tasks to do; but I will attempt this also. I believe that all the whole sum of things is ordered by Divine Providence, and that the brute creation are, among other created beings, under His government. Hence I believe that the state of things which I see existing in regard to them and their relations to man, are the results of His government, whether the particular enactment which brought about the present state, was a penal one or not. If, then, I found that all the world, or the largest part of it, at any time held and acted upon a certain view of the animal creation, I should say that that came of His government, and not by mere chance. If I found different orders in the animal creation, I should conclude they came by His appointment; such orders, e. g., as clean and unclean, or any other division you choose to make. And the same wise and good principle, whatever it was, which induced the Governor of the world, at one period of His government, to put some of these animals into one condition and some into another, may also have induced Him to put some beings of a higher grade into different positions analogous to these. We are told that there are different grades of beings even in Heaven, and that one star differeth from another star in glory (65). And unless we knew the whole system of things, and could define precisely how other orders of beings influenced us, as we influence lower orders of beings, we cannot at all tell but what such changes as I am speaking about may seem to beings of higher orders to have come about quite in the way of natural consequences. This we see, that brute beasts depend very much upon us for the degree of cultivation they obtain: they are, if one seriously reflects upon it, as capable, within certain limits, of having their rank in the creation elevated through the instrumentality of men, as men may be, for aught we know to the contrary, through the instrumentality of higher orders of beings. Elephants (66), for instance, may live and die to no purpose but those of a mere brute life; yet they are capable of being raised by training to a very high degree of tractableness and advantageousness to men. They display considerable signs of gratitude, malice, memory, adroitness, and half-reasoning powers, when they have been trained. And even those animals which are apparently of a viler grade, such as dogs and swine, may by kindness and skill be rendered available for many useful purposes. It is easy for a person who does not consider this world as God's world, to make mirth at all this: but when seriously considered, it shows that there are existing in this world of His, creatures capable of a state improved to a degree far above what we ordinarily call their natural state. And if this is so in the ordinary course of things, it is plain that any divine interposition, whether or no it suspended this ordinary course of things, might exercise a very great influence in increasing the capacities even of brute creatures for intercourse and familiarity with men. Hence the lower orders of the creation will not at all justify us in supposing that a natural state is one which precludes all improvement, although they show us most fully also that it is not all of these lower creatures, but only some of them, which the Almighty Disposer of the Universe, in that part of His scheme of government hitherto disclosed to us, puts into stations and conditions in which the way to improvement is open to them. And as they have capacities for improvement, so it appears also that they have capacities for degradation, so to speak. For early and long-continued ill-treatment, neglect, and even being in the way of other ill-tempered brutes, appears to have very considerable influence indeed in making them fiercer than they are naturally, and sometimes even irrecoverably untameable. Vain is the ridicule with which one foresees people of shallow minds will treat the idea of viewing these creatures as under GOD's government, and part of His world; for these are things which cannot be made light of without denying a Providence altogether. If, then, this is the case with the lower orders of creatures; if what, apart from the knowledge of a wise Governor of the world, would seem blind fate, finds its way into the brute creation, it is not at all unlikely that the same may be the case with respect to higher orders of beings also, and with whole classes of them, such as nations are. If, then, we turn to the state of things existing at one time more extensively than it does now, we shall see that there is very strong evidence of a design upon the part of Providence that there should be different religious situations assigned to creatures of like moral capacities: for we see that there are not only different orders of creatures in the world, but also that even the lower kinds of them are placed in situations where they have very different opportunities of being improved in those respects in which they are capable of improvement. Hence it seems to me clearly conceivable that it may have been a part of the original design of Providence that there should be slaves in different parts of the world, so far as we may speak of any of His dispensations in this way, and so far as the effects of sin (such as slavery is) can be considered to have been (67) anticipated and provided for in that design. Certain, however, it is, that slavery prevailed to a far greater extent than it now does, and that the encroachment that has been made upon it has been made by the slow working of Christianity. As for attempts to break through it by political overt acts, the success of them remains to be proved. But as I think the relation of Christianity to slavery has a most important bearing upon the question in hand, I shall add a few more remarks upon it here. Slavery, I have already said, came in my belief from sin; and the dispensation which professes to be and is the antagonist power to sin, has all along been operating slowly to the removal of it. Now it is a part of that dispensation that it makes known life and incorruptibility (68), and no two persons can well realize the fact that they stand together in this world before an Almighty Judge, who sees and will judge all they do in their present corruptible body, without feeling themselves reduced much more to a level than they before were: indeed their own differences sink into nothing when they consider the immense differences between themselves and their Judge. Now, if you look to the nations of the earth, you will, I think, find, that in proportion as they have treated slaves cruelly, they are sure to turn out to be unbelievers in a future state, and the converse: the one is an index of the other. The houses of the Romans (69) were not spattered with the blood of slaves, until they pretty generally took in the doctrines of Epicurus, who denied a future state. In Athens, a city of Greece famous for philosophers, we find that it was not uncommon for men to take their fill of lust and drunkenness (70) before death, as though they would have the last of their existence in brute enjoyment, and in this city slaves were commonly (71) killed without the least compunction, and a great philosopher among them, who held it to be a questionable thing if there were any future state of happiness (72), also held slaves to be property as cattle were, or to be personified tools for work, incapable of any civil relationship, but as things belonging to a master; whereas that philosopher (73) among them who most insisted on a future state was most kindly in his views of slaves, as was his disciple amongst the Romans. And if we look to the nation most of all like the Indians, the Egyptians, we find that they, held as it was before said they were, to be the inventors of the doctrine of a future state, had also gentle institutions for their slaves (74); and the kindness of the Jews, as a nation, to their slaves, should be noticed here as falling in with what I before urged respecting their belief of a future state, and confirming it. Now Christianity, by making what men only guessed at here and there before, to be a matter of moral certainty, also removed, though through a further and higher consideration of the relationship of Christian to Christian, the hard-hearted spirit of masters towards slaves. I do not think that where Christianity prevails in a real living way, we need fear much that liberty will ensue to all men; and without this, liberty is only a curse; for unless men's capacities of action correspond up to a certain extent with their external condition, and this with their capacities, happiness is impossible.

But besides slaves, whose condition it thus appears to have been the design of the Gospel to benefit, there existed another class of men of which I shall here say a few words: for on the subject of kindness to women, I need not tell you more than that the Greeks held them down in a state of miserable degradation, as did several of the western nations; and that Christianity has quite removed this, so furnishing a fact more to my purpose. I should, however, observe, that Christianity holds women to be a lower rank of beings than men, so far as not to allow them any priestly function. Still, as Sayána (75) says that women and Sudras were not allowed to study the Vedas, this ought not to be any objection in your eyes. But it should seem that, besides the relation of individual men towards one another in ancient times, whole nations were placed in a servile position towards one another. Thus, in the course of time, conquering nations made those who were overcome to work upon the land they had acquired; and this not in one or the other part of the West (76), but over almost the whole of it. Now these, who were free, seem to have come much nearer to your Sudras, who seem in the (77) Vishnu Purana to be spoken of as a people or race rather than as a lower grade of men. And I fear that in some measure your fathers ran into the habit of looking upon them in the same light as certain Western philosophers looked upon the barbarians whom they could conquer; as mere brutes almost, who could not be raised to the dignity of civilized men: a notion to which our experience even of the brute creation, as I have shown, affords material objections. Whether, however, they were a separate nation originally or not, is nothing to my purpose, which is to show that whole classes of men, once in a state of degradation, may be raised to a higher grade, or (which is the same thing, so far as I am concerned with it) may have no bar in their mere outward condition to their being so raised. As you have never (78) treated them, I believe, with the same barbarity that other nations did slaves, so it may come to pass that you may treat them as brethren. For you may by degrees come to take what I have tried to show you to be a more practical view of things, and, limiting your knowledge to the humble range of things which comes within experience, where you have no certain revelation (79) to guide you beyond that range, you may cease to think that a Sudra child comes into this world with any stain on it to prevent its becoming regenerate, and that with a far higher regeneration than you knew of before.

And let me also call your attention to another fact. I tried, you will remember, to show you that your Brahmans may have sprung from the tribe of Shem, the Priest-tribe of the whole earth. Now it is also matter of fact, under what we see of God's government, the very people who were the chiefest of the race of Shem, to whom, for several hundred years, the oracles of God were committed, are at last rejected from being a priest before God, and scattered abroad among the nations, doing the offices of Váisyas to the whole world. It is certain that the Jews are not a nation, and it does not seem at all likely that they ever will be again restored (80). They are, then, a standing proof that even priestly tribes may cease to be so; whatsoever becomes of theories, this certainly seems a fact much to be considered.

Next, as Israel is, according to their own books, the first-born of God, it follows that other nations (81) are also sons, and so the objects of His fatherly care; and therefore the disobedience of the first-born nation may lead to the instating of others in its dignity. The pre-eminence of that tribe to which they belonged, only originated with the times immediately subsequent to the Flood; a dispensation, therefore, which puts them upon a level with other nations, may not be any new thing under the sun, but that which hath been already. You must, I think, allow that your own books look back, in a way similar to what other nations (82) do, also to a Satya-kalpa, in which there was no distinction (83) of classes; instances occur of Xhatriyas becoming Brahmans; the Gargyas and Sainyas, though Xhatriyas by birth, became Brahmans (84), as did Kapi, the third son of Uraxhya. Now this would go to show that another state of things might exist under Providence. And if the existence of such distinctions in the world at one Kalpa is a proof of what His will was in regard to that Kalpa, the existence of no such distinctions in another Kalpa may be a proof of what His will is in regard to this last Kalpa. Going by matters of fact which we see about us, is as much a mode of arriving at His will as going by revelation is; only the latter is a speedy, the former a slow, way of arriving at knowledge. Thus proverbs, the result of experience, often fall in with the declarations of a revelation which they could not have copied after:—or, to take another instance, in some nations there is a custom for certain men to marry their sisters; now, supposing that there is no presage of conscience whatever against such matches, yet the fact that progeny produced from such unions, not only among mankind, but also among the brute creation, soon dwindle away and degenerate, is as much a declaration of His will against them as a presage of conscience beforehand would be. And seeing that mankind sprung originally from one pair, they seem to have been left very much to learn this by degrees, as time went on; neither is it at all clear that affinities of that kind can be proved (85) in any other way to be wrong, revolting as they are to us.

The fact, then, Rádhákánt, that such distinctions of classes has been wearing out all over the earth, must be taken for a declaration of GOD's will against their existence, unless any thing immoral can be shown to be involved in such a supposition. And perhaps we should also consider here the tendency (as such) of Christianity to obliterate all distinctions not founded upon inward and invisible gifts, and maintained by sanctity, as leading to the same conclusion, especially as that tendency has already in part become effect, and as it meets with so much in the constitution and course of nature to countenance it. For the sage Vishnu Serman says that the moon doth not withhold its light from the dwelling of the Chandála (86), and in the same way the Christian Church does not withhold Her blessings from any of the nations that flow in unto Her, but sets aside all distinction of Mlechchha, Sudra, bond or free (87), and bestows even her greatest honours upon men of meanest birth, provided they are regenerate with the true regeneration, and lead a holy life.

RAD. How great the changes have been in the whole commonwealth of things, how the lower orders have been or may be advanced, and how the higher may be degraded, you have told me. You have also hinted that we follow not the guidance of experience, but the roamings of our own fancy, when we consider the Sudra to come into this world with a stain from a state of pre-existence upon his soul, which prevents his attaining to a high degree. Yet certainly this would account for the existence of slavery and other like facts in the world. Now since you adopt the principle of holding what exists to exist by divine law, how can you deny that this distinction, existing as it does, is a fact which proves that theory of things to be a true one?

LAUR. All that we see in nature or in grace runs up into mystery: we see that there is a wonderful connexion between one event and another; there are reciprocal correspondences (88) and mutual relations, by which every thing is brought about; and so closely tied into each other are all things, that no one thing stands out clear and alone in the whole course of nature which we see before us. In other words, we do not know of any one single thing of which we can give a perfect account. But the theory that a Sudra was contaminated in a state of pre-existence will give a clear and perfect account of the way in which he comes to be what he is: it is too perfect a theory to be a true theory (89). It is a specimen of a theory which does not present the mind with something above experience, but something absolutely contradictory to it; and, though I may be wrong, I do not think any pure revelation would ever contradict experience, however much it may go beyond it. For experience, as I have so often suggested to you, is a record of GOD's dealings in one part of His government; and though, of course, in so vast (90) a system as that government is, it is likely that many things would at first sight appear to contradict each other, yet it is likely also the parts of that government would, upon reflection, turn out to be far more consistent with each other than at first sight they appear. And I think it is particularly the case with what I have just alluded to. Things in the system of grace appear to be far more mysterious than things in the system of nature; and this mysteriousness is a reason with some minds against believing them. But upon reflection it will turn out that things in the system of nature are, I will not say as mysterious as the other, but certainly far more mysterious than they are at first view taken to be, and that owing in a great measure to the wonderful connexions of things with others.

And I must think that the theory of pre-existence accounts by far too philosophically for the mysteries of the present course of GOD's government, to be a true theory. Experience teaches us that we cannot understand the whole of any thing, but that we know in part; whereas the theory of pre-existence is a perfect and entire account of the difficulty we feel at seeing divers opportunities and advantages bestowed on creatures of like capacities in other respects. I also think that it is one which cannot be proved to be revealed, and am sure that the information which some have pretended to have about it is far too precise to be true. When stated indefinitely, and used merely as a metaphysical speculation, it may possibly be not altogether inadmissible; but when you come to ground upon it a system which is practically contradicted by what we see even of the lower orders of creatures, I think you will, upon mature reflection, see that we are becoming vain in our imaginations when we insist upon it. I shall therefore leave you to reflect upon this, without further remarks upon it than these two. We have a difficulty (you say) in accounting for the origin of our knowledge without assuming certain precognita, for the sake of which we also assume a pre-existence. But there is the same difficulty as to the origin of our feelings. Let us, then, when we assume a pre-existence in which the former were planted, assume also a pre-existence in which the latter were planted, and let that be the period in which there existed no distinction of classes. Let us regard those feelings of mercy towards all creatures implanted in our breasts, as the voice of GOD within us; let us obey them with fear and reverence, and not "ensconce ourselves into seeming knowledge when we should submit ourselves to an unknown fear."

RAD. Doubtless there is something in what you

say about the difficulty of proving the pre-existence; but you bid me think over what you have said, so I will not ask any further questions now.

END OF THE SECOND DIALOGUE.

NOTES TO DIALOGUE II.

NOTE (1.) p. 144.

See Origen, c. Cels. p. 365. Beveridge ap. Cotel. Patres Apost. p. 464.

NOTE (2.) p. 144.

Aristotle ap. Jos. c. Apion. i. 22, is the person here alluded to: the passage is as follows. Ὅτι δὲ οὐ μόνον ἠπίσταντο τοὺς Ἰουδαίους, ἀλλὰ καὶ ἐθαύμαζον, ὅσοις αὐτῶν ἐντύχοιεν, οὐχ οἱ φαυλότατοι τῶν Ἑλλήνων, ἀλλ' οἱ ἐπὶ σοφίᾳ μάλιστα τεθαυμασμένοι, ῥᾴδιον γνῶναι. Κλέαρχος γὰρ ὁ Ἀριστοτέλους ὢν μαθητὴς, καὶ τῶν ἐκ τοῦ Περιπάτου φιλοσόφων οὐδενὸς δεύτερος, ἐν τῷ πρώτῳ περὶ ὕπνου βιβλίῳ φησὶν, Ἀριστοτέλην τὸν διδάσκαλον αὐτοῦ περί τινος ἀνδρὸς Ἰουδαίου ταῦτα ἱστορεῖν, αὐτόν τε τὸν λόγον Ἀριστοτέλει παρατιθείς. Ἔστι δὲ οὕτω γεγραμμένον, "Ἄλλα τὰ μὲν πολλὰ μακρὸν ἂν εἴη λέγειν· ὅσα δ' ἔχει τῶν ἐκείνου θαυμασιότητά τινα, καὶ φιλοσοφίαν ὁμοίως, διελθεῖν οὐ χεῖρον. Ὡς σαφῶς δὲ σοὶ εἰπεῖν, Ὑπεροχίδη, θαυμαστόν τι ὀνείροις ἴσα σοὶ δόξω λέγειν. Καὶ ὁ Ὑπεροχίδης εὐλαβούμενος, δι' αὐτὸ γὰρ, ἔφη τοῦτο, καὶ ζητοῦμεν ἀκοῦσαι πάντες. Οὐκοῦν, εἶπεν ὁ Ἀριστοτέλης, κατὰ τὸ τῶν ῥητορικῶν παράγγελμα, τὸ γένος αὐτοῦ πρῶτον διέλθωμεν, ἵνα μὴ ἀπειθῶμεν τοῖς τῶν ἀπαγγελιῶν διδασκάλοις. Λέγε, εἶπεν ὁ Ὑπεροχίδης, ὅτι σοι δοκεῖ. Καὶ ἐκεῖνος τοίνυν τὸ μὲν γένος ἦν Ἰουδαῖος ἐκ τῆς Κοίλης

Συρίας. Οὗτοι δέ εἰσιν ἀπόγονοι τῶν ἐν Ἰνδοῖς φιλοσόφων. Καλοῦνται δὲ, ὥς φασιν, οἱ φιλόσοφοι παρὰ μὲν Ἰνδοῖς Καλανοὶ, παρὰ δὲ Σύροις Ἰουδαῖοι, τὸ ὄνομα λαβόντες ἀπὸ τοῦ τόπου· προσαγορεύεται γὰρ ὃν κατοικοῦσι τόπον, Ἰουδαία. Τὸ δὲ τῆς πόλεως αὐτῶν ὄνομα πάνυ σκολιόν ἐστιν, Ἱερουσαλὴμ γὰρ αὐτὴν καλοῦσιν. Οὗτος οὖν ὁ ἄνθρωπος ἐπιξενούμενός τε πολλοῖς, καὶ ἐκ τῶν ἄνω τόπων εἰς τοὺς ἐπιθαλαττίους ὑποκαταβαίνων Ἑλληνικὸς ἦν, οὐ τῇ διαλέκτῳ μόνον, ἀλλὰ καὶ τῇ ψυχῇ. Καὶ τότε διατριβόντων ἡμῶν περὶ τὴν Ἀσίαν, παραβαλὼν εἰς αὐτοὺς τόπους, ἐν οἷς ἦμεν, ἐντυγχάνει ἡμῖν τε καί τισιν ἑτέροις τῶν σχολαστικῶν, πειρώμενος αὐτῶν τῆς σοφίας. Ὡς δὲ πολλοῖς τῶν ἐν παιδείᾳ συνῳκείωτο, παραδίδου τι μᾶλλον ὧν εἶχεν."

Note (3.) p. 144.

S. Cyril, c. Jul. p. 134. Ἀριστόβουλος δὲ οὕτω που φησὶν ὁ Περιπατητικός· Ἅπαντα μέν τοι τὰ περὶ φύσεως[1] εἰρημένα παρὰ τοῖς ἀρχαίοις λέγεται καὶ παρὰ τοῖς ἔξω τῆς Ἑλλάδος φιλοσοφοῦσι, τὰ μὲν παρ' Ἰνδοῖς ὑπὸ τῶν Βραχμαίων· τὰ δὲ ἐν τῇ Συρίᾳ ὑπὸ τοῦ [τῶν] καλουμένων Ἰουδαίων· which account is given also by St. Clem. Str. i. § 72, p. 360, Pott. to Megasthenes.

Note (4.) p. 147.

Waters are the recognized symbol for nations, not only in the Chaldee Paraphrast, Ps. xlvi. 5. cxliv. 7. Amos v. 8, &c., but also in the Revelation xvii. 15. (See Aretas' Commentary, p. 307. St. Aust. in Ps. lxxx. 11.)

[1] Τὰ περὶ φύσεως, with the ancients, is often taken to comprise much more than what is now called physical philosophy, and did not include only what could be taught demonstratively, but also much which could be gained by experience alone. See Michelet ad Aristot. Eth. N. p. 277, and Euseb. P. E. xi. 1, 2.

NOTE (5.) p. 148.

Schlegel, Essai sur la Langue, &c., des Indiens, p. 176: "Le Latin, par ses filles les langues Romanes, domine dans presque toutes les parties du monde ; l'Italien est la langue du commerce usitée dans le Levant, comme le Portugais sur des côtes de l'Afrique et des Indes. L'Espagnol est devenu l'idiome de la plus grande partie du nouveau monde. On sait l'influence, pour ainsi dire universelle, de la langue Française," &c.

NOTE (6.) p. 148.

This opinion is given by Ritter, Vorhalle zur Europ. Volkergesch. &c. pp. 286 and 316, as cited, though with disapproval, by Bähr on Herod. vol. ii. p. 666; while Windischmann, who was probably in a much better position of mind (so to speak) for passing a judgment, gives his sanction to it, p. 1206. It seems, from Molitor, i. § 115, that the Cabbalists yet hover about the Euxine Sea, and may furnish, possibly, at a future period, some further information as to the route followed by the disseminators of Indian doctrines. For Molitor thinks that they have many books hitherto unknown.

NOTE (7.) p. 148.

The Sacæ were a widely extended race. See Windis. as above; and Professor Wilson on the Vishnu P., p. 188, n. 43. The connexion between Sagax, Sacra, and Saca, is suggested by Wind. p. 525. See also Jablonski, Prolegg. to Panth. Ægypt. § 40, where the word Sach is made synonymous with ἱερογραμματεύς. Some think the Egyptian to belong to the Indo-Germanic class of languages, as Rhode, Heilige Sage, pp. 4—8; Ideler, Hermap. p. 58, who writes thus: "Quod si quis ex vocabulorum communium in linguis, quibus finitimæ gentes utuntur, copiâ communem originem vellet concludere, haud difficile foret demonstrare veteris Ægypti linguam Indo-Germanicæ stirpis fuisse." If, however, the different castes who carried on different occupations belonged originally to different nations, one can see how a number of common words may have existed in languages whose structure and family is entirely different. For Peyron. Gram. Copt. p. x. well says: "Linguarum affinitas ex intimâ grammaticarum indole ac vocabulorum originibus dijudicanda est, non vero ex minutis nominum verborumque formis aut accidentibus, quæ longa dies novare solet." And Ideler (l. c.) has suggested that the intercourse with Ethiopians and other Semitic nations gave rise to the *seeming* analogies between Coptic and these languages. If, however, the supposition that Hebrew roots are not triliteral, be (as I think probable) a well-founded one, we have the same root in שכל ܫܟ-ܠ. Dwelling thus upon one word would perhaps be frivolous, were it not that the opportunities of general remarks which one so finds seem to make it not unprofitable. Good instances of this may be found in Ihre's appendix to the fragments of Ulphilas, where he has shown the connexion between Mæso-Gothic and Greek and Latin. And this induces me to add here one remark more, which is, that the older the language is, the less distinction is found between words expressive of intellectual and moral faculties. Thus "sacer" is here made to be connected with words of an intellectual bearing. "*Cor*datus" (in olden Latin) was used for "clever;" לב (a heart), in Hebrew, is used for "wisdom," and a *heart* in China was also a symbol for the same. See Gesen. Lex. Maj. p. 739. Thus, that believing is with the heart, was what the intuition of unsophisticated nature readily entered into; while the distinctions of more modern languages are less philosophical. Well did De Maistre say: "La langue la plus philosophique est celle dont la philosophie s'est le moins mêlée."

NOTE (8.) p. 148.

See Vish. Pur. p. 62, where a passage from the Vayu P. is given by Professor Wilson.

NOTE (9.) p. 149.

Bopp, Vergl. Gramm. Vorrede, p. ii. "Wer hätte vor einem halben Jahrhundert es sich träumen lassen, dass uns aus dem fernsten Orient eine Sprache würde zugeführt werden, die das Griechische in allen seinen ihm als Eigenthum zugetrauten Form-Vollkommenheiten begleitet, zuweilen überbietet, und überall dazu geeignet ist, den in Griechischen bestehenden Dialecten Kampf zu schlechten," u.s.w. As to the other part—the way in which customs were cleared up by a knowledge of things accessible through Sanscrit—it was suggested by a passage in De Maistre, Soirées de St. Petersbourg, Entr. ii. p. 102, ed. Bruxelles. He has some excellent remarks upon language, although his instances are ludicrous, in most cases. As I have omitted to notice down instances, I must remind the reader that the text is only an illustration, which if fictitious would serve my purpose, although I have wished to convey information by all parts of that illustration. For it has a general aim as well as particular ones: the *general* aim is to introduce to the mind that peculiarity of some parts of Scripture, if not all, which is most clearly exhibited, perhaps, in Jotham's fable; the primary interpretation of which evidently does not account for several expressions in it, and so leads us to look for an explanation of the explanation. The *particular* aims are: first, to introduce to the mind some of the perplexities and wonders of the material world; secondly, the connexion of different languages with each other, and the things to be learned from it. This I leave for others to follow out if thought expedient. Thirdly, the illustration deals only with the Indo-Germanic or Japhetic branch, as feeling it to be uncertain if there is any such thing as an orthodox Semitic nation now, which, if the case, is too awful a thing not to influence one in the choice of the nations used to illustrate the diffusion of primitive tradition. This will be enough to suggest to the reader that I have wished to look several ways in things seemingly incidental, though anxious to have the main thing attended to, and not these incidental ones. A fictitious instance, then, may be given, to throw a light on my meaning, in what I have said of customs in the text. Suppose the word "superstitio" (whose etymology is so controverted) meant the duty of *survivors*, as such, to their ancestors; when we see the importance attached in the Hindu law to the worship of Pitris, or forefathers, this custom throws a light upon the primary sense of that word.

Note (10.) p. 149.

This is Westergaard's opinion, in the preface to his Radices L. Sanscritæ, p. xii. "Quarto jam sæculo ante Christum natum, lingua Sanscrita ex ore et quotidiano usu recessisse, et, præter viros nobiles et sacerdotes illam edoctos, cæteri dialectos e linguâ sacrâ ortas, sive, si vis, linguam Sanscritam corrupte et barbare locuti esse videntur."

Note (11.) p. 149.

The waters of Babylon (in conformity with what was said in the ninth note) mean, not the nations of Babylon only, but, in the ultimate explanation of it, those nations as a type of the world. It is the primary explanation with which we are here dealing. Now though it must, I think, be allowed that the influence of Hebrew through different translations of the Bible has had an incalculable influence upon European and other modes of thought and expression, yet in clearing up the etymological difficulties of these people, the Semitic languages did little or nothing. Even real resemblances seemed absurd, from want of the intervening links supplied by ancienter languages, such as the Sanscrit or Zend. I have seen somewhere mentioned a treatise of Ernesti's on the Semitic roots traceable in Greek and Latin; but his manner of disposing of facts, when they controvert his preconceived theories, is too well known, from his edition of Cicero, to make one care to consult him. Of modern writers, Fürst, in the portion of his Aramaic Grammar which is published, and in his Concordance (though often justly censured by Gesenius for fancifulness) has yet paved the way to a comparison between the Semitic and Indo-Germanic classes of languages. He has shown that among Semitic languages there are several words of like signification, two letters of which words are alike (ab. p. 194). He assumes that these two are the radical letters, and then proceeds to confirm this by the fact that this residuum from the triliteral roots meets its counterpart in the monosyllabic Sanscrit roots. In this opinion he is followed by Delitzsch, Redslob, and others. It is desirable to state this, lest the text should seem in any degree to countenance the belief of a separate fount of language, so to speak.

NOTE (12.) p. 149.

Vish. P. p. 228. Bhag. Pur. i. 1. 15.

NOTE (13.) p. 149.

The use of Mantras, or forms of prayer, in divers ceremonies, would be an instance of this belief. Compare Origen c. Cels. p. 20. S. Athan. c. Ar. iii. 28, says, τὴν ἀκοὴν τὴν ῥυπωθεῖσαν ἀπὸ τῶν βλασφήμων ῥημάτων ἀπονίψασθε τοῖς τῆς εὐσεβείας λόγοις· which passage may suggest, that such a use of words in false religions may be another instance of the way in which evil spirits inspired their votaries with anticipations of the true. In Manu, xi. 33, we meet with the following example of this belief:

वाक् शस्त्रं वै ब्राह्मणस्य तेन हन्याद्रीन् द्विजः

"A Brahman's weapons are his words; with them let the regenerate smite his foes."

NOTE (14.) p. 149.

See Majer, Mytholog. Lex. in v. Ganga.

NOTE (15.) p. 149.

Quoted by Windis. p. 1903. In the Vish. Purana, p. 495, Brahma, amongst other things, is said to be the spirit who is language[2]. The question as to the origin of language will probably be always settled according to the temper of the minds which discuss it: Aristotle and Plato took opposite views about it, as may be seen by referring to Origen c. Cels. p. 18, and Spencer's note upon it. Plato, as there quoted, says, *μείζω τινὰ δύναμιν εἶναι ἢ ἀνθρωπείαν τὴν θεμένην τὰ πρῶτα ὀνόματα τοῖς πράγμασιν*. (Cratyl. v. fin.) Aristotle, on the contrary, that they were *κατὰ συνθήκην*. (De Interp. 2.) Perhaps the latter, if hardpressed, would have owned to holding a belief in the theory of a civil compact (see Eth. Nic. viii. 11, p. 1160, a. 10), which is the counterpart in morals to this theory of language in intellectual matters. Even Mohammed found it advisable to keep to the higher theory. Koran, Sura ii. 29. وعلم ادم الاسما كلها "So he (God) taught Adam the names of them all." Other authorities may be found in Walton's Prolegom. i. § 1, &c. Dathe's Pref. p. vi. &c. De Maist. Entret. ii. Diod. Sic. i. 8.

[2] Possibly the word "Devanagari" contains a trace of some tradition to the same effect; it reminds one of the Literæ Angelorum among the Jews. See Thomæ Bang Cœlum Orientale, p. 96.

Euseb. P. E. p. 516. It is amusing for those who take Plato's view, to see the endless speculations formed by the opposite party—one assuming that prepositions and pronouns are only modified verbs (e. g. Hupfeld in Ewald's Zeitschrift für K. des Morgenl.) ; another (e. g. Redslob de Part. כי) contending that they are apocopated verbs ; while all seem unwilling to acknowledge any thing divine in the matter. I shall avoid any further discussion here, and content myself with quoting Dante's words de Vulg. Eloquio, i. 5. "Opinantes autem non sine ratione tam ex superioribus quam ex inferioribus sumptâ, ad ipsum Deum primitus hominem direxisse locutionem, rationabiliter diximus ipsum loquentem primum, mox, postquam afflatus est ab animante Virtute, incunctanter fuisse locutum. Nam in homine sentiri humanius credimus quam sentire, dummodo sentiatur et sentiat tanquam homo. Si ergo Faber ille atque perfectionis Principium et Amator primum hominem omni perfectione complevit, rationabile nobis apparet nobilissimum animal non ante sentire quam sentiri cœpisse. Si vero quis fatetur contra objiciens, quod non oportebat illum loqui, cum solus adhuc homo existeret, et Deus omnia sine verbis arcana nostra discernat, etiam ante quam nos; cum illâ reverentiâ dicimus quâ uti oportet cum de æternâ Voluntate aliquid judicamus, quod licet Deus sciret, immo præsciret (quod idem est quantum ad Deum) absque locutione conceptum primi loquentis, voluit tamen et ipsum loqui, ut in explicatione tantâ dotis gloriaretur Ipse qui gratis dotaverat. Et ideo divinitus in nobis esse credendum est quod actu nostrorum affectuum ordinato lætamur; et hinc penitus eligere possumus locum illum, ubi effutita est prima locutio : quoniam si extra Paradisum afflatus est homo, extra ; si vero intra, intra fuisse locum primæ locutionis convicimus."

Note (16.) p. 149.

The *Finger* of God is synonymous with the Holy Ghost (see St. Matt. xii. 28, as compared with St. Luke xi. 20); and the thing here supposed is, that this Indian legend was based possibly on a diabolic imitation of the truth; for the phrase is frequently so used in the Old Testament. See Ps. viii. 3, as compared with Job xxvi. 13.

Note (17.) p. 150.

These words are taken from St. Gregory of Nyssa, i. p. 189.

Note (18.) p. 151.

S. Iren. lib. iii. 4, § 1, 2. "Quid autem si neque Apostoli quidem Scripturas reliquissent nobis, nonne oportebat ordinem sequi Traditionis, quam tradiderunt iis quibus committebant Ecclesias? Cui ordinationi assentiunt multæ gentes barbarorum, eorum qui in Christo credunt, sine chartâ et atramento scriptam habentes per Spiritum in cordibus suis salutem, et veterem traditionem diligenter custodientes, in unum Deum credentes. . . . Hanc fidem qui sine literis crediderunt, quantum ad sermonem nostrum barbari sunt, quantum autem ad sententiam et consuetudinem et conversationem, propter fidem perquam sapientissimi sunt, et placent Deo, conversantes in omni justitiâ et castitate et sapientiâ." So Plato, Phædr. § 133—135, thought the invention of letters contributed to the perversion of truth rather than otherwise; and it must be obvious, to any one who thinks at all, that oral teaching has its advantages, which advantages would gradually be lost sight of in proportion as written teaching took its place. By this, of course, it is not intended to deny that written teaching is a blessing to men when too corrupt to be trusted with oral teaching, but merely to intimate that we do not well to pride ourselves upon having a medicine healthful to us.

Note (19.) p. 151.

Pseudo-Aust. de Nativ. Serm. 22. "Deus per Angelum loquebatur, et Virgo per aurem impregnabatur," quoted by Assemanni, B. O. i. p. 91, when speaking of a similar passage in St. Ephrem, ii. p. 328 b. "By the voice Mary conceived the Might, that came to her body."

Note (20.) p. 152.

See Windisch. p. 224, who mentions that the Chinese argued, from the universality of the language of brute creatures, that man must have forfeited that universality by sin. Compare also, for other traditions on the subject, Abydenus, ap. Cyr. c. Jul. p. 9, and Note g to the preface of Meninski's Lexicon, Sect. i.

Note (21.) p. 152.

The matter here is borrowed from St. Ephrem's commentary upon Genesis i. p. 59:

ܡܛܠ ܕܐܒܘܗܘܢ ܗܘܐ ܠܟܠܗܝܢ ܝܘܐ ܦ"

Note (22.) p. 153.

The whole subject of the interference of Satan in the world before Christ is one which I have already touched upon in page 90 and page 108. If it seems, at first, strange to assume that evil spirits coined resemblances to the truth, and those often minute ones, or stole from the prophets a knowledge of things to come, I am persuaded that this strangeness arises merely from not having thought of the subject. It will wear off as men come to reflect upon it, especially if habits of self-examination shall have predisposed them, from a knowledge of Satan's mode of dealing with individuals, to think that there is an antecedent probability in the view of his government, which it is hoped the following passages from the Fathers will put before the reader. For whether it be from a preternatural intelligence of the meaning of the least outward movements of our features, or (what seems to me most probable) from some more recondite mode of access to our thoughts, that Satan is permitted to know what goes on in our minds, with a view to avail himself of it; certain it must be, to any one who attempts a strict watch over himself, that he does exercise a marvellous foresight in dealing with us, to effect if possible our ruin, and does set before us counterfeits of our true good, to bring about that end. Hence it would seem to be antecedently credible that his more extended government should be carried on upon the same rule, that there should be amongst the heathen external resemblances to Catholic doctrines and practices, which men who unhappily have never been led to look deeper than at the outside of things, ever have made, and probably ever will make, in one way or other, an excuse for their rejection of the truth. The following texts of Scripture may be cited, as showing that it is distinctly revealed to us that the heathen did worship devils. Levit. xvii. 7. "They shall not offer their sacrifices any more unto devils (לשעירים), after whom they go a whoring." Deut. xxxii. 17. "They sacrificed unto devils that are not gods." (יזבחו לשדים לא אלה. Syriac, ܕܒܚܘ ܠܫܐܕܐ ܕܠܐ ܗܘܘ ܐܠܗܐ) 2 Chron. xi. 15. "He ordained him priests for the high places and for the devils (לשעירים), and for the calves which he had made." Ps. cvi. 37. "So they sacrificed their sons and their daughters unto devils (לשדים), and shed innocent blood, even the blood of their sons and their daughters, whom they sacrificed to the *idols of Canaan*." 1 Cor. x. 20, &c. The Gentiles "sacrifice to devils and not to God," *δαιμονίοις καὶ οὐ Θεῷ*. Syr. ܠܫܐܕܐ. 1 Tim. iv. 1. "In the latter times some shall depart from the faith to seducing spirits and doctrines of devils;" where St. Paul is plainly speaking of heresies which borrowed from pagan systems most largely. Rev. ix. 20. "They should not worship devils and idols of gold," &c. To which add Ps. xcv. 5, in the LXX., a text much quoted by the Fathers: πάντες οἱ θεοὶ τῶν ἐθνῶν δαιμόνια· which version shows that the opinion of the Jews of the time coincided with the subsequent teaching of St. Paul. These texts, then, show first, that devils were worshipped by the heathen; secondly, that the sacrifices offered to them put men into connexion with those evil spirits, and so had more than an external resemblance to the true sacrifice; and thirdly, that there was seductive *doctrine* conveyed by them to men, Satan being able to transform himself into an angel of *light*. Let us next proceed to some passages of the Fathers, which will but form a comment upon these passages.

Tertul. Apolog. adv. Gentes, c. xxii. "Operatio dæmonum est hominis eversio; sic malitia spiritalis a primordio auspicata est in hominis exitium. Itaque corporibus quidem et valetudines infligunt et aliquos casus acerbos; animæ vero repentinos et extraordinarios per vim excessus. Suppetit illis ad *utramque* substantiam hominis adeundam subtilitas et tenuitas sua; multum spiritalibus viribus licet, ut invisibiles et insensibiles in effectu potius quam in actu suo appareant: si poma, si fruges, nescio quod auræ latens vitium in flore præcipitat, in germine exanimat, in pubertate convulnerat, ac si cæcâ ratione tentatus aer pestilentes haustos suos offundit. Eâdem igitur obscuritate contagionis adspiratio dæmonum et angelorum mentis quoque corruptelas agit furoribus et amentiis fœdis, aut sævis libidinibus cum erroribus variis; quorum iste potissimus, quod eos ipsos captis et circumscriptis hominum mentibus comedat, ut et sibi pabula propria sudoris et sanguinis procuret simulachris imaginibusque oblata; et quæ illi accuratior pascua est, hominem a cogitatu veræ divinitatis avertat præstigiis falsis, quas et ipsas quomodo operetur expediam. Omnis spiritus ales est; hoc angeli et dæmones. Igitur momento ubique sunt. Totus orbis illis locus unus est; quid ubique geratur *tam facile sciunt quam enunciant*. Velocitas, divinitas creditur; quia substantia ignoratur. Sic et auctores interdum videri volunt eorum quæ annunciant; et sunt plane malorum nonnunquam, bonorum tamen nunquam. *Disposiones etiam Dei, et nunc prophetis concionantibus excerpunt, et nunc lectionibus resonantibus carpunt.* Ita et hinc sumentes quasdam temporum sortes æmulantur divinitatem, dum furantur divinationem. In oraculis autem quo ingenio ambiguitates temperent in eventus, sciunt Crœsi, sciunt Pyrrhi. Ceterum testudinem decoqui cum carnibus pecudis, Pythius eo modo renunciavit, quo supra diximus; momento apud Lydiam fuerat. Habent de incolatu aerio, et de viciniâ siderum, et de commercio nubium, cœlestes sapere paraturas; ut et pluvias quas jam sentiunt repromittant. Benefici plane, et circa curas valetudinum. Lædunt enim primo, dehinc remedia præcipiunt ad miraculum nova," &c. Cf. de Baptismo, v. "Nam et sacris quibusdam per lavacrum initiantur (nationes extraneæ) Isidis alicujus aut Mithræ . . . quo agnito hic quoque studium diaboli recognoscimus, res Dei æmulantis." And as Tertullian says this of one Sacrament, so of another, St. Just. Mart. pro Christ. Apol. ii. p. 98 b, says: Οἱ ἀπόστολοι ἐν τοῖς γενομένοις ὑπ' αὐτῶν ἀπομνημονεύμασιν, ἃ καλεῖται εὐαγγέλια, οὕτως παρέδωκαν ἐντετάλθαι αὐτοῖς τὸν Ἰησοῦν, λαβόντα ἄρτον εὐχαριστήσαντα εἰπεῖν, Τοῦτο ποιεῖτε εἰς τὴν ἀνάμνησίν μου· τοῦτό ἐστι τὸ σῶμά μου· καὶ τὸ ποτήριον ὁμοίως λαβόντα καὶ εὐχαριστήσαντα εἰπεῖν, Τοῦτό ἐστι τὸ αἷμά μου· καὶ μόνοις αὐτοῖς μεταδοῦναι. Ὅπως καὶ ἐν τοῖς τοῦ Μίθρα μυστηρίοις παρέδωκαν γίνεσθαι μιμησάμενοι οἱ πονηροὶ δαίμονες· ὅτι γὰρ ἄρτος καὶ ποτήριον ὕδατος τίθεται ἐν ταῖς τοῦ μυουμένου τελεταῖς μετ' ἐπιλόγων τινῶν, ἢ ἐπίστασθε, ἢ μαθεῖν δύνασθε· to which a parallel imitation already referred to (Dial. i.

page 135) existed amongst the Chinese and the Americans. To proceed with St. Just. Mart. Dial. cum Tryph. Jud. p. 294 d. Εὖ ἴσθι οὖν, ὦ Τρύφων, λέγων ἐπέφερον, ὅτι ἃ παραποιήσας ὁ λεγόμενος διάβολος ἐν τοῖς Ἕλλησιν λεχθῆναι ἐποίησεν, ὡς καὶ διὰ τῶν ἐν Αἰγύπτῳ μάγων ἐνήργησε, καὶ διὰ τῶν ἐπὶ Ἡλίᾳ ψευδοπροφητῶν, καὶ ταῦτα βεβαίαν μου τὴν ἐν ταῖς γραφαῖς γνῶσιν καὶ πίστιν κατέστησεν. Ὅταν γὰρ Διόνυσον μὲν υἱὸν τοῦ Διὸς ἐκ μίξεως, ἣν μεμίχθαι αὐτὸν τῇ Σεμέλῃ, γεγενῆσθαι λέγωσι, καὶ τοῦτον εὑρετὴν ἀμπέλου γενόμενον, καὶ διασπαραχθέντα καὶ ἀποθανόντα ἀναστῆναι, εἰς οὐρανόν τε ἀνεληλυθέναι ἱστορῶσι, καὶ οἶνον ἐν τοῖς μυστηρίοις αὐτοῦ παραφέρωσιν, οὐχὶ τὴν προλελεγμένην ὑπὸ Μωσέως ἀναγραφεῖσαν Ἰακὼβ τοῦ πατριάρχου προφητείαν μεμιμῆσθαι αὐτὸν νοῶ; ἐπὰν δὲ τὸν Ἡρακλέα ἰσχυρὸν καὶ περινοστήσαντα πᾶσαν τὴν γῆν, καὶ αὐτὸν τῷ Διῒ ἐξ Ἀλκμήνης γενόμενον, καὶ ἀποθανόντα εἰς οὐρανὸν ἀνεληλυθέναι λέγωσιν, οὐχὶ τὴν ἰσχυρὸν ὡς γίγας δραμεῖν ὁδὸν αὐτοῦ περὶ Χριστοῦ λελεγμένην γραφὴν ὁμοίως μεμιμῆσθαι νοῶ; ὅταν δὲ τὸν Ἀσκληπιὸν νεκροὺς ἀνεγείραντα, καὶ τὰ ἄλλα πάθη θεραπεύσαντα παραφέρῃ, οὐχὶ τὰς περὶ Χριστοῦ ὁμοίως προφητείας μεμιμῆσθαι τοῦτον καὶ ἐπὶ τούτῳ φημί; Here there are a number of minutiæ observed, such as to justify the allusions made in the text, p. 153, to the story of Crishna.

Dial. cum Tryph. Jud. p. 296. Ὅταν δὲ οἱ τὰ τοῦ Μίθρου μυστήρια παραδιδόντες, λέγωσιν ἐκ πέτρας γεγενῆσθαι αὐτὸν, καὶ σπήλαιον καλῶσι τὸν τόπον, ἔνθα μυεῖν τοὺς πειθομένους αὐτῷ παραδιδῶσιν, ἐνταῦθα οὐχὶ τὸ εἰρημένον ὑπὸ Δανιὴλ, ὅτι λίθος ἄνευ χειρῶν ἐτμήθη ἐξ ὄρους μεγάλου, μεμιμῆσθαι αὐτοὺς ἐπίσταμαι, καὶ ταῦτα ποιῆσαι ὁμοίως, οὗ καὶ τοὺς λόγους πάντας μιμήσασθαι ἐπεχείρησαν· δικαιοπραξίας γὰρ λόγους καὶ παρ' ἐκείνους λέγεσθαι ἐτεχνάσαντο. If the passage of Tertullian remind us of Satan's power to pass through the world in a moment of time, these serve to recal to our recollection his boldness in mingling with the angels, even when presenting themselves to God (Job i. &c.). If he dared to be among them, much more would he venture into places where upon earth he might attain to a knowledge of God's designs for his purposes. Again, p. 308, he says: Εἶπε γὰρ ὅτι φονεύεσθαι καὶ μισεῖσθαι διὰ τὸ ὄνομα αὐτοῦ μέλλομεν, καὶ ὅτι ψευδοπροφῆται καὶ ψευδόχριστοι πολλοὶ ἐπὶ τῷ ὀνόματι αὐτοῦ παρελεύσονται, καὶ πολλοὺς πλανήσουσιν· ὅπερ καί ἐστι· πολλοὶ γὰρ ἄθεα καὶ βλάσφημα καὶ ἄδικα ἐν ὀνόματι αὐτοῦ παραχαράσσοντες ἐδίδαξαν, καὶ τὰ ἀπὸ τοῦ ἀκαθάρτου πνεύματος διαβόλου ἐμβαλλόμενα ταῖς διανοίαις αὐτῶν ἐδίδαξαν, καὶ διδάσκουσι μέχρι νῦν. Hence we see that St. Justin recognizes a parallel mode of acting upon the part of devils before and after Christ's coming, although we may notice with Molitor, iii. § 59, that Satan is spoken of in the Old Testament as having a much freer access to the court of Heaven than in the New Testament. S. Clem. Alex. Strom. lib. i. § 81, p. 366. Ναὶ φασὶν γεγράφθαι, πάντες οἱ πρὸ τῆς παρουσίας τοῦ Κυρίου κλέπται εἰσὶ καὶ λησταί· πάντες μὲν οὖν οἱ ἐν Λόγῳ, οὗτοι δὴ οἱ πρὸ τῆς τοῦ Λόγου σαρκώσεως, ἐξακούονται καθολικώτερον· ἀλλ' οἱ μὲν προφῆται, ἅτε ἀποσταλέντες καὶ ἐμπνευθέντες ὑπὸ τοῦ Κυρίου, οὐ κλέπται, ἀλλὰ διάκονοι. Φησὶ γοῦν ἡ γραφὴ, ἀπέστειλεν ἡ σοφία τοὺς ἑαυτῆς δούλους, συγκαλοῦσα μετὰ ὑψηλοῦ κηρύγματος ἐπὶ κρατῆρα οἴνου. (Prov. xi. 3.) Φιλοσοφία δὲ οὐκ ἀπεστάλη ὑπὸ Κυρίου, ἀλλ' ἦλθε, φησὶ, κλαπεῖσα, ἢ παρὰ κλέπτου δοθεῖσα· εἴτ' οὖν δύναμις ἢ ἄγγελος μαθών τι τῆς ἀληθείας, καὶ μὴ καταμείνας ἐν αὐτῇ, ταῦτα ἐνέπνευσε καὶ κλέψας ἐδίδαξε, οὐχὶ μὴ εἰδότος τοῦ Κυρίου τοῦ τὰ τέλη τῶν ἐσομένων πρὸ καταβολῆς τοῦ ἕκαστου εἶναι ἐγνωκότος, ἀλλὰ μὴ κωλύσαντος· εἶχεν γάρ τινα ὠφέλειαν τότε ἡ εἰς ἀνθρώπους ἐρχομένη κλοπὴ, οὐ τοῦ ὑφελομένου τὸ συμφέρον σκοπουμένου, κατευθυνούσης δὲ εἰς τὸ σύμφερον τῆς Προνοίας τὴν ἔκβασιν τοῦ τολμήματος[3]. Potter's note upon this place may be worth adding:—"Clemens superius memoravit nonnullos fuisse qui diabolum philosophiæ auctorem existimarent, Strom. i. § 18, p. 326. Putarent enim e veteribus non pauci, angelos malos, sive feminarum amore captos, sive ut homines in errores traherent, varias illis artes ac disciplinas revelasse. Tatianus Orat. ad Græc. pp. 28, 29. Ὑπόθεσις δὲ αὐτοῖς τῆς ἀποστασίας οἱ ἄνθρωποι γίνονται· διάγραμμα γὰρ αὐτοῖς ἀστροθεσίας ἀναδείξαντες, ὥσπερ οἱ τοῖς κύβοις παίζοντες, τὴν εἱμαρμένην εἰσηγήσαντο λίαν ἄδικον· Defectionis occasio ipsis et scopus sunt homines. Figuras enim positionis siderum hominibus ostendentes, tanquam in testarum ludo, fatum, rem prorsus iniquam, introduxerunt. Hermias philosophus, cum Tatiano editus, pp. 213, 214. Δοκεῖ γάρ μοι (σοφία) τὴν ἀρχὴν εἰληφέναι ἀπὸ τῆς τῶν ἀγγέλων ἀποστασίας. Videtur enim mihi sapientia ab angelorum defectione principium habuisse. Tertullianus, Apolog. cap. 35. Qui astrologos, et aruspices, et augures, et magos de Cæsarum capite consultant, quas artes ut ab angelis desertoribus proditas, et a Deo interdictas, ne suis quidem causis adhibent Christiani. Idem de Idololatr. cap. 9. Angelos esse illos desertores, amatores feminarum, proditores hujus curiositatis (astrologiæ) proinde quoque damnatos a Deo. Idem de Cultu Femin. lib. i. cap. 2. Nam et illi qui ea constituerunt damnati in pœnam mortis deputantur: illi scilicet angeli, qui ad filias hominum de cœlo ruerunt, ut hæc quoque ignominia feminæ accedat. Nam et cum materias quasdam bene occultas, et artes quasdam non bene revelatas, sæculo multo magis imperito prodidissent, (siquidem et metallorum opera nudaverant et herbarum ingenia traduxerant, et incantationum vires provulgaverant, et omnem curiosi-

[3] Compare what has been said above, p. 90. "First, the truth," &c.

tatem usque ad stellarum interpretationem designaverant,) proprie et quasi peculiariter feminis instrumentum istud muliebris gloriæ contulerunt lumina lapillorum quibus monilia variantur, et circulos ex auro, quibus brachia arctantur, et medicamenta ex fuco, quibus lanæ colorantur, et illum ipsum nigrum pulverem, quo oculorum exordia producuntur. Clemens postea, Strom. v. p. 650. Οἱ ἄγγελοι ἐκεῖνοι, οἱ τὸν ἄνω κλῆρον εἰληχότες, κατολισθήσαντες εἰς ἡδονὰς, ἐξεῖπον τὰ ἀπόῤῥητα ταῖς γύναιξιν, ὅσα τε εἰς γνῶσιν αὐτῶν ἀφῖκτο, κρυπτόντων τῶν ἄλλων ἀγγέλων, μᾶλλον δὲ τηρούντων εἰς τὴν τοῦ Κυρίου παρουσίαν. Conf. Strom. vi. p. 822. Pædag. lib. iii. c. 2. extremum, et quæ ibi adnotata sunt. Porro his aliisque hujusmodi opinionibus originem præbuisse videtur Enochi liber supposititius, qui Spicileg. Patrum, sec. 1, a Joan. Grabio editi p. 350, de quodum lapso angelo hæc continet: Ἐδίδαξε γὰρ τὰ μυστήρια, καὶ ἀπεκάλυψε τῷ αἰῶνι τὰ ἐν οὐρανῷ· ἐπιτηδεύουσι τὰ ἐπιτηδεύματα αὐτοῦ, εἰδέναι τὰ μυστήρια τολμῶσιν οἱ υἱοὶ τῶν ἀνθρώπων. Secreta palam fecit, et ista quæ in cœlis occlusa erant sæculo revelavit. Genium ejus student assequi, et arcana quæque perscrutari non verentur filii hominum." This passage, however, of the book of Enoch is, in part, in the ancient Æthiopic version (ix. 5), which, if a *liber supposititius*, certainly contained much ancient tradition, while the fact that the Fathers in general (i. e. the Holy Spirit in them possibly, as in St. Jude) recognized a certain part of it to contain divine teaching, is additional reason for reverencing such parts.

Origen c. Cels. lib. iii. p. 129. Ἐπεὶ δὲ μετὰ ταῦτα καὶ περὶ τοῦ Κλαζομενίου ὁ Κέλσος εἶπε, προσθεὶς ἐπὶ τῆς κατ' αὐτὸν ἱστορίας, "μῶν οὐ τοῦτό φασιν, ὡς ἄρα ἡ ψυχὴ αὐτοῦ πολλάκις ἀπολιποῦσα τὸ σῶμα περιεπολεῖ ἀσώματος; καὶ οὐδὲ τοῦτον ἐνόμισαν Θεὸν οἱ ἄνθρωποι·" καὶ πρὸς τοῦτο φήσομεν, ὅτι τάχα πονηροί τινες δαίμονες τοιαῦτα ᾠκονόμησαν ἀναγραφῆναι (οὐ γὰρ πιστεύω ὅτι καὶ γενέσθαι ᾠκονόμησαν)· ἵνα τὰ προφητευθέντα περὶ τοῦ Ἰησοῦ, καὶ τὰ λεχθέντα ὑπ' αὐτοῦ, ἤτοι ὡς πλάσματα ὅμοια ἐκείνοις διαβάλληται, ἢ ὡς οὐδὲν πλεῖον ἑτέρων ἔχοντα, μὴ πάνυ θαυμάζηται. And so again, ibid. lib. iv. p. 228. Εἰ δὲ ὑπὲρ τοῦ ἐξετάσαι τὰ Κέλσου τἀκόλουθον σκοποῦμεν, δῆλον ὅτι κατ' αὐτὸν ἱερώτεραι τῶν σεμνῶν Φερεκύδου, καὶ Πυθαγόρου, καὶ Σωκράτους, καὶ Πλάτωνος, καὶ τῶν φιλοσόφων ὁμιλιῶν εἰσιν αἱ τῶν ἀλόγων ζώων· ὅπερ ἐστὶ καὶ αὐτόθεν οὐ μόνον ἀπεμφαῖνον, ἀλλὰ καὶ ἀτοπώτατον· ἵνα δὲ καὶ πιστεύσωμεν, τινὰς ἐκ τῆς ἀσήμου φωνῆς τῶν ὀρνίθων μαθόντας ὅτι ἀπίασί ποι οἱ ὄρνιθες, καὶ ποιήσουσι τάδε ἢ τόδε, προδηλοῦν· καὶ τοῦτ' ἐροῦμεν ἀπὸ τῶν δαιμόνων συμβολικῶς ἀνθρώποις δεδηλῶσθαι, κατὰ σκοπὸν τὸν περὶ τοῦ ἀπατηθῆναι ὑπὸ τῶν δαιμόνων τὸν ἄνθρωπον, καὶ κατασπασθῆναι αὐτοῦ τὸν νοῦν ἀπ' οὐρανοῦ καὶ Θεοῦ ἐπὶ γῆν καὶ τὰ ἔτι κατωτέρω. It seems to have been a common plan with the Platonists afterwards to avail themselves of such incidents as those here alluded to, in order to show that they could produce a parallel to our Lord's history. This, then, might furnish a good instance of Satanic foresight.

St. Athanasius, de Incar. Verbi Dei, § 11. p. 56. Τοσοῦτον δὲ ἠσέβουν ὅτι καὶ δαίμονας ἐθρήσκευον λοιπὸν καὶ θεοὺς ἀνηγόρευον, τὰς ἐπιθυμίας αὐτῶν ἀποπληροῦντες· θυσίας τε γὰρ ζώων ἀλόγων, καὶ ἀνθρώπων σφαγὰς, ὥσπερ εἴρηται πρότερον, εἰς τὸ ἐκείνων καθῆκον ἐπετέλουν, πλεῖον ἑαυτοὺς τοῖς ἐκείνων οἰστρήμασι καταδεσμεύοντες. διὰ τοῦτο γοῦν καὶ μαγεῖαι παρ' αὐτοῖς ἐδιδάσκοντο, καὶ μαντεῖα κατὰ τόπον τοὺς ἀνθρώπους ἐπλάνα, καὶ πάντες τὰ γενέσεως, καὶ τοῦ εἶναι ἑαυτῶν τὰ αἴτια τοῖς ἄστροις καὶ τοῖς κατ' οὐρανὸν πᾶσιν ἀνετίθουν, μηδὲν πλέον τῶν φαινομένων λογιζόμενοι. καὶ ὅλως πάντα ἦν ἀσεβείας καὶ παρανομίας μεστὰ, καὶ μόνος ὁ Θεὸς οὐδὲ ὁ τούτου Λόγος ἐπεγινώσκετο, καίτοι οὐκ ἀφανῆ ἑαυτὸν τοῖς ἀνθρώποις ἐπικρύψας, οὐδὲ ἁπλῆν τὴν περὶ ἑαυτοῦ γνῶσιν αὐτοῖς δεδωκὼς, ἀλλὰ καὶ ποικίλως καὶ διὰ πολλῶν αὐτὴν αὐτοῖς ἐφαπλώσας.

Page 88, § 47. Καὶ πάλαι μὲν τὰ πανταχοῦ τῆς ἀπάτης τῶν μαντείων ἐπεπλήρωτο, καὶ τὰ ἐν Δελφοῖς, καὶ Δωδώνῃ, καὶ Βοιωτίᾳ, καὶ Λυκίᾳ, καὶ Λιβύῃ, καὶ Αἰγύπτῳ, καὶ Καβείροις, μαντεύματα καὶ ἡ Πυθία ἐθαυμάζοντο τῇ φαντασίᾳ τῶν ἀνθρώπων. νῦν δὲ ἀφ' οὗ Χριστὸς καταγγέλλεται πανταχοῦ, πέπαυται καὶ τούτων ἡ μανία, καὶ οὐκ ἔστιν ἔτι λοιπὸν ἐν αὐτοῖς ὁ μαντευόμενος. καὶ πάλαι μὲν δαίμονες ἐφαντασιοσκόπουν τοῖς ἀνθρώποις, προκαταλαμβάνοντες πηγὰς, ἢ ποταμοὺς, ἢ ξύλα, ἢ λίθους, καὶ οὕτω ταῖς μαγγανείαις ἐξέπληττον τοὺς ἄφρονας. νῦν δὲ τῆς θείας ἐπιφανείας τοῦ Λόγου γεγενημένης, πέπαυται τούτων ἡ φαντασία. τῷ γὰρ σημείῳ τοῦ σταυροῦ καὶ μόνον ὁ ἄνθρωπος χρώμενος, ἀπελαύνει τούτων τὰς ἀπάτας. καὶ πάλαι μὲν τοὺς παρὰ ποιηταῖς λεγομένους Δία καὶ Κρόνον καὶ Ἀπόλλωνα καὶ ἥρωας ἐνόμιζον οἱ ἄνθρωποι θεοὺς, καὶ τούτους ἐπλανῶντο σέβοντες· ἄρτι δὲ τοῦ Σωτῆρος ἐν ἀνθρώποις φανέντος, ἐκεῖνοι μὲν ἐγυμνώθησαν ὄντες ἄνθρωποι θνητοὶ, μόνος δὲ ὁ Χριστὸς ἐν ἀνθρώποις ἐγνωρίσθη Θεὸς ἀληθινὸς Θεοῦ Θεὸς Λόγος. Τί δὲ περὶ τῆς θαυμαζομένης παρ' αὐτοῖς μαγείας ἄν τις εἴποι; ὅτι πρὶν μὲν ἐπιδημῆσαι τὸν Λόγον, ἴσχυε καὶ ἐνήργει παρ' Αἰγυπτίοις καὶ Χαλδαίοις καὶ Ἰνδοῖς αὕτη, καὶ ἐξέπληττε τοὺς ὁρῶντας· τῇ δὲ παρουσίᾳ τῆς ἀληθείας, καὶ τῇ ἐπιφανείᾳ τοῦ Λόγου, διηλέγχθη καὶ αὕτη, καὶ κατηργήθη παντελῶς. And to this opinion thus expressed in his earlier work, he appears to allude in a later one, as follows: cont. Arianos, i. § 43, p. 447. Οὐκέτι δὲ μόνος ὁ Ἰσραὴλ, ἀλλὰ καὶ πάντα τὰ ἔθνη λοιπὸν, ὡς προείρηκεν ὁ προφήτης, τὰ μὲν εἴδωλα ἑαυτῶν καταλιμπάνουσι, τὸν δὲ ἀληθινὸν Θεὸν τὸν τοῦ Χριστοῦ πατέρα ἐπιγινώσκουσι, καὶ ἡ μὲν τῶν δαιμόνων φαντασία κατήργηται, μόνος δὲ ὁ ὄντως Θεὸς ἐν τῷ ὀνόματι τοῦ Κυρίου ἡμῶν Ἰησοῦ Χριστοῦ προσκυνεῖται.

St. Cyril of Alexandria, de Ador. p. 185, says, as the

reason why Christ bade the devils to hold their peace, even when they spoke the truth, was for our good. Τὸ γάρ τοι, he adds, *μὴ δεῖν τοῖς παρ' ἐκείνοις προσκεῖσθαι λόγοις, κἂν εἰ αὐτὴν ἐθέλοιεν ἀναφωνεῖν τὴν ἀλήθειαν, καὶ τὰ ἐναργῶς ἔτυμα λέγειν διὰ τοῦτο παιδευόμεθα. Ἀναπλέκοντες γὰρ ἔσθ' ὅτε τῇ ἀληθείᾳ τὸ ψεῦδος κατασίνονται τοὺς ἀκροωμένους, οὐ καθ' ἕτερον οἶμαι τρόπον ἢ καθ' ὃν θεῷτό τις τοὺς τῇ τοῦ μέλιτος μίξει παραιτουμένους τὴν αἴσθησιν τῶν πικρῶν, καὶ τῇ τῶν γλυκέων ἐπιπλοκῇ κατασυλᾶν ἐθέλοντας τὸ ἔσθ' ὅτε λυποῦν.* And again, p. 190 E, he lets us see how Satan promised oracles through the same channels in different ages of the world. . . . *εἶτα φησίν· Ἀνάγαγέ μοι τὸν Σαμουὴλ, οὐχ ὡς τῆς ἐπῳδῆς ἤτοι τῆς μάγων τέχνης τὴν τοῦ ἁγίου ψυχὴν παρενεγκεῖν δυναμένης, ἀλλ' ὡς ἀεὶ τῶν μαντευομένων τῇ τοιᾷδε κεχρημένων φωνῇ· ἐπυθόμην δὲ ὅτι λόγοις τισὶν ἀποῤῥήτοις καταγοητεύοντες τὰ δαιμόνια, καὶ ὕδατι κατεπᾴδοντες εἴδωλα καὶ σκιὰς καὶ ὡς ἐν ἐσόπτρῳ μορφὰς καταθεῶνταί τινων, τάχα που τῶν δαιμονίων καταπλαττομένων ἀστείως τὰ τῶν λεγομένων ἀποκομιεῖσθαι σχήματα.* And again, ibid. p. 322 A, he speaks of earthly wisdom as *ἐξ ἀνθρωπίνων ἐννοιῶν καὶ δαιμονιώδους ἐμπνοίας ἐξευρημένον.*

St. Ephr. ii. p. 478, speaking of the belief of certain heretics, that good angels went in to the daughters of men, says: "If the angels gendered children, then were it easy for devils at all times to commit whoredom with women and gender children. Lo! there are devils and women! consider of these, and see if they have had children. Let the virgins confute them, who, apart from men, have never borne children at any time. Mary alone it was that bore a Child without a man! for to God all things are easy. But if angels gendered children, no marvel then any more would be the virginity that bore our Saviour. For Satan, sure, would fain have had that virgins should conceive, that by a virgin he might make a semblance of the Virgin Mary. His fraud made semblances of every thing, ܐܦܩܗ ܠܟܠܐ ܕܡܘܬ. By virginity alone was he conquered, so as to be unable to counterfeit it." The stories of Mars being the father of Romulus and Remus, and other kindred lies, appear to be on St. Ephrem's mind here. Ibid. p. 533. "Errors as coin did the evil one strike out; and in all ages did he melt iniquity, and in all times did stamp fraud," &c.: and presently after, "These things did he introduce among the Greeks according to fit season, and other ones among the diverse nations, mischiefs suited to each generation: and among the Hebrews he mingled his own feasts with their feasts; among the priests, priests of Baal; and sacrifices amid sacrifices; amongst prophets, prophets of fraud." So, too, vol. iii. p. 92, after noticing again how Satan despoiled all generations, he gives us the clue to his mode of doing so, in the following awful words:—"Who would not be ashamed that his own soul is so foolish? that the evil one dwells within it, and it feeleth not his intimate access? He lets himself not be seen to the eye nor touched by the hand, neither is he to be tasted, that it should know that he is bitter, neither yet can he be smelt, that it should perceive that he is brimstone. Blessed be He that makes him to be without effect! The soul, then, perceiveth not the devil, though he dwells in it; yet does it not perceive his approach, nor his creeping up to it. And if he camp against it, yet doth it not find out his access; and if he be in its neighbourhood, or if even in its own self, the soul doth not perceive it. Let us bewail our having boldly scrutinized the Son of our Creator." This passage is quoted with a wish to make people consider, whether Satan's present mode of dealing with those he tempts, does not make it credible that he is, even after the Incarnation of our LORD, allowed a wonderful power of access to our souls, so as to be able to inspire them with bad thoughts even now. Neither do I think that any supernaturally accurate observance of external features, &c., will account for all his modes of tempting; since, when he finds a proposition in our minds, which we use as an argument against him, he raises up another to meet it, or endeavours to make us believe that this case is an exception. However, to proceed: we have here a witness from the great Syriac Father to the same doctrine which, as we have seen, was taught by St. Justin Martyr, Tertullian, and several of the Alexandrine Fathers, the most learned and acute writers of Christian antiquity. The same doctrine is also held by Pseudo-Basil in Es. § 218. Euseb. P. E. p. 161 c. p. 329 d. Cyril of Jerusalem, Catech. xv. 11. (quoted by Dr. Pusey on Tertullian, p. 55.) who mentions his counterfeits of the birth from a virgin; Jerome on Esai. xli. p. 158. Erasm. Methodius, Conv. Virg. x. 4 & 5. Aretas on the Apocalypse, p. 382, l. 21. p. 440, l. 28. The doctrine thus generally held is stated in several places by St. Augustine, who reviewed the teaching of earlier writers, and often systematized it, thus standing as a particularly Catholic writer. Some of these are the following:—

C. Faustum, lib. xx. c. 21. "Sed maledicendi cupiditate Faustus qui profiteretur, oblitus est; aut forte dormitans umbras somniando dictavit, nec cum verba sua legeret evigilavit. Populus autem Christianus memorias Martyrum religiosâ solemnitate concelebrat, et ad excitandam imitationem, et ut meritis eorum consocietur, atque orationibus adjuvetur; ita tamen ut nulli Martyrum, sed ipsi Deo Martyrum, quamvis in memoriis Martyrum, constituamus altaria. Quis enim antistitum in locis sanctorum corporum assistens altari aliquando dixit, Offerimus tibi, Petre, aut Paule, aut Cypriane? sed quod offertur, offertur Deo, qui Martyres coronavit, apud memorias eorum quos coronavit; ut ex ipsorum locorum admonitione affectus major exsurgat, ad acuendam caritatem, et in illos quos imitari possumus, et in Illum quo adjuvante possumus. Colimus ergo Martyres eo cultu dilectionis et societatis, quo et in hac vitâ coluntur sancti homines Dei, quorum cor ad talem pro evangelicâ veritate passionem paratum esse sentimus. Sed illos tanto devotius, quanto securius post certamina superata; quanto etiam fidentiore laude prædicamus, jam in vitâ feliciore victores, quam in istâ adhuc usque pugnantes. At illo cultu, quæ Græce λατρεία dicitur, Latine uno verbo dici non potest, cum sit quædam proprie Divinitati debita servitus, nec colimus, nec colendum docemus, nisi unum Deum. Cum autem ad hunc cultum pertineat oblatio sacrificii, unde idololatria dicitur eorum, qui hoc etiam idolis exhibent; nullo modo tale aliquid offerimus, aut offerendum præcipimus, vel cuiquam martyri, vel cuiquam sanctæ animæ, vel cuiquam angelo; et quisquis in hunc errorem delabitur, corripitur per sanam doctrinam, sive ut corrigatur sive ut caveatur. Etiam ipsi enim sancti, vel homines vel angeli, exhiberi sibi nolunt, quod uni Deo deberi norunt. Apparuit hoc in Paulo et Barnaba, cum commoti miraculis quæ per eos factæ sunt Lycaonii, tamquam diis immolare voluerunt; conscissis enim vestimentis suis, confitentes et persuadentes se Deos non esse, istoc sibi fieri vetuerunt. Apparuit et in angelis, sicut in Apocalypsi legimus, angelum se adorari prohibentem, et dicentem adoratori suo, Conservus tuus sum, et fratrum tuorum. Ista sibi plane superbi spiritus exigunt, diabolus et angeli ejus, sicut per omnia templa et sacra gentilium. Quorum similitudo in quibusdam etiam hominibus superbis expressa est; sicut de Babyloniæ quibusdam regibus memoriæ commendatum tenemus. Unde Sanctus Daniel accusatores et persecutores pertulit, quod regis edicto proposito, ut nihil a quoquam deo peteretur nisi a rege solo, Deum suum, hoc est unum et verum Deum, adorare deprecarique deprehensus est. Qui autem se in memoriis Martyrum inebriant, quomodo a nobis approbari possunt, cum eos, etiam si in domibus suis id faciant, sana doctrina condemnet? Sed aliud est quod docemus, aliud quod sustinemus, aliud quod præcipere jubemur, aliud quod emendare præcipimur, et donec emendemus, tolerare compellimur. Alia est disciplina Christianorum, alia luxuria vinolentorum, vel error infirmorum, veruntamen et in hoc ipso distant plurimum culpæ vinolentorum, et sacrilegorum. Longe quippe minoris peccati est, ebrium redire a Martyribus, quam vel jejunum sacrificare Martyribus. Sacrificare Martyribus, dixi; non dixi sacrificare Deo in memoriis Martyrum; quod frequentissimè facimus, illo duntaxat ritu, quo sibi sacrificari Novi Testamenti manifestatione præcepit; quod pertinet ad illum cultum, quæ *latria* dicitur, et uni Deo debetur. Sed quid agam, et tantæ cæcitati istorum hæreticorum quando demonstrabo, quam vim habeat quod in Psalmis canitur, Sacrificium laudis glorificabit me, et illic via est, ubi ostendam illi salutare meum? Hujus sacrificii caro et sanguis ante adventum Christi per victimas similitudinum promittebatur; in passione Christi per ipsam veritatem reddebatur; post adscensum Christi per sacramentum memoriæ celebratur; ac per hoc tantum interest inter sacrificia Paganorum et Hebæorum, quantum inter imitationem errantem, et præfigurationem prænuntiantem. Sicut autem non ideo contemnenda vel detestanda est virginitas sanctimonialium, quia et Vestales virgines fuerunt; sic non ideo reprehendenda sacrificia Patrum, quia sunt et sacrificia gentium! quia sicut inter illas virginitates multum distat, quamvis nihil aliud distet, nisi quæ cui voveatur atque reddatur; sic inter sacrificia Paganorum et Hebræorum multum distat, eo ipso, quod hoc solum distat, quæ cui sint immolata et oblata; illa scilicet superbæ impietati dæmoniorum id ipsum sibi ob hoc arrogantium, quo haberentur dii, quia divinus honor est sacrificium; illa vero uni Deo, ut ei offerretur similitudo promittens veritatem sacrificii, cui erat offerenda ipsa reddita veritas in passione corporis et sanguinis Christi."

Austin, contr. Faustum, lib. xxii. c. 17. "De sacrificiis vero nihil aliud mihi Paganus objiceret, nisi cur apud eos illa reprehendamus, cum in nostris libris veteribus talia sibi Deus noster jussisse legeretur offerri. Hic ego de verò sacrificio latius fortasse disserens, demonstrarem id non deberi nisi uni vero Deo, quod ei unus verus Sacerdos obtulit, Mediator Dei et hominum; cujus sacrificii promissivas figuras in victimis animalium celebrari oportebat, propter commendationem futuræ carnis et sanguinis per quam unam victimam fieret remissio peccatorum de carne et sanguine contractorum; quæ regnum Dei non possidebunt, quia eadem substantia corporis in cœlestem commutabitur qualitatem; quod ignis in sacrificio significabat, velut absorbens mortem in victoriam. In eo autem populo hæc rite celebrata sunt, cujus et regnum et sacerdotium prophetia erat venturi Regis et sacerdotis ad regendos et consecrandos fideles in omnibus gentibus, et introducendos in regnum cœlorum et sacrarium angelorum ac vitam æternam. Hujus itaque veri sacrificii sicut religiosa prædicamenta Hebræi celebraverunt, itā sacrilega incitamenta Pagani; quoniam quæ immolant gentes, ait Apostolus, dæmoniis immolant, et non Deo. Antiqua enim res est prænuntiativa immolatio sanguinis, futuram passionem Mediatoris ab initio generis humani testificans; hanc enim primus Abel obtulisse, in sacris literis invenitur. Non igitur mirum est, si prævaricatores angeli, quorum duo maxima vitia sunt superbia atque fallacia, per hunc aërem volitantes, quod uni vero Deo deberi noverant, hoc sibi a suis cultoribus exegerunt, a quibus Dii putari voluerunt, dante sibi locum vanitate cordis humani: maxime cum ex desiderio mortuorum constituerentur imagines, unde simulacrorum usus exortus est; et majore adulatione divini honores deferrentur tamquam in cœlis receptis, pro quibus se in terris dæmonia colenda supponerent; et sibi sacrificari à deceptis et perditis flagitarent. Sacrificium ergo non solum cum juste imperat verus Deus, sed etiam cum superbe exigit falsus deus, satis ostendit cui debeatur."

St. Aust. De Trinitate, lib. iv. 13. "Quia enim non pervenerat diabolus quo ipse perduxerat, (mortem quippe spiritus in impietate gestabat, sed mortem carnis non subierat, quia nec indumentum susceperat) magnus homini videbatur princeps in legionibus dæmonum, per quos fallaciarum regnum exercet, sic hominem per elationis typhum, potentiæ quam justitiæ cupidiorem, aut per falsam philosophiam magis inflans; aut per sacra sacrilega irretiens, in quibus etiam magicæ fallaciæ curiosiores superbioresque animas deceptas illusasque præcipitans, subditum tenet; pollicens etiam purgationem animæ, per eas quas τελετὰς appellant, transfigurando se in angelum lucis per multiformem machinationem in signis et prodigiis mendacii. Facile est enim spiritibus nequissimis per aërea corpora facere multa, quæ mirentur animæ terrenis corporibus aggravatæ, etiam melioris affectûs. Si enim corpora ipsa terrena nonnullis artibus et exercitationibus modificata, in spectaculis theatricis tanta miracula hominibus exhibent, ut ii qui nunquam viderunt talia, narrata vix credant, quid magnum est diabolo et angelis ejus, de corporeis elementis per aërea corpora facere quæ caro miretur; aut etiam occultis inspirationibus ad illudendos humanos sensus phantasmata imaginum machinari, quibus vigilantes dormientesve decipiat, vel furentes exagitet? Sed sicut fieri potest ut homo vitâ ac moribus melior, spectet nequissimos homines, vel in fune ambulantes, vel multimodis motibus corporum multa incredibilia facientes, nec ullo modo facere talia concupiscat, nec eos propterea sibi præponendos existimet; sic anima fidelis et pia, non solum si videat, verum etiam si propter fragilitatem carnis exhorreat miracula dæmonum, non ideo tamen aut non se posse talia dolebit, aut ob hoc illos meliores esse judicabit, cum sit præsertim in societate sanctorum, qui per virtutem Dei cui cuncta subjecta sunt, et minime fallacia, et multo majora fecerunt, sive homines, sive angeli boni. Nequaquam igitur per sacrilegas similitudines et impias curiositates et magicas consecrationes animæ purgantur et reconciliantur Deo; quia falsus mediator non trajecit ad superiora, sed potius obsidens intercludit viam per affectus, quos tanto maligniores, quanto superbiores, suæ societati inspirat; qui non possunt ad evolandum pennas nutrire virtutum, sed potius ad demergendum pondera exaggerare vitiorum, tanto gravius animâ ruiturâ, quanto sibi videtur evecta sublimius." To this may be subjoined a passage which, though it in part only applies to the present subject, yet also contains much which bears upon other matters treated of in these dialogues. It occurs in lib. xii. § 24, of the same treatise. "Plato ille philosophus nobilis persuadere conatus est vixisse hic animas hominum, et antequam ista[4] corpora gererent; et hinc esse quod ea quæ discuntur reminiscuntur potius cognita, quam cognoscuntur nova. Retulit enim puerum quendam, nescio quæ de geometricâ interrogatum, sic respondisse tanquam esset illius peritissimus disciplinæ. Gradatim quippe atque artificiose interrogatus, videbat quod videndum erat, dicebatque quod viderat. Sed si recordatio hæc esset rerum antea cognitarum; non utique omnes vel pene omnes, cum illo modo interrogarentur, hoc possent. Non enim omnes in priore vitæ geometræ fuerunt, cum tam rari sint in genere humano ut vix possit

[4] I may notice here, what I ought to have noticed before, that in ecclesiastical Latin, borrowed perhaps, as it was, from the poor who had the Gospel preached to them, *iste* is used for *hic*; as, Dignare, Domine, die *isto* sine peccato nos custodire.

aliquis inveniri; sed potius credendum est mentis intellectualis ita conditam esse naturam, ut rebus intelligibilibus, naturali ordine, disponente Conditore, subjuncta sic ista videat in quadam luce sui generis incorporeâ, quemadmodum oculus carnis videt quæ in hâc corporeâ luce circumadjacent, cujus lucis capax eique congruens est creatus. Non enim et ipse ideo sine magistro alba et nigra discernit quia ista jam noverat, antequam in hac carne crearetur. Denique cur de solis rebus intelligibilibus id fieri potest, ut bene interrogatus quisque respondeat quod ad quamque pertinet disciplinam, etiamsi ejus ignarus est? Cur hoc facere de rebus sensibilibus nullus potest, nisi quas isto vidit in corpore constitutus, aut iis quæ noverant indicantibus credidit, seu literis cujusque seu verbis. Non enim adquiescendum est iis qui Samium Pythagoram recordatum fuisse ferunt talia nonnulla quæ fuerat expertus, cum hic alio jam fuisset in corpore; et alios nonnullos narrant alii ejusmodi aliquid in suis mentibus passos; quas falsas fuisse memorias, quales plerumque experimur in somniis quando nobis videmur reminisci, quasi egerimus aut viderimus quod nec egimus omnino nec vidimus; et eo modo affectas esse illorum mentes etiam vigilantium, instinctu spirituum malignorum atque fallacium (quibus curæ est de revolutionibus animarum falsam opinionem ad decipiendos homines firmare vel serere) ex hoc conjici potest, quia si vere illa recordarentur quæ hic in aliis antea positi corporibus viderant, multis ac pene omnibus id contingeret, quandoquidem ut de vivis mortuos, ita de mortuis vivos, tanquam de vigilantibus dormientes, et de dormientibus vigilantes sine cessatione fieri suspicantur[5]."

So, again, the same great writer speaks (as St. Clemens

[5] The fact that magnetized persons pretend to such reminiscences is a ground, not for unbelief in what really happens to such persons, but for "trying the spirits" who so influence them.

does) of their philosophers as follows: xiii. § 24. "Illi præcipui gentium philosophi, qui invisibilia Dei per ea quæ facta sunt intellecta, conspicere potuerunt, tamen quia sine Mediatore, id est, sine homine Christŏ, philosophati sunt, quem nec venturum Prophetis, nec venisse Apostolis crediderunt, veritatem detinuerunt, sicut de illis dictum est, in iniquitate. Non potuerunt enim in his rerum infimis constituti nisi quærere aliqua media per quæ ad illa quæ intellexerant sublimia pervenirent, atque ita in deceptores dæmones inciderunt, per quos factum est ut immutarent gloriam incorruptibilis Dei in similitudinem imaginis corruptibilis hominis, et volucrum, et quadrupedum, et serpentium. In talibus enim formis etiam idola instituerunt sive coluerunt."

Such, then, is the concurrent testimony of the Fathers to the doctrine that all the gods of the Gentiles were demons; and that these beings revealed to men resemblances of the truth, with a view, by such anticipations of it, to keep them from the truth. It follows from this, that no external resemblances to any part whatever of the Catholic system, form any kind of presumption against that *system*, seeing that such anticipations of *parts* of it are, upon this theory, to be expected. And in regard to the credibility of the theory itself, the proper question for serious people to ask themselves, before rejecting it, seems to be the same as in other cases of concordant testimony of the Fathers—whether or no they believe the Holy Spirit in any sense to guide the Church into all truth; and if they do, whether they can refuse to believe that He does so guide her in cases of universal consent: or whether they will run the *risk* of blasphemy against Him by making light of what, perchance, He has guided the Church to. It does seem that if Christians will not fearlessly and uncompromisingly ask themselves these questions, they are coming before God, as revealing His will in His word, with their own idols in their hearts; and one cannot be surprised if He will not be at all inquired of by them. For opinions, self-chosen and without submission to the Church, are as much idols as solid things are: there is no worshipping of God, save as she teaches; all others worship idols, i. e. creations of their own heart. The Mohammedans do not worship the same God as the Church does; and others who affect an abhorrence of idols may, we know, commit sacrilege. Upon this ground it may be that idolatry was looked upon of old as the type of heresy, and the threats of Scripture against the former to be now-a-days applicable to the latter.

In conclusion, it may be proper to add, that the power of Satan and his angels extends of course only so far as God permits it. The claim to have all the kingdoms of the world, and the glory of them, is a lie of his, which he endeavoured to use against the Truth Himself, before he knew to Whom he was speaking. His dealing with the Son of Man does, however, confirm the doctrine that has been here stated, and show (what is very fearful) that he has an intimate acquaintance with Holy Writ; for he was able to quote it with an adroitness which (as has been observed of St. Paul in regard to heathen authors) shows that he did not possess a mere chance knowledge of it. His omission of the context of Psalm xci. 12—14, in the Temptation, also seems a type of his way of teaching doctrine by parts only, so that it amounted to error at last.

Of course it should be carefully remembered, then, that Satan could have no power, unless by permission from above; and therefore it must not be assumed that the Fathers meant to teach that the world was governed by demons, which is indeed a lie that the father of lies uttered to our Lord, (St. Luke iv. 6.) but is often contradicted by those writers. See S. Irenæus v. 21, § 2. 22, § 2, &c. S. Aust. Civ. D.

libb. vi. viii. S. Cyril. c. Jul. p. 124. Indeed the reader will have perceived that they have in some of the passages quoted guarded themselves against such a misrepresentation, as also that they do not contemplate the rites, &c., so far as they were witnesses to what was good to good men, but so far as they were a cunningly devised scheme to anticipate, and so make men satisfied while rejecting the teaching of the Church.

Note (23.) p. 153.

See above on Dial. i. Notes 27 and 28.

Note (24.) p. 154.

Orig. c. Cels. p. 377. *Φαύλους δὲ δαίμονας οὐ μόνοι λέγομεν ἡμᾶς, ἀλλὰ καὶ σχεδὸν πάντες ὅσοι δαίμονας τιθέασιν εἶναι.* See Berkeley, Min. Philos. vi. § 12. Phocylides ap. Clem. Strom. v. § 128, p. 726.

Note (25.) p. 154.

Wind. p. 1931. "Das Dharma ist ihm (dem Kanada,) der Inbegriff von heiligen Gesetzen, Gebräuchen, und Uebungen, wodurch Brahma-erkentniss erreicht und das Böse für immer entfernt wird. Dies aber kann nicht geschehn ohne festen Glauben an etwas besseres als Menschenzeugniss, an den Veda, der göttlichen Ursprungs und die Rechtschnur (Sastra) des Lebens ist."

Note (26.) p. 154.

Ibid. p. 1896. "Beide Schule halten," &c.

Note (27.) p. 154.

This is taken from St. Ephr. adv. Scrut. p. 107. The passage may be given at length :—" Who hath searched out his soul, and touched it ever with his hand, how and where it culls and lays up in itself its harvest of knowledge, supplying by repetition books which are in its heart, gathering by recollection, multiplying by reflection, minishing by remitted exertion? for in all these there is a wonder, and musings on Thy Majesty. Who is there that can enter into it, and understand how that place sufficeth for so much knowledge, and yet the soul lacketh? And is there any wonder at all greater than the memory that taketh in, yet filleth not, that giveth and yet lacketh not? in the heart there is every thing, while yet there is nothing in it. Who can gaze upon the brightness of the memory, which is a shadow of the Creator, who cannot be comprehended, what He is? It taketh in without trouble the names of the creatures, and though there be no space in it, yet for every thing is there space in it. And how doth it by the names contain all things, while its strength weareth not out? Who can enter into the midst of the memory, and feel where they are, those names of the creatures, since neither it nor they are to be felt? in the mind and in the Essence they wholly dwell. Thus in the Very Father is the Very Son, while neither He nor they may be felt [to know] where they are."

NOTE (28.) p. 155.

Aristot. Topic. viii. 14. p. 163. b 29. Ἐν τῷ μνημονικῷ νόμον οἱ τόποι τεθέντες εὐθὺς ποιοῦσι μνημονεύειν.

NOTE (29.) p. 155.

Aristot. Polit. viii. 4. Τοὐναντίον ἑκάτερος ἀπεργάζεσθαι πέφυκε τῶν πόνων, ἐμποδίζων ὁ μὲν τοῦ σώματος πόνος τὴν διάνοιαν, ὁ δὲ ταύτης τὸ σῶμα. That this was Aristotle's own case we learn from Censorinus de D. N. cap. xiv. extr., who expresses his surprise that, suffering as he did from continual indigestion, he should yet have done so much. Origen's language, c. Cels. p. 393, may be added to this: Ἢ ἑορτάζων τις τῷ πνεύματι κακοῖ τὸ σῶμα, μὴ πεφυκὸς διὰ φρόνημα τῆς σαρκὸς ἑορτάζειν μετὰ τοῦ πνεύματος· ἢ ἑορτάζων κατὰ σάρκα, οὐ χωρεῖ καὶ τὴν κατὰ πνεῦμα ἑορτήν.

Note (30.) p. 156.

It may be as well to suggest to persons unacquainted with chemistry, that the cases in which fuel of any kind, or other matters, are converted apparently or really into air, are not cases in which the substances used are destroyed; for air is ponderable, and may in some instances be made to surrender up again the substances combined with it. Whether, indeed, ponderable matter may, under any circumstances, be converted into imponderable or radiant matter, is (I am kindly informed by an experienced chemist whom I have consulted upon this subject) a question that may be entertained, yet could not affect the statement in the text, whichever way it was decided; for imponderable matter would still continue to be matter.

Note (31.) p. 158.

Justin Martyr, p. 267. Οἷς οὐ συντίθεμαι· . . . ἐπειδὴ οὐκ ἀνθρωπείοις διδάγμασι κεκελεύσμεθα ὑπ' αὐτοῦ τοῦ Χριστοῦ πείθεσθαι, ἀλλὰ τοῖς διὰ τῶν μακαρίων προφητῶν κηρυχθεῖσι καὶ τοῖς δι' Αὐτοῦ διδαχθεῖσιν.

Note (32.) p. 159.

On the bearing of the Mosaic code upon polytheism, whether as formally developed by the servants of Satan in earlier times, or as subsequently adopted in an unconscious way by heretics, the reader may be referred to St. Athanas.

c. Arian. iii. 8. Εἶπε τοσαῦτα (after quoting Deut. vi. 4. xxxii. 39, &c.) οὐκ εἰς ἀναίρεσιν τοῦ Υἱοῦ, οὐδὲ δι' αὐτόν ἐστι τὰ τοιαῦτα ῥητά· ἀλλ' εἰς ἀθέτησιν τοῦ ψεύδους. Ἐξ ἀρχῆς γοῦν ὁ Θεὸς οὐκ εἶπε τῷ Ἀδὰμ τὰς τοιαύτας φωνὰς, καίτοι ὄντος τοῦ Λόγου σὺν αὐτῷ, δι' οὗ τὰ πάντα ἐγένετο· οὐ γὰρ ἦν χρεία μήπω γενομένων εἰδώλων, κ. τ. λ.

Note (33.) p. 159.

Colebrooke, Ess. i. p. 196. "Five great sects exclusively worship a single deity: one recognizes the five divinities which are adored by the other sects respectively, but the followers of this comprehensive scheme mostly select one object of daily devotion, and pay adoration to other deities on particular occasions only. Even they deny the charge of polytheism, and repel the imputation of idolatry. They justify the practice of adoring the images of celestial spirits, by arguments similar to those which have been elsewhere employed in defence of angel and image worship." Possibly Colebrooke takes rather an external view of things here, seeing the Church early recognized the distinction between λατρεία and other worship. See St. Austin, as quoted above, p. 214, and de Trin. i. § 13, in Ps. cxxxv. § 3.

Note (34.) p. 159.

The traditions of a purer or golden age, so common in the world, cannot be looked upon as *mere* witnesses to the fall of man, as something past. For had there been nothing in the continual declension of manners to keep up the tradition by falling in with it, man's pride would surely have forgotten it. Homer's words attest this belief:

Παῦροι γάρ τοι παῖδες ὁμοῖοι πατρὶ πέλονται·
Οἱ πλέονες κακίους· παῦροι δέ τε πατρὸς ἀρείους.

Odyss. ii. 275.

as do those of Aratus, Phæn. 135.

Οὐδ' ἔτ', ἔφη [ἡ Δίκη], εἰσωπὸς, ἐλεύσεσθαι καλέουσι·
Οἵην χρύσειοι πατέρες γενεὴν ἐλίποντο
Χειροτέρην, ὑμεῖς δὲ κακώτερά τ' ἐξείεσθε.
Καὶ δή κου πύλεμοι καὶ δὴ καὶ ἀνάρσιον ἅμα
Ἔσσατ' ἐν ἀνθρώποισι· κακοῦ δ' ἐπικείσεται ἄλγος.

and Horace, Od. iii. vi. 46, on which place Döring quotes these passages, attesting a belief in a degeneracy.

Note (35.) p. 159.

Herodotus (i. 131) tells us of the Persians and (iv. 59) of the Scythians, that they had neither images (ἀγάλματα) nor altars to the gods: the same Varro (ap. Aug. Civ. D. iv. 9) assures us was the case with the Romans in early times, as Bardesanes (ap. Eus. P. E, p. 274. d., 275. b.) does of the ancient Seres and Brahmans; and Euseb. (p. 29. d.) thinks it was the case with most ancient nations. Tacitus (Germ. c. 9) mentions the same of the ancient Germans, as does Windisch. (p. 348) of the Chinese; and Carli Rubbi (xi. p. 171) remarks of the Americans what will apply to other nations: "La superstitione si modificò in proportione che la dottrina teologica si corruppe. Le rappresentazione della Divinità si multiplicarono. Queste divennero altrettanti oggetti di adorazione. Così i tempj, gli oratorj, e le piramidi, si propagarono in onore degli Dei particolari o penate." See also Cyril. c. Jul. p. 193, and Menard on Diog. Laert. ii. p. 159, ed. Hübner.

Note (36.) p. 159.

See St. Luke xviii. 8. For a description of the Kaliyúga, or last age, see the Vish. Purana, bk. vi. ch. 1. The following is a part of it:—"The laws that regulate the conduct of husband and wife will be disregarded, and oblations to the gods with fire no longer be offered. In whatever family he may be born, a powerful and rich man will be held entitled to espouse maidens of every tribe. A regenerate man will be initiated in any way whatever, and such acts of penance as may be performed will be unattended with any results. Every text will be Scripture that people choose to think so; all gods will be gods to them that worship them, and all orders of life will be common alike to all persons. In the Káli age, fasting, austerity, liberality, practised according to the pleasure of those by whom they are observed, will constitute righteousness," &c. The lawlessness of the last times contemplated in Scripture is here also spoken of, as by Aratus, Phænom., as just quoted.

Note (37.) p. 160.

See 1 Cor. x. 20. Ps. xvi. 5, &c. St. Austin in Ps. cxxxv. 3, upon those words of the Septuagint, Ps. xcv. 4, "Dii Gentium dæmonia," thus observes: "Hoc quidem in Hebræo dicitur non ita esse scriptum, sed, 'Dii Gentium simulacra.' Quod si verum est, multo magis credendi sunt Septuaginta Divino Spiritu interpretati, quo Spiritu et illa dicta sunt quæ in Hebræis literis sunt: eodem namque operante Spiritu etiam hoc dici oportuit quod dictum est: 'Dii Gentium dæmonia,' ut intelligeremus sic in Hebræo positum, 'Dii Gentium simulacra,' ut dæmonia potius quæ sunt in simulacris significarentur. Nam quod attinet ad ipsa simulacra quæ Græce appellantur idola . . . ait Apostolus, 'Scimus quia nihil est idolum;' hoc enim retulit ad materiam terrenam sensu carentem. Item ne quisquam putaret non esse aliquem viventem sentientemque naturam, quæ Gentium sacrificiis delectetur, adjunxit, 'Sed quæ immolant Gentes, dæmoniis immolant et non Deo. Nolo enim vos socios fieri dæmoniorum.'"

Note (38.) p. 160.

St. Austin in Ps. cxiii. En. ii. § 5. "Quis autem adorat, vel orat intuens simulacrum, qui non sic afficitur, ut ab eo se exaudiri putet, ab eo sibi præstari quod desiderat speret? Itaque homines, talibus *superstitionibus obligati*, plerumque ad ipsum solem," &c.: and in § 6, "Plus simulacra valent ad *curvandam infelicem animam*, quod os habent, oculos habent," &c.

Note (39.) p. 163.

In Wilson's Theatre of the Hindus, i. p. 293.

Note (40.) p. 163.

See Bopp's Nalus, p. 11.

Note (41.) p. 164.

It may be as well to make a few remarks upon the text here, in order to secure it against mistakes that possibly may arise from it.

1. Moral *laws* are here spoken of as mutable, only in the sense in which they are expressions of a moral law which cannot be wholly enunciated in words. Thus when St. Paul says that all the special commandments are "briefly comprehended in this saying, Thou shalt love thy neighbour as thyself," the former (viz. the special commandments, "Thou shalt not kill," &c.) are what are here meant by moral laws: the latter is a close approximation to what is meant by *a* moral law. Now it may be made a question whether this moral law is dependent upon the mere will of the Almighty, or whether there is an eternal, *immutable* fitness in it; and the reason why I wished to avoid entering into this question in the text is, because it appears to me to partake, in one light at least, of the temper of that insolent remark made by Aristotle's pupil, Agatho—viz. that "God cannot

undo what is once done." As if, where there is Omniscience to foresee, and Omnipotence to prevent withal, it were by any means possible that He could wish a thing undone! And in a like way, if there be a law written on our consciences, which has no appearance of having changed, to what purpose is it to inquire whether such a decree of God can be undecreed by Him? Surely He foreknew the consequences of such His unchanged decree, and does reward or punish, and has ever done so, those who abide by or depart from it. The very notion of a law, in this view of it, implies subjection and creatureship. And to suppose any immutable thing which bound God to act so and so, and not otherwise, would be to suppose Him to give up His attributes as Creator. This, indeed, He did at the Incarnation, yet so as that He became obedient to the Law only so far forth as He was man. See St. Cyril Al. c. Nest. ii. p. 40. b.

But if by moral law is meant, not a decree which renders it obligatory on creatures to act so and so, and not otherwise, but an attribute of God displaying itself to us and in us, as Christ is said to be made unto us righteousness and sanctification and the like, then this Moral Law[7] *is* Christ, and so immutable. This is that Law of which the Psalmist saith that it converteth the soul, that Law which is the Truth, and so the Way and the Life. To discuss whether it is mutable would be the same with discussing whether God Himself is mutable. If God maketh a decree no otherwise than by His Word, we ought to consider how weak our conceptions are at best concerning His Word who is God, before we pry overmuch into His Word, as He is Law.

It may suffice thus to have touched upon this in-

[7] It is worth observing that a personality was commonly attributed to Law or Duty in the East. See Tholuck, Speculative Trinitats-Lehre, p. 43.

tricate question, which cannot be fully treated without going into the doctrine of Ἰδέαι. Enough, however, has been said to show what is meant by speaking of the further question, whether moral law is dependent upon arbitrary will.

But besides this question, which deals obviously with law in a high and transcendental sense, there is another question far more important to the present subject, which is, whether the laws—i. e. the expressions into which the Moral Law is thrown in order to its being audible to us, so to speak—admit of change. And this they cannot be said to do in the natural course of things; in a supernatural one (that is, one in which God discloses His will in regard to individual acts) they are mutable. Thus, if love be the fulfilling of the Law, and we are not judges, from partial knowledge, what *is* our neighbour's greatest good, then Divine knowledge may reveal what this is, though He do not show us *how* it is the greatest good. It may be a good to a reprobate to be cut off in his sins, if his further continuance in this state of probation would only entail upon him greater punishment in the next world. The knowledge of the whole of the case may constitute an act moral, which in ordinary cases were not so. It would not be moral in a parent to kill his son, or a host his guest; but God, who may take away life when He wills, and does take it away in many cases by rules of which we are entirely ignorant, may command any person to do so, and therefore may command a father to do so, as He did Abraham; or a host to kill a guest, as He did Jael, whom His prophetess would else not have praised. So, again, to tell a lie is immoral; yet we often are obliged to say things to those to whom we do say them, in the hearing of those to whom we do not say them, and to which last they convey a false impression. Hence, if we suppose the cloud of witnesses, of saints and angels, present, when the saints of old were commissioned to teach things to these principalities and powers in heavenly places, it may have been for these last, and not for man, that they were speaking; and this must necessarily make a great difference in those actions of Abraham, Isaac, and Jacob, for instance, which at first sight appear to result from want of faith. Saints in all ages have been "as deceivers, and yet true;" men of the world "daily mistake their words," because they live not in the same world of angels *and* men in which the saints do live. To take an illustration from revelation itself: men of letters are at great pains to defend, even if they do not recklessly pronounce spurious, whole passages of holy writ, because not historically accurate: but if (not historical accuracy, but) the grouping of events, *real* in themselves, in such way as may best typify things to come (see p. 74), was the object of the authors, then the events, unseen except by faith, in this case as in that, alter the character of the act of the writer or agent. What I am contending for is, that it is more credible that great saints of old were inspired, under a supernatural system, to do typical actions, which without sufficient thought appear unsaintly, than that Scripture should have pandered to men's captiousness, in giving evidence of its own honesty, by recounting their failings.

I would not, however, be misunderstood to imply that the moral lessons to be drawn from the appearance of failings in the old saints were not *intended:* I think their actions might be intentionally so framed as to teach moral lessons to those who went no deeper, but to have far sweeter and deeper teaching for those who, not finding it in them to think aught amiss of the saints of God, believe that it was of the Lord that Samson sought a Gentile spouse, and Sarah drove out her which should be in bondage with her children—believe that the outward violations of the moral law in the saints were obedience and love, when looked at from within. Is the love and awe of God in the saints now-a-days never mistaken for mere prudence or politeness, or some other low worldly principle? Happy they whose delight (as their Master's was) is in the saints that are upon the earth, and such as excel in virtue; for by so delighting in them, they at times see the fulfilling of their Master's Law converting the soul; while others have but the gloomy sight of slavery to the world. Happy they who have opportunities of learning from the world's treatment of holy men now, to amend their own opinion of the old saints, and see the deeper view of their conduct, according to which they were obeying, not written laws, but Christ, who is the Law, as He is the Way, the Truth, and the Life.

The reader may find the distinction between moral and positive laws drawn out by Bishop Butler, Analogy, part ii. chap. i., and between the injunction of acts and that of habits in part ii. chap. iii. Upon the subject of man's obligation to obey the voice of conscience, considered as the pulse (so to speak) indicative of the Divine Will, he will find very valuable remarks in Bishop Berkley's Sermon on Passive Obedience, § viii. &c.

Note (42.) p. 164.

Aristot. Eth. Nic. v. 10, p. 1134. b. 25 . . . τὸ μὲν φύσει ἀκίνητον καὶ πανταχοῦ τὴν αὐτὴν ἔχει δύναμιν, ὥσπερ τὸ πῦρ καὶ ἐνθάδε καὶ ἐν Πέρσαις καίει· τὰ δὲ δίκαια κινούμενα ὁρῶσιν· τοῦτο δὲ οὐκ ἔστιν οὕτως ἔχον, ἀλλ' ἔστιν ὥς· καίτοι παρά γε τοῖς θεοῖς ἴσως οὐδαμῶς· παρ' ἡμῖν δ' ἐστὶ μέν τι καὶ φύσει, κινητὸν μέντοι πᾶν, ἀλλ' ὅμως ἐστὶ τὸ μὲν φύσει, τὸ δ' οὐ φύσει.

Note (43.) p. 164.

St. Aust. de Doct. Christianâ, iii. § 21, 22. "Quicquid

congruit consuetudini eorum cum quibus vita ista degenda, vel necessitate imponitur vel officio suscipitur a bonis et magnis hominibus, ad utilitatem et beneficentiam referendum est, vel proprie sicut et nos debemus, vel figurate sicut Prophetis licet. In quæ facta legenda cum incurrunt indocti alterius consuetudinis, nisi auctoritate reprimantur, flagitia putant; nec possunt animadvertère totam conversationem suam, vel in *conjugiis*, vel in conviviis, vel in vestitu cæteroque humano victu atque cultu, aliis gentibus et aliis temporibus flagitiosam videri. Qua varietate innumerabilium consuetudinum commoti quidam dormitantes, ut ita dicam, qui neque alto somno stultitiæ sopiebantur, neque in sapientiæ lucem poterant evigilare, putaverunt nullam esse justitiam per seipsam, sed unicuique genti consuetudinem suam justam videri, quæ cum sit diversa omnibus gentibus, debeat autem incommutabilis manere justitia, fieri manifestum, nullam usquam esse justitiam. Non intellexerunt, ne multa commemorem, *Quod tibi fieri non vis, alii ne feceris*, nullo modo posse ullâ eorum gentili diversitate variari. Quæ sententia, cum refertur ad dilectionem Dei, omnia flagitia moriuntur, cum ad proximi, omnia facinora." He had spoken of marriage in § 18, see Note 50; and for more upon the subject of the polygamy of the patriarchs and others, see de Civ. Dei, xvi. 34, and c. Faust. xxii. 30, &c. The language in Canticles vi. 8 will show that Scripture does use the word "concubines" as figuratively descriptive of somewhat relating to Christ; and so of course the *thing* might also be, unless a person denies "multis uxoribus caste uti quenquam pro tempore posse," as St. Austin speaks, de D. Christ. ib. § 27.

Note (44.) p. 164.

Plato, Rep. i. 5. Ὅταν τις ἐγγὺς ᾖ, &c. Butler, Anal. i. iii. p. 75, and below, Note 24 to Dial. iii.

Note (45.) p. 165.

In the text allusion is made to the acute remark of De Maistre, du Pape, conclus. § xiv. "Il n'y a rien de si infaillible que l'instinct de l'impiété."

Note (46.) p. 165.

See Cyril c. Jul. as quoted above, p. 64.

Note (47.) p. 166.

For instances of such departures see the Notes to p. 45.

Note (48.) p. 166.

S. Cyril, c. Julian. lib. ix. p. 313 b. Μετεῤῥυηκότων δὴ εἰς ἀλήθειαν τῶν πραγμάτων καὶ τῶν ἐν τύποις καὶ αἰνίγμασι τὴν εἰς τὰ ἀμείνω λαβόντων μεταβολὴν, οὐ καταλελύσθαι φαμὲν τὸν Νόμον, ἐκπεπεράνθαι δὲ μᾶλλον ἐπὶ καιροῦ, καθ' ὃν ἡμῖν ἐπέλαμψεν ἡ ἀλήθεια, τουτέστι Χριστός· εἰ δὲ, ὅτι τῶν τύπων ἀπεχόμεθα, καὶ ἰσχνοῖς διανοίας ὄμμασι τὸ τῆς ἀληθείας καταθρήσαντες φῶς, τὴν τοῖς Ἰουδαίοις ἀνεπιτήδευτον πολιτείαν κατορθοῦν ᾑρήμεθα, τὴν πνευματικὴν τιμῶντες λατρείαν, ἐν αἰτίᾳ ποιεῖται τὰ καθ' ἡμᾶς· ἐπιπληττέτω καὶ ταῖς ἑτέραις τῶν ἐπιστημῶν, καὶ τοῖσδ' αὐτῶν ἰέναι σπουδάζουσι, ἐπείτοι μεθεῖσι τὰ ἐν ἀρχαῖς καὶ τὰ τῶν μαθημάτων εἰσαγωγικὰ, τὸ ἐν καλῷ γενέσθαι τῶν ἐσπουδασμένων διὰ πολλῆς γέγονεν αὐτοῖς φρόντιδος. Where there is more on the same *analogy:* ἀλλ' οὐχὶ φωράσων ἔγωγ' εἰσέρχομαι, as the comedian says.

Note (49.) p. 167.

See more at length Note 20, p. 72, &c.

Note (50.) p. 168.

The word "wives" is added, to suggest a way of meeting difficulties arising out of such cases as Hos. i. 2. St. Aust. de D. C. iii. § 10, says concisely, "Quod in aliis personis plerumque flagitium est, in divinâ vel propheticâ personâ magnæ cujusdam rei signum est. Alia est quippe in perditis moribus, alia in Oseæ prophetæ vaticinatione conjunctio meretricis; nec si flagitiose in conviviis temulentorum et lascivorum nudantur corpora, propterea in balneis nudum esse flagitium est." As there was a difference of opinion about the passage alluded to, it is open to me to add here two or three remarks upon it.

1. The sanctity of marriage depends upon God's having joined the persons (supposed to be fit recipients) together: this He does by particular outward rites in ordinary cases; but in some few cases, for which the reason can generally be discovered, He has dispensed with these rites.

2. The fitness of the recipients depends also upon God's grace, whereby alone marriage with one person can be chaste (see above, p. 120); by which a man might be enabled, as St. Austin suggests of the patriarchs, to use many wives chastely under the old dispensation; by which harlots could be called into His kingdom before such Pharisees[8] as were formalists, and held the truth in unrighteousness.

3. As of our Lord's female ancestors three were harlots, Thamar, Rahab, and she that had been the wife of Uriah, so it is likely that the coming in of the nations should be prefigured by the prophet's marriage with a harlot.

4. The nature of marriage seems to depend most intimately upon the nature of the union of Christ with the Church. When He intended one day to give the Jewish Law and Church (see Rom. vii. 1, &c. Isai. l. 1) a writing of divorcement, He permitted divorces; but after that

[8] It is of the utmost importance, in understanding the New Testament, to know that Jewish authorities mention seven kinds of bastard Pharisees, each of which has its counterpart in the New Testament, while St. Paul and Nicodemus, and others, which believed, would belong to the true Pharisees, who held fast the traditions, not of men, but of Moses—i. e. of God. See Molitor, i. p. 232.

everlasting union with the Church, whereof Hosea speaks in the second chapter, divorce was no longer permitted, save for that which destroyed all membership with Him.

These remarks will, I hope, make it clear how, under a *miraculous* dispensation, seeming violations of the sanctity of matrimony cannot well have been so; for the temper[9] of mind of even a harlot may, by possibility, be far better than that of a formalist, who walks undismayed in the very midst of holy things, and uses the chiefest means of grace, fasting, alms, and prayer, as cloaks for unbewailed and unpunished wickedness.

Note (51.) p. 168.

This is the way in which the Fathers in general argue against Gnostics, Manicheans, and others. Molitor, in his book upon Jewish tradition, endeavours to show that a real pollution was, under the old dispensation, conveyed from matter, iii. § 159. This mode of viewing things I suspect to have had its origin in the pantheistic theories which the cabbalists seem to have fallen into. It is, however, not necessarily a Manichean way of viewing them in Molitor; for he would of course hold that matter was created, and only affected by the fall in such and such ways. The theory which some hold, that the descent from the material blood of Adam is the reason of men's being born in original sin, will, however, be rather countenanced by such a doc-

[9] That such was Thamar's temper is rendered credible from the following striking words of St. Ephrem, Hom. in Nativ. vol. ii. p. 421. f. "Holy was the whoredom of Thamar for Thy sake [O Lord]. Thee it was she thirsted after, O pure Fountain! Judah defrauded her of drinking Thee! The thirsty womb stole a draught of Thee from the spring thereof! She was a widow for Thy sake! Thee did she long for; she hasted and was also a harlot for Thee. Thee did she vehemently desire, and was sanctified because it was Thee she loved," &c. So also St. Just. Mart. p. 314. St. Cyril Glaphyr. p. 196. St. Aust. c. Faust. xxii. 60—62, 83—86.

trine, to which it affords a strong parallel, the Catholic doctrine being that the φρόνημα σαρκὸς, i. e. somewhat immaterial, lying in the will of the parents, is the source of original sin. Its presence forms the opposite of that Power which overshadowed St. Mary. See above pp. 119, 120.

NOTE (52.) p. 169.

The breaking of the Sabbath in going round Jericho was often noticed of old in this light, as by St. Aust. c. Faust. xii. 31. Tertull. c. Jud. 4. Greg. Nyss. ap. Gall. vi. p. 590. Origen and S. Ephrem on the place. Cyril. Collect. p. 17.

NOTE (53.) p. 169.

Passages of this kind, if not in *all* cases the same, are cited by St. Greg. Nyss. ap. Gall. vi. 589; by St. James of Nisibis, ibid. v. pp. xciii.—xcv. Cyril of Alex. c. Jul. p. 309.

NOTE (54.) p. 170.

S. Hil. de Trinit. lib. v. p. 44. "Cum lex umbra sit futurorum, veritatem corporis umbræ species expressit." So St. Cyril. c. Nest. p. 81, c. speaking of the appearance to Jacob, says, Σύνες οὖν ὅπως, οὐχ ὡς ἀσώματός τε καὶ ἀναφὴς Λόγος ἠξίου φαίνεσθαι τῷ πατριάρχῃ τοτηνικάδε τὸν τοῦ μυστηρίου τύπον προαναφαίνων αὐτῷ. On the subject of these appearances, St. Aug. de Trin. ii., and particularly § 27, § 32, § 33, may be referred to. They are noticed here only as showing how, under the law, almost every thing was but an unsubstantial shadow of the things to be revealed. The first and second lessons for Trinity Sunday exhibit the shadows of the Law in striking contrast with the mysteries of the Gospel.

NOTE (55.) p. 171.

Allusion is here made to the words of the Vishnu Purana, p. 327. "He will, with the permission of the Brahmans, give food to any guest who arrives at the time (of the Sraddha) or who is desirous of victuals, or who is passing along the road; for holy saints and ascetics, benefactors of mankind, are traversing this earth, disguised in various shapes." This reminds one of Hebrews xiii. 2. "Be not forgetful to entertain strangers, for thereby some have entertained angels unawares."

Note (56.) p. 172.

I have ventured to let the words of Scripture, "Sons of God," stand unexplained, because it does not (as Dr. Pusey observes on Tertullian, p. 54) appear that such a title is any where applied to men in the Old Testament. Hosea, cap. ii., speaks of it as a name to be given at some future time. The phrase "Sons of the Most High," in Ps. lxxxii. 6, comes nearest to it. If the "vir prudentissimus," whom S. Jerome quotes on Isaiah liv. p. 200, be, as one may suspect, St. Ambrose, who wrote a commentary, now lost, upon Isaiah, (see S. August. c. Jul. Pel. ii.) then we should see that he did not think it incredible that *demons* might have gone in to the daughters of men. For references to passages on the subject see Dr. Pusey as above, and Gallandi, i. p. 223. My main object is to guard against its being assumed that we can argue with certainty from the present course of nature, what the course of nature was before the flood: and it is plain that such arguing is best guarded against, not by stating a positive opinion, but by showing that there are difficulties in the way of our coming to such an opinion.

Note (57.) p. 172.

After Aristeas, ed. Hody, p. 18, some of the most learned Fathers notice this as the ground why some birds are classed as unclean; as Origen (Cont. Cels. p. 225) in Levit. p. 226, where Ruæus quotes Tertull. c. Marc. Theodoret has the same sentiment.

Note (58.) p. 173.

Aristotle, Eth. iv. 6, notices this of his μεγαλοπρεπὴς, περὶ ταῦτα μᾶλλον δαπανᾷ ὅσα πολυχρόνια τῶν ἔργων.

Note (59.) p. 173.

See Rev. xv. 4, where *Moses' hymn* is sung in heaven; (whence also the words עזי וזמרת יה are quoted from it in Ps. cxviii. 14, and Is. xii. 2, which both relate to Christian times.) Hence, in the Law, rites are said to be by an ordinance *for ever*, because they typify something external. See also St. Cyril. c. Jul. p. 322, αἰώνιος τοίνυν ὁ νόμος, κ. τ. λ. p. 243. Moses is like Christ, not as he is a king or a priest, but as a prophet, foreshowing that heavenly temple for which the saints long. See S. Methodius, Conv. Virg. v. 7; and St. Ambrose in Ps. xxxviii. 25, "Umbra in Lege, imago vero in Evangelio, veritas in cœlestibus. Umbra Evangelii et Ecclesiæ congregationis in Lege, imago futuræ veritatis in Evangelio, veritas in judicio Dei." Compare S. Irenæus, ii. 28, who assigns as the reason why Scripture is not here fully understood, ἵνα ἀεὶ μὲν ὁ Θεὸς διδάσκῃ, ἄνθρωπος δὲ διὰ παντὸς μανθάνῃ παρὰ Θεοῦ.

Note (60.) p. 174.

This is well observed by St. Cyril, de Adoratione in Spiritu et Veritate, p. 498, d. Ἔστι δὴ οὖν οὐκ ἀσυμφανὲς, ὅτι βεβηλοῖ μέν τι τῶν ὄντων ἥκιστα μὲν ὁ νόμος, πάντα δὲ οἶδε καθαρὰ τοῖς καθαροῖς· ἀλλ' εἰς ἠθῶν ποιότητας ἀνθρωπίνων τὸ ἑκάστου ζώου φυσικὸν εὖ μάλα παραλαβὼν ὀνίνησιν οὐ μετρίως. Μάθοις δ' ἂν ὅ φημι δὴ κἀκ τῶνδε πάλιν ἀληθὲς ὅτι καὶ ἀναμφίβολον. Τὰ γάρ τοι πᾶσι κατεγνωσμένα, καταμυσάττεσθαι δεῖν ὁρᾶται προστεταχὼς κάμηλον δὴ λέγων καὶ τὸν χοιρογρύλλιον, νυκτικόρακα, καὶ τὸν καταῤῥάκτην, καὶ ἀσκαλαβώτην, καὶ μυγαλὴν, καὶ τὰ ἔτι τούτων αἰσχίονα . . . Εἰς ἠθῶν οὖν ποιότητα μετακομιστέον εὖ μάλα τὰ φυσικῶς ἐνόντα τισὶ τῶν ἀλόγων ζώων, ἑκάστου φέρε εἰπεῖν καταγράφοντος, ὥσπερ ἐν ἑαυτῷ τὸν τοῦ δεῖνος τρόπον, καὶ ἐν οἷς ἂν εἴη κατασημαίνοντος.' Ἢ γὰρ οὐχὶ καὶ ἡμεῖς αὐτοὶ κατειθίσμεθά πως τοὺς μὲν ἄγαν θερμοὺς καὶ εὐσθενεστάτους καὶ θράσει τῶν ἄλλων ὑπερφέροντας σῦς ἢ λέοντας ἤ τι τῶν τοιούτων ἕτερον ἀποκαλεῖν; τοὺς δὲ πραεῖς καὶ ἠρεμαίους, κ. τ. λ. It was strikingly said by Confucius (in Windischm. p. 159), that the later ages ran into superstition by taking the symbol for the reality, yet that this ought not to hinder the due use of the symbol; and doubtless much light will be thrown upon the whole question of symbols, such as those just noticed, by the study of hieroglyphics, which will, further, either show the naturalness of particular symbols, or else force us to assume of others that they were traditional. In the latter case they may be said to throw light upon Scripture symbols, as history is said to throw light on prophecy. Each, by reflecting the light of Scripture, throws it on to us, and makes us conscious of it.

NOTE (61.) p. 173.

Aristot. Hist. An. ix. p. 608. b 4. Τούτων δὲ ἴχνη μὲν τῶν ἠθῶν ἐστιν ἐν πᾶσιν ὡς εἰπεῖν μᾶλλον φανερώτερα ἐν τοῖς ἔχουσι μᾶλλον ἦθος, καὶ μάλιστα ἐν ἀνθρώπῳ· τοῦτο γὰρ ἔχει τὴν φύσιν ἀποτετελεσμένην, ὥστε καὶ ταύτας τὰς ἕξεις εἶναι φανερωτέρας ἐν αὐτοῖς. To this may be subjoined a passage from Quain's Anatomy, which, though not obviously bearing upon the text in this place, will be conveniently put in juxtaposition with this passage of Aristotle. It is important to put down the *analogies* between our past existence in the womb and that of other animals, lest by not stating them one should seem not to have thought of them, while in reality they are mere analogies, upon which we have no right whatever to build hypotheses as to any future changes in our mode [1] of existence; changes, I mean, which if not allowed to be at once actually against revelation, are certainly unrevealed by God. For it can hardly be observed too often that analogy alone will not serve as a guide to the truth: it presupposes a revelation, or somewhat claiming to be a revelation, which it may confirm or clear up. And the use of it in confuting false revelations is this: that, as nature and real revelations come from one Author, false revelations will only have partial, temporary, and fanciful coincidences with nature. One need not fear but that the false will, sooner or later, be found to conflict with it. Dr. Quain writes as follows, § 61. "In reviewing the succession of changes during the progress of development, we recognize each of them as a temporary or transition stage, which, while it lasts, bears a certain degree of analogy to a *fixed* condition of the circulating apparatus in some of the lower orders of animals. Thus, when in the embryo of a vertebrate animal, a single vessel, without any cardiac dilatation, runs along the back, it at once suggests the idea of the dorsal vessels in insects. When at the anterior part of this vessel an enlargement occurs, where the 'punctum

[1] I may remind the reader here, that the doctrine of transmigrations originated, possibly, in the perversion of symbolical expressions for the belief of the continuance of habits after death. E. g. a man might be said to become a swine, when it was meant that he would be "filthy still" in a future state. And if such perversion of symbols took place through man's ceasing to "hold fast the traditions," it is quite credible that there should be things in nature seeming to confirm the error, as there are things in Scripture seeming to confirm heresy; and, for all one knows, designedly seeming so. Or again, if arts are under a divine superintendence in one view, hieroglyphics may, from the first, have been overruled so as to subserve this retributive dispensation.

saliens' is seen, and which assumes the character of a ventricle, it is the analogue of what is found in the higher crustacea. In the next stage, where two cavities exist, one just before the other, representing an auricle and ventricle, it corresponds with the condition of the central organ in the mollusca. When the auricle ascends and the ventricle comes forward (the bulbus arteriosus reaching upwards from its base), it is like the heart of fishes, in which it is called branchial or respiratory, from its sending the blood into the gills or respiratory organs solely, and therefore discharges the function of the right or pulmonic heart in higher animals. When the auricular cavity becomes separated into two chambers by the growth of the septum, the ventricle still remaining single, it passes into the condition of the organ in the batrachial reptile. In the next place, as the development of the ventricular septum proceeds from the apex upwards to the base, before it is completed, a communication will still remain at this point. The heart in this stage, consisting of two auricles and a partially divided ventricle, represents the condition of the organ in the ophidian reptile; and were its growth arrested at this point (of which many instances have occurred), that form of congenital malformation will remain through life in which the two sorts of blood are blended, owing to the imperfection of the septum. Lastly, even when all communication between the ventricular cavities is cut off by the completion of the septum, the streams issuing from them are still, to a certain extent, blended by means of the current which passes from the pulmonary artery through the ductus arteriosus into the aorta. Hence, until this diverticulum is closed, an analogy will still remain between the conformation of the organs of the fœtus of the human subject, and the higher animals, with that of the reptile. It is finally cut off at the moment of birth, when the condition of the circulating apparatus in the new being passes from that of the cold-blooded to that of the warm-blooded animal."

NOTE (62.) p. 163.

Tertull. de Idol. at the close, where see Dr. Pusey's note. Of the ass, St. Aust. on Ps. xxxi. En. ii. § 23, says: "Populus mitis et mansuetus, portans bene Dominum, asellus est, et tendit in Jerusalem;" and so in the opposite corner of the Church, St. Ephrem on Judg. v. 10, "*Ye that ride on white asses.* These are mystically interpreted of the Apostles, who are exalted in the assembly of the faithful, and [the latter are] they who are clad with white garments spiritually in holy baptism." An attempt has been made, in "Nature a Parable," to put this kind of interpretation more fully out, to which I must refer.

NOTE (63.) p. 173.

"Rerum ignorantia facit obscuras figuratas locutiones, quam vel animalium vel lapidum[a] vel herbarum naturas," &c. S. Austin de Doct. Christian. ii. § 24 or 16.

NOTE (63*) p. 174.

St. Cyril, c. Jul. p. 322. *Αἰώνιος τοίνυν ὁ νόμος ὁ πάλαι μὲν παρ' Ἰουδαίοις αἰνιγματώδως, ὁ αὐτὸς δὲ νῦν παρ' ἡμῖν νοητῶς καὶ πνευματικῶς καὶ κατά γε τὸ ἀληθές·* and presently, *Καὶ γοῦν ὁ Μώσης τὰς πρός γε τοὺς Ἰουδαίους διαλέξεις ποιούμενος κάλυμμα ἐτίθει ἐπὶ τὸ πρόσωπον αὐτοῦ, μονονουχὶ βοῶν διὰ τοῦ πράγματος ὡς τὸ ἀληθὲς τοῦ νόμου πρόσωπον ἄποπτον ἦν αὐτοῖς.* And so St. Chrys. vol. vi. p. 657, Savile, *Εἰ μὴ δόξαν εἶχεν ἀπρόσιτον ὁ νόμος*

[a] Would not the work of Garuda throw light on these? It were to be wished that such works as this, Al-Damiri, &c. were made accessible by a text and a translation.

οὐχ ἂν ἐδεήθη καλύμματος· and St. Basil, Hex. vi. 2, Πανταχοῦ τῇ ἱστορίᾳ τὸ δόγμα τῆς θεολογίας μυστικῶς συμπαρέσπαρται.

NOTE (64.) p. 176.

The original is given by Prof. Wilson, note to Vishnu Purana, p. 202.

क्वचित् क्वचित्पुराणेषु विरोधो यदि लक्ष्यते
कल्पभेदादिभिस्तत्र व्यवस्था सद्भिरिष्यते

NOTE (65.) p. 177.

S. Ephrem, adv. Scrut. iii. p. 9. "When the watchers (i. e. angels) seek to learn the generation of the Son, their questions do they direct to them that are higher than they, and even these high ones learn by the hinting of the Spirit. As are the degrees of the angels, so are the questions of the angels. None is there among them that boldly seeks to partake of aught that is beyond his measure. To this doth nature witness by the gradation that is in it; for order leadeth to order until that which is the summit. The counsels of Jethro also made gradations from rank to rank, even unto Moses." See above, Note 25 on Dial. i. St. Austin, de Gen. ad literam v. cap. xix., was of opinion that the angels knew of the Incarnation long before; nor does his language, in his Retractations, appear to imply that he retracted this, but only the use made of a certain text to confirm it.

NOTE (66.) p. 178.

The process of taming elephants in India is described at length by Arrian in his Indica, p. 535. Strabo, p. 1030. It shows how untractable many of them are before the operation.

Note (67.) p. 180.

The following passage from S. Ath. c. Arian. (ii. 75) will show that it is in a certain way allowable to speak of God's dispensations as anticipating and providing for the effects of sin. Ἡ παρὰ τοῦ Σωτῆρος εἰς ἡμᾶς γενομένη χάρις ἄρτι μὲν ἐπεφάνη (ὡς εἶπεν ὁ ἀπόστολος) καὶ γέγονεν ἐπιδημήσαντος Αὐτοῦ· προητοίμαστο δὲ αὕτη καὶ πρὶν γενέσθαι ἡμᾶς, μᾶλλον δὲ καὶ πρὸ τῆς καταβολῆς τοῦ κόσμου· καὶ ἡ αἰτία χρηστὴ καὶ θαυμαστή πώς ἐστιν. Οὐκ ἔπρεπε τὸν Θεὸν ὕστερον περὶ ἡμῶν βουλεύεσθαι ἵνα μὴ ὡς ἀγνοῶν τὰ καθ' ἡμᾶς φαίνηται· κτίζων τοίνυν ἡμᾶς διὰ τοῦ ἰδίου Λόγου ὁ τῶν ὅλων Θεὸς, καὶ εἰδὼς τὰ ἡμῶν ὑπὲρ ἡμᾶς, καὶ προγιγνώσκων τε ὅτι καλοὶ γενόμενοι ὕστερον παραβαταὶ τῆς ἐντολῆς ἐσόμεθα, καὶ ἐκ τοῦ παραδείσου ἐκβληθησόμεθα διὰ τὴν παρακοὴν, φιλάνθρωπος καὶ ἀγαθὸς ὢν, προετοιμάζει ἐν τῷ ἰδίῳ Λόγῳ, δι' οὗ καὶ ἔκτισεν ἡμᾶς, τὴν περὶ τῆς σωτηρίας ἡμῶν οἰκονομίαν, ἵνα κἂν ἀπατηθέντες παρὰ τοῦ ὄφεως ἐκπέσωμεν, μὴ τέλεον ἀπομείνωμεν νεκροὶ, ἀλλ' ἔχοντες ἐν τῷ Λόγῳ τὴν προητοιμασμένην ἡμῖν λύτρωσίν τε καὶ σωτηρίαν, πάλιν ἀναστάντες ἀθάνατοι διαμείνωμεν, ὅταν αὐτὸς ὑπὲρ ἡμῶν ἀρχὴ τῶν ὁδῶν κτισθῇ, καὶ ὁ Πρωτότοκος τῆς κτίσεως γένηται πρωτότοκος ἀδελφῶν, καὶ αὐτὸς ἀπαρχὴ τῶν νεκρῶν ἀναστῇ. If any one reflect how intimately all changes, on a large scale, in the outward circumstances of man, are connected with changes preceding them in his inward constitution, this passage will be seen to have a much more particular bearing upon the text than, at first sight, it appears to have. It is by a conflict with harder external circumstances, that man is enabled to recover, in some degree, his primitive power of self government. Discipline, in all degrees of severity (see Butler, Anal. i. v. p. 137), such as slavery would be, may be necessary for fallen beings such as those under the slavery of sin are, and the providing of such discipline may be necessarily implied in the providing for the consequences of sin. If it is wrong to say that slavery was originally contemplated, then it would be wrong to say, as St. Athanasius implies, that the taking of the form of a slave (μορφὴν δούλου) was originally contemplated. That outward condition of slavery which yielded a temptation, both to the master and to the slave, to different forms of sin, did He take upon Him to make us free indeed.

Note (68.) p. 180.

The words φωτίσαντος ζωὴν καὶ ἀφθαρσίαν διὰ τοῦ εὐαγγελίου are differently commented upon by different writers, some insisting on the word φωτίσαντος as meaning, throwing light upon an already existing belief. (See Sherlock's Sermon on the text, and compare Pocock, quoted p. 121.) As the Vulgate, Syriac, and (to judge from the Latin) the Coptic, and also seemingly the Arabic in Walton's Polyglott, (وفقد البلي) keep the word *incorruption*, one cannot but think there is something emphatic in the word, although ἀφθαρσία may be in some places used of imperishableness, as distinct from incorruption, which seems properly to apply to a body. The resurrection of the body would be a natural thing to allude to, as being a great Christian doctrine, and forming the contrast to 'death' (which was just before mentioned), as in 1 Cor. xv.

Note (69.) p. 181.

Much here said is noticed by Möhler in a tract to be found in vol. ii. p. 54 of his works, in Döllinger's edition. The connexion of this with the last note will be plainer, if we remember how the bringing to light of the incorruptibility of the body, when once raised again, must necessarily affect all δουλαγωγία[3] of the body, whether sinful or virtuous. Here, however, the thing dwelt upon is, that any belief of a future state, at all practically felt, necessarily must influence the treatment of slaves.

Of the Romans, see Juv. Sat. iii. 261, and Rupert on the place. Cato de R. R. i. p. 12. Bip. "Vendat boves vetulos, &c.; plostrum vetus, servum senem, servum morbosum." Cicero has somewhere observed, that the introduction of a denial of a future state was a recent one in Rome; and Lucretius, lib. i. and elsewhere, speaks of the introduction of such principles as a modern advantage, in his view of it. See Möhler as above, p. 69.

Note (70.) p. 181.

Plato, Phædo, § 151. Οἶδα καὶ ἄλλους πάνυ ὀψὲ πίνοντας, ἐπειδὰν παραγγέλθῃ αὐτοῖς, καὶ ξυγγενομένους γε ἐνίους ὧν ἂν τύχωσιν ἐπιθυμοῦντες.

Note (71.) p. 181.

Id. Euthyphr. § 4, where a specimen of the coolness with which slave-murder was treated may be seen. The beginning of the Nubes will suggest much to the same effect.

Note (72.) p. 181.

In his Politics, vii. 15, Aristotle says, Εἴ τινές εἰσιν, ὅπερ οἱ ποιηταί φασιν, ἐν μακάρων νήσοις. It is true that Cicero spoke in a similar way of "insulæ beatorum, ut fabulæ ferunt" (ap. S. Aug. de Trin. xiv. 11), but the other writings of the two authors colour their meaning. Atticus (ap. Euseb. P. E. p. 809; see above, p. 124) well asks, Τίς οὖν ἐστι ὁ πρῶτος ἐγχειρήσας ἀντιτάξασθαι ἀποδείξεσι καὶ τὴν ψυχὴν ἀφελέσθαι τῆς ἀθανασίας, καὶ τῆς ἄλλης πάσης δυνά-

[3] 1 Cor. ix. Οὕτω πυκτεύω, ὡς οὐκ ἀέρα δέρων. Ἀλλ' ὑπωπιάζω μου τὸ σῶμα καὶ δουλαγωγῶ· μήπως ἄλλοις κηρύξας, αὐτὸς ἀδόκιμος γένωμαι.

μεως; τίς ἕτερος ἢ ὁ Ἀριστοτέλης; I give this as embodying an impression I had come to before I read the passage of Atticus. Compare Origen c. Cels. p. 67. To show how he speaks of slaves, I may quote his Met. xi. 10. p. 1075. a. 16. Πάντα συντέτακταί πως, ἀλλ' οὐχ ὁμοίως, καὶ πλωτὰ καὶ πτηνὰ καὶ φυτά. καὶ οὐχ οὕτως ἔχει ὥστε μὴ εἶναι θατέρῳ πρὸς θάτερον μηθὲν, ἀλλ' ἐστί τι· πρὸς μὲν γὰρ ἓν ἅπαντα συντέτακται, ἀλλ' ὥσπερ ἐν οἰκίᾳ ἥκιστα ἔξεστι ὅτι ἔτυχε ποιεῖν, ἀλλὰ πάντα ἢ τὰ πλεῖστα τέτακται, τοῖς δὲ ἀνδραπόδοις καὶ τοῖς θηρίοις μικρὸν τὸ εἰς τὸ κοινὸν, τὸ δὲ πλεῖστον ὅτι ἔτυχεν· τοιαύτη γὰρ ἑκάστου ἀρχὴ αὐτῶν ἡ φύσις ἐστίν. See also Eth. N. v. 10, p. 1134. b. 10. p. 1136. b. 30. Polit. i. 1—7. In Eth. Nic. viii. 13, he calls the slave an ἔμψυχον ὄργανον, incapable of civil rights. And in the Politics, lib. i., he seems to hold that some men might be made slaves, by capture, &c. Aristotle[4] was an acute observer of facts: may he not here be faithfully recording then an actually existing dispensation of Providence, and so be a witness in favour of the supposition (noticed in Note 68) that slavery was intended to exist for a time—*was* winked at, as perhaps in part it *is* still?

NOTE (73.) p. 181.

Möhler, as above, p. 62, has shown that the passage (Polit. p. 113, Bip. § 46) in which Plato speaks with apparent harshness of slaves, is capable of being interpreted of the slavishness resulting from vice; and also is careful to distinguish things which Plato puts into the interlocutor's mouth as suited to his character, from his own opinion, which he thinks more kindly than that of Aristotle. The Euthyphro would seem to show what his bias was,

[4] It is to be regretted that what he says in Polit. vii. 10, extr., Διότι βέλτιον πᾶσι τοῖς δούλοις ἆθλον προκεῖσθαι τὴν ἐλευθερίαν, ὕστερον ἐροῦμεν, contains a promise, to us as good as unfulfilled.

though at that time in Athens people were obliged to be careful what they said. Euseb. P. E. (though at 609 he speaks otherwise) at p. 713 indeed attributes very different sentiments to Plato, but it may be doubted if he does not make the confusion Möhler has pointed out. I give these passages, which contravene the statements in the text, for fairness' sake, and not at all as doubting the general truth of the position there stated. It is confirmed by Cicero's way of speaking of slaves, de Off. i. c. 13. "Meminerimus autem etiam adversus infimos justitiam esse servandum; est autem infima conditio et fortuna servorum; quibus non male præcipiunt qui ita jubent uti, ut mercenariis, operam exigendam, justa præbenda." And that he carried out this lenient view of them, we see from the following words (ad Att. i. 12, p. 53, ed. Schutz.) "Quod præterea ad te scribam, non habeo. Et mehercule eram conturbatior: nam puer festivus, anagnostes noster Sositheus discesserat, meque, plus quam servi mors debere videbatur, commoverat:" a passage which at once shows his own kindliness and the heartlessness of the generality towards slaves.

Note (74.) p. 181.

Herod. ii. 113, mentions a temple of Hercules, to which, if slaves fled, and had sacred marks branded on them (*ἐπιβάληται στίγματα ἱρὰ*), and gave themselves to the god, they might not be touched; which law, he adds, continued from early times to his own day. Diod. Sic. i. 77, p. 88, has the following passage, which further shows their kindness to slaves. Εἰ δέ τις ἑκουσίως ἀποκτεῖναι τὸν ἐλεύθερον ἢ τὸν δοῦλον, ἀποθνήσκειν τοῦτον οἱ νόμοι προσέταττον, ἅμα μὲν βουλόμενοι μὴ ταῖς διαφοραῖς τῆς τύχης, ἀλλὰ ταῖς τῶν πράξεων ἐπιβολαῖς εἴργεσθαι πάντας ἀπὸ τῶν φαύλων, ἅμα δὲ διὰ τῆς τῶν δούλων φρόντιδος ἐθίζοντες τοῖς ἀνθρώποις πολὺ μᾶλλον εἰς τοὺς ἐλευθέρους μηδὲν ὅλως ἐξαμαρτάνειν. This, as Wesseling observes, agrees well with the Law of God, Ex. xxi. 20. And so we find Garcilasso di Vega, in his Commentarios Reales de los Incas, v. cap. 12, tells us of the Incas' kindness to their vassals, whose belief in the immortality of the soul he elsewhere mentions, as follows: "Aquellos Reyes del Peru, por aver sido tales, fuesen tan amados y queridos de sus vasallos, que oy los Indios, con ser yá Christanos, no pueden olvidarlos; antes en sus trabajos y necessidades, con llantos y gemidos á voces y alaridos, los llaman uno á uno por sus nombres: por que no se lee, que ninguno de los Reyes antiguos de Asia, Africa, y Europa, aia sido para sus naturales vasalles tan cuidadoso, tan apacible, tan provechoso, franco, y libero, como lo fueron los Reyes Incas para con los suios." I may observe, in case any one wishes to try how far this holds in other cases, that care should be taken not to confound the treatment of slaves by one branch or caste of a nation with that by another. Thus, if it seems (from Cæsar, B. G. vi. 13) that the military part of the Gauls ill used their slaves, this will not show any thing as to the treatment of the ἱερόδουλοι by the Druid class; that is, will not show that those who did believe in a future state were not influenced by it in their way of treating their slaves. The openly sanctioned unnatural sins of the Gauls, spoken of by Ar. Pol. ii. 9 (Κελταὶ, Γάλλοι, Euseb. P. E. p. 276. a.) evidently apply to the warlike part of the race (στρατιωτικὸν καὶ πολεμικὸν γένος), and seem to show that there was but little practical belief of a future state among them, whatever the doctrines of the Druids may have been.

Any one who watches himself will, I think, allow that kindness towards inferiors is not only a duty which he feels he ought to *force* upon himself, but one which it comes naturally to him to exercise, in proportion as he realizes a world to come. And if this is so, we may almost settle the matter *à priori*, that where slaves are ill-treated, there men have no active belief of a future state.

With regard to the Jews, their kindness to slaves is noticed by Molitor, iii. § 47. § 99; as by Euseb. p. 713; by St. Clem. Strom. ii. § 91, p. 476. P.; and by St. Cyril de Ad. in S. et V. p. 263, who ends his remarks upon it with these words: Προσεθίζει δὲ καὶ ἑτέρως ὁ νόμος ἡμᾶς εἰς φιλαλληλίαν τιμᾷν ἀναπείθων τὸ συγκαθίστασθαι τοῖς ἐγγὺς καὶ τοὺς τῆς ἀνισότητος, καταμυσαττόμενός τε καὶ κολάζων τρόπους. Creuzer also, c. iv. abt. i. p. 23, considers the Jewish law herein to be an anticipation of Christianity.

Note (75.) p. 183.

This is mentioned by Burnouf in the preface to his edition of the Bhagavat Purana, p. xx.

Note (76.) p. 183.

The "Clientela" appears in one form or another amongst the whole, almost, of the nations of the West. See for instances, Clinton, F. Hellen. i. p. 28. ii. p. 412. Pollux iii. 83. Livy xxvi. v. fin., where they are mentioned as in Spain. Herod. vii. 155, &c.

Note (77.) p. 183.

See on the Vish. Pur. p. 195, n. 153, where Mr. Lassen's conjecture, that the Sudras or Sudrakas were the 'Οξυδράκαι of the Greeks, is mentioned with approval.

Note (78.) p. 184.

Arrian, pp. 529, 530, with other Greek writers, notices that the Indians were all free. Though Sudras and others were looked upon with contempt, still the notion so common amongst pantheists of Ahinsa, i. e. the duty of abstaining from injury to any thing living, secured them as well as animals from ill treatment, and is obviously a useful substitute for the true principles of loving kindness, where these have not been published.

Note (79.) p. 184.

Plato, Phæd. § 94. Ἐγὼ δὲ τοῖς διὰ τῶν εἰκότων τὰς ἀποδείξεις ποιουμένοις λόγοις ξύνοιδα οὖσιν ἀλαζόσι καὶ ἄν τις αὐτοὺς μὴ φυλάττηται, εὖ μάλα ἐξαπατῶσι καὶ ἐν γεωμετρίᾳ καὶ ἐν ἄλλοις ἅπασιν. Ὁ δὲ περὶ τῆς ἀναμνήσεως καὶ μαθήσεως λόγος δι' ὑποθέσεως ἀξίας ἀποδέξασθαι εἴρηται· which is an acknowledgment, seemingly, that the doctrine of ἀνάμνησις cannot be demonstrated. Origen well urges the want of demonstrative evidence for the ἐκπυρώσεις and κατακλυσμὸς among heathens, as a reason why Celsus should not condemn Christians for believing upon faith. (p. 16.) The proper question in such cases is, of course, whether the revelation which tenders things to be believed is or is not a certain one.

Note (80.) p. 184.

A careful examination of the context will, I think, generally show that such passages as are most strong at first sight for the return of the Jews, in a literal outward sense, are to be understood of the Jews in a spiritual sense—the Jews which are Jews inwardly, and children of the faith of Abraham. This, I think, would be the result of such examination, if made by a person ignorant of the opinions of the Fathers and others upon the subject. Tertullian, Origen, S. Jerome, and St. Ephrem (in Esai. v. fin.), thought they would not be restored; and with these St. Chrysostom and Josephus agree. See Spencer ad Orig. c. Cels. iv.

p. 174. Of the same opinion, among great Hebrew scholars, is the learned Pocock, ii. p. 67, &c.; and I may refer also to Dr. Pusey on Tertullian, p. 123—126.

NOTE (81.) p. 185.

St. Cyril, c. Julian. p. 105. Εἴπερ ἐστὶ Θεοῦ πρωτότοκος ὁ Ἰσραὴλ, ἔχει πάντως που καὶ ἀδελφοὺς ἑτέρους, ὡς ὑπὸ πατέρα τὸν Θεόν.

NOTE (82.) p. 185.

See Möhler's treatise, p. 73, quoting Macrob. i. x.

NOTE (83.) p. 185.

Professor Wilson on the Vishnu Purana, p. 406, says that "the existence of but one caste in the age of purity, however incompatible with the legend which ascribes the origin of the four first tribes to Brahma, is every where admitted."

NOTE (84.) p. 186.

See ibid. p. 451.

NOTE (85.) p. 186.

The following passage from St. Augustine will justify the language in the text: de Civ. Dei, xv. 16. "Esset enim unus homo filiis suis fratri scilicet sororique conjugibus, et pater et socer, et avunculus, &c. Omnes autem istæ consuetudines, quæ uni homini tres homines connectebant, novem connecterent, si essent in singulis singulæ, ut unus homo haberet alteram sororem, alteram uxorem, alteram consobrinam, alterum patrem, alterum avunculum, alterum socerum, alteram matrem, alteram amitam, alteram socrum, atque ita se non in paucitate coartatum, sed latius atque numerosius propinquitatibus crebris vinculum sociale diffunderet. Quod, humano genere crescente et multiplicato, etiam inter impios deorum multorum falsorumque cultores sic observari cernimus, ut etiamsi perversis legibus permittantur fraterna conjugia, melior tamen consuetudo ipsam malit exhorrere licentiam, et cum sorores accipere in matrimonium primus humani generis omnino licuerit, sic aversetur quasi nunquam licere potuerit. Ad humanum enim sensum vel alliciendum vel offendendum mos valet plurimum. Qui cum in hac causa immoderationem concupiscentiæ coerceat, eum dissignari atque corrumpi merito esse nefarium judicatur. Si enim iniquum est aviditate possidendi transgredi limitem agrorum, quantò est iniquius libidine concumbendi subvertere limitem morum? Experti autem sumus in connubiis consobrinarum etiam nostris temporibus propter gradum propinquitatis fraterno gradu proximum, *quam raro per mores* fiebat quod fieri per leges licebat, quia nec id divina prohibuit, et nondum prohibuerat lex humana. Veruntamen factum etiam licitum propter vicinitatem *horrebatur* illiciti; et quod fiebat cum consobrina pene cum sorore fieri videbatur." The sin of incest, we here see, is represented as a sin which had no place in primeval times; the feeling against it is so strong, as to offer a curious instance of a development of a new moral instinct in our nature—new, that is, inasmuch as it is subsequent to the original instinctive feelings, as far as one can perceive. And as probably there was a time when marriage with sisters was not fully recognized to be disgusting and revolting, so there may be times when other alliances, in their degree disgusting and revolting, will not be fully recognized as such without a legal enactment. This, the Benedictine editor informs us, was the case with the marriage of cousins (the feeling against which St. Augustine implies was on the decline), against which they make it probable that Theodosius promulgated a law.

NOTE (86.) p. 186.

Hitopad. l. 368.

न हि संहरते ज्योत्स्नां चन्द्रश्चाण्डालवेश्मनि

NOTE (87.) p. 187.

See Origen, c. Cels. iv. p. 166. Εἰσί τινες εἱρμοὶ καὶ ἀκολουθίαι ἄφατοι καὶ ἀνεκδιήγητοι περὶ τῆς κατὰ τὰς ἀνθρωπίνας ψυχὰς διαφόρου οἰκονομίας. And see Butler's Anal. i. chap. vii. p. 177.

NOTE (88.) p. 187.

This was suggested by De Maistre, though I am unable to find the passage.

NOTE (89.) p. 188.

Aristotle, in his Metaphysics, p. 993. b. 6, (α. ἔλαττον init.) notices the vastness of the system of things, as creating such difficulties. Τὸ ὅλον τι ἔχειν καὶ μέρος μὴ δύνασθαι δηλοῖ τὸ χαλεπὸν αὐτῆς· ἴσως δὲ καὶ τῆς χαλεπότητος οὔσης κατὰ δύο τρόπους οὐκ ἐν τοῖς πράγμασιν, ἀλλ' ἐν ἡμῖν τὸ αἴτιόν ἐστιν αὐτῆς. Ὥσπερ γὰρ τὰ τῶν νυκτερίδων ὄμματα πρὸς τὸ φέγγος ἔχει τὸ μεθ' ἡμέραν, οὕτω καὶ τῆς ἡμετέρης ψυχῆς ὁ νοῦς πρὸς τὰ τῇ φύσει φανερώτατα πάντων· οὐ μόνον δὲ χάριν ἔχειν δίκαιον, κ. τ. λ. as above, p. 63.

END OF NOTES TO DIALOGUE II.

DIALOGUE III.

OUR MORE IMMEDIATE RELATIONS TO SYSTEMS OF MATTER.

"Ut carnis restitutio negetur, de unâ omnium philosophorum scholâ sumitur."—TERT. PRÆSC. 3.

DIALOGUE THE THIRD.

LAUR. You recollect, Rádhákánt, that we were to recur again to our relations to matter. Now if you look back with a wise mind upon all upon which we have been discoursing, you will see that I have been exercising a sort of general government over what we discoursed of, whereby our conversation was, upon the whole, confined to the use which is made, in the present world, of sundry things which could not come about without what we call matter. The purity and impurity of men, the cleanness and uncleanness of animals, the freedom or the servitude of particular classes of men, are several pairs of things which all depend upon matter. If matter be a non-existence, then how can it make men pure or impure, or how can one animal be clean and another unclean, or one man be by birth free, another not free? The means whereby all these ideas come before us, in our present state of existence, all depend upon matter in some way or another. The existence of any one living creature is made to depend upon matter, from its first conception (1) to its death. All, then, whereof we have hitherto discussed has a bearing upon the relation in which we stand to matter; and as there are several systems of matter in the universe, whereof some affect the soul through other systems of matter (as e. g., systems of matter at a distance through the medium of other natural or artificial systems of matter at hand), so also there is a system of matter which affects the soul without the intervention of any third thing of which we are conscious. Thus diseases in this system of matter, which we call our body, impair the vigour of the soul, without the intervention of any other system of matter. Now I may say that it is the view which a revelation takes of systems of matter, which forms its distinguishing character. The old systems of theology treated man as if he had some impurity conveyed to him by being born of a bad race, which runs up, if you reflect upon it, into the belief that certain degradations were conveyed to him by matter. And Moses' system, amongst the rest, has the outward appearance of recognizing this view of things. Different forms of matter are there spoken of as conveying impurity, people of certain races are discarded from the congregation for religious rites for a certain time, and every thing in the code bears the appearance of recognizing this distinction, outwardly at least.

But different inward aspects very often alter the whole view we take of a code. Some, for instance, held that all matter was an originally evil principle, and have gone so far as to think that water could not be made a means of purification, because it was matter (2). And wherever the belief that matter was eternal existed, every rite would probably derive a new meaning and colouring from this: the outward ceremonial must be viewed in relation to the inward theory.

Now the inward theory of Moses' law does not appear in any place to recognize matter (as such) as the source of evil; in such sense the source, as that impurity came from it by itself alone. Its inward theory does not seem to have been much concerned with questions of an abstract kind as to the nature of matter, but simply to look upon some kinds of it as the channels whereby pollution came, through which it was conveyed, not in which it was inherent. And even this seems to be a mere accident to the main object of the legislator, which was to make a system which should foreshadow and be only an imperfect development of another system. Hence it seems that permission was given the Jews, so soon as they should be settled in the Holy Land, to eat animals of every sort in their private dwellings; they were not forbidden to eat any thing save the blood. Now this may be taken as a proof that under the Mosaic dispensation there was no distinction between unclean and clean animals, save in order to show something to come (3). We have, however, said enough concerning the relations to matter into which the Mosaic code views mankind as placed. The exception, however, of blood is one (4) which, under the Christian system, long continued in force.

We may then avail ourselves, Rádhákánt, of this to pass on now to the relations to matter into which the Christian system views man as placed. And though I cannot at all go into all the points in which the Christian view of our relation to systems of matter comes in, yet I may, I think, say, that if you go on to become a perfect Christian, you will find them to be very numerous, and to be concerned with almost the whole circuit of actions, from the highest privilege of our religion to the commonest act of common life. I should say, then, that relations to matter (5) into which we are viewed as placed by any religion, must form a very prominent feature in that religion.

RAD. This seems an unusual way of looking at a revelation. You have pointed out how the Law of Moses, viewed from without, represents man, as our laws do, as capable of sundry pollutions from matter: and this whole way of looking at man and matter may, I readily see, be called the doctrine of man's relations to matter. But I am desirous now to know further what the Christian doctrine of our relations to matter may be, and how far it agrees with the Indian schools or not.

LAUR. If I mistake not, the Vedantists would hold that all pollutions from matter are in fact unrealities (6), and take place in the world of unrealities; that the reason why the devout must abstain from them is because he cannot otherwise get free from the world of unrealities, and arrive at that state of mind in which spirit alone is discerned to exist. All that the senses convey to you they hold to be unreal: they think that the existence of the world of the senses is a mere deception altogether, and that the spirit could perform all its functions without them. If, then, you wish to see how your views and the Christian stand related to each other, we must first consider this.

And to show you that I do not omit taking in what may be the case in regard to the soul's capacity for acting without the senses, I will state that I think the senses, as Gotama (7) says, merely prepare things for our minds, and are not at all themselves organs of perception save as connected with the mind. Hence I can clearly see how, in visions (8) or other ecstatic conditions, the functions of one sense might be performed by another. Things, for all we know, might, if our souls were once set free from the body, come (as far as the possibilities of the matter are concerned) to the soul immediately, without any intervention of the senses whatever. What is possible, and what we think possible, are two very distinct things, which we are exceeding liable to confuse; but if we look, not to these, but to what actually takes place, I fear we shall find that we are far less independent of the body than we are minded sometimes to think. Every thing that we know of by experience leads to a contrary impression: an act of memory, for instance, is never in such sense an act of the soul alone as to dispense with the preceding operations of the bodily senses, through which it was, mediately or immediately, furnished with matter for recollection. Even your writers who speak of recollecting actions of a former life, mean, it seems, actions done in a former body, so that body is essential to the performing of those things which memory remembers. And I do not know that any of those who have laid the greatest claims to memory of such acts, have ever succeeded in finding language (9) which could represent them in such way as to avoid allusions to the body: which all seems as if we were dealing with something not meant for man, when we speak of the possibility of the soul existing, during all periods of its being, apart from the body; since it seems that, for all we know, being embodied at some time is an essential condition to its existing at all. But what would your sages say of the soul's connexion with the body?

RAD. Our sages would teach that the soul is imprisoned in this body for past sins in order to do penance here, which penance, according to the degree of it, is looked upon as the means of liberation from the body for a longer or a shorter period. It is one blessing of the Yoga (as they teach) to be free from the iron fetters of the body (10) for ever. For the great end of our philosophy is to divest men of unrealities of every kind, and therefore to be divested of body is a blessing.

LAUR. Hence, I suppose, it was that your ancestors used to burn (11) themselves sometimes; and we, too, hold that it is a blessing to be set free from the body; only we hold it so, in a very different light to what you do. For with us the separate existence of the soul is not looked upon as a blessing in and by itself, but in that it is a step towards a final union with the body, which union is to be eternal. In your view, then, the spirit's relation to that system of matter which we call our body is the relation which a spirit, interrupted for a time from its highest state by the body, holds to that body. In our view the soul's relation to that system is an eternal one, interrupted for a time by death. We look upon the compounded state, so to speak, in which soul and body are united, as essential to full and perfect happiness: you regard it as an obstacle to that happiness. The whole of our books teem with this doctrine. We are to be judged by a GOD who can ruin both body and soul in hell. And this is not a mere speculation with us, but an essential fundamental (12) doctrine of Christianity, insomuch that it is expressed in all our short summaries of belief, and cannot be denied by any man without his giving up the whole of Christianity as a distinctive system. It was, then, in this view that I said that our relations to matter, as recognized by the Christian system, were of the utmost importance. And the least possibility that such a doctrine should be true, ought to make it worth your while duly to consider it; for if it is true, it is most awful, and throws a new light over all our actions.

RAD. You seem, then, to be an advocate for the eternity of matter.

LAUR. By the eternity of matter you mean the existence of matter from everlasting; and so you have, I perceive, a very confused notion of what I mean. That which I assert is a very different position, viz. that the same GOD who created matter, at the time when He created it, or at any other subsequent time, or in any particular instances and kinds of it, had and has power to bestow upon it eternity; and this eternity is not a retrospective eternity from everlasting, but a prospective eternity to everlasting. As the soul is a created thing, and had a beginning, yet will last to eternity, so will the body, which had a beginning, also last to eternity. But I fear that you are so far in the habit of looking upon all created things as subject, from the very fact of their being created things, to destruction, that I shall not readily make myself intelligible to you.

RAD. I own, Laurence, that it does seem to me a most incredible doctrine that a soul should lose all connexion whatever with a system of matter, and yet at some time or another resume its connexion with that system.

LAUR. Let us, then, address ourselves to this difficulty first. To me it seems very much more credible that the soul, supposing it can be demonstrated to have lost all connexion with any given system of matter (which I do not think it can), should return to that system and vivify it again, than that it should vivify any other. Probability is the guide of life, and by some strange process of recondite reasoning in the mind, when a thing has once happened, it is natural to us to expect that it may happen again. Our souls, then, having been once in connexion with one particular system of matter, may with the least improbability be thought likely to resume that connexion at a future period. Neither is this likely only, but far more likely (13) than that they should become connected with any other system of matter. But you, who believe the transmigration of souls into other bodies, believe the more unlikely, and therefore ought not to hesitate at the less. It does, I confess, seem to me a very curious phenomenon, that those who discard Christianity upon the score of its containing in it some things incredible (14), may almost always, upon examination, be shown to believe somewhat more incredible themselves. No man ever objects to the Truth, who does not himself believe something harder to believe than the Truth.

RAD. But I cannot see that that is the case here. It seems to me reasonable enough to suppose that, if men are to be punished, they should be degraded in the creation; and that their souls should, in order to degradation, migrate into other animals, is perfectly reasonable also. Neither do I see how your mode of arguing from experience can come in here at all.

LAUR. Of course, if you think it decidedly revealed, then we must discuss, not the doctrine, but the genuineness of the revelation which teaches it. But as we have given sufficient time to that already, and as the notion of transmigration is completely at variance with our revelation; as, consequently, we have two conflicting revelations, we cannot do better than see whether there are not some things in experience which go against this notion also. Now, as we should both allow that the senses cannot perceive, except as instruments, it being the soul which perceives, it will follow that the body must have a certain adaptation to the soul, and the soul also to the body; they correspond to one (15) another. And even when limbs are cut off, it seems that the powers of motion in that direction which the soul had before, still reside in it, so as that the living being who has suffered the loss would be capable of moving as before, if it had another limb to move with. Thus it would be of no use to men to have in their souls a power of moving any limb which they have not, as, for instance, the trunk of an elephant; neither have we any evidence that they have any such power. But the motive powers of the soul are precisely those which are correlative to the body, if any are. So, too, the body of man is capable of expressing shame, which is a passion, as far as I know, peculiar to man; neither can I well conceive of its belonging to a creature of a higher or lower grade of being. And so great is the adaptation of the body to the soul (16), that it is not without an effort that men can undergo certain passions, and yet not feel the corresponding symptoms in their body (17), nor throw their body into the attitudes of rage or other passions, without feeling those passions in part. Every thing, then, leads us to suppose that the soul is framed to suit a certain body, and not another; not to mention that it seems that men who have certain passions strong by nature have certain indications more or less palpable (18) in their outward make and constitutions answerable to them. Experience, then, leads us to think that men have no capacities for entering into other bodies. And this experience extends over the whole of a man's duration, so far as we have means of knowing any thing of it; for the powers that the soul exercises in the conformation of the body (19) in the womb, appear to be the same powers as those which it subsequently has; and the other powers appear to exist there also, though not in actuality, owing to there being no scope for their exercise. And the notion which in the West was ascribed to your fathers, whereby they seem to have held that death put a man into a larger sphere of existence, as birth does (20), would seem to be an admission that those living powers continued both throughout the whole period of his duration which comes under our experience, and probably beyond it also. If, then, as far as we know, it is one soul which has actuated one body, both before that body was visible and after; and if, arguing from what we know, it is probable that the soul is incapable of actuating any other kind of body, I contend that experience does make it more probable that the soul should be joined to the same body, at some subsequent period, than that it should be joined to any other body.

We have, then, two revelations; one teaching that the soul will actuate other kinds of bodies, and another that it will actuate the same body at a future period. And both these revelations pretend to come from the same GOD, who is the Lord and Governor of the world; but the things which happen under the visible part of His government contravene the one revelation, do not contravene the other. As, then, both cannot be true, I think that the things happening under that part of His government must be taken as some kind of proof which of the two is the true one. And though, of course, it is wrong to lower revelation to the standard of experience, yet it cannot be wrong, when two revelations are before us, to choose that which does not conflict with our experience in preference to that which contradicts it, until some further evidence gives the latter a preponderance. Perhaps, however, I ought to let you know that I make the fullest allowance for your having been long attached to one system, and do not at all suppose that a man can alter his belief at a moment's notice, as soon as arguments overbear him. And this, perhaps, will make you not unwilling to allow me to proceed with further arguments from experience in favour of the resurrection of the body.

RAD. What you have urged upon the subject of the mutual correspondence between soul and body has certainly in it some weight; but I have one fact which appears to me to make very strongly against it, which is, that we have actual experience of certain insects actuating different kinds of bodies. Now, as our knowledge of what is or is not possible in the whole sphere of the creation is excessively limited; and as I hold it to be revealed that men's souls may migrate into different animals, why may I not also argue that my revelation does not contradict experience, since this is a fact which falls in with that revelation and confirms it?

LAUR. There seems to me to be this simple objection to your argument, which is, that however sudden such changes may be, there is no evidence that in those cases the living powers of the insect have ever been separated from that system of matter which they originally actuated: and therefore it would be fairer to urge such changes as parallel to the changes in a human body, which, though not so great perhaps, are yet surprisingly great (21). That the same living powers produce a given number of modifications in one system of matter with which we have never seen them unconnected, is no kind of ground for thinking that those living powers can actuate any other system of matter, subsequently to their having left that with which they are at present connected. But if you suppose the living powers of the worm to be other than the same with those of the fly, then plainly there is no further room for the comparison. Have you any further objection to make?

RAD. I do not know that this answer perfectly satisfies me, but shall turn it over in my mind some other time. There is, however, another objection, which seems also a strong one. Persons are possessed of a power of seeing things in ecstasies and dreams as if they were present to them, without their making any use of their organs of sense in order to see them. Now this seems to show that the present organs are far from being indispensable to the soul, that it may maintain its identity, in this life, without them, and that consequently it might maintain its identity with some other organs than the present.

LAUR. What you argue, then, is this; that the soul can act without any organs; therefore it might act with other than the present organs. But I never at all denied the possibility of the soul's existing separately, which all Christians believe that it will do, in the intermediate state between death and the resurrection of the body. All that I contended for was, that we had no ground for thinking that it could be embodied in any other system of matter than the present one, or one like it. But to say that because it may continue to exist without the present use of the body, therefore it might exist in another body, is to betake yourself to mere guess-work, whereas we were examining, how far what we know by experience fell in with our revelation, or with yours. However, I am glad you mentioned this, because it gives me an opportunity of saying that, if we had had any experience of any other life than the present, we should have recollections of it, as this analogy of dreams leads us to see. For we recollect, in many instances, the whole particulars of a dream, or, at all events, that we have been dreaming (22); whereas we cannot recollect any of the particulars of a whole life before the present, or even that we ever did live before. Neither does it seem to me of any avail to urge that some men have thought they could remember a previous existence: since, if this were a true account of things, all men would recollect (23) some facts in regard to their pre-existence, or, at least, that one fact that they had existed before, whereas I never met any one who did recollect such a fact. Again, if incorporation produces oblivion, then we cannot know that we existed in a former state. So that experience, even during the widest range that memory can extend over, cannot offer any proof to a revelation which teaches this as an essential part of its system.

RAD. Return then, Laurence, to the arguments in favour of the resurrection of the body, since we seem not likely to agree upon this point, and you dissuade any sudden change of opinions.

LAUR. All that we have said of the mutual correspondence between the soul and the body will, if upon further reflection you judge it true, be found to fall in with the doctrine of the resurrection of the body: since, if the soul requires the body here in order to its performing several functions, the likelihood is that it will also require it in a future state of existence, and not the contrary. When once the doctrine has been put before us, the fact of the soul's present dependence upon the body begets a likelihood that that doctrine is true rather than the reverse. And I think, when we come to dwell a little upon particulars, we shall see that this gives further weight to that general credibility drawn from the mere fact of the present dependence of the soul upon the body. Let us, then, proceed to notice some of the particulars, which I urge not as proving the doctrine apart from revelation, but as making the doctrine probable from experience, when it has been brought before us by revelation. First, all those who have dwelt upon the immortality (24) of the soul in a practical way have supposed that there was a future state of torment for the wicked, and with this Manu and your Purana agree. But, when they come to speak at all in detail of that torment, they suppose men endued with certain forms analogous, at least, to our present bodies. Their whole language upon the subject is just what one could conceive that of men with some naturally implanted (25) forebodings of the Christian view of future punishment would be. Hence these natural forebodings are a presumption strong, in proportion to the universality of them, in all nations in favour of the Christian doctrine, so far as the wicked are concerned. Secondly: the condition of our present life is such, that of three sorts of pains, those inflicted by Heaven, those of the body, and those of the soul, none appears to go on without the body (26). For the distresses of the mind affect the body, seemingly, in all cases; and in some cases to a degree almost miraculous, both for intensity and suddenness (27). And the inflictions of Heaven are of course resolvable into one or the other of these two classes of pain, and do come under the same observation. This is particularly the case in regard to hereditary disorders, whether of the mental or bodily constitution. This observation, then, that all pain appears to take place through, or, at least, not without the instrumentality of the body, would seem to make it (28) likely that pain may be executed in a future state by its means. Thirdly: a further confirmation is given to this fact by considering with what wonderful capacities for suffering we are endued; capacities to which our capacities for enjoyment bear no sort (29) of proportion, so far as we see them in this present portion of our existence. And it seems, from what was just said, as if no intense suffering was capable of taking place here without the body being affected by it. If, then, this life presents us with instances of protracted misery which are effected by the body, or not without it, the probability is that the sufferings of the wicked to all eternity will be carried on by means of the body, which is a probability that the bodies of the wicked will be restored in order to their future and durable state of suffering. Neither can the fact, that virtuous joys are in a great measure independent of the body, be made any presumption that the good will be liberated from the body. For this fact in itself would hardly afford any presumption one way or the other, since the case of dreams shows that the soul's capacity for independent action of some kinds will not at all disprove that it is embodied. But it seems fully met by several other things which might be noticed.

1. In the first place, there is often a positive pleasure in bearing pain submissively, with a sense that we are in a state of trial here, which submissiveness often displays itself in a wonderful sweetness and serenity upon the outward features. This submissiveness, then, may be looked upon as in some measure, though in a very slight one, rewarded openly here in this life through the body.

2. Again, there are several virtues, such as temperance and chastity (30), which seem to be virtues of the body almost as much as of the soul. And there are cases in which these virtues cannot be attained to, or at least preserved, without great toil and even pain to the body. And to this must be added that people's temptations to behave (31) ill seem to depend very much upon their natural constitution of body, even in the case of other vices than those directly connected with the body. Hence the presumption that the body will be rewarded arises not only from the consideration of one or two virtues in which it obviously has a large share, but also from that of others in which it has its share, though not as obviously so. For if all good government avails itself of pains and deprivations to check vice, then good self-government will do so likewise; and, as pain is effected by the body, self-government must

work upon the soul through the body even in these cases. And the soul must be supposed to exist in a future state along with those particular affections which must be supposed to remain, though subjugated; since it is proportionately credible, when put before us, that the body, though brought into subjection, should remain also in order to have its toils rewarded. But, as experience shows that it does not remain, the next credible thing is that it should be restored, since there is evidently no more difficulty to the Almighty in restoring it than in originally attaching it to the soul. As the recollection of past victories over passion (32) in itself is a natural source of pleasure and even joyousness of heart, which joyousness does not arise from the passions being eradicated and so no longer there, but from the sense that, though they are there, they are brought into captivity; so, if the body also, by means of which and in which they have been chastised, were likewise to remain (33), it would furnish additional happiness. Hence the Christian doctrine, that perfect happiness will not be attained until the restoration of the body, is a doctrine which is confirmed even by what we see of the purest pleasures, viz. those resulting from the recollection of past virtues.

4. But the general fact that there are several very innocent pleasures which the soul does not have without the body, such as the sight of the sun and the stars, and of the green fields, the smells of flowers and rain, the taste of food when hungry and of drink

when thirsty, the joyousness of a temperate meal, the happiness of shaking hands with those we love, and many other things, seems to intimate that there may be other pleasures conveyed to us in a future state through the body.

However, supposing it could not be made at all credible from reason that the body was requisite in order to perfect happiness, as well as in order to perfect pain; supposing, that is, that the Author of Nature had not placed within the reach of our unassisted reason any thing which should lead us to anticipate the need of our bodies in order to perfect happiness, as He has placed several which lead us to anticipate its need in order to perfect pain; still there would be an obvious reason why we should have stronger evidence for this latter than for the former. For mankind are in no need (34) of arguments for pleasure; whereas there is a constant need of their being kept in awe of punishment, especially when the punishment is at a great distance off. And it seems as if the sense of shame which is felt at past sin, even a very long time after it has been forsaken, was a witness in the natural government of God (35) (who knows best men's needs) of the exceeding need we have of the fear of punishment to keep us from going wrong. For whoever considers what shame is, will see that it is a fear of punishment of some kind or other. Yet I think the soul's dependence upon the health of the body for many of its present functions, in itself is to be taken as a token of what may be the case in a future state. And I must again remind you that I am not attempting to prove the doctrine as a mathematician would a theorem, but merely to show that, when it has been put before us, there is nothing impossible in the thing itself, that there are traditions and analogies within all men's reach which fall in with it, and that all we know of pleasure and pain is not against the doctrine, but rather for it.

RAD. There seem, Laurence, to be two things which I hold to be of considerable weight against all you have said. You argue, as far as I understand the general drift of your argument, that our connexion with a certain system of matter called our body in this present life, is of such a nature as to beget a presumption that we shall at some time resume that body and "not another[1]." And, in particular, the agency of that system in producing pleasure and pain was very much insisted upon, they being the means of reward and punishment. Now, although I have other objections of a deeper kind to this doctrine, yet there are one or two which lie against the surface of it, which I wish to ask you about. First, then, it seems to me that it is not that system of matter which we call our bodies, but the world's vastidity, which acts upon us in order to produce pleasure and pain. Parts of this larger system of matter, at a great distance off, Surya and Soma,

[1] Job xix. 27.

and the rest, act upon us in several ways. Why then, if present connexion is any ground whatever for assuming future connexion, am I not to conclude by parity of reasoning that the devout will take this whole system also to heaven with him? This, then, is one objection; and there is another connected with it, which is, that from the instances you gave of innocent pleasures conveyed through the body, one might justly conclude that you expected eating and drinking in this new heavens and new earth, which seem to be required in order to make your doctrine consistent.

LAUR. Let me take your last objection first. Although the Kingdom of Heaven be not meat and drink, according to our great Doctor, yet, had I asserted that it was so, I do not think you would have any right to object. For all nations, and the Indians amongst them, have supposed some Amrita, whereby the (36) immortals were sustained. And though the Chhandogya speaks of the sight only as sufficient to sustain them, still that sight presumes the existence of the matter as necessary in order that they may be supported in their immortal conditions. And our books also speak of Angels as having (37) meat which has been also bestowed on men. And so of old the Soma drink was thought to confer immortality. Now much as there is of truth (38) at the bottom of these universal traditions, I shall not notice it here any more than I have done; but shall merely caution you against supposing that we can understand with what body men come into Heaven. There all is spiritual; spiritual bodies, spiritual sustenance, spiritual joys. Without at all presuming to define what the Supper may be whereof our books speak, I merely say thus much, that so far am I from denying that spiritual bodies may need their proper support, that I know not but that even souls would come to utter annihilation (39) without support ministered to them by God. And therefore, provided you confuse not the heavenly with the gross and earthly, I have no reason for wishing to elude your assertion that I hold that there may be support to be ministered in Heaven. For we see that matter is capable of undergoing such astonishing changes here without ceasing to be the same matter, that we know nothing at all of the inherent capacities or needs of special kinds of it. Hence we know not what change our bodies may undergo. Thus when a seed is put into the ground it dies, and recovers (40), and gains a form which, antecedently to experience, would have been incredible; and yet, in a loose and popular way of speech, we may justly say that the life and organization of the plant which were contained in the seed are the same as those afterwards developed (41). If, then, the capacities of immortality are sown within our bodies here, they may be raised in a spiritual condition hereafter, and to a sphere of agency with limits (42) indeed, yet of far wider extent than any of which we have any present conception. And whether or no there are to be new heavens and a new earth in the sense you anticipate, certain it is that our books do speak as if such were to be the case (43) in some sense. And without going at all into any particulars of the case, I am sure you must see that, if you once admit that a man will exist in a future state, you must of necessity assume him to be in a world suited to those appetites, passions, and affections which he shall then have: our nature corresponds now and, for all we can see, always must correspond to our external condition, and our external condition to it. The existence, then, of that nature with a renewed body necessarily supposes a sphere of action over against it, and correspondent to it. So that without determining what will be the employment and happiness (44), the particular life, of good men hereafter, there must be some determinate capacities, some necessary character and qualifications, without which persons cannot but be utterly incapable of it; and the converse. Yet I think there is also a great difference between our interest in a system of matter so intimately united to us as our bodies are, and any external system of matter which can only act upon us through the body; and although there may be very great difficulty in stating in what the identity of the body to be raised is to consist, yet it seems a clear way of speaking enough to say that, if all the particles which ever entered into the composition of our bodies were brought together, we should have a far more intimate connexion with them than with any other particles.

And to suppose that God does not know which out of all the particles (45) they were, or is unable to decide which are most properly and especially ours, is plainly to set limits to omniscience. Let me, then, beg you not to raise too many objections (46), which may always be raised against the verbal statement of a doctrine: when people discuss a thing together, they are more likely to deceive themselves than they are when thinking them quietly over (47) alone; and that, in a great measure, owing to the imperfections of language. Consider, then, the thing in a practical light, and remember that probability is the guide of life; that, when we have a chance of being brought before a judge in this life, we behave in all respects as if we were sure of it, because that is the safest way to meet the trial (48). For, if it should by any chance turn out true that we are to receive in the body the things done in the body, then will it be woe to him who has had the evidence of it put before him, and has not acted upon it. Woe will it be to him that has polluted himself at the feasts of idols, when he finds that, in spite of the obscurity of the evidence, the thing is true, and that when his limbs come together again, they have in them the stains of past sin, and he sees the Judge before him like a refiner's fire, and a hell which no revolution of Kalpas will ever bring to an end prepared from of old for all that live ungodly, but chiefly for those that defile the flesh and speak evil of authorities. The danger, Rádhákánt, is very great, and enough to rouse up the whole energies of our soul, and make us awake to the slightest evidence, lest we displease Him who will destroy both soul and body in hell.

RAD. This is certainly a ground of terror, and one which I trust I shall not recklessly put aside. Yet I before said that there were other objections to the doctrine which I thought lay deeper, and to which I shall be most desirous to see what you have to say. I begin now to see very clearly why you made such an attack upon the Vedánta system; since, if it were true, Christianity must be false, according to your representation of it. Still it has been my habit to think that the constant flux of the whole material world was a proof of its perishableness, and that spirit only will ultimately survive all these changes which we see, and those which we have been taught to expect. Soul, by being associated with Pracriti, appears to us to be vitiated (49), and assume the qualities of grosser natures, although essentially distinct from them and incorruptible. Now it is the object of the Yogi to attain to discriminative knowledge, and thereby to be liberated ultimately from existence, and become one with the Supreme. And it seems to me that this view has much to commend it, and might be true even though it could be proved that matter has a real existence, since that real existence may be temporal. We hold further that the soul consists of two parts, the Manas and the Paramâtma, and that by this latter men are capable of union with the Supreme, of such kind that at the end of the life of Brahma they will be absorbed into him and become identified (50) with him. And we believe that the Paramâtma is now identical with Achyuta, only that through want of Vijnana men do not see it.

LAUR. If, then, I understand you, the Paramâtma is the only real part of a man, and the body and Manas are but appearances and unrealities; and the main business of the devout is to attain, through Vijnana, to the understanding or perception of that reality and this unreality.

RAD. Rightly understood, Laurence. Now tell me what Christians will say to this immaterial view of things.

LAUR. I fear, Rádhákánt, that you mistake me when you speak, as you do now of yours, as an immaterial view of things. The Christian religion, by holding that there is an intermediate state in which the soul exists separately from the body, is an antagonist to materialism, to say nothing of its opposing a belief in the retrospective eternity of matter, which is an essential part of materialism. And by asserting that our bodies will be raised again, it is an antagonist to the Vedánta system, because such an assertion implies the reality of matter. But you must see at once that such a view of things, *à fortiori*, would assert the individuality and real personality of the soul. You, I know, hold existence to be pain, and absorption—i. e. annihilation of individual existence—to be the only true happiness. Let me, then, put before you a little more distinctly what the Christian view of man's nature is, as more immediately opposed to the one which you have just stated.

We hold, then, as well as you, that there is a three-fold division of man into spirit, soul, and body; but of these three (51), two, the soul and the body, are, logically speaking (in the Christian view), far more essential to man than the other—the spirit. The soul may, in some sense, be said to be the essence of man, as the body may be supposed to be removed from him, and is removed from him, in the intermediate state, without destroying his individuality. With the body he continues in the visible world, and through it he receives all the greatest blessings bestowed on him during this portion of his existence, whether those blessings are of a transient nature or of a permanent one. And this body, we believe, will be raised up in consequence of the redemption of man by the Incarnation (52). And though the body is essential to our present notion of a man, yet, as it is plain that he can exist without it, we may call it an accident of his essence, though it is more inseparable from our notion of man than spirit is, since the damned in hell are to be cut off from the spirit, and are to consist only of body and soul. Spirit, then, whereby man communes with heavenly things, is not, as your system represents it, the only part of man which subsists eternally, but a divine gift, which may be removed from him without destroying his everlasting subsistency. According to your doctrine, the end of the present Kalpa will be the end of all existence, the spirits of the good losing their individuality, and becoming one with the Supreme; according to ours, the good will not only retain their individuality to all eternity, but will, at the end of the present dispensation, resume their bodies also. The bad, on the contrary, instead of being destroyed, are to undergo a second (53) death; and as in the death of this Kalpa there is a separation between the parts of the compound (54) being into body and that which is incorporeal, so in the second death there will be (55) also a separation of the spirit from the soul now united indissolubly to the body, and one with it eternally for eternal pain and misery.

And our great doctors view this gift of the Spirit, not as you do, as one with Achyuta, and not as if man had never fallen from it (56), but as the very thing which through the fall of man was forfeited to him, which it is the great glory of Christianity to have restored to him, and which can only be entirely forfeited again by gross sin or long-continued carelessness. And so very great is this gift, that the possession of it makes all outward distinction to sink into nothing in comparison of it. Hence we do not teach that there are spiritual (57) castes in the world by birth, but that the gift is not by birth but by grace; and that it is open to all men alike who, by repentance and self-abasement, seek it. Neither Mlechchha, nor Sudra, nor Chandála, is excluded from receiving it. And little as I care myself for seeing these distinctions violently done away with, much indeed do I desire to see that inward and invisible gift of glory imparted to all, since, when it is once imparted, much as it may be abused by many, it will work its way through all outward distinctions and gently level them, as men are fit for it, and feel indeed that they are all brethren. For be assured, Rádhákánt, that all these outward distinctions are as nothing in the sight of the Most High. Already He declares it through the works of Nature—none of the gods of the nations can give rain as He does, even to the unthankful and the evil, as well as to the just, that He may win, if possible, all to Himself through the food and gladness which He distributes indiscriminately to all. Already has this inward and spiritual gift broken down before its unseen agency many of the distinctions which existed in the world, and it will still work far and wide. And if men will persist in pampering their bodies through luxury, or their souls through pride, so that they will not yield to this mighty decree of Heaven, they can only hold out against it for a very little while. And consider what I am saying: if by any possibility the Christian, and not the Indian, should be the true account of the case; if the Lord God of Christians has made a decree to give a new birth to all that ask it, which makes the slave that has it better than the king that has it not, and the Chandála that enjoys it nobler than the noblest-sprung of all the Saraswatas; if He for His wise purposes has winked at those distinctions for many generations, but now, by taking upon Himself our nature, has read with a voice of thunder to us the lessons of humility; how dreadful, if by any chance this be so, will it be to resist His will, who setteth up one and putteth down another, who cares not whether men come from the east or from the west, or from the north or from the south, or for any outward distinction, but for those, and those only, who have, or by obedience are seeking to have, this great and glorious gift of spiritual new birth, which is a fountain open to all men! And if you do resist, you cannot do so long; for He has appointed a day in the which He will judge all men by our Lord and Master—all men will be gathered before Him, Christians and Gentiles, Jews and Barbarians, Sacæ and Indians, Brahmans and Chandálas; and all of them will be raised again with their bodies, that all flesh may see the salvation of our God. And when they have received their new bodies, every knee shall bow before the Lord, and every tongue shall confess, and give an account of himself to God. And all men, when they see this great miracle, shall be at length humbled before Him, from the highest priest to the lowest slave: all distinctions will then be *seen* to be, what they now at this moment are, as nothing and less than nothing before Him. In vain will men here have resisted His scheme for levelling all men of all classes, when they all stand before this judgment-seat. Consider, then, how you will feel, if these things are true; if you rise up clothed with an imperishable body which no revolutions or transmigrations shall ever undo or dissolve; if with that body you shall have to go into eternal misery, provided you despise the lowest Sudra who shall have the gift of the Spirit. For me, I own that I am horribly afraid when I consider how even Christians ill-treat servants at times: still more am I afraid for those who live in continual estrangement from any class of men save those whose sins make it necessary. And the reason is, because that day will come so soon (considering the short-lived nature of all human things); and, when I know that angels and apostles, and saints and Gentiles, will all be present at that great confession, I marvel and am exceedingly afraid at what our books say: "The LORD *alone* shall be exalted in that day."

END OF THE THIRD DIALOGUE.

NOTES TO DIALOGUE III.

NOTE (1.) p. 259.

St. Justin Martyr, Apol. p. 65. b. Ἡμεῖς τὰ νεκρούμενα καὶ εἰς γῆν βαλλόμενα πάλιν ἀπολήψεσθαι ἑαυτῶν σώματα προσδοκῶμεν, ἀδύνατον μηδὲν εἶναι τῷ Θεῷ λέγοντες, καὶ κατανοοῦντι ἀπιστότερον ἂν μᾶλλον δόξαι ἢ εἰ σώματι μὴ ὑπήρχομεν, καί τις ἔλεγεν ἐκ μικρᾶς τινὸς ῥανίδος τῆς τοῦ ἀνθρωπείου σπέρματος δυνατὸν ὀστέα τε καὶ νεῦρα καὶ σάρκας εἰκονοποιηθέντα, οἷα ὁρῶμεν γενέσθαι· ἔστω γὰρ νῦν ἐφ' ὑποθέσεως λεγόμενον· εἴ τις ὑμῖν μὴ οὖσι τοιούτοις μηδὲ τοιούτων, ἔλεγε τὸ σπέρμα ἀνθρώπειον δεικνὺς, καὶ εἰκόνα γραπτὴν, ἐκ τοῦ τοιοῦδε οἷόν τε γενέσθαι διαβεβαιόμενος, πρὶν ἰδεῖν γενόμενον ἐπιστεύσατε; οὐκ ἄν τις τολμήσειεν ἀντειπεῖν· τὸν αὐτὸν οὖν τρόπον, διὰ τὸ μήπω ἑωρακέναι ὑμᾶς ἀναστάντα νεκρὸν, ἀπιστία ἔχει. The same mystery is noticed by S. Method. de Resur. § 14, p. 780, Gallandi; Const. Ap. v. 8; S. Greg. Nyss. (or probably Nemesius) de Op. Hominis, p. 119, cap. xxvii.; and by St. Dionysius of Alexandria, though with a different reference, ap. Euseb. P. E. p. 779. "—— Unde autem mens humana dies istos commutationis speculari et arcana naturæ rimari potuerit, nemo miretur. Hæc enim frequens medicorum experientia pervidit, qui cum multas animadverterint semen non retinere conceptum, compertum habuerunt, quod intra sex dies septemve ejiciebatur esse *lacteum*, et vocaverunt ἔκρυσιν, quod postea autem sanguineum atque ἐκτρωσμὸς appellabatur," as Censorinus de D. N. xi. notices. The same is noticed also by Holy Scripture, Job x. 10. "Hast thou not poured me out as *milk*, and curdled me like cheese? Thou hast clothed me with skin and flesh, and hast fenced me with bones and sinews;" which passage is quoted by St. Dionysius. See also Ps. cxxxix., which is evidently looking to this passage. Of either place we may use the words of St. Gregory the Great on Job, l. c.: "Angusta Dei laus est descriptio creati corporis, nisi etiam subsequenter exprimatur mira aspiratio vivificationis." Censorinus, in another place (v. 3), also says: "Illud quoque ambiguam facit inter auctores opinionem, utrumne ex patris tantummodo semine partus nascatur . . . . an etiam ex matris;" on which Gruber observes: "Veteres philosophi de hac re valde dissenserunt, ut noster docet; recentiores medici vero probarunt, utrumque maris æque ac fœminæ semen ad procreandum sobolem esse necessarium." When, therefore, Scripture speaks of Levi as in the loins of his father, it of course can only mean the matter out of which his *body* was in part to be formed: it must not be so understood as if it implied a materialist view of the origin of life. The existence of matter in the woman, requisite also for the formation of a man in her, leads one to very awful thoughts, were this the place to enter upon them. See below, Note 19.

Note (2.) p. 261.

The Cainites followed out the doctrine of impurity of matter so far as to reject baptism by water. See Dr. Pusey on Tertull. p. 255, and Spencer ad Orig. c. Cels. iii. p. 119.

Note (3.) p. 261.

In Deut. xii. 15. "Notwithstanding thou mayest kill and eat flesh in all thy gates, *whatsoever thy soul lusteth after*, according to the blessing of the Lord thy God which he hath given thee: the unclean and the clean may eat thereof, as of the roebuck, and of the hart. Only ye shall not eat the blood." This text seems to show that whatever the soul lusteth after, might lawfully be eaten by the Jews in their own houses; that *there* no distinction of kinds of flesh prevailed, but only in the holy place. The word "notwithstanding" obviously contrasts this with the preceding verse, "In the place which the LORD shall choose in one of thy tribes, *there* thou shalt offer thy burnt-offerings, and *there* thou shalt do all that I command thee." Verse 15 then states the exception to this obligation, as 16 states the exception to the permission; each, in the original, begins with the same particle, רק, which the Chaldee, Syriac, and Greek also keep the same. Verse 20 contains the same permission: "When the LORD thy God shall enlarge thy border, as he hath promised thee, and thou shalt say, I will eat flesh, (because thy soul lusteth to eat flesh,) thou mayest eat flesh, whatsoever thy soul lusteth after." In the next verse, if we introduce a semicolon after the words, "As I have commanded thee," which will be authorized by the Athnach in the Hebrew, it will then state the obligation with the same exceptions as before. Rabbi Ismael (in the Pesikta, Ugolini, xvi. p. dccccxxi.) says that "the text shows that Israel was forbidden flesh that they lusted after in the wilderness, but when they came into the land, the Scripture allowed them this." And there would be a reason for this in what Porphyry says, iii. 18: that GOD forbad eating animals, ἡδονῆς χάριν, which may be taken as a specimen of heathen faith upon the subject, and is the denial of the text in question. For this, as well as Genes. ix. 3, quoted above, p. 113, seems to give men an arbitrary power over the brute creation; by which is not meant the right to kill wantonly, but the right to kill all and any species of animal that they fancy for food. The principle here implied has been already given in a passage from St. Cyril, Note 60 on Dial. ii. The text seems, however, to contain an anticipation of Christian times, as is well observed by an anonymous author in the Σειρὰ ο' Πατρῶν, p. 1483. Μᾶλλον προφητεύει, he says, περὶ τῶν ἀληθῶς Ἰσραηλιτῶν, λέγω δὴ περὶ τῶν Χριστοῦ δούλων τῶν καὶ κρέα ἕτερα ἐσθιόντων παρὰ τὰ εἰρημένα καθαρά. A Jewish gloss, which has been adopted in the Vulgate, prevents our having the opinion of the Latin Fathers on the Hebrew text; yet St. Austin, c. Adim. xv. 1, says (after quoting Mark vii. 15. Matt. xv. 11. Rom. xiv. 21), "Dum cupit de Novo Testamento Veteri adversari, *ubi* dictum est, Secundum desiderium animæ tuæ occide, et manduca omnem carnem?" He presently after notices how the distinction between clean and unclean was adopted to signify the characters of such as were inadmissible into the Church.

Note (4.) p. 261.

On the subject of the allowableness of eating blood, the reader will find a disquisition at the end of Tertullian's Apology, as edited by Dr. Pusey.

Note (5.) p. 262.

St. Paul, Galat. iv. 3, speaks of being in bondage under the elements of the world; and perhaps, if we consider how many legal enactments were restrictions upon the use of matter in one way or other, there will be no need to take the word 'elements' in other than its ordinary sense. Compare Note 7 on Dial. iv.

Note (6.) p. 262.

See Frank's Vedánta Sara, p. 6 of translation. "Das Wesen ist das seyende, denkende, seelige, nicht entzweiete Subject-object (Brahma). Die *ganze Vielheit des Unempfindlichen* von dem Bewusstlosen Anfangend ist das Nichtwesen." Scarcely any thing is more terrible than a belief in the unreality of matter seems calculated to become in wicked hands.

Note (7.) p. 263.

Canada held that the senses only prepared things for the mind (Windis. p. 1933); and Gotama maintained (ibid. p. 1912) that they acted not independently, but by means of the five elements which had a relation to them, and by which they saw, heard, &c. See Manu, i. 75. Plato Theæt. § 102. Σκοπεῖ ἡ ἀπόκρισις ποτέρα ὀρθοτέρα ᾧ ὁρῶμεν τοῦτο εἶναι ὀφθαλμοὺς ἢ δι' οὗ ὁρῶμεν· καὶ ᾧ ἀκούομεν, ὦτα ἢ δι' οὗ ἀκούομεν; κ. τ. λ. And so Aristot. de Animâ, i. 4. p. 408, b. 20. iii. 1, 2.

Note (8.) p. 263.

Aretas in Apoc. p. 193. Ταὐτὸν ἡ πνευματικὴ ἀκοὴ τῇ βλέψει. S. Austin. de Trin. xv. 18. "Nec tamen quia dicimus locutiones cordis esse cogitationes, ideo non sunt etiam visiones exortæ de notitiæ visionibus, quando veræ sunt. Foris enim cum per corpus hæc fiunt, aliud est locutio, aliud visio: intus autem cum cogitamus, utrumque unum est." Comp. de Civ. D. xi. c. 27.

Note (9.) p. 264.

If St. Paul (2 Cor. xii. 2) was, when in an ecstasy [1], independent of the senses, still what he then saw could not be uttered: ἄῤῥητα ῥήματα ἃ οὐκ ἐξὸν ἀνθρώπῳ λαλῆσαι· on which St. Clement, Strom. v. 80, observes: Οὐ νόμῳ καὶ φόβῳ παραγγελίας τινὸς τὸ οὐκ ἐξὸν προστιθεὶς, δυνάμει δὲ ἁγίᾳ ἄφθεγκτον εἶναι τὸ θεῖον μηνύων, εἴγε ὑπὲρ οὐρανὸν τὸν τρίτον ἄρχεται λαλεῖσθαι, ὡς θέμις τοῖς ἐκεῖ μυσταγωγεῖν τὰς ἐξειλεγμένας ψυχάς. p. 293, Pott.

[1] S. Aust. in Ps. lxvii. § 36, thus defines ecstasy: "Ecstasis est mentis excessus, quod aliquando pavore contingit; nonnunquam vero per aliquam revelationem, alienatione mentis a sensibus corporis, ut spiritui quod demonstrandum est, demonstretur."

Note (10.) p. 264.

The bodies through which a person had gone are compared by Patanjali, in Windisch. p. 1589, to iron fetters. A kindred notion occurred among the Jews (v. Buxtorf in v. נדן) and the Stoics (see Gatak. ad Anton. ix. 3), and was afterwards adopted by the Manicheans, who called bodies "carceres Dei." S. Aust. c. Faust. xx. 22. Tit. Bostr. c. Manich. i. 13, 29.

Note (11.) p. 264.

See Wilson in v. पंचाग्नि St. Clement, ii. 125, p. 494, quotes a Stoic as saying he would rather see one Indian roasting himself, than hear any number of demonstrations to show that pain is nothing. Strabo, p. 1006, mentions an Indian who burnt himself at Athens.

Note (12.) p. 265.

It would be endless to quote passages from the Fathers, in which the resurrection of the body is pointed out as a distinctive doctrine of Christianity. St. Justin Martyr, p. 26, appears to think that Plato had some notion of it. Pantheistic heresies, as borrowing from heathen systems, very commonly deny it, and it is to be feared that too many Christians live from day to day in a practical disbelief of the doctrine.

Note (13.) p. 267.

This argument was very often urged by the Fathers: for references, see Dr. Pusey's note on Tertullian's Apology, c. 48.

Note (14.) p. 267.

S. Austin somewhere says: "Fit credibiliorum fides ex incredibilioribus creditis." Similar words occur de C. D. xxii. 5.

Note (15.) p. 268.

Aristot. de An. i. 3, extr. Ἐπιχειροῦσι μόνον λέγειν ποῖόν τι ἡ ψυχὴ, περὶ δὲ τοῦ δεξομένου σώματος οὐθὲν ἔτι προσδιορίζουσιν, ὥσπερ ἐνδεχόμενον κατὰ τοὺς Πυθαγορικοὺς μύθους τὴν τυχοῦσαν ψυχὴν εἰς τὸ τυχὸν ἐνδύεσθαι σῶμα· δοκεῖ γὰρ ἕκαστον ἴδιον ἔχειν εἶδος καὶ μορφήν. And in his Prior Analytics, ii. 27. p. 70, b. 7. Τὸ δὲ φυσιογνωμονεῖν δυνατόν ἐστιν, εἴ τις δίδωσιν ἅμα μεταβάλλειν τὸ σῶμα καὶ τὴν ψυχὴν ὅσα φυσικά ἐστι παθήματα, κ. τ. λ. The principle here stated is carried out in his Physiognomonica. The latter passage tends to show the existence of subsequent reciprocal changes; the former, of an original correlativeness between the soul and body. This correlativeness is further dwelt upon by Origen in the following words, c. Cels. iv. p. 203. Ἔτι δὲ καὶ τοῦτό φαμεν τῷ Κέλσῳ εἰπόντι ὅτι ψυχὴ μὲν Θεοῦ ἔργον, σώματος δὲ ἄλλη φύσις· καὶ οὐ μόνον ἀκατασκευάστως τὸ τηλικοῦτον δόγμα ῥίψαντι, ἀλλὰ καὶ ἀδιορίστως· οὐ γὰρ ἐσαφήνισε, πότερον πᾶσα ψυχὴ Θεοῦ ἔργον, ἢ μόνη ἡ λογική· φαμὲν τοίνυν πρὸς αὐτὸν, εἰ μὲν πᾶσα ψυχὴ Θεοῦ ἔργον, δηλονότι καὶ τῶν ἀλόγων καὶ εὐτελεστάτων· ἵνα καὶ παντὸς σώματος ἄλλη φύσις ᾖ παρὰ τὴν τῆς ψυχῆς· ἔοικε μέν τοι ἐν τοῖς ἑξῆς, ἐν οἷς καὶ θεοφιλέστερα τὰ ἄλογα ζῶά φησιν ἡμῶν, καὶ τοῦ θείου τὴν ἔννοιαν ἔχειν καθαρωτέραν, παριστάνειν, ὅτι οὐ μόνον ἡ τῶν ἀνθρώπων, ἀλλὰ πολὺ μᾶλλον καὶ ἡ τῶν ἀλόγων ζώων ψυχὴ ἔργον ἐστὶ τοῦ Θεοῦ· τοῦτο γὰρ ἀκολουθεῖ τῷ θεοφιλέστερα λέγεσθαι ἐκεῖνα ἡμῶν. Εἰ δὲ μόνη ἡ λογικὴ ψυχὴ Θεοῦ ἔργον ἐστὶ, πρῶτον μὲν οὐκ ἐσαφηνίσας τὸ τοιοῦτον· δεύτερον δὲ ἀκολουθεῖ τῷ ἀδιορίστως εἰρῆσθαι περὶ τῆς ψυχῆς, ὡς οὐ πάσης, ἀλλὰ μόνης τῆς λογικῆς οὔσης Θεοῦ ἔργον, τὸ μηδὲ παντὸς σώματος εἶναι φύσιν, εἰ δὲ μὴ παντὸς σώματος ἄλλη φύσις, ἀλλ' ἑκάστου δὲ τὸ σῶμα ζώου ἀνάλογον τῇ ψυχῇ· δῆλον ὅτι οὗ ψυχὴ Θεοῦ ἔργον ἐστὶ, διαφέροι ἂν τὸ ταύτης σῶμα σώματος, ἐν ᾧ οἰκεῖ ψυχὴ οὐκ οὖσα ἔργον Θεοῦ. Καὶ οὕτω ψεῦδος ἔσται, τὸ μηδὲν διοίσειν νυκτερίδος, ἢ εὐλῆς, ἢ βατράχου σῶμα παρὰ τὸ τοῦ ἀνθρώπου· καὶ γὰρ ἄτοπον, λίθους μὲν λίθων, καὶ οἰκοδομήματα οἰκοδομημάτων νομίζεσθαι εἶναι καθαρώτερα ἢ μιαρώτερα, παρὰ τὸ εἰς τιμὴν τοῦ θείου κατεσκευάσθαι, ἢ εἰς ἀτιμοτάτων σωμάτων καὶ ἐναγῶν ὑποδοχήν· σώματα δὲ σωμάτων μὴ διαφέρειν, παρὰ τὸ λογικὰ εἶναι τὰ ἐνοικήσαντα, ἢ ἄλογα, καὶ λογικῶν τὰ σπουδαιότερα, ἢ τοὺς φαυλοτάτους ἀνθρώπους. Τὸ τοιοῦτόν γε πεποίηκε τολμῆσαί τινας ἀποθεῶσαι μὲν τὰ τῶν διαφερόντων σώματα, ὡς δεξάμενα ψυχὴν σπουδαίαν· ἀποῤῥίψαι δὲ ἢ ἀτιμάσαι τὰ τῶν φαυλοτάτων· οὐχ ὅτι πάντως τὸ τοιοῦτον ὑγιῶς γεγένηται, ἀλλ' ὅτι ἀπό τινος ἐννοίας ὑγιοῦς ἔσχε τὴν ἀρχήν· ἢ ὁμοίως ὁ σοφὸς μετὰ τὴν τελευτὴν Ἀνύτου καὶ Σωκράτους φροντίσει τῆς ταφῆς τοῦ Σωκράτους σώματος καὶ τοῦ Ἀνύτου; καὶ τὸ παραπλήσιον ἀμφοτέροις κατασκευάσει ἠρίον ἢ τάφον; καὶ ταῦτα διὰ τὸ 'ὧν οὐδὲν ἔργον Θεοῦ' (τοῦ ὧν ἀναφερομένου ἐπὶ τὸ τοῦ ἀνθρώπου σῶμα, ἢ τῶν ἐκ τοῦ σώματος ὄφεων· καὶ ἐπὶ τὸ βοὸς, ἢ τῶν ἐκ τοῦ σώματος βοὸς μελισσῶν· καὶ ἐπὶ τὸ ἵππου, ἢ ὄνου, καὶ τῶν ἐξ ἵππου μὲν σφηκῶν, ἐξ ὄνου δὲ κανθάρων·) δι' ἃ ἠναγκάσθημεν ἐπαναλαβεῖν καὶ τὸ 'ψυχὴ μὲν Θεοῦ ἐστὶν ἔργον, σώματος δὲ ἄλλη φύσις.' Εἶθ' ἑξῆς φησιν, ὅτι κοινὴ ἡ πάντων τῶν προειρημένων σωμάτων φύσις καὶ μία ἐς ἀμοιβὴν παλίντροπον ἰοῦσα καὶ ἐπανιοῦσα· καὶ πρὸς τοῦτο δὲ δῆλον ἐκ τῶν προειρημένων, ὅτι οὐ μόνον τῶν προκατειλεγμένων σωμάτων κοινή ἐστιν ἡ φύσις, ἀλλὰ καὶ τῶν ἐπουρανίων, κ. λ. To which may be added a passage from the work attributed to St. Gregory Nyssen,—De Hominis Opificio, p. 125, c. Ὥσπερ τελειωθεὶς ὁ ἄνθρωπος ἐν τοῖς μείζοσιν, ἔχει διαφαινομένην τῆς ψυχῆς τὴν ἐνέργειαν· οὕτως ἐν ἀρχῇ τῆς συστάσεως τὴν κατάλληλόν τε καὶ σύμμετρον τῇ παρούσῃ χρείᾳ συνέργειαν τῆς ψυχῆς ἐφ' ἑαυτοῦ διαδείκνυσι, ἐν τῷ κατασκευάζειν αὐτὸν ἑαυτῇ διὰ τῆς ἐντεθείσης ὕλης τὸ προσφυὲς οἰκητήριον· οὐδὲ γὰρ εἶναι δυνατὸν λογιζόμεθα, ἀλλοτρίαις οἰκοδομαῖς τὴν ψυχὴν ἐναρμόζεσθαι, ὡς οὐκ ἔστι τὴν ἐν τῷ κηρῷ σφραγῖδα πρὸς ἀλλοτρίαν ἁρμοσθῆναι γλυφήν· καθάπερ γὰρ τὸ σῶμα ἐκ βραχυτάτου πρὸς τὸ τέλειον πρόεισιν, οὕτω καὶ ἡ τῆς ψυχῆς ἐνέργεια καταλλήλως ἐμφυομένη τῷ ὑποκειμένῳ, συνεπιδίδωσι καὶ συναύξεται· προηγεῖται μὲν γὰρ αὐτῆς ἐν τῇ πρώτῃ κατασκευῇ οἷον ῥίζης τινὸς ἐν τῇ γῇ κατακρυφθείσης ἡ αὐξητική τε καὶ θρεπτικὴ δυνάμις μόνη· οὐ γὰρ χωρεῖ τὸ περισσότερον ἡ τοῦ δεχομένου βραχύτης.

This belief that the soul passed into different bodies Aristotle evidently takes to have been *literally* maintained; as did the Fathers, several passages from whom have been collected by Ritterhuis on Porphyr. de Vita Pythag. p. 159, ed. Kiessling. In later times some have endeavoured to defend the ancients, as though it was only a symbolical mode of speaking with them. Olearius on Philostratus, iii. 16, p. 108, maintains that Philostratus intended to represent even Iarchas (the Indian of whom Apollonius learnt) as holding this opinion. Now, though I do not feel satisfied with his evidence, yet I think it immaterial if true; for after our Lord's time those who adhered to heathenism endeavoured to explain, as allegorical, the pagan stories of the gods, and so to set up a counter-system to the allegory of the Church. As Apollonius imitated, by Satanic instinct, the kindness of Christianity towards slaves (Philostr. iv. 34), so he may have acted in regard to explanation of myths also. For this was a common practice of Platonists (see Van Goens's Diss. i. § 3, ad Porph. de Antro Nymph.), who did well to try and rid themselves by allegory of their obscene absurdities, yet had no systematic creed to be a standard whereby they could allegorize aright. Hence their attempt to reverse the process, which, as Confucius says, led them into error (see above p. 240), did but expose their inconsistency the more, seeing they did it not from a love of truth, but for the maintenance of their own opinion. Origen well observes, c. Cels. p. 123. Ἐὰν δὲ . . . ἐπὶ ἀλληγορίας καταφεύγωσιν ἰδίᾳ μὲν ἐξεταστέον τὰς ἀλληγορίας εἰ τὸ ὑγιὲς ἔχουσιν, κ. τ. λ. This soundness they cannot have, as not being guided by a definite creed, the ignorance of which often leads even Christians to suppose that by allegorizing any thing may be made of any thing.

I take it, then, for certain that the ancients did believe in a literal metensomatosis, though it might have originated in a symbolical way of expressing truths. (See above, p. 241, note; and, for further confirmation, see Plutarch, as quoted p. 109.) And it seems that this doctrine came from India, through Ethiopia, into Egypt, and thence into Greece and Italy. (See Olear. ad Philostr. iii. 18.)

It was held amongst the Gauls by the Druids (Cæsar, B. G. vi. 14), though only in part, probably; and by the Chaldees (Porphyr. V. Pyth. p. 25) if the doctrine of abstaining from meats implies it. Origen also (in Joan. vi. § 7) mentions that metempsychosis was a part of the secret teaching of the Jews, who perhaps in later times drew it from heathen sources (see Justin M. c. Tryph. p. 222; comp. St. Austin in Joan. iv. 4); and though outwardly abstaining from heathen idolatry, fell inwardly into errors less revolting at first sight. Thus entirely does the world seem to be given up to error, even when holding a belief of a future state, and so much to need that preaching of life and incorruptibility which the Gospel brought to light!

Note (16.) p. 268.

Butler, Serm. p. 4, has an observation quite falling in with that of Aristotle at the beginning of the last note. "The several members having distinct offices implies the mind." And so St. Irenæus, ii. 19, § 6. "Animæ ipsæ corporis habent figuram: ipsi enim adaptatæ sunt vasi." S. Archel. Caschar. c. Manet. xviii. extr. "Ostendere possumus consonantiam esse virtutum in utrâque, id est corporis atque animæ substantiâ, in quà ait Scripturarum doctor maximus Paulus Deum in corpore sicut voluit unumquodque membrum posuisse." St. Augustine's words, from his De Gen. ad lit. may be added: "Animam vero non esse corpoream me putare sed plane scire, audeo profiteri, tamen habere posse similitudinem corporis et corporalium omnino membrorum quisquis negat potest negare animam esse, quæ in somnis videt vel se ambulare, vel sedere, vel hac atque illac gressu atque etiam volatu ferri ac referri, quod sine quadam similitudine corporis non fit. Proinde si hanc similitudinem etiam apud inferos gerit non corporalem sed corpori similem; ita etiam in locis videtur esse non corporalibus, sed corporalium similibus, sive in requie sive in doloribus." xii. 62.

Note (17.) p. 268.

See Burke on the Sublime and Beautiful, iv. 4.

Note (18.) p. 269.

Aristot. Physiog. cap. 2, p. 806, a. 28. Ἔκ τε τῶν κινήσεων φυσιογνωμονοῦσι καὶ ἐκ τῶν σχημάτων καὶ ἐκ τῶν χρωμάτων καὶ ἐκ τῶν ἠθῶν ἐπὶ τοῦ προσώπου ἐμφαινομένων, καὶ ἐκ τῶν τριχωμάτων καὶ ἐκ τῆς λειότητος καὶ ἐκ τῆς φωνῆς καὶ ἐκ τῆς σαρκὸς, καὶ ἐκ τῶν μερῶν καὶ ἐκ τοῦ τύπου ὅλου τοῦ σώματος. He then goes on to give instances, and argues from the development of certain qualities conformably with certain external constitutions in brutes (i. e. in creatures, where reason does not intervene to check this), to the existence of the same thing in men, in tendency at least. I confess I do not see, myself, any great improbability in the further idea that where reason does check inward bad propensities, the exterior conformation also gradually alters; only it is a further idea. See also Note 14 on Dial. iv.

Note (19.) p. 269.

Aristot. E. N. i. 13. Τοῦ ἀλόγου τὸ μὲν ἔοικε κοινῷ καὶ φυτικῷ, λέγω δὲ τὸ αἴτιον τοῦ τρέφεσθαι καὶ αὔξεσθαι· τὴν τοιαύτην γὰρ δύναμιν τῆς ψυχῆς ἐν ἅπασι τοῖς τρεφομένοις θείη τις ἂν καὶ ἐν τοῖς ἐμβρύοις· τὴν αὐτὴν δὲ ταύτην καὶ ἐν τοῖς τελείοις· εὐλογώτερον γὰρ ταύτην εἶναι ἢ ἄλλην τινά. And see the author de Hom. Opif. cap. viii. p. 59, and p. 125, as quoted above, p. 298. This assertion of the existence of the soul from the first, though at first displaying a part only of its faculties, as it is of the utmost weight against the sin of procuring abortions (see St. Clement as above, p. 106), so it has another important bearing, which may be suggested by the following passage of St. Cyril, against Nestorius, i. p. 18. Τίκτεται μὲν γὰρ ἀπὸ σαρκὸς ἡ σὰρξ ὁμολογουμένως· ὁ δέ γε τῶν ὅλων δημιουργος, καθ' ὃν εἶδε τρόπον τε καὶ λόγον ποιεῖται τὴν ψύχωσιν· ἀλλ' ἡ τεκοῦσα γυνὴ καίτοι μόνης οὖσα πηγὴ τῆς σαρκὸς ἄνθρωπον ὅλον ἀποτεκεῖν πιστεύεται, τὸν ἐκ ψυχῆς δὴ λέγω καὶ σώματος, καίτοι πρὸς τὴν τῆς ψυχῆς ὕπαρξιν τῶν παρ' ἑαυτῆς συνεισενεγκοῦσα μηδέν· ὁ δέ γε ἄνθρωπον εἰπὼν συνεσήμηνέ που πάντως τῷ σώματι τὴν ἑνωθεῖσαν αὐτῷ ψυχήν· ὥσπερ οὖν ἡ γυνὴ καίτοι τεκοῦσα τὸ σῶμα μόνον τὸν ἐκ ψυχῆς καὶ σώματος ἀποτίκτειν λέγεται· διαλυμανεῖται δὲ τοῦτο τοῖς τῆς ψυχῆς λόγοις οὐδὲν, ὡς σάρκα τὴν ἀπὸ τῆς ἰδίας ὑπάρξεως λαμβανούσης ἀρχήν· οὕτω καὶ ἐπὶ τῆς μακαρίας Παρθένου· εἰ γὰρ ἡ Μητήρ ἐστι τῆς ἁγίας Σαρκὸς, ἀλλ' οὖν ἐκτέτοκεν ἑνωθέντα αὐτῇ κατ' ἀλήθειαν τὸν ἐκ Θεοῦ Θεὸν Λόγον· κἂν εἴ τις λέγῃ Θεότοκον αὐτὴν οὐχὶ δή που πάντως καθοριεῖ τοῦ Θεοῦ Λόγου τὸ νεώτερον, οὔτε μὴν τῆς ἰδίας ὑπάρξεως τὴν ἀρχὴν πεποιῆσθαι τὴν σάρκα.

Note (20.) p. 269.

See the well-known passage of Strabo, quoted by Bishop Butler, Anal. i. 1, p. 40.

Note (21.) p. 271.

Butler, Anal. p. 18. "The states of life in which we ourselves existed formerly in the womb, and in our infancy, are almost as different from our present in mature age, as it is possible to conceive any two states or degrees of life can be. Therefore that we are to exist hereafter in a state as different (suppose) from our present as this is from our former, is but according to the analogy of nature," &c. Compare the passage from Dr. Quain above, p. 241.

Note (22.) p. 273.

Dan. ii. 10, where Nebuchadnezzar is conscious of having dreamt a dream, which he had forgotten in substance, though it contained an outline of God's government over four vast empires; a remarkable instance of what is noticed in the text.

Note (23.) p. 273.

S. Iren. ii. 33. "De corpore autem in corpus transmigrationem ipsorum subvertamus ex eo, quod nihil omnino eorum quæ ante fuerint, meminerint animæ. Si enim ob hoc emittebantur, uti in omni fierent operatione; oportebat deas meminisse eorum, quæ ante facta sunt, uti ea quæ deerant, adimplerent, et non circa eadem semper volutantes continuatim, miserabiliter laborarent; (non enim poterat corporis admixtio in totum universam ipsorum, quæ ante habita erant, exstinguere memoriam et contemplationem,) et maxime ad hoc venientes. Quomodo enim nunc soporati et requiescente corpore quæcumque anima ipsa apud se videt, et in phantasmate agit, et horum plura reminiscens communicat cum corpore; et est quando et post plurimum temporis, quæcumque per somnium quis vidit, vigilans annuntiat: sic utique reminisceretur et illorum, quæ antequam in hoc corpus veniret, egit. Si enim hoc quod in brevissimo tempore visum est, vel in phantasmate conceptum est, ab ea sola per somnium, postquam commixta sit corpori, et in universum membrum dispersa, commemoratur: multo magis illorum reminisceretur, in quibus temporibus tantis et universo præteritæ vitæ sæculo immorata est. Ad hæc Plato vetus ille Atheniensis, qui et primus sententiam hanc introduxit, quum excusare non posset, oblivionis induxit poculum, putans se per hoc aporiam hujusmodi effugere; ostensionem quidem nullam faciens, dogmatice autem respondens, quoniam introeuntes animæ in hanc vitam, ab eo qui est super introitum dæmone, priusquam in corpora intrent, potantur oblivione. Et latuit semetipsum in alteram majorem incidens aporiam. Si enim oblivionis poculum potest, posteaquam ebibitum est, omnium factorum obliterare memoriam, hoc ipsum unde scis, O Plato, quum sit nunc in corpore anima tua, quoniam priusquam in corpus introeat a dæmone potata est oblivionis medicamentum? Si enim dæmonem, et poculum, et introitum reminisceris, et reliqua oportet cognoscas: si autem illa ignoras, neque dæmon verus neque artificiose compositum oblivionis poculum."

Note (24.) p. 274.

Butler, Anal. i. 2, p. 58. "The reader is desired to observe that Gentile writers, both moralists and poets, speak of the future punishment of the wicked, both as to the duration and degree of it, in a like manner of expression and of description, as the Scripture does." With this statement St. Just. Martyr, Apol. i. § 20, p. 66, agrees, as does St. Clem. Strom. v. 91, and § 122, where he gives the following striking passage from Diphilus, a comic poet:

Οἴει σὺ τοὺς θανόντας, ὦ Νικήρατε,
τρυφῆς ἁπάσης μεταλαβόντας ἐν βίῳ,
πεφευγέναι τὸ θεῖον ὡς λεληθότας;
ἔστιν Δίκης ὀφθαλμὸς, ὃς τὰ πάνθ' ὁρᾷ.
καὶ γὰρ καθ' Ἅιδην δύο τρίβους νομίζομεν,
μίαν δικαίων χἀτέραν ἀσεβῶν ὁδόν.
κεἰ τοὺς δύο καλύψει γῆ φύσει παντὶ χρόνῳ,
ἅρπαζ' ἀπελθὼν, κλέπτ', ἀποστέρει, κύκα.
μηδὲν πλανηθῇς. ἔστι κἀν Ἅιδου κρίσις,
ἥνπερ ποιήσει Θεὸς ὁ πάντων δεσπότης,
οὗ τοὔνομα φοβερὸν, οὐδ' ἂν ὀνομάσαιμ' ἐγώ·
ὃς τοῖς ἁμαρτάνουσι πρὸς μῆκος βίον
δίδωσιν· εἴ τις δ' οἴεται τοὐφήμερον
κακόν τι πράσσων τοὺς θεοὺς λεληθέναι,
δοκεῖ πονηρὰ, καὶ δοκῶν ἁλίσκεται,
ὅταν σχολὴν ἄγουσα τυγχάνῃ Δίκη.
ὁρᾶθ' ὅσοι δοκεῖτε οὐκ εἶναι Θεόν·
ἔστιν γὰρ, ἔστιν· εἰ δέ τις πράττει κακῶς
κακὸς πεφυκὼς, τὸν χρόνον κερδανάτω·
χρόνῳ. γὰρ οὗτος ὕστερον δώσει δίκην.

Συνᾴδει δὲ τούτοις ἡ τραγῳδία διὰ τῶνδε·

ἔσται γὰρ, ἔσται κεῖνος αἰῶνος χρόνος,
ὅταν πυρὸς γέμοντα θησαυρὸν σχάσῃ
χρύσωπος αἰθὴρ· ἡ δὲ βοσκηθεῖσα φλὸξ
ἅπαντα τἀπίγεια καὶ μετάρσια
φλέξει μανεῖσα.

Of philosophers, Plato, in the Gorgias, § 171, speaks of men suffering τὸν ἀεὶ χρόνον·—and Naraka, or Hell, forms a common subject of terror to the wicked, in Manu and elsewhere, among the Hindus. In the Vish. Purana, p. 309, we read as follows: "He who commits adultery is punished both here and hereafter; for his days in this world are cut short, and when dead he falls into hell:" and p. 210, "The sinner goes to Naraka, who neglects the due expiation of his guilt;" where the different punishments there inflicted are described. St. Austin also, De Gen. ad lit. xii. § 62, says, "Possumus ostendere illorum quoque sapientes de inferorum substantiâ minime dubitasse, quæ post hanc vitam excipit animas mortuorum."

Note (25.) p. 274.

Origen, c. Cels. p. 6, magnificently remarks: *Οὐδὲν θαυμαστὸν τὸν αὐτὸν Θεὸν ἅπερ ἐδίδαξε διὰ τῶν Προφητῶν καὶ τοῦ Σωτῆρος, ἐγκατεσπαρκέναι ἐν ταῖς ἁπάντων ἀνθρώπων ψυχαῖς, ἵν' ἀναπολόγητος ἐν τῇ θείᾳ κρίσει πᾶς ἄνθρωπος ᾖ, ἔχων τὸ βούλημα τοῦ Νόμου γραπτὸν ἐν τῇ ἑαυτοῦ καρδίᾳ.*

Note (26.) p. 274.

Aristot. Physiog. cap. 4, init. p. 808. *Δοκεῖ δέ μοι ἡ ψυχὴ καὶ τὸ σῶμα συμπαθεῖν ἀλλήλοις, καὶ ἡ τῆς ψυχῆς ἕξις ἀλλοιουμένη συναλλοιοῖ τὴν τοῦ σώματος μορφὴν, πάλιν τε ἡ τοῦ σώματος μορφὴ ἀλλοιουμένη συναλλοιοῖ τὴν τῆς ψυχῆς ἕξιν.*

Note (27.) p. 275.

Tertull. Apol. cap. 48, says that "the soul can suffer nothing by itself without connexion with a material substance;" which is an over-strong statement, and one which, as Dr. Pusey observes on the place, Tertullian modified afterwards, but which shows how strongly he felt their mutual connexion.

Note (28.) p. 275.

Butler, Serm. vi. p. 87. "Suppose we are capable of happiness and of misery in degrees equally intense and extreme, yet we are capable of the latter for a *much* longer time beyond all comparison. We see men in the tortures of pain for hours, days, and (excepting the short suspensions of sleep) for months together, without intermission; to which no enjoyments of life do, in degree and continuance, bear any sort of proportion."

NOTE (29.) p. 275.

Origen, in a fragment, De Resurr. vol. i. p. 33, Delarue, has the following wonderful remark:—"Quomodo enim non videtur absurdum, ut hoc corpus, quod pro Christo pertulit cicatrices, et pariter cum animâ persecutionum toleravit sæva tormenta....ac diversa pœnarum genera perpessus est, tantorum certaminum præmiis defraudetur? Quippe si sola anima, quæ non sola certaverit, coronetur, et corporis sui vasculum, quod ei cum magno labore servivit, nulla agonis et victoriæ præmia consequatur, quomodo non contra omnem rationem esse videtur, ut naturalibus vitiis atque ingenitæ libidinis propter Christum caro resistens, et virginitatem obtinens cum ingenti labore, qui continentiæ labor utique aut major corporis quam animæ est, aut certe utriusque æqualis est, præmiorum tempore altera veluti indigna rejiciatur, altera veniat ad coronam? Quæ res sine dubio aut injustitiæ alicujus Deum, aut impossibilitatis accusat."

NOTE (30.) p. 276.

Butler, Anal. ii. ch. vi. p. 326, speaks of the natural constitution of body and temper as a temptation to go wrong. Aristotle, in his Problemata, xxx. 1, has some speculations upon this subject, as well as in the Physiognomonica, as above referred to. So in Eth. Nic. x. 8, he says, *Ἔνια (ἤθη) συμβαίνειν ἀπὸ τοῦ σώματος δοκεῖ.* And Plato, though with a different view, observes, (Phædo, § 30.) *Καὶ γὰρ πολέμους καὶ στάσεις καὶ χάμας οὐδὲν ἄλλο παρέχει ἢ τὸ σῶμα καὶ αἱ τούτου ἐπιθυμίαι.* To prevent a misconstruction being put upon such a fact, we may add the following passage of St. Aust. c. Jul. Pel. iv. § 16. "Qui dicit impium justum esse maledictus erit populo et odibilis in gentibus (Prov. xxiv. 24). Etiam virtutibus veris gentiles prædices abundare; quanto, inquam, satius hæc ipsa in iis dona Dei esse fatereris, sub cujus occulto judicio nec injusto, alii fatui, alii tardissimi ingenii et ad intelligendum quodammodo plumbei, alii obliviosi, alii acuti memoresve nascuntur, alii utroque munere præditi, et acute intelligentes et tenacissimæ memoriæ thesauro cognita recondentes; alii naturâ lenes, alii levissimis causis irâ facillimâ ardentes, alii ad vindictæ cupiditatem inter utrosque mediocres; alii spadones, alii in concubitu ita frigidi, ut vix omnino moveantur, alii libidinosissimi, ut vix omnino teneantur, alii inter utrosque et moveri faciles et teneri; alii timidissimi, alii audacissimi, alii neutrum; alii hilares, alii tristes, alii ad nihil horum proclives; nec eorum quæ commemoravi aliquid instituto ac proposito, sed *naturâ;* unde medici *audent* ista tribuere temperationibus corporum. Quod etsi probari vel nullâ existente, vel omni finitâ quæstione potuisset; numquid sibi quisque corpus condidit, et hoc ejus tribuendum est voluntati, quod mala ista naturalia magis minusve perpetitur? Nam prorsus ea non perpeti, cum hic vivitur, nullo modo, nullâ ratione quisquam potest. Nec tamen, sive a maximis sive minimis urgeatur, fas est ut dicit Ei, qui se finxit, quamvis omnipotenti, justo, et bono, Quare sic me fecisti? Et de jugo gravi quod est supra filios primi Adam, nemo liberat nisi secundus Adam. Quanto ergo tolerabilius illas quas dicis in impiis esse virtutes divino muneri potius, quam eorum tribueres tantummodo voluntati, licet ipsi hoc nesciunt donec, si ex illo sunt prædestinatorum numero, accipiant Spiritum qui ex Deo est, ut sciant quæ a Deo donata sunt iis." St. Augustine here admits the fact of natural constitutions forming a temptation to particular sins; and argues that those heathens who overcame such temptations did it by GOD's hidden grace [a], being powerless, without that aid, to overcome in their own strength.

NOTE (31.) p. 276.

S. Hil. in S. Aust. ibid. ii. 27. "Memores et conscii illa ipsa corpora nostra omnium vitiorum esse materiam, per quam polluti et sordidi nihil in nobis mundum, nihil innocens obtinemus, gaudeamus nobis esse hostem, in cujus concertatione quodam concertationis nostræ (nostri?) bello dimicemus." Comp. S. Archel. Casch. c. Manet. xviii. "Gaudet anima corpore, et diligit et colit illud; nihilominus etiam corpus gaudet, ab animâ se vivificatum. Quod si maligni opus dicat esse quis corpus; cum sit et corruptibile ac vetustum atque deterrimum, non potest ferre spiritus virtutem, nec animæ commotionem et ejus splendidissimam creaturam."

NOTE (32.) p. 277.

Aristot. E. Nic. i. § 5. Συναριθμουμένην δὲ δῆλον ὡς αἱρετωτρέαν μετὰ τοῦ ἐλαχίστου τῶν ἀγαθῶν.

NOTE (33.) p. 277.

Ibid. ii. v. fin. Ἐν παντὶ δὲ μάλιστα φυλακτέον τὸ ἡδὺ καὶ τὴν ἡδονήν· οὐ γὰρ ἀδέκαστοι κρίνομεν αὐτήν.

NOTE (34.) p. 278.

Plato de Legg. i. 14. Τί δ' ὅταν ἐπιχειρῶμέν τινα φοβερὸν ποιεῖν μετὰ δίκης, ἆρ' οὐκ ἀναισχυντίᾳ ξυμβάλλοντας

[a] *Grace* is sometimes used in a limited sense, as signifying the gift of glory and of grace, whereby Christians are zealous of and able to do good works; sometimes in a wider one, as signifying the assistance offered by GOD to heathens and others out of the Church. The latter may be compared to heat from the sun, as far as it is from without; the former to vital warmth, which is inherent and from within.

αὐτὸν καὶ προσγυμνάζοντας νικᾷν δεῖ ποιεῖν διαμαχόμενον αὐτοῦ ταῖς ἡδοναῖς; ἢ τῇ μὲν διαίτῃ τῇ ἐν αὐτῷ προσμαχόμενον καὶ νικῶντα αὐτὴν δεῖ τέλεον οὕτω γίγνεσθαι πρὸς ἀνδρίαν, ἄπειρος δὲ δή που καὶ ἀγύμναστος ὢν τῶν τοιούτων ἀγώνων ὁστισοῦν οὐδ' ἂν ἥμισυς ἑαυτοῦ γένοιτο πρὸς ἀρετήν; σώφρων δὲ ἄρα τελέως ἔσται μὴ πολλαῖς ἡδοναῖς καὶ ἐπιθυμίαις προτρεπούσαις ἀναισχυντεῖν καὶ ἀδικεῖν διαμεμηχανημένος καὶ νενικηκὼς μετὰ λόγου καὶ ἔργου καὶ τέχνης, ἔν τε παιδίαις καὶ ἐν σπουδαῖς καὶ ἀπαθὴς ὢν πάντων τῶν τοιούτων . . . φόβου φάρμακον ἔσθ' ὅστις Θεὸς ἔδωκεν ἀνθρώποις, ὥστε ὁπόσῳ πλέον ἂν ἐθέλοι τις πίνειν αὐτοῦ, τοσούτῳ μᾶλλον αὐτὸν νομίζειν δυστυχῆ γενέσθαι καὶ φοβεῖσθαι τὰ παρόντα καὶ τὰ μέλλοντα αὐτῷ πάντα, κ. τ. λ. And in iii. § 14. Ἐπὶ τῆς ἐλπίδος ὀχούμενοι ταύτης εὑρίσκον καταφυγὴν αὐτοῖς εἰς αὐτοὺς μόνους εἶναι καὶ τοὺς θεούς· ταῦτ' οὖν αὐτοῖς πάντα φιλίαν ἀλλήλων ἐνεποίει ὁ φόβος ὁ τότε παρὼν, ὅτε ἐκ νόμων τῶν ἔμπροσθεν γεγονὼς, ὃν δουλεύοντες τοῖς πρόσθεν νόμοις ἐκέκτηντο, ἣν αἰδῶ πολλάκις ἐν τοῖς ἄνω λόγοις εἴπομεν, ᾗ καὶ δουλεύειν ἔφαμεν δεῖν τοὺς μέλλοντας ἀγαθοὺς ἔσεσθαι, ἧς ὁ δειλὸς ἐλεύθερος καὶ ἄφοβος. And in the Protagoras, § 35. Καὶ νόμον θὲς παρ' ἐμοῦ τὸν μὴ δυνάμενον αἰδοῦς καὶ δίκης μετέχειν κτείνειν ὡς νόσον τῆς πόλεως. From these passages it appears what great importance Plato attached to shame as available in education.

Note (35.) p. 278.

Aristot. Rhet. ii. 6. Ἔστω δὴ αἰσχύνη λύπη τις ἢ ταραχὴ περὶ τὰ εἰς ἀδοξίαν φαινόμενα φέρειν τῶν κακῶν, ἢ παρόντων, ἢ γεγονότων, ἢ μελλόντων. And again, τοὺς ΑΕΙ παρεσομένους μᾶλλον αἰσχύνονται.

Note (36.) p. 280.

Aristot. Metaph. p. 1000, a. 9. Οἱ περὶ Ἡσίοδον καὶ πάντες οἱ θεολόγοι μόνον ἐφρόντισαν τοῦ πιθανοῦ τοῦ πρὸς αὐτοὺς, ἡμῶν δὲ ὠλιγώρησαν· θεοὺς γὰρ ποιοῦντες τὰς ἀρχὰς καὶ ἐκ θεῶν γεγονότας τὰ μὴ γευσάμενα τοῦ νέκταρος καὶ τῆς ἀμβροσίας θνητὰ γενέσθαι φασὶν, δῆλον ὡς ταῦτα τὰ ὀνόματα γνώριμα λέγοντες αὐτοῖς· καὶ τὰ περὶ αὐτῆς τῆς προσφορᾶς τῶν αἰτίων ὑπὲρ ἡμᾶς εἰρήκασιν· εἰ μὲν γὰρ χάριν ἡδονῆς θιγγάνουσιν, οὐθὲν αἰτία τοῦ εἶναι τὸ νέκταρ καὶ ἡ ἀμβροσία· εἰ δὲ τοῦ εἶναι, πῶς ἂν εἶεν ἀΐδιοι δεόμενοι τροφῆς; See Windisch. p. 1511, who mentions that the Chhandogya says that certain deities live by eating the amrita—the very word, almost, which the Greeks had, only they made it a fluid.

NOTE (37.) p. 280.

The main Scripture ground for speaking of the angels as nourished is the phrase לחם אבירים, which occurs in Ps. lxxviii. 25, which was taken of old (see Wisdom xvi. 20, and the LXX.) to mean the bread of angels, and explained by a Midrash (or ancient mystical commentary) to mean the food eaten by angels. In Tobit xii. 19, the angel's words seem to imply that he had other meat to eat, though of course it would be of a spiritual nature. A few passages of the Fathers may be given here in illustration of this. St. Just. Mart. Dial. cum Tryph. p. 279, says of the angels sent to Abraham: Ἄγγελοι τῷ ὄντι ἦσαν καὶ ἐν τοῖς οὐρανοῖς δῆλόν ἐστιν ἡμῖν τρεφόμενοι, κἂν μὴ ὁμοίαν τροφὴν ἧπερ οἱ ἄνθρωποι χρώμεθα, τρέφονται. S. Athan. in Ps. lxxvii. 24. Οὐ μόνον τῷ μάννα τὰ σώματα ἔτρεφεν, ἀλλὰ καὶ λογικῇ τινι καὶ οὐρανίῳ δυνάμει διέτρεφεν αὐτῶν τὰς ψυχὰς, ὥσπερ ἀμέλει διατρέφει καὶ τοὺς ἀγγέλους· καὶ τοῦτο μὲν ἐστὶ καὶ ἐκ τοῦ συνδεσμοῦ ἰδεῖν, τῷ ὥσπερ ἐν ἐπαγωγῇ εἰπεῖν τὸ Καὶ ἄρτον οὐρανοῦ ἔδωκεν αὐτοῖς. Ἔστι δὲ οὐδὲν ἧττον καὶ ἐκ τοῦ Ἀποστόλου μαθεῖν περὶ αὐτῶν εἰρηκότος ὡς πνευματικὸν ἔφαγον βρῶμα· τοῦτο δὲ ἦν ὁ νῦν ἄρτος ἀγγέλων ὀνομαζόμενος. The question whether angels are nourished runs very much into the questions, what a spiritual body is, and whether the angels have such as Tertull. de C. Christi, vi. xi. S. Cyril. de Ador. p. 214. A, and others have thought: questions which may be even healthful to those who are led by them not to think meanly of the nature of the holy angels, but with reverence and godly fear of that of bodies. And the following words of St. Cyril are of help towards bearing this in mind: p. 233. d. Ἄρτον ἀγγέλων ἔφαγεν ἄνθρωπος, τὸ μάννα λέγων οὐρανοῦ καὶ ἀγγέλων τρόφον, ἵνα τῶν αἰσθητῶν καὶ ὁρατῶν τὸν οἰκεῖον ἱέντες ἐπέκεινα νοῦν, τὴν πνευματικὴν καὶ θείαν κατασκεπτώμεθα χορηγίαν, ἣν ταῖς τῶν ἁγίων ψυχαῖς ἐνίησι Θεὸς, τὸν ἀγγέλους τρέφοντα καὶ ζωογονοῦντα τοὺς ἀνθρώπους Θεὸν Λόγον ἐγκαταυλίζεσθαι ποιῶν τοῖς τὴν πίστιν εἰσδεδεγμένοις· κατῴκηκε γὰρ ὁ Χριστὸς ἐν ταῖς καρδίαις ἡμῶν διὰ τοῦ Ἁγίου Πνεύματος, καὶ Ἄρτῳ ζῶντι καὶ ἐξ οὐρανοῦ τρεφόμεθα πρὸς εὐεξίαν τε καὶ ἰσχὺν πνευματικήν. And so again, at p. 339, he says, after quoting the words of the Psalm again, Τρέφεται γὰρ τὸ πνεῦμα πνευματικῶς, σῶμά τε αὖ κατ' ἰδίαν φύσιν τοῦτ' ἔστι σωματικῶς· τροφὴ δὲ ἀγγέλων καὶ ἄρτος ὁ πρέπων ἀγγέλοις καὶ τοῖς ἄνω πνεύμασιν ὁ ἐκ Θεοῦ Πατρὸς Λόγος. And so St. Aust. Serm. de Temp. 194, 2. 196, 3. Greg. Naz. S. 37. Origen. de Orat. p. 94, Fell. Greg. Nyss. de Hom. Opif. p. 95, who notices that it is not by gross food, but by every word that proceedeth out of the mouth of God, that man liveth. Neither is a difference of opinion implied by such as speak of having wisdom and knowledge as the food of angels, seeing that it is in Christ that all treasures of wisdom and knowledge are hidden, and by Him it is, whether by word or by wisdom, or by knowledge or by bread, or by manna, that God the Father upholdeth all things in heaven and in earth and under the earth.

Note (38.) p. 280.

See above, p. 135 and p. 205.

Note (39.) p. 281.

S. Aug. c. Jul. Pelag. vi. 59. "Si bonitas operationis ejus subtrahatur formandis promovendisque seminibus, et vivificandis quibusque viventibus, non solum gignenda non aguntur, sed ad nihilum penitus etiam genita rediguntur."

Note (40.) p. 281.

Butler, Diss. i., discusses the use of the word 'same,' as applied to plants; and contends that, strictly, it is inapplicable to them at different periods of their existence. St. Clem. Str. ii. § 101, seems to think they had some living principle, to which he gives the name of 'soul:' neither is it immediately obvious that there is not something analogous to a soul in them, possessing those powers only which the soul of animals does in the womb. I am not stating an opinion here, for I have none on the subject; I am merely noticing what St. Clement says as falling in with the Indian division of things into *mobile* and *immobile*, the latter of which is subdivided into those which have and those which have not life.

Note (41.) p. 281.

The analogy between man's growth and that of a plant is often noticed in Scripture, as in Job xiv. 1 Cor. xv. &c.: as such it is often insisted on by the Fathers also.

Note (42.) p. 281.

Whoever attempts to form an idea of a finite *spirit*, will, I suspect, find it a very difficult task. It seems easier far to me, to conceive spirits, as such, to be ubiquitous than finite. "Not but that I think (with Bishop Butler, letter iv. p. 489) that there is somewhat in the manner of the existence of spirits that more directly answers to the manner of the existence of body; but what that is, or of the manner of their existence, I cannot possibly form an idea." St. Basil, Ep. viii. 2, observes that an angel may be said to be numerically one, but that, as in the case of a man, because he is not uncompounded, *οὐσίαν γὰρ μεθ' ἁγιασμοῦ τὴν τοῦ ἀγγέλου ὑπόστασιν ἐννοοῦμεν.* Perhaps this bears materially upon the question, since all beings who are what they are by participation of somewhat in another, must necessarily be subject to some limitations, possibly some in regard to space, as participation implies the having of a part only of what another has. Yet even this does not seem to clear up the difficulty; as it is so difficult to determine what space is, and more still "what relation the self-existent Being hath to space," as Butler goes on to remark. And even if spirits, either angels or men, are limited to space, their powers of seeing, hearing, and the like (or those analogous to them), may be of incomparably wider range than ours, as St. Gregory, Moral. ii. 3, teaches; may not be impeded by things, which are an impediment to our souls, acting as they do through the medium of a gross body. (See Note 44.) A reflecting mind will find these are questions of the greatest importance to have the most *probable* opinions upon, even though demonstration be impossible. For *probability* is the guide of life; and this, as most metaphysical speculations, runs up into practical bearings.

NOTE (43.) p. 282.

The Scripture says expressly that GOD has established the earth *for ever*, לְעוֹלָם יסדה, Ps. lxxviii. 69, and speaks of its being made so fast that it cannot be moved, Ps. xcvi. 10; and of the heavens, it says, He hath made them to stand for ever and ever, לָעַד לעולם, Ps. cxlviii. 6; and in conformity with this the Fathers generally teach that the earth is not to be annihilated, but to be renewed after its *dissolution* (2 Pet. iii. 10). Thus Tertullian, de Cor. vi.,

"Dei æmulus universam conditionem, certis usibus homini mancipatam, cum homine corrupit. Unde eam et Apostolus invitam ait vanitati succidisse:" upon which passage Dr. Pusey has the following note:—"Comp. adv. Herm. c. 11. The Apostle is understood to speak of a restoration of the natural creation, by S. Irenæus, (5, 32, 1. [and 36, 1.]) S. Hilary, (in Ps. clxviii. § 2.) S. Ambrose, (Prol. in Expos. Ev. sec. Luc. Hexaem. i. 7. § 22, but including the human soul, Ep. 34, ad Horont.) Origen, (Hom. 4, in Ezek. § 2.) S. Gregory Naz. (Orat. 1, in Julian. iv. 15.) S Chrysostom, (in loc.) Theodoret, (in loc. and Gal. vi. 15.) Proclus ap. Epiphan. (Hær. lxiv. 31.) Œcumenius, (ad 2 Pet. iv.) Gaudentius, (Serm. 3, init. Bibl. P. v. p. 948.) S. Jerome, (in Is. xxiv. fin. 51, 6 seqq.) Maximus Taur. (Bibl. Pat. t. vi. p. 48.) Ambrosiaster, (ad loc.) Auct. de Prom. Dimid. Temp. (ap. Prosper. c. 20.) the later Sedulius, (Collectanea, ad loc. B. P. vi. p. 518.) This liberation of the creature they state, according to Scripture, will take place through its destruction. 'For good will He destroy the world. For there will be a new heaven, and there shall be no more night.' Ambr. de Elia, c. 21, fin. § 80. 'From which (Ps. cii. 26) it appears that the perishing of the heavens denotes not their utter destruction, but change for the better,' Jerome in Is. li. 6. Comp. S. Aug. de Civ. D. xx. 16. Chrys. ad loc. Method. de Res. § 32. S. Cyril, Jer. xv. 2. S. Athanas., Euseb., Prosper., Cassiodorus, in Ps. ci. 26. Proclus, l. c. and § 32. Œcumen. l. c. Gaudentius, l. c. Greg. M. Moral. xvii. 9, in Job xxv. 24. Auct. de Prom. Dimid. Temp. l. c. Hesychius also, l. v. in Lev. (c. 18.) understands by 'the creature,' the natural creation [as does St. Ephrem in Joel i. fin. ii. p. 250. E.]. On the other hand, S. Augustine understands it to be 'human nature,' in those who actually, or who shall hereafter, believe, (Quæstt. 83, qu. 67. Propos. de Ep. ad Rom. Prop. 53, in Prisc. et

Orig. c. 8, in Ps. cxxv. § 2.) in which he is followed by Greg. M. (Mor. iv. 34, in Job iii. 18.) and Gelasius i. (Tr. 3, c. Pelag. ap. Labbe Conc. t. i. p. 1248.) Origen (ad loc.) seems, in like way, to suppose it chiefly to relate to the soul sympathizing with the body; but also (wherein he is followed by Sedulius, l. c.) to include angels and even archangels, in that they 'fight' for us (Dan. x.). S. Hilary (de Trin. xii. 5.) and S. Cyril Alex. (Thes. xiv. 1. t. v. p. 170, ed. Par.) employ the text against the Arians, since the Son, if created, must have been liable to all here spoken of; they must then have held all creatures, even the highest, to be included; the holy angels are also regarded by Theodoret (ad loc.) as included in the '*whole* creation,' and apparently by S. Greg. Naz. l. c." Perhaps, as the majority seem agreed on the application in the text, the passage in the following note may be taken as giving it a decided preponderance.

NOTE (44.) p. 282.

Butler, Anal. p. 115. "One thing is set over against another, as an ancient writer expresses it. Our nature corresponds to our external condition. Without this correspondence there would *be no possibility* of any such thing as human life and human happiness; which life and happiness, therefore, are a result from our nature and condition jointly; meaning, by human life, not living in the literal sense, but the whole complex notion commonly understood by those words. So that without determining what will be the employment and happiness, the particular life of good men hereafter, there must be some determinate capacities, some necessary character and qualifications, without which persons cannot but be utterly incapable of it: in like manner as there must be some without which men would be incapable of their present state of life." And so, p. 40, i. i. he says, "Death may put us into a higher and more enlarged *state of life*, as our birth does." The one is presupposed by the other; the state of life by the capacities.

NOTE (45.) p. 283.

St. Aug. Conff. ix. 28. . . . "Quærentibus utrum non formidaret tam longe a suâ civitate corpus relinquere. Nihil, inquit, longe est a Deo; neque timendum est, ne Ille non agnoscat in fine sæculi, unde me resuscitet.

NOTE (46.) p. 283.

Aristot. Anal. Post. i. 10, p. 76, b. 23. Οὐκ ἔστιν ὑπόθεσις οὐδ' αἴτημα ὃ ἀνάγκη εἶναι δι' αὐτὸ καὶ δοκεῖν ἀνάγκη· οὐ γὰρ πρὸς τὸν ἔξω λόγον ἡ ἀπόδειξις, ἀλλὰ πρὸς τὸν ἐν τῇ ψυχῇ, ἐπεὶ οὐδὲ συλλογισμός· ἀεὶ γὰρ ἔστιν ἐνστῆναι πρὸς τὸν ἔξω λόγον, ἀλλὰ πρὸς τὸν ἔσω λόγον οὐκ ἀεί. And so St. Hilary de Trin. x. p. 197. "Secundum humanæ naturæ consuetudinem nullus est sermo non obnoxius contradictioni."

NOTE (47.) p. 283.

Aristot. Soph. Elench. cap. vii. p. 169, a. 37. Ἡ ἀπάτη γίνεται μᾶλλον μετ' ἄλλων σκοπουμένοις ἢ καθ' αὑτούς· ἡ γὰρ μετ' ἄλλων σκέψις διὰ λόγων, ἡ δὲ καθ' αὑτὸν οὐχ ἧττον δι' αὐτοῦ τοῦ πράγματος.

NOTE (48.) p. 283.

Origen. in Levit. ix. 7. "Cum lasciviunt oculi vel per illicitas concupiscentias vel per spectacula diabolica, quid aliud nisi ignem sibi congregant? Cum aures non avertuntur ab auditu vano, ac derogationibus proximorum; cum manus a cæde nequaquam nec a rapinis ac deprædationibus continentur; cum pedes veloces sunt ad effundendum sanguinem; cumque corpus non Domino sed fornicationi tradimus, quid aliud nisi totum corpus tradimus in gehennam? At hæc cum dicuntur, contemtui habentur. Quare? quia fides deest.

Alioquin si tibi hodie diceretur quia judex sæculi vult te crastino vivum exurere, et his auditis si esset unius diei spatium liberum, quanta faceres? quomodo et per quos discurreres? quam lugens et quam sordidus oberrares? Nonne effunderes omnem pecuniam tuam in eos quorum intercessione evadere posse te crederes? Nonne omnia quæ possides redemptionem faceres animæ tuæ? Quod si etiam aliquis te retardare aut impedire tentaret, nonne diceres, Pereant omnia pro salute meâ, nec quicquam remaneat tantum ut ego vivam? Hoc quare faceres? quia inde non dubitares: hinc dubitas. Et ideo bene Dominus dicit, *Putas veniens Filius Hominis inveniet fidem super terram?* Et quid ego de certis indubitatisque periculis? Tantummodo si causa dicenda sit apud judicem terrenum, quæ aliquem metum ex legibus habere videatur, nonne omnibus vigiliis excubatur, advocato patrono munera præparantur, etiamsi anceps periculum sit, aut etiam solius notæ metus vel damni ratio? Nos quare non credimus quod *omnes adstabimus ante tribunal Dei, ut reportet unusquisque propria corporis prout gessit sive bona sive mala?*"

NOTE (49.) p. 284.

In the Vedas the impassibility of the soul is taught. "We do not recognize the doctrine that supposes the slayer to slay, or the slain to be killed: this (spiritual existence) neither kills nor is killed," quoted by Professor Wilson, Vish. Purana, p. 135, note. And again, p. 252, "Union of self with supreme spirit is said to be the great end of all: but this is false; for one substance cannot become substantially another." Upon which it is observed in the note, that "this is to be understood as applying to the doctrines which distinguish between the vital spirit (Jivátma) and the supreme spirit (Paramátma), the doctrine of the Yoga. It is here argued, that it is absurd to talk of effecting a union between the soul of man and supreme soul; for if they are distinct essentially, they cannot combine; if they are already one and the same, it is nonsense to talk of accomplishing their union. The great end of life or truth is, not to effect the union of two things, or two parts of one thing, but to know that all is unity." And so also at p. 650, "The properties of pain, ignorance, and impurity, are those of nature (Pracriti), not of soul. . .. When a soul is associated with Pracriti, it is vitiated by egotism and the rest, and assumes the qualities of grosser nature, though essentially distinct from them and incorruptible." Burnouf, Pref. to Bhag. Puran. xlvi., note, says: "La destruction dite A'tyantika, c'est à dire définitive, est l'identification de l'âme individuelle avec le suprême Brahma, identification à laquelle le Yogin parvient par la science."

Note (50.) p. 285.

Vish. Purana, p. 633, note. Those sainted mortals who have diligently worshipped Vishnu, and are distinguished for piety, abide at the time of dissolution in the Maharloka, with the Pitris, Manus, the seven Rishis, the various orders of celestial spirits, and the gods. These, when the heat of the flames that destroy the world reaches to Maharloka, repair to Janaloka in their subtle forms, destined to become re-embodied in similar capacities to their former, when the world is renewed at the beginning of the succeeding Kalpa. This continues throughout the life of Brahma; at the expiration of his life all are destroyed: but those who have then attained a residence in the Brahmaloka, by having *identified* themselves in spirit with the supreme, are finally resolved into the sole-existing Brahma.

Note (51.) p. 286.

The words of St. Paul, to which allusion is made in the text, stand as follows, 1 Thess. v. 23. Αὐτὸς δὲ ὁ Θεὸς τῆς *εἰρήνης ἁγιάσαι ὑμᾶς ὁλοτελεῖς· καὶ ὁλόκληρον ὑμῶν τὸ πνεῦμα καὶ ἡ ψυχὴ καὶ τὸ σῶμα ἀμέμπτως ἐν τῇ παρουσίᾳ τοῦ Κυρίου ἡμῶν Ἰησοῦ Χριστοῦ τηρηθείη.* St. Hilary well says (De Trin. iv. p. 33), "In divinis rebus non frequentius dicta sed tantum dicta sufficiunt:" and therefore, if the division of man's nature here given occurred no where besides, it would be still a text of importance. But, as now-a-days the doctrine mentioned in it hardly enters at all into the theology of some people; as it is of the utmost importance in practical theology; as, further, it is one met with in divers parts of Scripture, I shall speak upon it here somewhat more at length, at the risk of repeating things already noticed in the text.

1. Upon the passage itself it may be observed, that St. Paul implies that the Christians he addresses are already in possession of certain things which may be called faculties or gifts, and which may be forfeited in different degrees: otherwise he would not pray that they might be preserved wholly and unblameably. He prays to the God of peace, as though he would beg that there might be no schism in the three specified, and uses a singular verb to the three nouns, after the manner in which, in the Old Testament, the unity and eternal peace of the most blessed Trinity is hinted at by joining a plural noun with a singular verb, as ברא אלהים, &c.

2. The spirit here spoken of is that supernatural gift whereby Adam was what he was in Paradise. It is sometimes called the gift of glory and of grace, sometimes glory, sometimes the breath of life (נשמה). This is the stricter and more limited sense in which it is used, although in other passages the word 'spirit' is used in a laxer way, as synonymous perhaps with soul, although possibly a more rigid examination of such passages might lead to a different conclusion. Thus, when St. Paul, 2 Cor. vii. 1, speaks of filthi-

ness of flesh and spirit (μολυσμὸς σαρκὸς καὶ πνεύματος), he may mean pollution resulting from the body or from an unclean spirit.

3. There are several texts, in which the same division is implied, where either all the three are specified, or at least the distinction between soul and spirit. Of this distinction, Origen (in Joan. vi. § 7) says, there are countless passages which observe it. I shall put three or four passages together, without separating the former class from the latter. "Oh my *soul* come not thou into their secret, into their assembly my *glory* be not thou united," אל תחד כבדי, Gen. xlix. 6. . . "My *glory* rejoiceth, my *flesh* also shall rest in hope, for thou wilt not leave my *soul* in hell," Ps. xvi. 9, 10, which passage is urged against the Apollinarians by St. Cyril de Inc. xix. ap. Mai. Coll. Nova, vii. "Let the enemy persecute my *soul*, and take it; let him tread down my life upon the earth, and lay my *glory* in the dust," Ps. vii. 5. Again, "And Mary said, My *soul* doth magnify the Lord, and my *spirit* hath rejoiced in God my Saviour." Luke ii. 46. "Awake up, my *glory;* awake, harp and lute; I will awake right early," where the *glory* is distinguished from himself. Ps. lvii. 9. "My *heart* is fixed; I will sing and give praise; yea, my *glory* shall" (אף כבודי), cviii. 1[3]. Baruch iii. 1 (quoted by Athan. c. Serap. i. 7), "The *soul* in anguish, the troubled *spirit* crieth unto Thee." Song of Three Children, "O ye *spirits* and *souls* of the righteous." Lastly, in Hebrews iv. 12, "The Word of the Lord . . . pierceth even to the dividing asunder of the *soul* and *spirit*, and of the joints and marrow."

4. The division of man into spirit, soul, and body, is of

[3] See Mr. Newman's Lectures on Justification, p. 186, for further observations on the word *glory*. The Old Testament, more particularly the Psalms, being ultimately designed for Christians, the prophets *need* not have ministered to themselves at all in such expressions, but unto us. See, however, presently, § 5.

course not a logical division: for a logical division is one into this, and that, i. e. into two only. And properly speaking it is not man, but Christian, which is so divided (non-logically): Ἡμεῖς γὰρ οὐ μάτην αὐτόν φαμεν ἐπὶ τοῦ πνευματικοῦ μὴ προστεθεικέναι τὸ Ἄνθρωπος· κρεῖττον γὰρ ἢ ἄνθρωπος ὁ πνευματικὸς, τοῦ ἀνθρώπου ἤτοι ἐν ψυχῇ ἢ ἐν σώματι ἢ ἐν συναμφοτέροις χαρακτηριζομένου, οὐχὶ δὲ καὶ ἐν τῷ τούτων θειοτέρῳ πνεύματι, οὗ κατὰ μετοχὴν ἐπικρατοῦσαν χρηματίζει ὁ πνευματικός. Orig. in Jo. ii. § 15. Body, then, is almost essential to the idea, man: it may be logically divided into body and soul: but man and this gift (i. e. spirit) together make up the idea, Christian. Body is only separated from man's soul during the brief space of death; in hell and in heaven it is united with the soul, and is part of the man. The natural man is here meant, and not the Christian man.

5. The Christian man is this natural man with that supernatural gift which Adam had, restored to him. This St. Cyril teaches, contr. Anthropom. 2. Ἐπεὶ οὐ μόνον λογικὸν ἐχρῆν εἶναι, ἀλλὰ καὶ Πνεύματος ἁγίου μέτοχον, ἵνα λαμπροτέρους ἔχῃ τοὺς χαρακτῆρας τῆς θείας φύσεως ἐν αὐτῷ, ἐνεφύσησεν αὐτῷ πνοὴν ζωῆς. Τοῦτο δέ ἐστι τὸ δι' Υἱοῦ τῇ λογικῇ κτίσει χορηγούμενον Πνεῦμα, καὶ διαμορφοῦν αὐτὸ εἰς εἶδος τὸ ἀνωτάτω, τοῦτ' ἔστι τὸ θεῖον· ὅτι γὰρ οὐκ εἰς ψυχὴν ἀνθρώπῳ τὸ ἐμφυσηθὲν αὐτῷ γέγονε πνεῦμα, οὔτε μὴν εἰς νοῦν, ὡς οἴονταί τινες, ἔστιν ἐντεῦθεν ἰδεῖν. Πρῶτον μὲν ὁ ἐμφυσήσας Θεὸς νοεῖται, τὸ δὲ ἐμφυσηθὲν ἐξ αὐτοῦ πάντως που νοεῖται· καὶ ἴδιον αὐτοῦ, ἤτοι τῆς οὐσίας αὐτοῦ· εἶτα πῶς ἂν τὸ ἐκ Θεοῦ πνεῦμα μεταβέβληται εἰς φύσιν ψυχῆς; κ. τ. λ. And presently, speaking of what Christ said to the Apostles when He breathed on them, "Receive ye the Holy Ghost," he says: Ἀνανέωσις γὰρ τῆς ἀρχαίας ἐκείνης δωρεᾶς καὶ τοῦ δοθέντος ἡμῖν ἐμφυσήματος τὸ διὰ Χριστοῦ γέγονεν ἀναμορφοῦν ἡμᾶς εἰς τὸν πρῶτον ἁγιασμὸν, καὶ ἀνακομίζον τὴν ἀνθρώπου φύσιν ὡς ἐν ἀπαρχῇ τοῖς ἁγίοις ἀποστόλοις εἰς

τὸν ἄνωθεν καὶ ἐν πρώτῃ κατασκευῇ δοθέντα ἡμῖν ἁγιασμόν[4]. This supernatural gift may be called *our* spirit, in the same way as the spirits of the prophets are said to be subject to them, as if they were their possessions; as Origen remarks (in Joan. vi. 7) Δεδωρημένα αὐτοῖς ὑπὸ Θεοῦ, οἱονεὶ ἐκείνων ὀνομάζεσθαι κτήματα. As the one supernatural gift may be abused, so the other, which we are here considering, may also. This gift it is which sanctifies the soul and the body, which gives the soul the preponderance over the body, which enables it to converse with the other world in prayer and meditation. Its efficacy is pointed out by the same wonderful writer on Levit. ii. 2. "*Anima quæcunque peccaverit coram Domino, non voluntate.* Recte animam dicit quam peccare describit; non enim spiritum vocasset quem diceret peccaturum. Sed ne hominem quidem hunc diceret, in quo nequaquam imago Dei peccato interveniente constaret. Non ergo est spiritus ille qui peccat; *Fructus enim* spiritus est, ut describit Apostolus, *charitas, gaudium, pax, patientia*, et cætera his similia, quæ etiam fructus vitæ appellantur. Denique et alibi dicit: *Qui seminat in carne, de carne metet corruptionem: et qui seminat in spiritu, de spiritu metet vitam æternam.* Quoniam ergo alius est qui seminat et alius est in quo seminatur, seminatur autem vel in carne cum peccatur, ut metatur corruptio, vel in spiritu cum secundum Deum vivitur, ut metatur vita æterna; constat animam esse quæ vel in carne vel in spiritu seminat, et illam esse quæ vel in peccatum ruere possit vel converti a peccato. Nam corpus *sequela* ejus est ad quodcunque delegerit, et spiritus *dux* ejus est ad virtutem, si eum sequi velit." However, though this gift is in a special sense

[4] See further, in Bishop Bull's treatise on the state of man before the fall, particularly pp. 90—94, who curiously enough saw the importance of a doctrine which Möhler, in his Symbolik, makes the 'Standpunkt' for attacking heresies current abroad.

Christian, insomuch that till it came, the Spirit was (St. John vii. 39) said to be not yet; still it may have been in part enjoyed by the Patriarchs, and in some faint degree even by the heathen, only with this difference, that they arrived at it as the reward of long labours, the Christian has it bestowed upon him in baptism at once. How far all Jewish rites were anticipations, though feeble ones, of Christian rites, not only outwardly, but also inwardly, I shall not here discuss; but shall content myself with saying that it seems probable that the Patriarchs, at least, were in some measure partakers of the overflowings of the grace which in their language they anticipated. It may be interesting upon the other case—that of the heathen—to add here two or three passages from the Fathers. St. Justin Martyr. c. Tryph. p. 221, speaks as follows: *Φησὶ γὰρ Πλάτων, αὐτὸ τοιοῦτον εἶναι τὸ τοῦ νοῦ ὄμμα, καὶ πρὸς τοῦτο ἡμῖν δεδόσθαι, ὡς δύνασθαι καθορᾷν αὐτὸ ἐκεῖνο τὸ ὂν εἰλικρινεῖ αὐτῷ ἐκείνῳ, ὃ τῶν νοητῶν ἁπάντων ἐστὶν αἴτιον, οὐ χρῶμα ἔχον, οὐ σχῆμα, οὐ μέγεθος, οὐδὲ οὐδὲν ὧν ὀφθαλμὸς βλέπει, ἀλλά τι ὂν τοῦτ' αὐτὸ φημὶ. ὂν ἐπέκεινα πάσης οὐσίας, οὔτε ῥητὸν οὔτε ἀγορευτὸν, ἀλλὰ μόνον καλὸν καὶ ἀγαθὸν, ἐξαίφνης ταῖς εὖ πεφυκυίαις ψυχαῖς ἐγγινόμενον διὰ τὸ συγγενὲς καὶ ἔρωτα τοῦ ἰδέσθαι. τίς οὖν ἡμῖν, ἔλεγε, συγγένεια πρὸς τὸν Θεόν ἐστιν; ἦ καὶ ἡ ψυχὴ θεία καὶ ἀθάνατός ἐστι, καὶ αὐτοῦ ἐκείνου τοῦ βασιλικοῦ νοῦ μέρος; ὡς δὲ ἐκεῖνος ὁρᾷ τὸν Θεὸν, οὕτω καὶ ἡμῖν ἐφικτὸν τῷ ἡμετέρῳ νῷ συλλαβεῖν τὸ θεῖον, καὶ τὸ ἐντεῦθεν ἤδη εὐδαιμονεῖν; πάνυ μὲν οὖν ἔφην.* Tatian also, although a writer not so much to be depended on, has much to the same effect, of which the following is a small part, p. 150. *'Απώλεσεν ἡμᾶς τὸ αὐτεξούσιον, δοῦλοι γεγόναμεν οἱ ἐλεύθεροι, διὰ τὴν ἁμαρτίαν ἐπράθημεν. οὐδὲν φαῦλον ὑπὸ τοῦ Θεοῦ πεποίηται, τὴν πονηρίαν ἡμεῖς ἀνεδείξαμεν. οἱ δὲ ἀναδείξαντες δυνατοὶ πάλιν παραιτήσασθαι· δύο πνευμάτων διαφορὰς ἴσμεν ἡμεῖς, ὧν* τὸ μὲν καλεῖται ψυχή· τὸ δὲ, μεῖζον μὲν τῆς ψυχῆς, Θεοῦ δὲ εἰκὼν καὶ ὁμοίωσις, ἑκάτερα δὲ παρὰ τοῖς ἀνθρώποις τοῖς πρώτοις ὑπῆρχεν, ἵνα τὸ μέν τι ὦσιν ὑλικοὶ, τὸ δὲ ἀνώτεροι τῆς ὕλης. So, too, St. Clement, Strom. v. § 89, p. 698, Ἐντεῦθεν οἱ ἀμφὶ τὸν Πυθαγόραν θείᾳ μοίρᾳ τὸν νοῦν εἰς ἀνθρώπους ἥκειν φασὶ, καθάπερ Πλάτων καὶ Ἀριστοτέλης ὁμολογοῦσιν· ἀλλ' ἡμεῖς μὲν τῷ πεπιστευκότι προσεπιπνεῖσθαι τὸ ἅγιον Πνεῦμα φαμὲν, οἱ δὲ ἀμφὶ τὸν Πλάτωνα νοῦν μὲν ἐν ψυχῇ θείας μοίρας ἀπόῤῥοιαν ὑπάρχοντα, ψυχὴν δὲ ἐν σώματι κατοικίζουσιν, ἀναφανδὸν γὰρ διὰ Ἰωὴλ ἑνὸς τῶν δώδεκα προφητῶν εἴρηται· "Καὶ ἔσται μετὰ ταῦτα, ἐκχεῶ ἀπὸ τοῦ Πνεύματός μου ἐπὶ πᾶσαν σάρκα, καὶ οἱ υἱοὶ ὑμῶν καὶ αἱ θυγατέρες ὑμῶν προφητεύσουσιν·" ἀλλ' οὐχ ὡς μέρος Θεοῦ ἐν ἑκάστῳ ἡμῶν τὸ Πνεῦμα· ὅπως δὲ ἡ διανομὴ αὕτη καὶ ὅ τι ποτέ ἐστι τὸ ἅγιον Πνεῦμα ἐν τοῖς περὶ προφητείας κἀν τοῖς περὶ ψυχῆς ἐπιδειχθήσεται ἡμῖν· ἀλλὰ τὰ μὲν τῆς γνώσεως βάθη κρύπτειν 'ἀπιστίῃ ἀγαθῇ' καθ' Ἡράκλειτον, ἀπιστίη γὰρ διαφυγγάνει μὴ γιγνώσκεσθαι. Compare the passage from St. Austin, c. Jul. Pel., quoted above, p. 308.

Plato also saw (see Tennem. Platon. Philos. iv. p. 34,) that man was not willingly and of his own accord wicked, although his wicked acts were voluntary acts. Hence there is an appearance of there being a double will, and so a double personality, in a man—a difficulty which the doctrine we have been upon comes in to explain. For it being the soul which sins (see Origen, as just quoted), the flesh which is attached to it gives it the propension to sin, while the spirit which is superadded to it gives it a propension towards virtue and holiness. Hence the appearance of a double will, from the soul being, so to say, intimately interpenetrated by two opposite powers. The heathens, who expressed their consciousness of such opposite powers at work in them, are witnesses to the fact that they enjoyed the gift in some measure, though doubtless in a slight one.

How can a *law* be said to be in our *members* unless there is that wonderfully close connexion between the soul and the body whereby the law which properly belongeth to mind is said to dwell in them? "Spiritus spiritali munere adjutus adversus carnis concupiscentiam concupiscit," said St. Aust. c. Jul. Pel. v. § 56. The heathen, then, though they received not the promise, yet had such tokens and marks of grace upon them as showed that they were sprung from a fallen parent, not from a parent who had no grace to fall from. The natural man needed the supernatural gift, to be able to fulfil his own longings: the fables of a golden age were but the external circumstances in imagination, suited to the internal condition which those longings witnessed the loss of.

As the mind of *man* is present in all parts of the body, and sees, and hears, and feels in every way in it and by it, so that there is no conscious interval between the act of the body and of the mind; as all its temptations, or by far the larger part of them, are felt by the body, and executed by it, if carried into act, so that the mind which yields to them is said to be carnal, not that it becomes material in a literal sense, but in that it is under the gross influence of matter: so, on the other hand, the spirit of a *Christian* is present in all acts of the mind, and through the mind in several acts of the body also; the inducements to go right, in a Christian sense, are through the spirit; through it the mind feels aright, i. e. has awe and love; through it, sees aright, i. e. has faith; through it, hears the inward communings of the Spirit of God, tastes His graciousness and the powers of the world to come, and smelleth the sweet-smelling savour of heavenly incense. Through it both body and soul become spiritual, partake of a spiritual and heavenly nature, become mysteriously blended in a mysterious union and peace.

6. But as the body may become spiritual (for there is a spiritual body), so it may forfeit the gift of the spirit through

the sins which in it and with it the soul committeth. As the Word of God is able to divide asunder the soul and the spirit, so He will, through His angels, cut them asunder in him whose soul sinneth, and appoint him his portion with the unbelievers. This is the true death of man; as the separation of soul and body is the natural death, so the final separation of the spirit from these is everlasting death. This may be illustrated by the following passage of St. Irenæus, v. 6. "Quum Spiritus hic commixtus animæ unitur plasmati; propter effusionem Spiritus, spiritualis et perfectus homo factus est: et hic est qui secundum imaginem et similitudinem factus est Dei. Si autem defuerit animæ Spiritus, animalis est vere, qui est talis, et carnalis derelictus imperfectus erit: imaginem quidem habens in plasmate, similitudinem vero non assumens per Spiritum. Sicut autem hic imperfectus est; sic iterum si quis tollat imaginem, et spernat plasma, jam non hominem intelligere potest, sed aut partem aliquam hominis, quemadmodum prædicimus, vel aliud aliquid præter hominem. Neque enim plasmatio carnis ipsa secundum se homo perfectus est, sed corpus hominis et pars hominis. Neque enim et anima ipsa secundum se homo; sed anima hominis et pars hominis. Neque Spiritus homo: Spiritus enim, et non homo vocatur. Commixtio autem et unitio horum omnium perfectum hominem efficit. Et propter hoc Apostolus se ipsum exponens explanavit perfectum et spiritualem salutis hominem, in primâ Epistolâ ad Thessalonicenses dicens sic: Deus autem pacis sanctificet vos perfectos, et integer vester spiritus, et anima, et corpus sine querelâ in adventum Domini Jesu Christi servetur. Et quam utique causam habebat his tribus, id est, animæ et corpori, et spiritui, integram et perfectam perseverationem precari in adventum Domini, nisi redintegrationem et adunitionem trium et unam et eandem ipsorum sciebat salutem? Propter quod et perfectos ait eos, qui tria sine querelâ exhibent Domino. Perfecti igitur, qui et Spiritum in se perseverantem habuerint Dei, et animas et corpora sine querelâ servaverint; Dei, id est, illam, quæ ad Deum est, fidem servantes, et eam quæ ad proximum est justitiam custodientes." And again, ii. 33. Πάντες οἱ εἰς ζωὴν ἐγγραφέντες ἀναστήσονται ἴδια ἔχοντες σώματα καὶ ἰδίας ψυχὰς καὶ ἴδια πνεύματα ἐν οἷς εὐηρέστησαν τῷ Θεῷ. Οἱ δὲ τῆς κολάσεως ἄξιοι ἀπελεύσονται εἰς τὴν αὐτὴν καὶ αὐτοὶ ἰδίας ἔχοντες ψυχὰς καὶ ἴδια σώματα, ἐν οἷς ἀπέστησαν ἀπὸ τῆς τοῦ Θεοῦ χάριτος. Cf. v. 7. S. Ephr. S. in Ps. cxl. 3, fin. With this compare St. Basil, De Sp. Sancto, xvi. § 40. Οἱ λυπήσαντες τὸ Πνεῦμα τὸ ἅγιον τῇ πονηρίᾳ τῶν ἐπιτηδευμάτων αὐτῶν ἢ οἱ μὴ ἐπεργασάμενοι τῷ δοθέντι, ἀφαιρεθήσονται ὃ εἰλήφασιν, εἰς ἑτέρους μετατιθεμένης τῆς χάριτος, ἢ κατά τινα τῶν εὐαγγελιστῶν καὶ διχοτομηθήσονται παντελῶς, τῆς διχοτομίας νοουμένης κατὰ τὴν εἰς τὸ παντελὲς ἀπὸ τοῦ Πνεύματος ἀλλοτρίωσιν. Οὔτε γὰρ σῶμα διαιρεῖται ὡς τὸ μὲν παραδίδοσθαι τῇ κολάσει τὸ δὲ ἀφίεσθαι. Μυθικὸν γὰρ τοῦτό γε, καὶ οὐ κατὰ δίκαιον Κριτὴν ὅλου ἡμαρτηκότος, ἐξ ἡμισείας εἶναι τὴν κόλασιν. Οὔτε ψυχὴ διχῇ τέμνεται, ὅλη δι' ὅλου τὸ ἁμαρτωλὸν φρόνημα κεκτημένη καὶ συγκατεργαζομένη τῷ σώματι τὸ κακόν. Ἀλλὰ διχοτομία, ὥσπερ ἔφην, ἡ ἀπὸ τοῦ Πνεύματος εἰς τὸ διηνεκὲς τῆς ψυχῆς ἀλλοτρίωσις. Νῦν μὲν γὰρ εἰ καὶ μὴ ἀνακέκραται τοῖς ἀναξίοις, ἀλλ' οὖν παρεῖναι δοκεῖ πως τοῖς ἅπαξ ἐσφραγισμένοις τὴν ἐκ τῆς ἐπιστροφῆς σωτηρίαν αὐτῶν ἀναμένον· τότε δὲ ἐξ ὅλου τῆς βεβηλωσάσης Αὐτοῦ τὴν χάριν ψυχῆς ἀποτμηθήσεται. Διὰ τοῦτο οὐχ ἔστιν ἐν τῷ ᾅδῃ ὁ ἐξομολογούμενος οὐδὲ ἐν τῷ θανάτῳ ὁ μνημονεύων Θεοῦ, οὐκέτι τῆς βοηθείας τοῦ Πνεύματος συμπαρούσης.

7. Lastly, it may be observed that the distinction into spirit, soul, and body, is capable of being made the basis, or *tessera*, of a system of devotional meditation. For we find that the body is mentioned in Scripture as in some way

mysteriously connected with the Holy Spirit: it is called the Temple of the Holy Spirit. And texts might be noticed which would show the connexion of the soul with the Son, as also that of the spirit with the Father, e. g. Rom. viii. 15, &c. Weak and feeble as all resemblances in the creature to the Creator must needs be, still the spirit tends in man to make the three co-equal and, prospectively, co-eternal, if such awful words may be applied to aught relating to a creature: for it tends to make the body spiritual and the soul spiritual. In the Fathers one commonly sees that the mention of any *three* things in Scripture sets them upon searching well to see if somewhat concerning the Trinity be not there concealed, or rather reservedly revealed; and this may be the case with regard to the following passage of St. Ephrem, who more than once speaks in the same way of this division of man. Vol. iii. p. 34, he says, "If the spirit suffer, it is wholly sealed with the Father; if the soul suffer, it is wholly blended with the Son; if, again, the body confess and be burned, it partaketh wholly with the Holy Ghost." (See also vol. ii. p. 336.) This passage will, to a scripturally informed mind, afford ample matter for long meditation.

Note (52.) p. 286.

The body of man is to attain a more glorious resurrection through Christ's having taken a human body. See St. Athan. de Inc. § 21. c. Arian. iii. 34. St. Austin de C. D. xxii. 30, &c.

Note (53.) p. 287.

See above, p. 127, whence it appears that the Jews also held the doctrine of a second death; and see Jarchi on Gen. xlvi. 30.

Note (54.) p. 287.

Plato, Gorgias, § 168. Ὁ θάνατος τύγχανει ὢν, ὡς ἐμοὶ δοκεῖ, οὐδὲν ἄλλο ἢ δυοῖν πραγμάτοιν διάλυσις, ψυχῆς τε καὶ σώματος ἀπ' ἀλλήλοιν.

Note (55.) p. 287.

The second death, which takes place through sin, is noticed by St. Basil, as above, Note 51, by Aretas in Apoc. p. 207. Cyril, de Ador. in S. et V. p. 11. St. Aust. c. Jul. P. vi. 48. De Trin. iv. 5. "Sicut anima Deo deserente, sic corpus animâ deserente moritur."

Note (56.) p. 287.

Windischmann has somewhere noticed this. The identity of the Paramâtma (see Note 51) with Vishnu, who is called Achyuta, or the unfallen, will of course be equivalent to a proof of the statement in the text.

Note (57.) p. 287.

This was the doctrine of Basilides and other heretics. See Möhler as above, p. 60, where he points out the bearing of this upon castes, &c.

END OF NOTES TO DIALOGUE III.

DIALOGUE IV.

ON THE DISTINCT PERSONALITY OF MAN, AND THE THINGS IMPLIED IN IT.

"Obedire voluntati, habet exterioris necessitatem: facere voluntatem, proprium est unitati, cum factum sit voluntatis."

HILAR. *de Trin.* ix. p. 178.

DIALOGUE THE FOURTH.

LAURENCE. I felt, Rádhákánt, after leaving you the other day, that I had not at all come to the bottom of the Vedánta system. For in your account of things the influence of Yoganidri pervades all created beings, to whatever world they belong. And though what I have said may perhaps have led you to think how awful it is, if we really are endued with an unending individual existence, yet I feel doubtful whether I sufficiently instructed you as to the objections that there were against your theory of illusion. And therefore, as you said that you felt some objections to be against the surface of the Christian doctrine of our relations to matter, which we have discussed, let me now hear any objections which, according to your views, do not lie against the surface, but are of a deeper kind.

RAD. Our teachers hold that GOD includes all natures, as the sea does its waves, and that the notion of separate existences altogether is a mere deception, which it is the object of discrimination to remove. When the devout has obtained this, he sees that I and thou are but THAT, and that Siva is all things. Hence, as Siva is a spirit, and all things are ultimately to be absorbed into him, body must cease to exist, since it cannot become identical with spirit. And from the doctrine that Siva is all things, flows this also, that the distinction between right and wrong is only a deception, however necessary it may be for our guidance in this life.

LAUR. You make this last part of your theory consistent with the former part, at all events: for if men are indeed one with the Supreme Spirit, then what they are already, they cannot aim at attaining to; and therefore it cannot be union with Him, but the knowledge of that (already existing) union, at which the devout with you should aim: and since actions are done, not by bodies, but by the souls in them, it will follow that the Supreme Being does all actions. Since, then, you cannot ascribe wickedness to Him, those, out of all actions done by Him which seem wicked, cannot indeed be so, according to you: all actions you would hold to be mediately or immediately the fruit of His will, and so not really but apparently evil, there being no insulated spot, chasm, or solitude, which His Spirit does not pervade; no creature, which is not an organ of it, whereby it communicates good.

Now whatever becomes of this system in detail, there is this objection to it—an objection I so often feel to your views of things—that it is an imaginative system, not a practical one. You "body forth the forms of things unknown," and argue from them as though you saw far more clearly into the system of GOD's government than He permits you. For it is plain that it must involve what you have here fairly stated—the annihilation of all distinctions between right and wrong. But the world in which we are placed is one, in which this distinction is made to cling most pertinaciously to us; there is every reason to think that even the most abandoned men retain a sense of it, so far as to make them wish to be rid of the guilt of a wicked act, even when they would retain any advantages accruing from it.

If, then, this be so, and if, besides this, even when it is nearly effaced, the sense of this distinction often revives in full vigour upon the near approach of death, it is surely an unpractical system which treats men, even in theory, as if this distinction were unreal, although it lasts pertinaciously throughout the whole of that portion of their existence, with which experience makes us acquainted. In other words, we cannot succeed in divesting ourselves of the idea that they either are, or have been made, essentially distinct under that portion of GOD's government in which we His creatures are placed; and yet your theory of illusion, if followed out consistently, must make this distinction an unreal one; neither can I see how you will avoid coming next to the conclusion, that men's vices are the actions of the Supreme Being.

RAD. But we do not so hold indifference of actions; neither do we believe the fate which overrules the deeds of men to be any thing else than the result of actions done in a previous existence; which actions, in this way, entail a necessity of sinning.

LAUR. I must again insist on what I before urged, the danger of imagination in things of such high concernment to us. That forward and delusive faculty leads you to frame to yourselves what the rules (1) are by which GOD governs the world; and so you have, I fear, fallen into what we must account blasphemies against the Most High. Yet let me not be thought to assert, that all the evils in practice which generally follow from a false creed, have actually followed in your case. The high notions of self-denial held by your forefathers, and practised, more or less, during so many ages, may have exerted an influence not only in the way of example, but in some further and providential way, against the tendency of a wrong creed.

To proceed, however, with the discussion of your creed. It seems to me that you have a speculative, and also a practical view. The speculative view may be stated thus:—Siva being all creatures, produces all actions; certain actions appear to contradict this; therefore, since the first is true, the second is only an appearance; they do not really contradict it, and the apparent contradiction will be removed by Vijnana (discrimination). And what I call the more practical view is this: men's actions are the result of fate; but fate is itself the result of actions done in a previous existence. The former would be, I suppose, the language adopted when a man was arguing about the nature of GOD; the latter when he was treating of the rule of action. But if we look closely at the two, we shall see that one is incompatible with the other. For the latter shows plainly how men will allow themselves in any extent of imagination, which will delude their reason into a belief that after all they are not parting with the notion of moral responsibility. By weighing, then, the sentiments of the speculative view in the balance of the practical, we find that the practical view indirectly attests a truth which is subversive of the speculative view. For the notion of responsibility implies the notion of separate personality, and therefore contradicts the notion that Siva produces all actions.

Next, let us reverse the process, and see what will come of examining the practical view by the theoretical. All actions, you say, are the fruit of Siva's will: but under all actions are contained the actions done in a former existence; for if the actions of this existence themselves are the fruit of Siva's will, then the actions of a past existence, upon which those of the present depend, are the fruit of his will. From this it will follow that the difficulty I have alleged against your speculative view, viz. that it attributes wicked actions to GOD, is not destroyed, but only shifted into another existence by the practical theory, as I have called it. You do assert, theoretically at least, the indifference of actions right or wrong. And what I contend is, that the Almighty Dispenser of all things has placed us in a world, in which we are treated throughout as if the distinction between right and wrong was a real one; and that the Christian dispensation, coming as it does from the same GOD, is more probable than yours, because it confirms us in the idea, that this distinction is a permanent and eternal one.

But it will be well, perhaps, to assume next the truth of your practical view, in order to show more particularly how it disproves the notion, that Siva is all things. If, then, the condition of our present life depends upon actions done in a previous existence by us and not by any other being, we must assume the operation of independent wills, acting some in one direction and some in another direction. If, then, the one acted in conformity with Siva's will, and the other acted not in conformity with it, but against it, Siva's will is, upon this supposition, not the producer of all acts, but only of some acts. For it is as impossible to conceive of the same will operating in two different directions, as it is to conceive that an indivisible particle of matter can be at rest and in motion. You must, then, virtually admit, according to your practical view, that there are some independent, originative, sources of actions, endued with a personality distinct from Siva's personality, viz. those who oppose his will. And if it be plain that unanimity of will does not necessarily imply identity of person, then the good also must be capable of being conceived as distinct persons from Siva. The practical view then, in that it assumes independent action, though in a previous existence, is contrary to the speculative.

Again, will not this absurdity also follow from your view of things, that the present life is not at all a state of trial (2)? For if the Supreme Being rewards men according to their actions, He either rewards them according to their actions done in this life, or their actions done in a former life. If their future happiness or misery depends upon their making a right use of the opportunities offered in this life for all the different degrees of discipline, then this is the life upon which all depends, and therefore the doctrine of pre-existence is unnecessary. But, if He rewards them in proportion to the acts of a past existence, then their present existence ceases to be a state of trial, and your God will be made wantonly to expose His creatures to the pollutions of incorporation, when nothing that they can do in this life will alter their fate, once decided.

Neither will it avail to say that all have contracted some stains in a past existence, and that they are admitted here to a state of penance and purgation, in such way that their final destination can be reversed by neglect of the opportunities now offered them. Because in this way you will again be making our present existence to be, what Christians believe it is, that upon which our final destination after all depends, and so you will be admitting that a pre-existence is unnecessary.

I should also observe, that arguing from all we know of good men, there is every appearance that they also are mutable beings (3), and that their wills are at times opposed to what they will at other times. Hence, if God be immutable, and loveth righteousness and hateth iniquity, those creatures who are mutable, and love sometimes one, sometimes the other, are also endued with separate wills from Him, and so with separate personalities from His. But the whole economy of things, which you imagine for yourselves, is built upon the supposition that the subjects of it are mutable creatures, and so are distinct from an immutable Being. Neither do we know of any immutable Being but One: all others are by nature mutable, as the fall of some of them plainly shows, and they are therefore separate individuals from that one immutable Being. As, then, they have each a will of their own, which will may exercise itself in approximations to the Supreme will, or in declinations from it (4), this capacity of so exercising their will leads one to see at once, that there may be approximations in every different degree to the Supreme will, as well as deviations from it. As, further, will evinces its existence by energy, if we could suppose any two beings to have a will perfectly coincident, in the strictest logical sense of the word *perfectly*, we plainly must suppose their energies to be perfectly coincident. But to suppose this would be to suppose that they ceased to have an individual existence. And I own I am totally unable to conceive such a logically perfect coincidence between the wills and energies of any two created beings (5). For if their energies were perfectly coincident, they must have spheres of action perfectly coincident; else the will of one would be impeded, and consequently could not perfectly coincide with that of the other. If, then, you suppose a will perfectly coinciding with the Supreme will, you must suppose also an energy perfectly coinciding with the Supreme energy. And if you suppose that it is only through deception that we imagine ourselves distinct from the Supreme Being, you must suppose that our will is coincident with His will, and therefore infinite. But you also suppose creatures to be subject to change, as their being placed in different stations of probation would prove. And to suppose that a mûtable creature can become one with the immutable God is to suppose that there is a period, when advances towards an absolutely perfect Being, who never had any imperfection, come to a close. If, then, such advances come to a close, you must likewise imagine the past imperfections to be effaced from existence, otherwise a Being who never had any imperfection will be equalled by one, who has had imperfections.

I am indeed aware that you will say that you hold that after an Ahoràtri of Brahma, the good lose all individual existence, and are absorbed into the immutable ever-existing Being. And when it is so stated, it seems as if no answer could be made at once which should disprove it in the way of logical reasoning, however loudly a man's conscience may cry out against the thought of his becoming, in this sense, one with GOD, who is over all, blessed for ever! But the truth is, I believe, that it never could have been thus nakedly propounded to any thoughtful being for acceptation, and you do not yourselves so propound it. For this is only a part of the doctrine which you hold: for you believe that all spirits came out of Brahma, and were originally portions of him: that at the creation he unfolded (6) himself, i. e. separated from himself, both then and at subsequent times, portions of his essence. So that when we come to look at your doctrine as Christians, we feel at first sight a kind of suspicion that you are making GOD material, when you suppose men to have their whole essence absorbed into His essence at last. And a further examination of it leads us to fear that your god is, after all, but a subtle kind of matter. For the belief that spirits were originally separated from him, implies that he is discerptible, and so compounded. And in bringing it before you that your doctrines do lead to this blasphemy, I am not degrading the Indians to a lower rank than other nations not yet Christian. For I believe that a thoughtful examination of all errors and heresies whatsoever will show that they do ultimately run up to this (7). I think that you will find that the systems which suppose pre-existence, and periods in which men have lived before the present, are always accompanied with a virtual denial of free will, and a representation of GOD, which comes at last to identify Him with matter.

RAD. Yet surely the doctrine of a previous existence is a very ancient and widely diffused one: two things which ought to give it some claims to your regard.

LAUR. I think, indeed, that there are one or two great truths which it may be a mingled representation of, although I would not venture to dogmatize about this matter. Still, as far as I know, all error depends upon some truth for its subsistency (8), and therefore I suppose there is some truth disguised by the evil spirit, the father of this error. Yet when things very mysterious are so reduced to a form as to become no more mysterious, the error ceases to bear any great symptoms of ever having come from truth. Now we are told that GOD, before the foundation of the world, chose those whom He would save from the world, which is a very great mystery, and ought never to be treated of as if it were the act of a creature of time, such as you are. This, then, may be one truth which you have retained a trace of in your doctrine of a metempsychosis: you have not been content to treat it as a mystery belonging to a Being with whom the future is as the past, and to whom priority and posteriority cannot be ascribed: but you have worked it out into a system in order that you might contrive to fancy that you could reconcile it with what is most undeniably true—that men are free agents.

Or, again, this doctrine of transmigrations and periods may be looked upon in another light, viz. as keeping up a tradition of the fall of man from a higher and better state. For the books of Moses, in which I do not see any trace whatever of this doctrine of transmigrations, teach us that God made man upright; that afterwards his wife, whose body was mysteriously formed from his, led him into sin, and that in consequence they forfeited that happy state, and that also all who spring from him are under a state of punishment for his sin, by nature. And I think that, if you consider how readily men catch at any thing which will enable them to shift the responsibility (9) of wicked acts from themselves to some other being, or to necessity or fate, you must allow that this true history goes a good way towards accounting for the existence of your discoloured tradition.

Rad. Am I, then, to think that the sins of the parents in such ways limit man's free-will as to prevent his choosing what is good?

Laur. The power to choose good must certainly reside with us, otherwise we should not really be free beings at all. Upon what, indeed, that power depends is another question, which at some future time we may discuss. I think, however, that it is something which should be fully admitted and most attentively considered, that creatures endued with a power of doing right should so often choose what is wrong, in spite of that power. When we look back upon our misdeeds, we feel as if we could not deliberately have chosen them; so painful is it to realize to ourselves that our past conduct is ours, that upon cool reflection, we are completely at a loss to account for our inconsistency, and are fain to think that the power of acting aright, whatever it be, must have been withdrawn from us for the time. We cannot grasp the thought that we freely choose to do wrong; and it is in this state of mind that we are prone to adopt any theory which will shift the responsibility of the act off from ourselves. We see that there are in the world men who readily allow themselves to be led away by the false reasonings of others; and you may conclude that all men are in some degree, though in very different degrees, liable to the same thing (10) from their own selves. For we are plainly endued with a power of reflecting upon our own actions, which power, when it disapproves of past guilt, may be borne down by angry feeling at it, and not allowed to accuse us as it would do; i. e. may have its witness, that the act is our own act, set aside. Our inability, then, to realize to ourselves the distressing fact that we wilfully chose what was wrong, may be looked upon as a difficulty presented by our own mind in part, though not exclusively, to the belief that man is free: and perhaps there are other difficulties, and far greater ones, in the way of such belief, when we attempt to state to ourselves the mode in which wicked actions are controlled under divine Providence, and seem to make up a part of that whole system of things, which we believe to be under His government. And it seems to have been this sense that GOD does rule the world, that has led men so to forget that the government of the world is the concern of Him who is the Lord and Proprietor of it, as to imagine for themselves the rules by which He governs it. Hence they have come to implicate Him in the sum total of all actions, wicked as well as good, in a way which must, if carried out, obliterate all notions of free-will; along with those ideas of His own infinite perfections, which, though implanted by Him in men's minds, they need not retain of necessity in their knowledge (11).

But if the theory of free-will be liable to difficulties, which cannot perhaps be totally removed, the theory of necessity is liable to far greater difficulties, even in the most modified shape of it. For, in the first place, that world in which we are is under GOD's providence in every respect: for the fact that things apparently so trivial are often found to be so full of important bearing upon our interests, shows, beyond all contradiction, that if we admit a providence at all, we must admit a particular providence, since we are not at all judges of what is or is not a trivial event or action. Now among the particular things under GOD's government, we find that virtue is rewarded, and vice and carelessness punished, and this even in the smaller instances of it. And among the many ways in which this is effected, we find the ministration of other men to be a chief one, as the existence of courts of justice proves. If, then, according to your theory, creatures capable of improvement are admitted to penance in this life, for the imperfections of a past life, and if these imperfections are removed by the things which they suffer in this life, then what they suffer here is a purificatory process. And if purification be not administered by divine Providence, then you must give up the theory altogether. But if the purification be administered by Him, then the punishments which effect it are also. But the punishments which befall the virtuous in this life often befall them at the hands of wicked men, through oppression and violent perversion of judgment and justice in a province[1]; hence the divine Providence takes its rise and starting in them, so to say, and yet inflicts punishments upon those in whom, by birth, there is a capacity for amendment, not for that end, but on account of the virtues in them. And if this be so, you must, in your view of things, admit that the punishment is not unjust, and that the administrators of it act justly, or else that it is God who instigates them to do even wicked deeds (12). We, on the contrary, by believing that men's state of trial is here, and that their final condition depends upon their conduct in

[1] Eccles. v. 8.

this life, and not attempting to search out how it is that He overrules the actions of the wicked without instigating them, look rather to these confusions as proofs that men are free agents, endued with an individual existence, and placed in this world with a view to their being disciplined through the instrumentality of the things in it, accordingly as they avail themselves of the opportunities or not.

RAD. I can understand some things in what you say, and some things I must think over at another time. I can quite understand, for instance, how you mean that if all things done to us in this world, whether by good men or bad, go upon the supposition that we are free, we cannot suppose Siva to include all spirits, good and bad, but must assume that there are, as you say, other individual beings beside Siva in the world. Yet what you mean by saying that the theory of existence is false, though it bears witness to the true doctrine, that owing to the fall of one man others were condemned, I cannot understand. For you assert the individuality of the man who fell, because his will was opposed to GOD's will. And you deny the individuality of one man with another, and yet say that all are punished in consequence of one man's sin. Now this seems to amount to teaching the doctrine of dualism. For men, if they are all justly punished for this one man's sin, must all be one with this man; and as men, according to your views, are propagated by the agency of matter, you seem to me to be setting up a material principle, opposed to a spiritual principle; one which has a will energizing in one direction, and the other having a will energizing in an opposite direction.

LAUR. I think, Rádháḳánt, that this difficulty is one which is most fully met by observing some things which go on about us, which tend to show that we are going beyond our depth when we attempt to find out how it can be just for evil, of whatever kind it be, to be entailed from father to son. For the cases are numberless in which the innocent (13) suffer for the guilty, even where there is no such intimate dependency upon one another, as this of father and son is. Loss of property, good name, and many other things, put children in what seems, and often is, a far more disadvantageous position for growth in virtue and knowledge of religion. But, in particular, it is quite impossible to deny that there are many disorders which are entailed from father to son, and not unfrequently to the third and fourth generation; disorders which, in some instances, can be traced almost infallibly to the parent's misconduct: and there appear to be instances in which new disorders have been visited upon certain sins, which are hereditary, even when the sins are not imitated. And this is not a thing which was late observed, but early attracted the notice of physicians (14). Hence, as sins are committed by the soul, through the instrumentality of the body, the fact will amount to this, that for certain sins inherent in the soul of a man, certain inflictions are entailed upon the bodies (15) of his posterity: they suffer for his sins. This, then, is a fact in the course of GOD's ordinary government, which falls in with what our revelation teaches, concerning the entailment of the fruits of sin of a parent upon the souls of children, and completely removes all objection drawn from the supposed injustice of such punishment of the innocent for the wicked. But if you remember what was urged above, concerning the influence of bodily constitution upon the formation of character, it will also appear that the entailed consequences of sin, even in those instances where they come under our experience, and so belong to an ordinary, not a miraculous state of things, are to be viewed as something more than mere pains; for they are direct temptations to a peevish carelessness of mind in many cases, and temptations too which are carried about with men, and cannot be fled from, as other temptations can. Now the consideration of this fact, viz. that certain temptations to go wrong are entailed upon innocent children by the sins of their fathers, will, I think, lead you to see that whatever speculative difficulties you may raise to the Christian doctrine as involving a denial of the separate individuality of father and son, and so tending to a dualism, the very opposite is proved by this which I am now observing. For if a son, upon witnessing the folly and misery of his father's conduct, takes occasion to exert himself to overcome any temptations to sin, such as I have mentioned, then he plainly exerts his will in an opposite direction to what his father did, supposing the father to continue in sin to the last (16).

Now such a case as this is not merely hypothetical, but one of constant occurrence. Earth, in the Puránas (17), is made to bid children beware of their father's pride: which exhortation were useless unless they had both a tendency to go wrong, and also a power left to them of choosing what was right. Here, then, we have an instance of the will of the father going in one direction, and the will of the son going in another opposite direction. In this case, then, the material principle which you accuse me of setting up against the one spiritual principle, is found to be possessed of will, and will operating in two opposite directions, sometimes in accordance with, and sometimes in opposition to, the spiritual principle. And whether will can be, with any propriety, attributed to matter as such, I leave you to judge; to me it seems a contradiction in terms. But if there be any principle of unity between father and son, it is either material and discerptible, or it is immaterial and indiscerptible. If the former, then, as we have seen, a man is not precluded by it from having a will distinct from that of his father. If the latter, then it is also a contradiction in terms to say that a soul, which is an indiscerptible whole in itself, should will, and act upon that will, with one portion of itself in one direction, and with another portion in another direction. Yet this will be the only alternative left, unless you deny that the soul is an indiscerptible whole in itself, and so make it, in fact, the creature of destiny (18). For if it be not a whole in itself, then it must be part of something else, as you would say, of Siva; in which case, the absurdity above noticed will follow, for you will then make the Supreme Being to have, in one man, a will operating in one direction (19), and in another man a will operating in an opposite direction. Yet this is, as I said, equivalent to making him discerptible. For if any thing can make up an idea of a distinct being, it is a distinct will resulting in a distinct energy (20). If, then, the Supreme Being can become a number of distinct (21) wills and energies, He is discerptible.

Whether, then, the temptation to go wrong is transmitted to the soul of the sons from the father of all men, or to the body, is a further question, and one which it is nothing to the present purpose to discuss; since we see that facts which come under our observation abundantly prove the two things which I was desirous to show: viz. that the revealed account of transmitted guilt cannot be objected to as implying injustice, because, though there is enough to confirm our natural idea of GOD's justice (22), yet there are things which come under our observation in the course of GOD's ordinary government to show that we are not at all judges of what is just or unjust in the matter; and also that the existence of distinct wills evinced by the different conduct of different fathers and sons, is a proof that they are distinct individuals from each other and from God. For whether the particular propensions (23) to certain sins reside in the soul or the body, while they are present they must, at least in some degree, be an inducement to do what reason and conscience forbid: and when in one man we see that these propensions overcome reason, and in another remain, though in subjugation to reason, we cannot but see that there is an essential difference in the two men, such as fully to evince a distinct individuality; an *I* and a *Thou*, as your writers express it, which cannot be or become That (24), because our whole nature leads us to ascribe immutability, and all other perfections, to the Supreme Being. And let me again remind you how terrible it will be at the last day for those who have rejected the Christian scheme, when they might have known it: and how much more in conformity it would be with the wisdom which we do use in our temporal affairs, to act upon the safe side, when there is so tremendous an interest at stake. For it is not absorption into the Eternal for which Christians look, but for a day when the Lord God Almighty, who was, and is, and is to come, shall bring before Him all the whole sum of beings, which He gifted at creation with an individual eternal existence, not to absorb them into Himself, but to reward them, every one according to his works. What a man has done will then be the main thing; faith in Vishnu (25) will not then seem to be the only real thing, but good works in proportion to your knowledge; and they that have done good shall go into life everlasting, and they that have done evil into everlasting fire. Consider, then, well with yourself, that you may not treat it as a thing indifferent, whether you admit the truth of Christianity or not. For if I have put before you even evidence enough to make you feel doubts, whether after all it is not true, then you are bound to go on, and examine whether further evidence will not give strength to those doubts. For if this is our place of trial, and our only place of trial, as all Christians believe, then, if you reject the evidence here, you will not have any other opportunity between the time in which you are in this life, and the day of judgment and tribulation and wrath and anguish, when GOD ariseth to shake terribly the earth, and the elements shall be dissolved with a fervent heat. If all this should be true, what manner of persons ought you to be, and how attentive to all evidence upon the subject!

RAD. I had been told that the Christian scheme was a scheme of mercy; but in this view of it, it is a scheme of terror.

LAUR. Suppose, then, that we had been allowed to act on without the least knowledge of this great and dreadful and searching judgment, of the eternity of hell-fire, and the everlasting separation of the wicked from the good, for a certain period of our life; and that then a wise and good Being came and declared to us that all this was awaiting us, if we did not obey our consciences and live virtuously; would not the mere fact of this warning be in itself an act of the greatest loving-kindness?

RAD. Assuredly it would; yet one seems to want something more; one looks for forgiveness in some method: and it was in this light I thought the Gospel was a scheme of mercy.

LAUR. Doubtless you are right in this: the Gospel is a scheme of mercy or forgiveness. But then let us consider what forgiveness is. If it is in any sense the obliterating of the consequences of past sin, then it must be supposed to obliterate the worst consequences of it. Now nobody that at all makes it his business to obey GOD can have the slightest doubt that one of the worst consequences of past sin is inability to obey Him. Men would be angels if they could do His will on earth, as it is done in Heaven. Your own doctrine of metempsychosis is but one great and cumbrous expression of the plain truth, that the commission of sinful acts entails upon a man a necessity of sinning again, unless there be a very vigorous exertion of the moral principle upon his part. For if we substitute our brief life here for the period of a Manwantara, a man who sins in the Satyayuga of childhood often, in his after life comes to a Rajoyuga of peevishness and disobedience; and then follows the Tamoyuga of an undistinguishing spirit, and good and evil are confused before his spirit. This, then, is the most miserable of the effects of sin, that it disables men from obeying, and that forgiveness of sins which did not remove this disability would be no forgiveness at all. If a man's sins made him blind and lame, he could not be said to have those sins perfectly forgiven, until he could see and walk. Forgiveness of sins, then, and grace to walk uprightly for the future, are as inseparable from each other as the concave and convex of a circle. I am wholly unable to separate them even in thought, though I have often tried to do so. The Gospel, then, is a scheme of forgiveness, because it gives grace and strength to obey; it holds out divers means to this end; it professes to be a system under which GOD has chosen to Himself a peculiar people zealous of good works. And if it happens that men by leading careless lives make these means of no effect, that no more disproves that they did give spiritual life and strength, than the drunkenness of the vicious would disprove their having had natural life and strength. If ten lepers were cleansed, and only one of them was careful to maintain his restored health, this would not prove that the others had never been cleansed.

RAD. But if the object of Christianity was to make men lead better lives, and to give them strength to do so, it has surely failed most signally, from what I see of Christians. And after all, you must allow that a religion, which does not make men lead strict lives, is not worth so much as to make us leave our old profession for it.

LAUR. I think that the strongest possible argument for a religion is its influence upon the lives of its professors. Our books insist upon this most pointedly, as the best way of showing that God is really with us. Yet there are other arguments by which it may be sufficiently proved: and though I would not for a moment be thought to underrate your objection, (it cannot be set too high,) yet I think attention to the two following points will go far towards removing that objection.

1. Christians are entirely forbidden to strive and cry in the world, and try to display a front: I have no hesitation in saying that it is a false Christianity which attempts to do so. We are commanded most strictly to pray and give alms and fast in secret; and, in proportion as the whole body of Christians has among it those who do so, in that proportion is it rewarded openly. And from the continuance of Christ's kingdom upon earth, with its bishops as princes in all lands, I infer that these duties are still observed; and my belief is, that when the last day of account comes, we shall find that all the whole sum of outward and stirring exertion has done a mere nothing towards the promotion of His kingdom, when put in comparison with the effect of these unostentatious duties. Hence the side of Christianity which you see is just that which is the most contradictory to its distinctive characteristic as a practical system; whereas the side by which the Christian Church has power with God and prevails, is lonely weeping and supplication, which you do not see.

2. And this consideration, namely, that it is how men appear in GOD's sight, and not how they appear in man's, upon which the goodness of a religion depends, leads to another. For His all-seeing eye may see a rebellious stout-heartedness, where men think that devotion and self-denial reign: hence it may be a moral offence of the most heinous nature in His sight, when men disbelieve those revelations which He has made of Himself; or, in other words, the rejection of a sound creed may be, in the case of some minds, as thorough an act of rebellion against the Most High, as in the case of other men an act of sensuality would be. There are some people who, from their make and constitution, have little or no tendency to disregard the common rules of morality, but whose probation lies in their behaviour in regard to speculative difficulties.

Hence it is far from being clear that you can safely put Christianity aside, because it shows so little in the lives of most of its professors. For if its truest professors are those who least publicly profess it, on the one hand; and if, on the other hand, the moral improvement of mankind is far from being the whole of what it aims at, since the belief in its doctrines, in and by itself, is of the highest importance; it will follow that it is to be treated not only as a revelation of what GOD's will is, in regard to His creatures, but also as disclosing certain truths in regard to His own nature, which, for His wise purposes, He has made it our duty to hold religiously. And it is also very much to be observed, that knowledge is much more final than obedience is; obedience seems in all cases to lead to knowledge—obedience, I mean, not of the head or of the heart alone, but of the whole man, with all his mind as well as all his heart, and all his soul and all his strength—this obedience appears in all cases to lead to knowledge as a necessary attendant upon it; whereas knowledge, during a state of probation, seems in no case to lead necessarily to obedience. Now this being so, it becomes a question whether they who hold true doctrines in words only have any real hold of them, unless they live, or try to live, upright lives. It is stern obedience alone which will make men gentle towards others, and reverential towards God. For without a wish to obey, they cannot know of His doctrine; they think things absurd or nice distinctions (26) which are of the highest possible consequence: for it were hard indeed if, with a real wish to obey, issuing in a diligent use of all the means placed within their power, they could not attain to the truth. So firmly am I persuaded of this, that I should suppose there is always some real wrongness of heart, which perhaps confines its agency to mental acts alone, whenever people are careless about the creed they profess. False notions of God always prevent a good life (27): and from the very nature of imperfect creatures such as we are, it will follow that it is but a curious piece of trifling to attempt to decide precisely which comes first, the evil moral habit or the wrong creed. For as imperfect creatures advance gradually in corruption as well as in improvement, and never continue in one stay, evil or good habits, and wrong or right conceptions of God, keep giving birth to one another.

I am saying this with a view to show you that, although I by no means think moral improvement to be *the* end of the Gospel dispensation, yet it is one which is essentially bound up with it. For if the end of it be, as it much more correctly may be said to be, that certain of God's creatures should be the receptacles of that mystery of faith, which He has once delivered to them; and if there is every reason to think, that there is some impossibility in the nature of things that that mystery can be held in any thing but a pure conscience, then it appears clearly that Christianity, in order to effect this end, exacts of us a pure conscience—pure as well from mental contaminations of pride and self-satisfiedness, as from sensual ones of a grosser kind.

But besides, we are very greatly in the dark as to what the use of many moral habits, e. g. patience and temperance, will be in a future state of existence. We are obliged in childhood to learn many things which we do not see the use of; and perhaps it may be asserted, that to the very end of our present existence we are subjected to trials of various kinds, of the whole bearing of which upon our growth in holiness we can give a very slender account, at best. Hence many of the things which an infinitely wise and good Being bids us believe here, might be, in some unknown ways, the most absolutely necessary conditions of our further growth in holiness, in some wider sphere of existence. Hence it may be that He has chosen to try our teachableness and submission to superior wisdom, in the same way in regard to our whole duration, as we know that He has in regard to the different stages of it; for contempt of the undemonstrated decisions and opinions of the experienced in youth, is often followed by the greatest misery in after life (28). However, we Christians do see, though we cannot always express, the practical effect of a strict creed upon the heart, in humbling it, and exalting it too, by rendering it covetous after purity and unworldliness.

Nor ought it to be omitted that our books represent us as in the midst of other beings, as encompassed by a cloud of unseen witnesses; so that we know, I may say, nothing of the influence of the doctrines of the Church, as doctrines, upon principalities and powers in heavenly places. And perhaps the committing of these mysteries to our custody may contribute towards showing what is in our heart (29), not only to the few of God's creatures with whom sense makes us acquainted, but also to several unseen orders of beings, so that it may be known to God's creatures, by way of example, that we are thus and thus disposed of (30).

The very possibility, then, that a strictly orthodox creed may be absolutely necessary for our future happiness, makes it a moral obligation of the strongest kind not to set aside the evidence for the Christian religion all at once, particularly as we are such frail and exceedingly ignorant creatures, and know so very little upon what our real happiness may depend. You ought therefore to keep your mind open to every degree of evidence, and be particularly upon your guard against assuming that Christianity exerts no influence upon the minds of its professors, because that influence is not a visible one. For the kingdom of God cometh not with observation during any part of its continuance; and even that last and tremendous portion of it, the universal confession [2] of all the sins of all men, of their hearts as well as outward members, shall overtake men as a thief in the night.

RAD. All that you have told me makes me long to know somewhat more explicitly what these mysteries are whereof you speak. For to us, Christians appear to be worshippers of three Gods.

LAUR. I fear, Rádhakánt, exceedingly, now I have to answer you that question: for the other questions which you have asked me concerned the nature and destinies of man, but this will lead me to speak of Him which was and is and is to come. And these holy pearls cannot, without danger, be thrown before the unsanctified discretion of you that are heathens. I trust, then, that it is as an earnest inquirer that you ask, lest I should incur inexpiable guilt (31) by divulging them to one who is not in earnest. And I

[2] Rom. xiv. 11, 12. Psalm l. 21.

beg you not to think that the doctrine of the TRINITY is a simple and easy thing, which you can reduce to system without trouble. It is indeed easy for a common man to believe it, and praiseworthy for him to do so, though he understand not (32) what may be understood of so great a mystery. And I say this lest you should adopt the Christian system, and think to be able at once to discuss high doctrines in it; for though it be true that a man who is baptized, and becomes a Christian, has an inward power communicated to him in order to the understanding of these great truths, yet even then they are very full of difficulties, and require long study of the holy men of old, and a very holy life, before they will allow themselves to be as fully understood as they should be by those who deal with them as theologians, not as merely practical men. Feeling, then, that I am but little advanced in all these respects, I will endeavour to put only so much before you as is opposed to your own doctrines.

1. When we come to look at your theory of the Creation, there does seem ground for thinking that you deny the indiscerptibility of GOD, by representing all creatures as produced from His own essence, and not by Him, but from Him. We hold that it was on this wise. GOD is one Essence, but three Persons; and though all these three Persons were concerned in the Creation (33), yet it was by the Word, or second Person of this Trinity, that the worlds were made. And when GOD made the worlds by Him,

He did not separate Him from His Essence, but remained One with Him, and is One with Him, and ever will be One with Him. And to the creatures He gave a separate individuality; but He, being God, could not have a separate individuality from the Father, although He hath a distinct personality. For God is not divisible, as your books appear to make Him. For you represent Brahmá, Vishnu, and Siva (34), as denominations obtained by Him, according as His attributes display themselves, which is indeed like a certain heresy (35) against Christianity. Yet in other places they have been represented as at war with each other, so that they lose by this blasphemy all the attributes of divinity. Neither do we speak of the Divine Nature proceeding into three Avasthás (Hypostases) (36). For then we should make the Divine Nature, as such, to become something which it was not, and so destroy its eternity and unchangeableness. For "if it be not eternally that the Word is with the Father, then is not the Trinity eternal, but was a Monad aforetime, and from addition became afterwards a Triad (37)." Although, then, we hold that the Word of God proceeded (38) forth to create the worlds, yet we remember how little language can possibly do to express these mighty truths, and define not how He did so, though we know that He was not in any way separated from the Father, but is in all things "equal to the Father as touching His Godhead."

And as we believe that the doctrine of the Creation cannot be held aright (wherever the doctrine of the Trinity is revealed) save by belief in this doctrine, so neither is a right belief in God's omnipresence possible to one who has false notions of His creating. For you hold Him to be all things, and so confound the Creator with the created, by trying to explain His omnipresence. But we hold that He comprehendeth and surroundeth and pervadeth all things, upholding them by the Word of His power, yet not surrounded Himself, nor in space, but exceeding all space (39). This, then, is a mystery; whereas your belief that He is all things, and all things are He, is very hard to attain, and when attained is no mystery at all. His presence, according to you, is corporeal; according to us, is spiritual. When you have once let yourselves represent Him as separating parts of His Essence in order to create the world, then you easily pass on (40) to believing that He is what He has so created. But if this error extend to your views of all His ordinary dealings with men, in the course of nature, much more does it make you inconsistent also in those extraordinary and miraculous ones which you represent under the name of incarnations (Avatáras).

It is true, indeed, that all nations of which I know any thing to speak of, have had some faint traces of the doctrines of the Trinity (41) and the Incarnation; yet when we come to look at these traces, they are hardly deserving of the name of mystery. The doctrines implied in those traces amount, in both cases, to asserting the discerptibility of God. For you speak of a part of the Supreme Being becoming incarnate, or even of different parts of Him as incarnate at one and the same time. And as you explain Brahmá, and Vishnu, and Siva, to be different modes in which He manifests Himself, and so reduce your account of His Essence to one clear and intelligible to mortal finite man, you, by so doing, part with the right of explaining His noble acts by throwing yourselves upon His mysterious Nature. If, then, you excuse speaking of a part of Him as incarnate by the plea that His Nature is mysterious, you are doing what you have no right left to do: for there can be no parts or passions in a Spirit; but you have assumed that He has parts and passions, and so have reduced His Nature to one not mysterious. The Christian, on the contrary, by believing that three Persons are mysteriously united in one Nature from all eternity, is able to give a consistent account of the Incarnation. For he can, consistently with this belief, say that one Person of the Trinity took upon Him our nature, and remained undivided from God, retaining His Nature as God, and his distinct personality also, while He took the manhood into God. And this the Christian, by starting with the humble belief in the mystery of His divine Nature, has a right to do. He neither divides the substance of God, by saying that a part of Him became incarnate, instead of saying that one Person of the one Godhead took upon Him our nature; nor confounds the Persons, by calling them only three different manifestations of one Person. He would shrink with equal (42) horror from saying there are three Gods, and from saying that there is no distinction of Persons in the Godhead. By believing a Trinity of Persons, he is relieved from the blasphemy of asserting the discerptibility of God; and by believing a unity of Nature, from the folly of understanding the Essence of the Infinite.

And when he asserts that one Person of the all-glorious Trinity took upon Him our nature, he does not thereby assert His unchangeable Divine Nature to be subject to our passions, or diminish aught from His eternal perfections, but that He through His Divine Nature makes flesh to be divine, seeing (43) that He did not destroy His body, as in your stories Crishna is said to have done, but took it up into Heaven, whence it now ministereth unto Christians' good in divers manners. Neither did He often suffer by being incarnate (44) again and again, as your god is said to have done. For why should He, who is very God, and so Almighty, repeat His infinite condescension? or how could He remain one Person, if He were united in that high and mysterious way with many men, and not with one only? To believe Him to have taken into God our nature, is easier than to believe that (45) He is the soul of the world, and to believe that there are distinct Persons in the Godhead from all eternity, than to believe that He separated all creatures from His own Essence (46), and unfolded it into what was not: to believe that He has now a human body in Heaven, to which He will liken the bodies of the saints at last, according to the mighty working whereby He is able to subdue all things to Himself, is an easier task than to believe that this body we now have, and all the matter in the universe is an unreality (47). In our view it would be blasphemy, then, to assert that He destroyed that body, which, being a real body, He condescended to take upon Him, and to speak from, in the last dispensation, unto us when on earth, in which also He will judge all men at the last. For it is through our knowing of the eternity of His body that our flesh is able to rest in hope, trusting that we shall see Him at the last day, as will they also that pierced Him.

But I will not proceed further to speak of these great mysteries: I think that you have evidence enough before you to make you seriously inquire into the whole Christian system: you see how exceedingly important a right Creed may be, and I am sure that if, after a long and proper probation, you were baptized, you might then approach more safely to these awe-striking mysteries. I have only said so much of them because it seemed necessary, in order to prevent your thinking that your ancient writings taught you Christian truths, whereas they do but teach you things which have a kind of rude exterior resemblance to them.

These great doctrines of which I have been speaking, are the more marvellous because there are traces of them throughout the world, and because when known they show upon what truth these diabolical imitations were founded. They are more particularly remarkable as clearing up the ancient Jewish Scriptures, to which they, and they only, will give the full and consistent meaning which we might humbly expect to find in a revelation. And though they were doubtless known to the holier men among the Jews (48), still it was not till Christ came that they were fully disclosed, and began to be spread far and wide, and to be believed upon by the humble and unlearned as well as some of the wise. And they will continue to be believed until the world's end.

This, then, brings me to the close of what I wished to talk with you upon, save that I will just mention one thing—that when these doctrines were revealed, they unlocked also the whole of the books of prophecy. For the whole Christian scheme is contained in prophecy; and, along with it, the fates of divers nations, which perhaps shadow out the fates of other nations also. And though the whole argument from prophecy in favour of Christianity is one of very large compass, and has been so often treated of that I may point out books to you if you wish them, yet I cannot forbear dwelling a little longer upon one thing. Prophecy shows us that there will be a time when these doctrines shall be spread over the whole earth, as the waters cover the sea. It also shows the rejection of that nation who was most advantageously situated for the reception of them. Now this seems to me to disclose to us a general law and not a particular fact: namely, that those nations who, by the possession of the purest systems, would beforehand have seemed most likely to become Christian, really are the most slow in doing so. Semblances of the truth do but puff men up with pride. The Chaldeans, and Persians, and Indians, and Chinese, had the nearest approaches to the truth, and so they have kept furthest away from it. And to me it seems that the Chinese were wiser than you, and held of old a better system than was yours at its best estate. And this I am not saying to discourage you, but to lead you on. Your country it was who corrupted all the nations with the doctrines (49) of Buddha,—doctrines that have been, and perhaps I may say are, in one way or another, the basework of the most pernicious heresies that were ever wielded by the evil spirit against the kingdom of God and His Christ.

How glorious it would be if the wise people of India, by taking in the humbling foolishness of the Cross, found that she had become indeed wise,—was able to pave the way for the conversion of China; to send out, not Buddhist missionaries to pervert the nations of the earth, but Brahmans, now released from the obligation to stay in India by having become Christians, to undo, in the name of the holy and undivided Trinity, the baneful and far-spread heresy of Buddha! How much to be prayed for by us, that India, instead of sending only material frankincense to the Church, as of old, might swell with the prayers of her children the incense of the prayers of the saints; and, turning away from the idolatry of man, who is GOD's best work, might "worship Him who is GOD and Man, who draweth all things unto Himself" (50).

END OF THE FOURTH DIALOGUE.

NOTES TO DIALOGUE IV.

NOTE (1.) p. 336.

The words of Titus Bostr. c. Manich. i. 11, may be cited here: Δι' ἄγνοιαν τῆς τῶν πραγμάτων διαθέσεως καὶ τῆς θείας διοικήσεως γνῶσιν ἐσφαλμένην καὶ βλάσφημον ἑαυτοῖς ἐπραγματεύσαντο, δι' ἄγνοιαν ὧν γνῶναι ἔδοξαν, ἃ χεῖρον ἔγνωσαν ἢ ἠγνόουν, καὶ ὃ ἐζήτουν, ἀληθέστερον ἀπολέσαντες ἢ πρὶν ζητῆσαι. The great St. Athanasius (De Decr. S. N. § 24) points out a similar danger from heretical tendencies of an opposite character to those of Manes. Ἐξῃρήσθω ἐν τούτοις πᾶς λογισμὸς σωματικός· φαντασίαν τε πάσης αἰσθήσεως ὑπερβάντες, καθαρᾷ τῇ νοήσει καὶ μόνῳ τῷ νῷ νοοῦμεν Υἱοῦ πρὸς Πατέρα τὸ γνήσιον, κ. τ. λ. And so St. Ephrem, iii. p. 80. e. "Take thee heed, and make thee not an idol in thy prying search: take thee heed, nor shape thee in thine intellect thine own mind's guess-work, nor let the offspring of thy thought in the True One's offspring's place get shapen in thy fantasy." The passage of Butler, Anal. i. i. p. 24, is almost too well known to be worth referring to.

NOTE (2.) p. 339.

Orig. c. Cels. iv. p. 208. Οὐκ οἶδα πῶς χρήσιμον ἔδοξε τῷ Κέλσῳ καθ' ἡμῶν γράφοντι παραλεῖψαι δόγμα, πολλῆς δεόμενον κἂν δοκούσης ἀποδείξεως, κατὰ τὸ δυνατὸν παραστησάσης, ὅτι ὁμοία ἀπ' ἀρχῆς εἰς τέλος ἐστὶν ἡ τῶν θνητῶν περίοδος, καὶ κατὰ τὰς τεταγμένας ἀνακυκλήσεις ἀνάγκη τὰ αὐτὰ ἀεὶ καὶ γεγονέναι καὶ εἶναι καὶ ἔσεσθαι· ὅπερ ἐὰν ᾖ ἀληθὲς, τὸ ἐφ' ἡμῖν ἀνῄρηται. He mentions a little further on, that this was the opinion of the Stoics, who, however, differed from the Indians, in believing that the same actions were re-performed in each cycle. That a truth was attested by the view of the latter is observed by St. Austin, c. Jul. Pel. iv. extr. in these words: "Quis explicet omnia festinanter quibus gravatur jugum super filios Adam? Hujus evidentia miseriæ gentium philosophos nihil de peccato primi hominis sive scientes sive credentes compulit dicere, ob aliqua scelera suscepta in vitâ superiore pœnarum luendarum causâ, nos esse natos et animos nostros corruptibilibus corporibus .... tanquam vivos cum mortuis esse conjunctos." And, in § 60, he says of Cicero's expression, "homini inesse tanquam obrutum quondam ignem ingenii et mentis," "Latebat eum cur esset grave jugum super filios Adam .... quia sacris literis non eruditus ignorabat originale peccatum."

Note (3.) p. 340.

Aristot. Eth. N. vii. ver. fin. Πονηρὰ ἡ φύσις ἡ δεομένη μεταβολῆς, οὐ γὰρ ἁπλῆ οὐδ' ἐπιεικής. S. Athan. c. Ar. i. 51. Τῶν γενητῶν ἡ φύσις ἐστὶ τρεπτή· καὶ οἱ μὲν παρέβησαν, οἱ δὲ παρήκουσαν, ὥσπερ εἴρηται· ἥ τε πρᾶξις αὐτῶν οὐκ ἔστι βεβαία, ἀλλὰ πολλάκις ἐνδέχεται τὸν νῦν ἀγαθὸν μετὰ ταῦτα τρέπεσθαι καὶ ἕτερον γενέσθαι. S. Basil, Ep. viii. 2. Πᾶν ἅγιον, ὃ περιγραπτὴν ἔχει τὴν φύσιν καὶ ἐπίκτητον ἔχει τὴν ἁγιότητα, οὐκ ἀνεπίδεκτόν ἐστι κακίας. S. Austin, in Joann. i. § 8, "Omnis creatura mutabilis." See also c. Jul. Pel. i. § 37, in Note 11.

Note (4.) p. 340.

Butler, Sermons, p. 331. "Liberty, in the writings of the

New Testament, for the most part signifies being delivered from the bondage of the ceremonial law; or of sin and the devil, which St. Paul calls 'the glorious liberty of the children of God.' Rom. viii. 21. This last is a progressive state; and the perfection of it, whether attainable in this world or not, consists in that perfect love which St. John speaks of; and which, as it implies an entire coincidence of our wills with the will of God, must be a state of the most absolute freedom in the most literal and proper sense."

NOTE (5.) p. 341.

S. Basil, Ep. clxxxix. § 6. Ἐὰν μίαν νοήσωμεν τὴν ἐνέργειαν Πατρός τε καὶ Υἱοῦ καὶ Πνεύματος ἁγίου μηδενὶ διαφέρουσάν τι ἢ παραλλάσσουσαν, ἀνάγκη τῇ ταυτότητι τῆς ἐνεργείας τὸ ἡνωμένον τῆς φύσεως συλλογίζεσθαι. In connection with this it may be not improperly observed, perhaps, that the eternally distinct personality of each Person of the most holy Trinity in Unity helps us one step towards conceiving a communion of saints without a destruction of individuality. Our Lord (St. John xvii. 11. 21) prays that all His members may be one, *as* He and the Father are one. It may be argued by a person of a pantheistic cast from this, that if the Godhead is individual, then this implies that *all* the saints will *become* individual, i. e. will lose the individuality they now have taken one by one. And it is fair to reply to this, that not only is every likeness of a creature or number of creatures to the Creator necessarily a very imperfect likeness, but that the very mysteriousness of that unity, to which the Unity of the saints is compared, prevents our coming to any so definite determinations upon the nature of this last unity. It is not, of course, meant here to imply that personality and individuality are the same thing in the Most High; but merely to point out how this text, even if it were the only one upon the subject, would not show that Scripture in the least countenanced the pantheistic notion of man's individual soul being absorbed ultimately into the Deity. As in Scripture men are said to be gods from the indwelling of God in them, so may many be said to be one from the presence of Him who hath called them and is One in them. Ἀπόλλυται ὁ ἀριθμὸς τῇ τῆς Μονάδος ἐπιδημίᾳ, as St. Basil says, Ep. viii. 7. See also S. Athan. c. Ar. iii. 17, &c. S. Aust. de Trin. iv. 12. S. Cyril, Thes. p. 118—123. The words of St. Hilary, De Trin. viii. p. 122, extr. "Per honorem datum Filio, et a Filio præstitum credentibus, omnes unum sunt," will suggest much to the devout communicant upon the subject: "nam per sacramentum carnis et sanguinis naturalis communionis proprietas nobis indulgetur," as St. Hilary presently observes. For as the Father and the Son are one in the Holy Ghost by nature, so are Christians by imitation one, owing to the gift of the Spirit, which in diverse ways operates in them love and peace. The individuality of God's essence is set before them, not as that, in which they shall lose their own individuality, but as that, the oneness of whose nature they are to imitate by the unanimity of their own wills. The Fathers, as far as I know, are arguing against atheistic heresies when treating of this text: hence there is some difficulty in explaining it so as to obviate such a construction, as minds inclined to errors of an opposite cast may be induced, perhaps, to attempt to force upon it. For that there are such distinct classes of heresies is, I think, plain. See below, note, p. 396.

Note (6.) p. 342.

Orig. c. Cels. iv. p. 169. Ὁ τῶν Στωϊκῶν Θεὸς ἅτε σῶμα τυγχάνων, ὅτε μὲν ἡγεμονικὸν ἔχει τὴν ὅλην οὐσίαν, ὅταν ἡ ἐκπύρωσις ᾖ, ὅτε δὲ ἐπὶ μέρους γίνεται αὐτῆς, ὅταν ᾖ διακόσμησις· οὐδὲ γὰρ δεδύνηνται οὗτοι τρανῶσαι τὴν φυσικὴν τοῦ Θεοῦ ἔννοιαν ὡς πάντη ἀφθάρτου καὶ ἁπλοῦ καὶ ἀσυνθέτου καὶ ἀδιαιρέτου. And St. Athanasius, after pointing out how Arius, by denying the consubstantiality of the Son with the Father, implied that the creation might be destroyed and made again and again, observes: (c. Arian. iv. 13.) Τοῦτο δὲ ἴσως ἀπὸ τῶν Στωϊκῶν ὑπέλαβε διαβεβαιουμένων συστέλλεσθαι καὶ πάλιν ἐκτείνεσθαι τὸν Θεὸν μετὰ τῆς κτίσεως καὶ ἀπείρως παύεσθαι· τὸ γὰρ πλατυνόμενον ἀπὸ στενότητος πλατύνεται, καὶ τὸ ἐκτεινόμενον, συνεσταλμένον ἐκτείνεται. καὶ αὐτὸ μὲν ἐστὶ, πλέον δὲ οὐδὲν ἢ πάθος ὑπομένει . . . Ταῦτα δὲ καταψευδόμενος ἄν τις εἴποι τοῦ Θεοῦ σῶμα καὶ παθητὸν αὐτὸν εἰσάγων. Τί γάρ ἐστι πλατύνεσθαι, ἢ πάθος τοῦ πλατυνομένου; κ. τ. λ. Heresies, like heathen errors, do not escape from making God material: and physical philosophy, when irreligious, seems at this day to be making great approaches to the same debasing error. It may be useful to add, as bearing upon this, the following passage of Origen in Joan. Tr. xiii. § 21. Ἐὰν ἁπλούστερον τούτων (τοῦ Θεὸς φῶς ἐστι, κ. τ. λ.) ἀκούσωμεν, μηδὲν περὰ τῆς λέξεως περιεργαζόμενοι, ὥρα ἡμῖν λέγειν σῶμα εἶναι τὸν Θεὸν, τίνα δὲ ἡμᾶς διαδέχεται ἄτοπα τοῦτο λέγοντας οὐ τῶν πολλῶν ἐστιν εἰδέναι· ὀλίγοι γὰρ διειλήφασι περὶ τῆς τῶν σωμάτων φύσεως καὶ μάλιστα τῶν ὑπὸ λόγου καὶ προνοίας κατακοσμουμένων. . . . . Παρεδέξαντο δὲ τὰ ἀπαντῶντα τῷ λόγῳ αὐτῶν ἄτοπα οἱ θέλοντες εἶναι σῶμα τὸν Θεὸν, ἅτε μὴ δυνάμενοι ἀντιβλέπειν ἐκ λόγου ἐναργῶς παρισταμένοις. Ταῦτα δέ φημι καθ' ὑπεξαίρεσιν τῶν πεμπτὴν λεγόντων εἶναι φύσιν παρὰ τὰ στοιχεῖα. The heathens had recourse to the belief in this subtle matter (πεμπτὴ φύσις) as a mode of explaining physically many difficulties in nature. Strabo (p. 1040) mentions it as believed to exist by the Greeks in common with the

Indians. See further Olearius on Philostr. V. T. iii. 34. It was the ákása of the Indians, and the quinta essentia of Pythagoras, Aristotle, and the Stoics.

NOTE (7.) p. 342.

It is a further illustration of the principles alluded to in the last note, that heretics shift sometimes into heresies apparently opposite from those they hold. Thus a likeness may be traced, not only between the Arians and the Stoics, but also between them and the Manicheans. See Athan. c. Ar. ii. 11, 70. iii. 35, 50; and Mr. Newman's note on 3, § 8. So also St. Austin points out the way in which Pelagians, though seemingly opposed to Manicheans, eventually prove to be supporting them: c. Jul. Pel. i. § 3, § 36, &c. v. § 59, § 64. vi. § 66. The Pelagians say: "Non esse mala exorta de bonis." "Quibus vocibus conficitur," says St. Austin, "non esse mala exorta, nisi de malis." And as the dualist principles of the Manichees are but a short way removed from materialism, it is instructive to observe how Satan attempts to bring his children back towards a heathen creed, as well as heathen practice. Eunomius also, as St. Greg. Nyss. ii. p. 327, notices, ran very close upon thinking God to be material and discerptible: *ποικίλον τι χρῆμα καὶ σύνθετον*. On the whole, the power of rising above all that is material, to a conception (though feeble) of God as a Spirit, seems a Christian gift, and, as such, one of which the Fathers are continually exhorting their readers to a diligent use when contemplating the nature of God.

NOTE (8.) p. 343.

Plato, Phileb. § 153. *Ὧι μὴ μίξομεν τὴν ἀλήθειαν, οὐκ ἄν ποτε τοῦτο ἀληθῶς γίγνοιτο οὐδ' ἂν γενόμενον εἴη.*

NOTE (9.) p. 344.

See Mr. Newman's seventh University Sermon, p. 134.

NOTE (10.) p. 345.

Aristot. Soph. Elench. p. 175, b 9. Ὁ ὑφ' ἑτέρου ῥᾳδίως παραλογιζόμενος καὶ τοῦτο μὴ αἰσθανόμενος κἂν αὐτὸς ὑφ' αὑτοῦ τοῦτο πάθοι πολλάκις.

NOTE (11.) p. 346.

Didymus Alex., c. Manich. x. xi., writes as follows: Μηδεὶς δὲ ὑπολάβῃ ὅτι εἴδη λογικῶν πονηρῶν εἰρηκότες, οὐσίαν πονηρὰν λέγομεν. Ἔστιν γὰρ εἴδη καὶ γένη καὶ τῶν προαιρετικῶν ὑπαρχόντων. λέγομεν οὖν εἴδη σπουδαίου εἶναι δίκαιον, σώφρονα, φρόνιμον· ἐπεὶ γὰρ ἡ ἀρετὴ γένος εἰς εἴδη μεριζομένη εἰς δικαιοσύνην, σωφροσύνην, καὶ τὰ λοιπὰ, ἀνάγκη τὸν τοῦ γένους μετέχοντα σπουδαῖον, ὡσανεὶ γένος εἶναι τῶν μετεχόντων τῶν κατ' εἶδος ἀρετῶν. . . . κἂν τοίνυν πονηρῶν λογικῶν εἴδη λέγομεν, προαιρετικῶς πάντας τοὺς ὑπὸ τὰ εἴδη ταῦτα λέγομεν εἶναι τοιούτους. ἀμέλει γοῦν τὰ ὀνόματα τὰ προειρημένα πονηρὰ οὐκ οὐσιῶν, ἀλλὰ προαιρετικῶν ἐστιν ἐμφανιστικά. Τὸ γὰρ Διάβολος ὄνομα οὐκ οὐσίαν ἀλλὰ προαίρεσιν δηλοῖ· αὐτίκα γοῦν καὶ τὸν Ἰούδαν ἄνθρωπον ὄντα διάβολον ὁ Κύριος οὐ διὰ τὴν οὐσίαν, ἀλλὰ διὰ τὴν προαίρεσιν ὠνόμασεν, λέγων πρὸς πάντας ἅμα τοὺς μαθητὰς συναριθμῶν καὶ τὸν Ἰούδαν ἐν αὐτοῖς, Οὐχὶ τοὺς δώδεκα ὑμᾶς ἐξελεξάμην; κ. τ. λ. To this may be subjoined a passage from St. Austin, c. Jul. Pel. i. § 37. "Si quæratur qualis sit angelus vel homo malæ voluntatis, rectissime respondetur; Malus, magis accipiens qualitatis nomen ex voluntate malâ quam ex naturâ bonâ. Quoniam naturâ est ipsa substantia, et bonitatis et malitiæ capax: bonitatis capax est participatione boni a quo facta est; malitiam vero non capit ex participatione mali, sed privatione boni, id est, non cum miscetur naturæ quæ aliquod malum est, quia nulla natura, in quantum natura est, malum est; sed cum deficit a naturâ, quæ summum atque incommutabile est bonum; propterea quia non de illâ sed de nihilo facta est. Alioquin nec malum voluntatem habere posset, nisi mutabilis esset. Mutabilis porro natura non esset si de Deo esset, et non ab Illo de nihilo facta esset. Quapropter bonorum auctor est Deus, dum auctor est naturarum: quarum spontaneus defectus a bono non indicat a quo factæ sunt, sed unde factæ sunt. Et hoc non est aliquid, quoniam penitus nihil est; et ideo non potest habere quod nihil est."

NOTE (12.) p. 347.

A passage of St. Clement, not without several difficulties in it, was in my mind here. In his Stromatics, iv. § 90, p. 602, Potter, he writes as follows: Εἰ τοίνυν ἀπολογούμενός τις αὐτῶν λέγοι κολάζεσθαι μὲν τὸν μάρτυρα διὰ τὰς πρὸ τῆσδε τῆς ἐνσωματώσεως ἁμαρτίας, τὸν καρπὸν δὲ τῆς κατὰ τόνδε τὸν βίον πολιτείας αὖθις ἀπολήψεσθαι, οὕτω γὰρ διατετάχθαι τὴν διοίκησιν, πευσόμεθα αὐτοῦ εἰ ἐκ προνοίας γίνεται ἡ ἀνταπόδοσις. Εἰ μὲν γὰρ μὴ εἴη τῆς θείας διοικήσεως, οἴχεται ἡ οἰκονομία τῶν καθαρσίων καὶ πέπτωκεν ἡ ὑπόθεσις αὐτοῖς. εἰ δὲ ἐκ προνοίας τὰ καθάρσια, ἐκ προνοίας καὶ αἱ κολάσεις. Ἡ πρόνοια δὲ εἰ καὶ ἀπὸ τοῦ ἄρχοντος, ὡς φάναι, κινεῖσθαι ἄρχεται, ἀλλ' ἐγκατεσπάρη ταῖς οὐσίαις σὺν καὶ τῇ τῶν οὐσιῶν γενέσει πρὸς τοῦ τῶν ὅλων Θεοῦ. Ὧν οὕτως ἐχόντων ἀνάγκη ὁμολογεῖν αὐτοὺς ἢ τὴν κόλασιν μὴ εἶναι ἄδικον,—καὶ δικαιοπραγοῦσιν οἱ καταδικάζοντες καὶ διώκοντες τοὺς μάρτυρας—ἢ ἐκ θελήματος ἐνεργεῖσθαι τοῦ Θεοῦ καὶ τοὺς διωγμούς.

NOTE (13.) p. 349.

Sophocl. Antig. 582. Εὐδαίμονες, οἷσι κακῶν ἄγευστος αἰών· οἷς γὰρ ἂν σεισθῇ θεόθεν δόμος ἄτας οὐδὲν ἐλλείπει, γενεᾶς ἐπὶ πλῆθος ἕρπον. The analogy from entailed evils in the natural world to an entailed curse on the moral, is often noticed by St. Austin against the Pelagians. (See c. Jul. Pel. iii. § 13. § 37. § 55. § 56. § 60. iv. § 5. v. § 51. vi. § 17. § 55. § 82.) One is quite as unaccountable, upon principles of reason, as the other.

Note (14.) p. 349.

Hippocr. de Morbo Sacr. p. 303, Foes. b. 48, speaking of a disease among the Scythians, says: Ἄρχεται δὲ ὥσπερ καὶ κατ' ἄλλα νοσήματα κατὰ γένος· εἰ γὰρ ἐκ τοῦ φλεγματώδεος φλεγματώδης, καὶ ἐκ χολώδεος χολώδης γίνεται, καὶ ἐκ φθινώδεος φθινώδης, καὶ ἐκ σπληνώδεος σπληνώδης, τί κωλύει, ὅτου πατὴρ καὶ μήτηρ εἴχετο τούτῳ τῷ νοσήματι, τούτῳ καὶ τῶν ἐκγόνων ἔχεσθαί τινα; And in his De Aëre et Locis, p. 289, he notices instances of artificially obtained conformations becoming eventually hereditary. It is worth noticing here (what Hippocrates treats of at some length) the influence of climate in producing certain habits of mind and temper. Most men act by passion instead of acting by their better feelings; and consequently bodily constitution and climate, which, with all, are temptations to act in particular directions, with them become the causes of their becoming what all are tempted to become. Others (as Plato, Rep. iv. 11. Aristot. Polit. vii. 7, p. 1327. b. 20. Pliny, N. H. ii. 80. Cyril. c. Jul. p. 131, sqq. Cicero, De Lege Agr. ii. 35. De Rep. ii. 4. Philo ap. Euseb. P. E. p. 398. Windisch. p. 747—760.) have noticed this influence of climate, in the formation of national characters. Particular temptations to go wrong, forming, as they do, a part of the external condition of man (see Butler, quoted above, p. 316) in this state of probation, are in part afforded by climate and constitution. And if the triumph in the one over its temptations be in any sense a reason for expecting its renewal, then in a similar manner, though in a weaker degree, may we expect the renewal of the other[1]. And for aught one sees, there is something sobering in the thought that the scenes of our present temptation should become those of our triumph or disgrace. Πιστεύειν τάχα ἐξὸν τῇ δυνάμει τοῦ Θεοῦ καὶ τοὺς λίθους φωνὴν ἀφήσειν εἰς ἔλεγχον τῶν παραβεβηκότων—to *apply* St. Basil's words of the stone of witness set up by Joshua, de Sp. S. xiii. § 30.

NOTE (15.) p. 350.

See Note 13. S. Greg. Moral. xv. 57. "Peccatum originis a parentibus trahimus, et, nisi per gratiam baptismatis solvamur, etiam parentum peccata portamus: quia unum adhuc videlicet cum illis sumus. Reddit ergo peccata parentum in filios dum pro culpâ parentis anima polluitur prolis. Et rursum non reddit parentum peccata in filios; quia cum ab originali culpâ per baptismum liberamur, jam non parentum culpas, sed quas ipsi committimus, habemus." St. Gregory's expression "*unum* cum illis sumus" may *appear* at first sight to favour rather than to discountenance the error noticed in the text. The real meaning of it is, I believe, not to be seen without recollecting, that, as there is *one* mystical body of Christ, so there is also one mystical body of Satan, with many members in it. The former is (so to speak) filled with the Holy Spirit, the latter by the evil spirit. The proof of the existence of such a body of sin can only be shown from a number of texts indirectly bearing upon it in Scripture, although the idea of it seems clearly implied in the contrast drawn between partaking of the cup of the LORD and that of devils. Tichonius (ap. Austin. de D. Christianâ, iii. § 42. § 55,) in his famous rules of exegesis, notices this doctrine as one of the great principles

[1] Piorry, a French physician, has treated this subject and that of hereditary disorders. I have not been able to obtain a sight of his books.

requisite for a right understanding of Scripture; and that St. Gregory held it, is plain from iii. § 29. xiii. § 38. It is also noticed by Vincent. Lirin. c. xxvi. Origen on Josh. xv. § 5. S. Cyril in Hos. p. 106. c. S. Austin on Ps. lxxii. § 16. Jerome in Esai. p. 127. Aretas in Apocal. p. 432. A part of Origen's words appear to me worth adding, for the thoughts they may suggest. "... Non est putandum quod unus fornicationis spiritus seducat eum qui, verbi gratia, in Britanniis fornicatur et illum qui in Indiâ vel in aliis locis, neque unum esse iræ spiritum qui diversis in locis diversos homines agitet: sed puto magis principem quidem fornicationis spiritum *unum* esse, innumera vero esse qui in hoc ei officio pareant; et per singulos quosque homines diversi spiritus sub eo principe militantes, ad hujuscemodi eos peccata sollicitent. Similiter et iracundiæ .... et avaritiæ unum esse principem, sic et superbiæ et cæterarum malorum. Et ideo non unus principatus dicitur in contrariis ab Apostolo, sed plures adversum quos pugnam sibi esse et nobis omnibus scribit. Esse tamen reor horum omnium principem velut eminentiorem quendam in nequitiâ et in scelere celsiorem, qui totum mundum quem isti ad peccata singuli quique per peccatorum species pro parte sollicitant, solus velut omnium principum dux, et totius nefandæ militiæ magister exagitet." On what occurs presently in the text, see Note 30 to Dial. iii.

NOTE (16.) p. 351.

The doctrine implied in Ezek. xviii. has at first sight the appearance of contradicting that contained in Exod. xx. 5. The two passages may be reconciled by considering the natural course of things as parallel to the supernatural, and in some degree an outstanding type of it. In the natural course of things the children of good parents have good put before them; children of bad parents have bad put before them, "so that one is ready to think their difficulties and dangers are wholly *made* by the ill behaviour of others" (Analogy, i. iv. p. 107): still these external advantages and disadvantages may be overcome, as well as any entailed blessing or curse, by the moral conduct of the children. In Exodus, then, the natural course (so to speak) of God's love or justice is put before us; in Ezekiel the interruptions to that course from man's conduct, under the New Testament. See St. Aust. c. Jul. P. vi. 82.

Note (17.) p. 351.

See Vish. Pur. bk. iv., towards the close.

Note (18.) p. 352.

St. Clement, Strom. ii. 113, quotes a writer who has the following remark: Ἐάν τινι πεῖσμα δῷς ὅτι μή ἐστι ἡ ψυχὴ μονομερὴς, τῇ δὲ τῶν προσαρτημάτων βίᾳ τὰ τῶν χειρόνων γίνεται πάθη, πρόφασιν οὐ τὴν τυχοῦσαν ἕξουσιν οἱ μοχθηροὶ τῶν ἀνθρώπων λέγειν, ἐβιάσθην, ἀπηνέχθην, ἄκων ἔδρασα, μὴ βουλόμενος ἐνήργησα, τῆς τῶν κακῶν ἐπιθυμίας. αὐτὸς ἡγησάμενος καὶ οὐ μαχεσάμενος ταῖς τῶν προσαρτημάτων βίαις. For each man is but one person: see S. Austin, de Trin. xv. § 42. "Verum hæc quando sunt in una *personâ, sicut est homo,* potest nobis quisquam dicere, tria ista, memoria, intellectus, amor, mea sunt non sua; nec sibi sed mihi agunt quod agunt; immo, ego per illa," &c.

Note (19.) p. 352.

Origen, c. Cels. p. 169. See Note 6.

Note (20.) p. 352.

Aristot. Eth. Nic. ix. 7. p. 1168, a 5. Τὸ εἶναι πᾶσιν αἱρετὸν καὶ φιλητόν. ἐσμὲν δ' ἐνεργείᾳ. τὸ ζῆν γὰρ καὶ πράττειν.

NOTE (21.) p. 352.

The problem of (ἓν καὶ πολλὰ) unity and multiplicity occupied the attention of Indian and other Pantheists. If it is thereby meant to imply that the Deity is consubstantial with his works, as the Indians held, (see Windisch. p. 1626.) it is of course a gross error. And it may be doubted if heathen philosophers ever entirely escaped from such a confusion. If, on the other hand, it is intended as a formula to express a belief that the universe is a system, not a congeries of unconnected parts, as Dionysius (περὶ φύσεως, ap. Euseb. P. E. p. 772) seems to imply he thought heathens to mean it, then of course it is admissible[3].

NOTE (22.) p. 352.

Butler, Analogy, p. 12. "Our whole nature leads us to ascribe all moral perfection to GOD, and to deny all imperfection of Him. And this will ever be a practical proof of His moral character to such as will consider what a practical proof is, because it is the voice of GOD speaking in us." GOD's justice being proved to us by other considerations, our ignorance is a sufficient account of any apparent contradictions to it.

NOTE (23.) p. 353.

St. Basil c. Manich. ap. Aust. c. Jul. Pel. 1. § 16. "Si evenisset malum ita ut non valeret ulterius a voluntate removeri; id est, quamvis accidisset, si ita accidisset, ut sepa-

[3] In consulting Christian writers, and especially the earlier ones, who claim parts of heathen systems as coinciding with the Christian system, care should be taken not to overrate the amount of resemblance claimed—not to forget the side upon which the resemblances are contemplated. Otherwise Christian writers may be represented as favouring things which they would have abhorred. This is, of course, doubly necessary when people dip into books, and do not read them through.

rari ulterius a voluntate non valeret, merito dici posset substantiale quidem malum non esse, sed ipsam substantiam sine malitiâ quæ accidit jam esse non posse. Si autem accessit, et principium accessionis, non substantiam habuit sed voluntatem, facile potest malum' a substantiâ separari, ut et subjecta voluntati substantia munda possit per omnia possideri, ita ut nullius mali vel signa remaneant."

Note (24.) p. 353.

Vish. Pur. v. 33, p. 596. "That which I am, thou art; and that also is this world with its gods, demons and mankind. Men contemplate distinctions because they are stupefied by ignorance." '*That*' became a name for the Supreme Being. "The pronoun 'tat' thus emphatically used is understood to intend the Supreme Being, according to the doctrines of the Vedánta; when manifested by Creation, he is the entity 'sat,' while forms, being mere illusion, are non-entity." Colebrooke, i. p. 33. Cyril, c. Jul. p. 33 e, mentions something of the kind among the Egyptians, and the Jews also used זאת as a name of the Messiah. It has been a question whether the Cabbalists were Pantheists, and I have endeavoured in different parts of this book to notice any points of resemblance, which I happened to be led to, between the two. See Dr. Mill on the Pantheistic Theory, &c. p. 151, &c. Molitor, perhaps, is not very distinct upon the point—whether the Cabbalists held a theory of which Pantheism was the corruption, or whether they imported Pantheism into their actually existing traditive system.

Note (25.) p. 353.

Vish. Pur. p. 210. "Arduous penances for great sins, trifling ones for minor offences, have been propounded by Swyambhuva and others; but reliance upon Crishna is far better than any such expiatory acts, as religious austerity or the like. Let any one who repents of the sin of which he may have been culpable have recourse to this best of all expiations, remembrance of Hari: by addressing his thoughts to Náráyana at dawn, at night, at sunset, and mid-day, a man shall be quickly cleansed from all guilt; the whole heap of worldly sorrows is dispersed by meditating upon Hari," &c. A doctrine very pleasing to human indolence this! but the mark of what the Vish. Purana itself admits (p. 622) to be the corrupt age.

NOTE (26.) p. 359.

Aristot. Top. vi. 4. Δῆλον ὅτι οὐχ ὁριστέον διὰ τῶν ἑκάστοις γνωριμωτέρων, ἀλλὰ διὰ τῶν ἁπλῶς γνωριμωτέρων· μόνως γὰρ ἂν οὕτως εἷς καὶ ὁ αὐτὸς ὁρισμὸς ἀεὶ γένοιτο. ἴσως δὲ καὶ τὸ ἁπλῶς γνώριμον οὐ τὸ πᾶσι γνώριμόν ἐστιν, ἀλλὰ τὸ τοῖς εὖ διακειμένοις τὴν διάνοιαν, καθάπερ καὶ τὸ ἁπλῶς ὑγιεινὸν τὸ τοῖς εὖ ἔχουσι τὸ σῶμα. This contains the principle on which the remarks in the text are based; history and common life alike attest the truth of it.

NOTE (27.) p. 359.

Aristotle (Met. p. 1009, b 34) observes of those philosophers who deny the existence of truth apart from each man's own conception of it, Εἰ οἱ μάλιστα τὸ ἐνδεχόμενον ἀληθὲς ἑωρακότες (οὗτοι δ' εἰσὶν οἱ μάλιστα ζητοῦντες αὐτὸ καὶ φιλοῦντες) οὗτοι τοιαύτας ἔχουσι τὰς δόξας καὶ ταῦτα ἀποφαίνονται περὶ τῆς ἀληθείας, πῶς οὐκ ἄξιον ἀθυμῆσαι τοὺς φιλοσοφεῖν ἐγχειροῦντας· where we see also that he makes a *love* of the truth a condition for attaining it. Allusion is presently made to the words of S. Aust. de C. D. v. x. "Male vivitur, si de Deo non bene creditur."

NOTE (28.) p. 361.

Aristot. Eth. Nic. vi. 12. Δεῖ προσέχειν τῶν ἐμπείρων

καὶ πρεσβυτέρων ἢ φρονίμων ταῖς ἀναποδείκτοις φάσεσι καὶ δόξαις οὐχ ἧττον τῶν ἀποδείξεων· διὰ γὰρ τὸ ἔχειν ἐκ τῆς ἐμπειρίας ὄμμα ὁρῶσιν ὀρθῶς.

NOTE (29.) p. 361.

Tert. Præscr. i. "Ad hoc sunt hæreses, ut fides habendo tentationem habeat etiam probationem." Compare the Analogy, ii. 6. p. 317.

NOTE (30.) p. 361.

Butler, Anal. i. v. fin. p. 149. "It is not impossible that men's showing and making manifest what is in their heart, what their real character is, may have respect to a future life in ways and manners which we are not acquainted with; particularly it may be a means, for the Author of Nature does not appear to do any thing without means, of their being disposed of suitably to their characters, and of its being known to the creation *by way of example*, that they are thus disposed of." And Origen c. Cels. viii. p. 398, notices that the object of judgments, such as plagues, &c., is, ἵν' οἱ μὲν καὶ ἐν τοῖς τοιούτοις εὐσεβεῖς μένοντες, καὶ μηδαμῶς γιγνόμενοι χείρους φανεροὶ τέως τοῖς μὴ βλέπουσιν αὐτῶν τὴν ἕξιν ἀοράτοις καὶ ὁρατοῖς θεαταῖς γένωνται. οἱ δ' ἐναντίως μὲν διακείμενοι, κλέπτοντες δὲ τὴν τῆς κακίας ἐπίδειξιν, ἐλεγχθέντες ὑπὸ τῶν συμβαινόντων ὁποῖοί εἰσι, αὐτοί τε ἑαυτῶν συναισθηθῶσι καὶ δῆλοι τοῖς (ἵν' οὕτως ὀνομάσω) θεαταῖς γένωνται. Plato also thought the wicked who were not improved by the purgation he held them to undergo in a future state, were made examples of. Παραδείγματα ἀτεχνῶς ἀνηρτημένους ἐκεῖ ἐν Ἅιδου ἐν τῷ δεσμωτηρίῳ τοῖς ἀεὶ τῶν ἀδίκων ἀφικνουμένοις θεάματα καὶ νουθετήματα. Gorg. § 171. Theæt. § 86.

NOTE (31.) p. 362.

Hil. in Ps. cxviii. Beth. p. 849. "Novimus neque margaritas ante porcos projiciendas esse neque sanctum canibus dare oportere. Ergo intelligimus quædam nos cordis nostri secreto continere, quæ divulgata *inexpiabilis* peccati culpam comparabunt."

NOTE (32.) p. 363.

Id. de Trin. viii. p. 121. "Habet non tam veniam quam præmium ignorare quod credis." St. Cyprian, Ep. i. will offer an illustration of what follows: his words are (Epist. i.): "Ut ipse quam plurimis vitæ prioris erroribus implicitus tenebar, quibus exui me posse non crederem, sic vitiis adhærentibus obsecundans eram et desperatione meliorum malis meis veluti jam propriis ac vernaculis offavebam. Sed postquam undæ genitalis auxilio, superioris ævi labe detersâ, in expiatum pectus serenum ac purum desuper se lumen infudit: postquam cœlitus Spiritu hausto in novum me hominem nativitas secunda reparavit, *mirum in modum protinus* confirmare se dubia, patere clausa, lucere tenebrosa, facultatem dare, quod prius difficile videbatur," &c. Of course, ordinary Christians may not expect all that was conferred upon one designed to be a saint, yet that this sort of thing in its degree happens now in adult baptisms, where duly prepared for, no doubt will probably be entertained.

NOTE (33.) p. 363.

The operation of the three Persons at the creation was often noticed of old. Thus St. Basil de Sp. S. xvi., quoting Ps. xxxiii. 6. *Τρία τοίνυν νοεῖς τὸν προτάσσοντα Κύριον, τὸν δημιουργοῦντα Λόγον, τὸ στερεοῦν Πνεῦμα.* See Cyril c. Nest. p. 100. a. St. Austin in loc. &c.

Note (34.) p. 364.

In a note to the Vishnu Purana, p. 7, Professor Wilson quotes the Márkandeya as saying, "As the primal, all-pervading spirit is distinguished by attributes in creation and the rest, so he obtains the denomination of Brahmá, Vishnu, and Siva. In the capacity of Brahmá he creates the worlds; in that of Rudra, he destroys them. In that of Vishnu he is quiescent. These are the Avasthas (lit. hypostases) of the self-born: Brahmá is the quality of activity; Rudra that of darkness; Vishnu, the lord of the world, is goodness: so, therefore, the three gods are the three qualities. They are ever combined with and dependent upon one another: they are never for an instant separate; they never quit each other."

Note (35.) p. 364.

The heresy alluded to is that of the Sabellians. A heresy of this kind is noticed by Origen in S. Joan. Tr. x. § 21, who speaks of people that make the Father and the Son one, *οὐ μόνον οὐσίᾳ ἀλλὰ καὶ ὑποκειμένῳ τυγχάνοντας ἀμφοτέρους κατά τινας ἐπινοίας διαφόρους οὐ κατὰ ὑπόστασιν λέγεσθαι Πατέρα καὶ Υἱόν.* St. Athanasius also, c. Ar. iv. 2, 25, speaks of their making Son a mere name or quality of God. And St. Basil, Ep. 210, § 3, speaks of their calling the Holy Trinity *ἓν πρᾶγμα πολυπρόσωπον*, and so making God to consist of one Person only, and thereby also implying a denial of the Incarnation. He adds, in § 5, *Εὖ γὰρ εἰδέναι χρὴ, ὅτι ὥσπερ ὁ τὸ κοινὸν τῆς οὐσίας μὴ ὁμολογῶν εἰς πολυθεΐαν ἐκπίπτει, οὕτως ὁ τὸ ἰδιάζον τῶν ὑποστάσεων μὴ διδοὺς εἰς τὸν Ἰουδαϊσμὸν ὑποφέρεται.* The Sabellians thus denied a Trinity altogether. See St. Austin, de Trin. vii. 9.

Note (36.) p. 364.

S. Cyril, c. Jul. p. 34. *Πορφύριός φησι Πλάτωνος ἐκτιθέ-*

μενος δόξαν ἄχρι τριῶν ὑποστάσεων τὴν τοῦ θείου προελθεῖν οὐσίαν, εἶναι δὲ τὸν μὲν ἀνωτάτω Θεὸν τἀγαθόν· μετ' αὐτὸν δὲ, καὶ δεύτερον τὸν δημιουργόν· τρίτον δὲ καὶ τὴν τοῦ κόσμου ψυχήν· ἄχρι γὰρ ψυχῆς τὴν θειότητα προελθεῖν. See the note of Professor Wilson, referred to in Note 34. The Chinese had some of the closest approximations to the truth among them. See Windisch. p. 404, &c. Schmitt Uroffenbar, p. 184, &c.: at p. 188 he quotes a text of Lao-tseu: "Tao is one in nature; the first begat the second, both brought forth the third: the three made all things." And so among the Americans, three things were worshipped without an image, although G. di Vega says, (Com. Real. cap. xxi. p. 100,) it is false to consider them as supposed by the Americans themselves to be a trinity in unity. The Greeks and Romans will also furnish instances of trine divisions or names of the deity—all which are witnesses, more or less clumsy, of some antecedent belief, existing probably in its purest state amongst the Jews. A systematic treatment of the Gentile traditions on this subject would form a curious and useful book: but it probably could not be done without more accurate knowledge of the ancient Jewish belief upon the subject, than we possess: and certainly not without exact and scientific knowledge of the Christian doctrine. Compare Note 48.

NOTE (37.) p. 364.

Athan. c. Ar. i. 17. Εἰ γὰρ οὐκ ἀϊδίως σύνεστιν ὁ Λόγος τῷ Πατρὶ, οὐκ ἔστιν ἡ τριὰς ἀΐδιος· ἀλλὰ μονὰς μὲν ἦν πρότερον, ἐκ προσθήκης δὲ γέγονεν ὕστερον τριάς.

NOTE (38.) p. 364.

Bull, cited by Dr. Routh ad Hippol. p. 87. "Scilicet Domino triplicem nativitatem et filiationem attribuerunt veteres. Prima est, quâ ut Λόγος ex mente Patris ab æterno natus fuit. Ex hac nativitate perfecta hypostasis divina extitit: nec ipsi quicquam postea accessit, sed potius cæteræ nativitates συγκαταβάσεις fuerunt, sive condescensiones Filii Dei. Altera nempe nativitas est, quâ ὁ Λόγος a Deo Patre, apud quem, quum nihil adhuc præter Deum existeret adeoque ab æterno fuerat, κατ' ἐνέργειαν exivit, et tanquam ex utero ejus prodiit, seque dimisit ad condenda universa." Athan. c. Ar. ii. 64. Κατ' ἀρχὴν μὲν δημιουργῶν ὁ Λόγος τὰ κτίσματα συγκαταβέβηκε τοῖς γενητοῖς, ἵνα γενέσθαι ταῦτα δυνηθῇ, κ. λ., where the rest of Bishop Bull's statement is confirmed. So, too, S. Ephrem adv. Scrut. iii. p. 58. "Thou wert minished when Thou didst create; for from that majesty didst Thou come down to lowliness; for the creation were not possible, unless through condescension (ܐܬܪܟܢܘܬܐ)[4] Thou hadst come to stablish it. Condescension did He first put on, that He might be Creator: and how could He create unless He could condescend!" This is the doctrine of the προέλευσις, on which see further in Bull, Def. Fid. Nic. i. 2, 5. iii. 8, 7. Dr. Routh ad Hippol. p. 83. Vallars. ad Jer. c. Ruff. ii. 9; and compare Mr. Newman's Athanasius, p. 278.

Note (39.) p. 365.

Thus Origen says of the Stoics, c. Cels. p. 324. Διήκει ἡ ἐπισκοπὴ καὶ ἡ πρόνοια τοῦ Θεοῦ διὰ πάντων ἀλλ' οὐχ ὡς τὸ τῶν Στωϊκῶν πνεῦμα· καὶ πάντα μὲν περιέχει τὰ προνοούμενα ἡ πρόνοια καὶ περιείληφεν αὐτὰ, οὐχ ὡς σῶμα δὲ περιέχον περιέχει, ὅτι καὶ σῶμά ἐστι τὸ περιεχόμενον· ἀλλ' ὡς Δύναμις θεία καὶ περιειληφυῖα τὰ περιεχόμενα. And Tertull. c. Prax. xvi. "In Deo omnis locus, non ipse in loco." S. Clem.

[4] The same view of doctrine is contained here as in St. Athanasius, although the Syriac language cannot express it as exactly as the Greek. I may observe that the words σμικρυνθεὶς and μειωθεὶς are used by St. Methodius, Conv. V. viii. 11., in a similar way to what St. Ephrem uses the word ܐܬܪܟܢ.

Strom. ii. § 6, p. 431, Pott. Οὐκ ἐν γνόφῳ ἢ τόπῳ ὁ Θεὸς, ἀλλ' ὑπεράνω καὶ τόπου καὶ χρόνου καὶ τῆς τῶν γεγονότων ἰδιότητος. Hil. de Trin. viii. p. 128. "Deus immensæ virtutis vivens potestas, quæ nusquam non adsit nec desit usquam, Se omnem per sua edocet, et sua non aliud quam Se esse significat, ut ubi sua insint Ipse esse intelligatur; non autem corporali modo cum alicubi insit, non et ubique esse credatur, cum per sua in omnibus esse non desinat, non aliud autem sint quam quod est Ipse quæ sua sunt." In Ps. cxxxviii. p. 1107, b. Athan. de Decr. xi.; and Mr. Newman's note; c. Arian. i. 23. Austin, de Trin. vi. § 8. Cyril, c. Nest. p. 12. e. Greg. Mor. xvi. 38, &c.

Note (40.) p. 365.

The Deity is represented in Manu i. as becoming a body, and separating different classes from different parts of himself. See Windisch. p. 524, p. 636. This seems to be the Purusha of the Indians, and the אדם קדמון of the Cabbalists.

Note (41.) p. 365.

S. Hil. de Trin. iii. p. 24. "Manifestato nomine Patris hominibus hoc postulat, Sed quo nomine? Numquid nomen Dei ignorabatur? Hoc Moyses de rubo audivit, hoc Genesis in exordio creati orbis nunciavit, hoc lex exposuit, prophetæ prætulerunt, homines in his mundi operibus senserunt, *gentes etiam mentiendo veneratæ sunt.* Non ergo ignorabatur Dei nomen, sed Deus plane ignorabatur; nam Deum nemo noscit nisi confiteatur et Patrem, Patrem Unigeniti Filii, et Filium non de portione, aut dilatione aut emissione, sed ex eo natum inenarrabiliter," &c.

Note (42.) p. 367.

Basil, Serm. xvi. § 4. Πονηρὰ γὰρ κἀκείνη ἡ βλασφημία τῶν φύρειν τὰ πάντα ἐπιχειρούντων καὶ ἓν τὸ ὑποκείμενον λεγόντων Πατέρα καὶ Υἱὸν καὶ ἅγιον Πνεῦμα, προσηγορίας δὲ διαφορούσας τῷ ἑνὶ πράγματι ἐπιφημίζεσθαι. Πονηρὰ ἡ ἀσέβεια καὶ φευκτὴ οὐχ ἧττον τῶν ἀνόμοιον εἶναι κατ' οὐσίαν τὸν Υἱὸν τοῦ Θεοῦ, τῷ Θεῷ καὶ Πατρὶ βλασφημούντων.

Note (43.) p. 367.

Θεοποιεῖν τὴν Σάρκα is an expression often used of Christ. See Athan. iii. 48. So Origen, c. Cels. iii. p. 136, says, Τὸ θνητὸν Αὐτοῦ σῶμα.... εἰς Θεὸν μεταβεβηκέναι. Hilary de Trin. ix. p. 154. "Christus peccati nostri corpus assumens totus jam Deo vivit, naturæ nostræ societate in communionem Divinæ immortalitatis unitâ." And so St. Aust. de Trin. xiii. 18, f. xiv. 24. S. Cyril, c. Nest. p. 50, d. &c. Of Crishna see the Vishnu Purana, p. 612.

Note (44.) p. 367.

The Nestorians, by refusing to allow that the human nature of Christ never had any existence separate from the Godhead, thereby implied that in Christ God *dwelt* in a human being, but was not one Person in two Natures. But as God dwelleth in the saints, this was to make Christ to be as one of them, and not above His fellows. Hence He might, as St. Cyril urges, c. Nest. p. 26, 27, have been often incarnate. See also pp. 97, 98. 102, 103. His body saw no corruption, and therefore He needeth not to take any other body; but *in* It he received gifts for men (Heb. לקחת מתנות באדם), and by It evermore sustaineth them, evermore making intercession for them; and in that same body which they pierced through shall every eye behold Him when He cometh to judgment.

Note (45.) p. 367.

Athan. de Incarn. § 41, has a passage to this effect. The following is a portion of it: Εἰ τῷ κόσμῳ τοῦτον ἐπιβαίνειν καὶ ἐν ὅλῳ αὐτὸν γνωρίζεσθαι πρέπει, πρέποι ἂν καὶ ἐν ἀνθρωπίνῳ σώματι αὐτὸν ἐπιφαίνεσθαι καὶ ὑπὸ αὐτοῦ τοῦτο φωτίζεσθαι καὶ ἐνεργεῖν. Μέρος γὰρ τοῦ παντὸς καὶ τὸ τῶν ἀνθρώπων ἐστὶ γένος· καὶ εἰ τὸ μέρος ἀπρεπές ἐστιν ὄργανον αὐτοῦ γίνεσθαι πρὸς τὴν τῆς θεότητος γνῶσιν, ἀτοπώτατον ἂν εἴη καὶ δι' ὅλου τοῦ κόσμου γνωρίζεσθαι τοῦτον.

NOTE (46.) p. 367.

Origen, c. Cels. iii. p. 135, extr. Ἴστωσαν οἱ ἐγκαλοῦντες, ὅτι ὃν μὲν νομίζομεν καὶ πεπείσμεθα ἀρχῆθεν εἶναι Θεὸν καὶ Υἱὸν Θεοῦ, οὗτος ὁ αὐτολόγος ἐστὶ καὶ ἡ αὐτοσοφία καὶ ἡ αὐτοαλήθεια· τὸ δὲ θνητὸν αὐτοῦ σῶμα καὶ τὴν ἀνθρωπίνην ἐν αὐτῷ ψυχὴν, τῇ πρὸς ἐκεῖνο οὐ μόνον κοινωνίᾳ ἀλλὰ καὶ ἑνώσει καὶ ἀνακράσει τὰ μέγιστά φαμεν προσειληφέναι, καὶ τῆς ἐκείνου θειότητος κεκοινωνηκότα εἰς Θεὸν μεταβεβηκέναι. Ἐὰν δέ τις προσκόπτῃ καὶ περὶ τοῦ σώματος αὐτοῦ ταῦθ' ἡμῶν λεγόντων, ἐπιστησάτω τοῖς ὑπὸ Ἑλλήνων λεγομένοις, περὶ τῆς τῷ ἰδίῳ λόγῳ ἀποίου ὕλης ποιότητας ἀμφισκομένης, ὁποίας ὁ δημιουργὸς βούλεται αὐτῇ περιτιθέναι, καὶ πολλάκις τὰς μὲν προτέρας ἀποτιθεμένης κρειττόνας τε καὶ διαφόρους ἀναλαμβανούσης. S. Cyril also, c. Jul. p. 66, speaks as follows: Ἡμεῖς ἀγένητον ὄντα τὸν τοῦ Θεοῦ Λόγον συνυπάρχειν ἀναγκαίως τῷ φύσαντι διϊσχυριζόμεθα, καὶ ἐνυπάρχειν μὲν Αὐτῷ προελθεῖν δὲ γεννητῶς ἐξ Αὐτοῦ. Ὁ δέ γε τῆς Πλάτωνος εὑρεσιεπείας συνήγορος ἀκριβὴς ἀγέννητον μὲν εἶναί φησι τὸν ἀνωτάτω Θεὸν, ἐνυπάρχειν δὲ, καὶ ἐξ αὐτοῦ γεννηθῆναι καὶ προελθεῖν τοὺς παρ' αὐτοῦ γεγονότας, τὰ πάντα κυκῶν καὶ συγχέων, καὶ τὸ ἀκραιφνὲς εἰς θεοπτίαν τοῦ μηδενὸς ἀξιώσας λόγου· where the pantheistic theory of creation is contrasted with the Christian doctrine of the coming forth of the eternally subsistent Son to Creation.

Note (47.) p. 368.

The denial of reality of our blessed Lord's body formed a part of the system of several pantheistic[5] heretics, as the Gnostics, Docetæ, Manichæans, and others. See Fabricius, as cited by Dr. Routh ad Hippol. p. 89.

Note (48.) p. 369.

The degree of knowledge which the Jews possessed of the Trinity is a subject upon which one finds it difficult to state any thing with precision. One great reason of this is, that we possess definite gifts inward *and* outward, which enable us to receive it, and see into it to a certain extent, for the absence of which gifts it is scarcely possible by any powers of abstraction to make proper allowance. Recollecting, however, what was said above (p. 322) of the gift of the Spirit, as that to which patriarchs and others did in part ultimately attain, we shall be disposed to think that they, at least, could not have wanted the inward gift, requisite for such insight into the mystery, as man is capable of. And they who try to live holily, are perhaps, after all, the only persons that have such insight at any time; the patriarchs are vouchers for the existence of other, hidden, saints in their time, much as great doctors of the Church are also. Wisdom pours forth doctrine now, *as* she did prophecy then, (Ecclus. xxiv. 33.) developing the divine mysteries more and more to worthy men, till the Day of the Lord.

If this, then, be true, the only remaining question will be

[5] It had struck a very intimate friend (to whom I am indebted for several valuable hints when composing this work) as well as myself, that all heresies are either atheistic or pantheistic in their tendencies. Of the latter tendency are those mentioned above; of the former, Arianism, Socinianism, Rationalism, &c. By this, of course, it is not meant to imply that they never converge, though at first of seemingly opposite tendencies.

what evidence is there that there was any tradition putting such doctrine before them of old time; for that there was an explanative tradition has been, I trust, shown above. Here, then, I will give a brief sketch of what the evidence is for believing that the Jews held the doctrine of the Trinity in some sense, referring to Allix's Judgment of the Jewish Church, &c., for further information upon the subject.

1. We find no hint in the New Testament that what our LORD said of blasphemy against the Holy Ghost offended the Jews, *as* implying a plurality of Persons in the Godhead. Neither does it seem that any *doctrines* but those of the Incarnation and the Eucharist were really stumbling-blocks to them.

2. We find in Philo, and also in the Apocrypha, approximations to the Christian doctrine of the Trinity, and especially to the belief of the second Person in the Trinity.

3. We find the Chaldee Paraphrasts frequently introducing the name, the Word of GOD, for that of JEHOVAH, which implies their knowledge also of the same truth.

4. There are a number of passages in the Old Testament, which religious minds could not have failed to put together and compare, so as to arrive in part at the truth. For all we know of earlier Jewish books proves them to have had great powers of combining texts with a view to arrive at conclusions. Using, then, the tradition[6] of their Church as a rule, they might, by diligent reading of Scripture, find out much.

If, then, I may venture to give my own opinion upon a matter where I acknowledge there is some difference among the Fathers, I should do it in the words of Origen, in Josh.

[6] Comp. S. Athan. c. Arian. iii. 28. Τὸν σκοπὸν τῆς καθ' ἡμᾶς τοὺς Χριστιανοὺς πίστεως λάβωμεν καὶ τούτῳ ὥσπερ κανόνι χρησάμενοι προσέχωμεν, ὡς εἶπεν ὁ ἀπόστολος τῇ ἀναγνώσει τῆς θεοπνεύστου γραφῆς.

iii. 2. "Arbitror . . . quod et illi priores qui per legem agebantur, contigerint quidem scientiam Trinitatis, non tamen integre et perfecte, sed ex parte; deerat enim illis in Trinitate etiam Dei Unigeniti Incarnationem cognoscere," &c. And it is plain that the ignorance of the Incarnation, as a thing actually realized, must have had a very great influence on the rest of their belief; for nothing puts before us in so strong a light the distinction of Persons as this doctrine does.

Note (49.) p. 370.

S. Ephr. ii. p. 444, says, Manes drew his doctrine from India; as does Epiphanius, Hæres. lxvi. 1. Others, as Archel. Casch. lii. liii. (who, however, mentions Buddha as connected with the origin of it,) c. Aust. c. F. Manet. xii. 45, &c., say he drew from Persia. But as Persia and India were countries in intercourse with each other, as we learn from Philostratus (above, p. 70), the two accounts may probably be reconciled.

Note (50.) p. 371.

The last words are the concluding words of Windischmann's book. It is worth noticing, that Apollonius of Tyana and Manes seem both to have drawn from India. It was from India, also, that Buddhist missionaries came to intercept the Chinese when they sent an embassy to inquire after the dawn of Christianity. This is, I *think*, noticed by Schlegel, in his Lectures on the Philosophy of History.

END OF NOTES TO DIALOGUE IV.

GLOSSARY.

N. B. This Glossary is intended merely to furnish such an idea of the words used in it, as is sufficient to make the argument intelligible.

ACHYUTA, the unfallen, a name of Vishnu, 285, 287.

AHINSÁ, abstinence from injury to animals—one of the chief virtues with the Hindus, 30, 172.

AHORÁTRI, a day and night of Brahmá, consisting of an enormous period of years, after which all creatures were absorbed, 341.

AMRITA, nectar, 280.

BRAHMACHÁRI, a young Brahman in a state of pupillage, 14.

CHANDÁLA, an outcast, a man of the lowest grade, 287, 288, 289.

CHHANDAS, metre, intonation, 20.

CHHANDOGYA, an Upanishad, *q. v.*

CRISHNA, an incarnation or avatara of Vishnu, 367.

DEVANÁGARI, the Sanscrit alphabet, 18.

DHARMA, religious and moral duty, 154.

GANESA, the deity of wisdom, son of Siva, 7.

GOTAMA, a famous logician, 49, 154, 263.

GRIHASHTHA, a householder (see Sannyási), 29.

GURU, a spiritual preceptor, 14.

HARI, a name of Vishnu.

ÍSWARA, the Lord; a name applied to the Supreme Being, 4.

KÁLÍ, a terrific goddess, called also Durgá, the wife of Siva, 45.

KALIYUGA, the age of wickedness, 159.

KALPA, a period of 4,320,000,000 years (see Ahorátri), 46, 185, 287.

KANÁDA, the founder of a sceptical or rationalistic school of philosophy, 154.

KARMA-MÍMÁNSÁ, the same as the Púrva-mím. (See Mímánsá.)

MANAS, *mens*, mind, 284.

MÁNAVA-DHARMA-SÁSTRA, the book of the law of Manu, 5.

MANU, the legislator, 12.

MANWANTARA, the duration of a Manu; each Manu is supposed to reign during 306,720,000 years, 355.

MÍMÁNSÁ, an interpretative philosophy, consisting of two parts: the Púrva-mímánsá, relative to moral duties; and the Uttaramím., relating to the theory of being, &c., nearly identical with the Vedánta, 4.

MLECHCHHA, a barbarian, 186.

MUNI, a sage endowed with more or less of divinity, or attaining to it by penance, &c., 4.

NÁREDA, a son of Brahmá, inventor of the lute, 15.

NYÁYA, logical philosophy, 4.

PARAMÁTMÁ, supreme spirit, whether as self-existent, or as constituting man's nobler part, 284, 285.

PRADHÁNA, crude matter, 45.

PRAKRITI, matter, 284.

PRASÁDA, grace; influence proceeding from the Deity and calming the mind for devotion, &c., 10, 154.

PURANAS, sacred books later, but now more reverenced, than the Vedas, 45.

PURUSHA, Brahma as prolatus, προφορικὸς, the imaginary first man out of whom the different classes had their origin, 20.

RAJAYUGA, the third great period, the age of passion or rage.

RICH. See Veda.

SANHITÁ, a collection of the hymns, properly of the Veda, 42.

SÁNKHYA, the opposite of the Mímánsá system; a reasoning system, rejecting revelations, &c., 4.

SANNYÁSI, a Brahman, who having passed through the three grades of Brahmachári, Grihastha, and Vánaprastha, abandons all worldly affections and possessions, 143.

SATYAKALPA, the period of innocence, 31.

SATYAYUGA, the age of innocence or truth, 355.

SIVA (see Note 34 to Dial. iv.), a name or quality of GOD, 336.

SOMA, the moon; also the moon-plant, the Asclepias acida, or Sarcostema viminalis, 280.

SRÁDDHA, a funeral oblation to deceased ancestors, "offerings of the dead," 45.

SRUTI, a name for the Vedas, 19.

SÚDRAS, the lowest of the four great castes, 182, 183, 184.

SÚRYA, the sun, whether as visible, or as illuminating the mind, 6.

SWAYAMVARAM, the ceremony of choosing a husband, 163.

TAMOYUGA, the age of darkness, 355.

TAPAS, penance, 143.

UPANISHADS, certain scientific portions of the Veda, the same as the Vedánta: there are several of them, 20.

VAISYA, a man of the mercantile caste, 49.

Válmíki, a great poet, author of the Rámáyana, &c., 12.

Vedánta, a philosophy which treated the metaphysical portions of the Vedas systematically, 4.

Vedas (the), the scripture of the Hindus divided into four parts, three of which only are mentioned in Manu, the Rich, Yajur, and Sama, leaving out the Atharva, which is thought to be more recent.

Vedántists, 262, 284.

Vijnána, discrimination, the power of seeing the unreality of such notions as matter, individual, &c., 285, 336. See p. 319, Note 49.

Víná, the lute, 15.

Vishnu-serma, author of the Hitopadesa, 5.

Vyása, 'the *compiler*' of the Vedas, and some say of other books, 8.

Xhatriyas, the second or military caste, 185.

Yavanas, Greeks probably of Bactria; also used for other foreigners, and sometimes spelt Javanas; the same word as the Javan of Hebrew and Syriac.

Yoganidrá, the principle or goddess of delusion, 333.

Yogi, an ascetic, devoted to mystical contemplation, 284.

THE END.